The Poetics of Consent

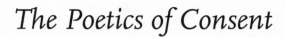

The Poetics of Consent

Collective Decision Making and the *Iliad*

DAVID F. ELMER

The Johns Hopkins University Press
Baltimore

© 2013 The Johns Hopkins University Press
All rights reserved. Published 2013
Printed in the United States of America on acid-free paper

2 4 6 8 9 7 5 3 1

The Johns Hopkins University Press
2715 North Charles Street
Baltimore, Maryland 21218-4363
www.press.jhu.edu

Library of Congress Cataloging-in-Publication Data
Elmer, David F.
The poetics of consent : collective decision making and the
Iliad / David F. Elmer.
pages. cm.
Includes bibliographical references and index.
ISBN 978-1-4214-0826-2 (hdbk. : alk. paper) —
ISBN 978-1-4214-0827-9 (electronic) —
ISBN 1-4214-0826-0 (hdbk. : alk. paper) —
ISBN 1-4214-0827-9 (electronic)
1. Homer. Iliad.   2. Consensus (Social sciences) in
literature.   I. Title.
PA4037.E55 2013
883'.01—dc23
2012020458

A catalog record for this book is available from the British Library.

*Special discounts are available for bulk purchases of this book. For more
information, please contact Special Sales at 410-516-6936 or
specialsales@press.jhu.edu.*

The Johns Hopkins University Press uses environmentally friendly
book materials, including recycled text paper that is composed of at
least 30 percent post-consumer waste, whenever possible.

For my parents, Russell and Julie

Contents

Acknowledgments

This book has been years in the making, and I have benefited from the advice, support, and friendship of many people along the way—too many, in fact, to list them all here. Some of my debts, however, are too great to go unmentioned.

No reader of the pages to follow will fail to notice how much I owe, intellectually and otherwise, to Greg Nagy, who has been a teacher, mentor, and friend for some seventeen years. I think it is safe to say that I would not have written this book—and perhaps not any other—without his encouragement.

John Hamilton and Richard Thomas, as readers of the dissertation in which this volume is rooted, helped me to craft the first rough framework for my ideas, and I have been very grateful to have both as colleagues in subsequent years.

I have drawn on the advice of a number of knowledgeable friends and colleagues, many of whom undertook to read all or part of the work in progress. Jason Aftosmis, Doug Frame, and Greg Nagy provided invaluable comments on a complete draft of the manuscript. Chapter 2 benefited from expert readings by Tim Barnes and Jeremy Rau; Jonas Grethlein's observations significantly improved chapter 3. Hillary Chute, Anna Henchman, Lenny Muellner, and Greg Nagy (all members of the so-called *atelier des anciens et modernes*) helped me with a generous discussion of chapter 5 (over pancakes). Correspondence with Joel Christensen was influential at an early stage of the work. Invigorating conversations with Barbara Graziosi and Johannes Haubold helped me to frame the project as a whole. James Townshend was an indispensable help in the preparation of the manuscript.

Papers deriving from this project were presented at the University of Oregon, the University of California, Santa Barbara, Harvard University, the University of California, Los Angeles, and the University of Missouri. I am grateful to the audiences on all those occasions for their reactions and thoughtful remarks, many of which have been incorporated into the book. One supportive listener from the last of these events—John Miles Foley—is now sorely missed.

The news of his death on May 3, 2012, cast a shadow over my final work on the manuscript. I am sorry that I did not have the opportunity to present him with a copy of the book, as I had promised.

Some of the early writing was done during my time as a Junior Fellow in the Harvard Society of Fellows. I am grateful to Wally Gilbert and Diana Morse for fostering such a genial atmosphere for conversation and reflection, and to all the junior and senior fellows of those years for many hours of stimulating discussion. Chapter 9 was written during three serene months as an unofficial guest at the Center for Hellenic Studies. I owe a great debt of thanks to the Center's staff, including Doug Frame, Sylvia Henderson, Cynthy Mellonas, Robin Olson, and Ruth Taylor, for making my stay possible.

For moral support at various stages of this project I am especially grateful to Dan Aaron, Tamar Abramov, Guillermo Bleichmar, Anna Bonifazi, Hillary Chute, Julia Faisst, and Scott Johnson, as well as to my parents, to whom I have dedicated this book, and my extended family.

Finally, I am grateful beyond words to Bonnie Talbert, whose love and encouragement mean more to me than I can ever say.

A Note on Texts, Translations, and Transliterations

Passages from the *Iliad* are quoted from T. W. Allen's *editio maior* (Allen 1931). Quotations from the *Odyssey* follow the Teubner edition of P. von der Mühll (von der Mühll 1962). Unless otherwise noted, all translations that appear in this book are my own. I have intended these to be useful rather than elegant. In transliterating proper names, I have adopted a hybrid system, using Latinized forms for names that are widely familiar but otherwise adhering to a precise transliteration of the Greek: so, Achilles and Menelaus (rather than Akhilleus and Menelaos), but Onkhēstos (rather than Onchestus). This is an uneasy compromise between convention and exactitude, but I ask the reader's forbearance. I use a circumflex to indicate the contraction in transliterations of Greek contract verbs.

Abbreviations

CID	*Corpus des inscriptions de Delphes*. 1977–. Paris.
FD	*Fouilles de Delphes*. III. *Épigraphie*. 1909–85. Paris.
FGrH	Felix Jacoby, ed. 1954–64. *Die Fragmente der griechischen Historiker*. Leiden.
IC	Margherita Guarducci. 1935–50. *Inscriptiones Creticae*. Rome.
IG	*Inscriptiones Graecae*. 1873–. Berlin.
LfgrE	Bruno Snell and Hans Joachim Mette, eds. 1955–. *Lexikon des frühgriechischen Epos*. Göttingen.
LSJ	H. G. Liddell, R. Scott, and H. S. Jones. 1996. *A Greek-English Lexicon*. 9th ed., with a revised supplement. Oxford.
PMG	Denys Page, ed. 1962. *Poetae Melici Graeci*. Oxford.
SEG	*Supplementum Epigraphicum Graecum*. 1923–. Leiden, Alphen aan den Rijn, Amsterdam.
SIG³	Wilhelm Dittenberger, ed. 1915–24. *Sylloge Inscriptionum Graecarum*. 3rd ed. Leipzig.
TGL	Henricus Stephanus. 1831–65. *Thesaurus Graecae Linguae*. 3rd ed. Paris.

The Poetics of Consent

From Politics to Poetics

At the conclusion of the chariot race described in the *Iliad*'s twenty-third "book"—to use the misleading but conventional modern term for what ancient scholars more accurately called *rhapsōidiai*, "rhapsodies" or "songs"—a question arises. An unforeseen and unaccountable mishap has caused the best team to come in last; how then should the prizes be awarded? This is a question of considerable importance in the context of a poem that has been propelled, from the very first book, by controversies over the rewarding of status and achievement, particularly as concerns Achilles. Now Achilles himself proposes a solution that is designed to recognize both the demonstrated worth of Diomedes, the first-place finisher, and the inherent worth of Eumēlos, who ought to have won: Diomedes will take first prize and Eumēlos second. This is a solution that appeals to all those in attendance, as the narrator immediately informs us: "So he spoke, and they all approved" (ὣς ἔφαθ᾽, οἳ δ᾽ ἄρα πάντες ἐπήνεον, 23.539). The narrator goes on to explain, in the next line, that this expression of approval ought to have meant, as a matter of course, the execution of Achilles' proposal: "and now he would have given [Eumēlos] the mare, for the Achaeans had approved" (καί νύ κέ οἱ πόρεν ἵππον, ἐπήνησαν γὰρ Ἀχαιοί).

The scene is evidently one of collective decision making, insofar as a proposition is put before a group on whose approval, notionally at least, the outcome depends.[1] In the event, Achilles' proposal is not carried out. But the narrator's remark about what *ought* to have happened, inconspicuous as it is, deserves closer scrutiny. The brief description of the normal order of things constitutes a rare instance of metanarrative, that is, of commentary, by the narrator himself, on the underlying rules and conventions of the narrative in progress. As in the case of Kalkhas' "folk definition of anger terms" (*Il.* 1.80–83), to which Thomas Walsh has drawn attention, the *Iliad* here records a gloss on a crucial element of its narrative apparatus, except that the gloss is no longer attributed to a character within the narrative but authorized by the narrator himself.[2] The simple act of stepping outside, however briefly, of the strict sequence of narration to make such a comment lays a certain amount of stress on this moment of collective approval, and we may justifiably wonder what motivates the emphasis. The chapters that follow formulate an answer to this question, by investigating the position of collective decision making in the *Iliad*'s narrative economy and by exploring the power ascribed to collective will in the context of deliberation.

These investigations ultimately permit me to extrapolate from the text of the poem as we have it an image of poetic tradition (more precisely, the Iliadic tradition) that privileges the collective judgment of an implied "interpretive community."[3] But there are many intermediate steps in the argument. For the purposes of this introduction, I begin with an observation made in 1948 by Louis Gernet, who, prompted by this same passage from Book 23, remarked that "the word *epaineîn*"—the verb that designates the approval of the Achaeans in both the lines quoted above—"often designates in Homer a quasi-juridical efficaciousness."[4] What Gernet meant by this is that the verb in question—which provides the Ariadne thread by which I trace my way through the poem in the chapters to come—conveys the sense ("often," in his words, but I will argue, *always*) of a certain formally recognizable procedure of ratification that has the effect, in ordinary circumstances, of actualizing the proposal to which it refers. When I say "formally recognizable," I do not mean to suggest that the Homeric heroes themselves acknowledge the existence of a system of formal rules and procedures to which they must adhere, as though their deliberations were to be conducted according to some version of *Robert's Rules of Order*. In spite of repeated appeals to what is *themis*, "established custom," for speakers in the assembly, one of the distinctive features of the Homeric portrayal of politics is its emphasis on the fluid, inchoate nature of collective dynamics, which offer, at best, a glimpse of incipient institutions.[5]

The formalization of these dynamics is rather a matter of the language and conventions of Homeric poetry, conventions on which the narrator himself comments in the passage I have taken as my starting point. These formalized, indeed, formulaic, conventions permit the attentive reader (and, at an earlier stage in Homeric reception, the attentive listener) to see in some ways more deeply into the process of collective decision making than the actors themselves seem capable of doing. As the narrator's metanarrative comment demonstrates, the gap between the represented world of the Homeric heroes and the representation of this world according to the conventions of traditional poetry enables the formulation of rules about political life even in situations in which those rules are suspended or contested.[6]

Gernet's insight about the "efficaciousness" of collective approval in Book 23 and elsewhere runs counter to a widespread view of Iliadic politics. Scholars routinely proclaim the irrelevance of popular sentiment to the decision-making process in the face of the supposedly incontestable authority of autocratic rulers. While allowance is often made for the influence such sentiment might exert informally on the "real" decision makers, nevertheless many critics have been inclined to second Moses Finley's judgment that "the king was free to ignore the expression of sentiment and go his way."[7] The writer of a recent study of ancient Greek political thought has even contended that, among the various assemblies depicted in the Homeric poems, "not one is truly a decision-making assembly," and that it is an "abuse of language to classify as a 'decision'" the response of the assembled Achaeans to Agamemnon's problematic proposal to return home in Book 2.[8] It is true that the Achaeans' mad dash for their ships cannot be counted as a proper "decision": as I argue in chapter 4, the scattering of the army on this occasion is a literal disintegration of collective structures—and not, therefore, the collective determination of a course of action. Yet, as I also show, the group, once reconstituted, does eventually come to a decision, a decision that arises precisely from the collective will of the assembled troops.

Some writers, especially in recent years, have shown a greater willingness to acknowledge the decision-making power vested in the community at large and to assign to the faceless crowds gathered in assembly a full measure of responsibility for the determination of communal affairs. Dean Hammer has, in this vein, usefully examined the relationship between leaders and groups in the *Iliad* in terms of Max Weber's model of plebiscitary politics, stressing the extent to which "the decisions of leaders derive at least part of their legitimacy from the acclaim, or perceived acclaim, of the people."[9] Still, Weber's model accounts more for the legitimation of decisions than their origination, and allows, even predicts, a substantial degree of independence from popular sentiment in a leader's exercise of decision-making power.[10] Closer to the spirit and the letter of Gernet's remark are the observations of William Allan and Douglas Cairns in a recent essay called "Conflict and Community in the *Iliad*," in which they contend (among other things) that "popular support matters" by distinguishing between de iure norms and de facto situations: among the Achaeans, decisions are de iure based on collective will but often undermined de facto by Agamemnon.[11] The *ius* in this formulation corresponds to the rule formulated by the narrator in Book 23, and the de iure / de facto distinction goes some way toward permitting us to reconcile the narrator's normative point of view with the reality of the often arbitrary exercise of power by Agamemnon—a reality that lies at the root of the position, maintained by Finley and others, that leaders are under no obligation to respect the will of their people.

The rule of collective decision making, as formulated by the narrator, hinges on the verb *epaineîn*, which lies at the heart of this study. To understand more clearly what is at stake in the use of this word—what it signifies or implies apart from a "quasi-juridical efficaciousness"—we may turn to another passage, one that is equally revealing of the framework that governs decision making in the poem. At the beginning of Book 4, the gods discuss what is to be done in response to the duel between Menelaus and Paris, which Paris has essentially forfeited. There are grounds for allowing, on the basis of this result, a negotiated settlement to the war, and Zeus proposes doing just that. Hera, however, with the silent support of Athena, objects. She invites Zeus to "do as you please—but we other gods do not all approve" (ἔρδ᾽· ἀτὰρ οὔ τοι πάντες ἐπαινέομεν θεοὶ ἄλλοι, *Il.* 4.29). Zeus immediately relents, albeit not without a commitment from Hera to allow the destruction of one of her beloved cities at some unspecified future time. As I argue in chapter 7, Hera's apparent invitation to Zeus to pursue a course of action that is in conflict with the express preferences of herself and others is nothing more than a rhetorical ploy; she and Zeus both know that, without the support of the group as a whole (signaled by *epaineîn*), no policy of consequence to the community can be sustained. The key word *epaineîn* therefore signals a form of collective approval that is not only sufficient to produce collective action (as emerges from the narrator's account of the awarding of prizes in Book 23) but also, at least in some circumstances, necessary. It is in recognition of this fact that Zeus acquiesces, reluctantly.

The process by which Zeus and the other gods negotiate their competing preferences to arrive at a decision—specifically, to foster the renewal of the fighting with an eye to Troy's eventual destruction—can be described, following Egon Flaig, in terms of consensus. In an important study of the *Iliad*'s "political reflections in atheoretical form," Flaig directs his attention to precisely this scene as an illustration of the principle of consensus (*das Konsensprinzip*).[12] This principle, as he expounds it, entails a number of specific conditions if it is to be instituted in practice, among which two may be singled out for special emphasis.[13]

In the first place, the parties to a decision must have acquired a disposition to yield ("eine Disposition des Nachgebens"): they must be willing and able to subordinate their own preferences to the (stronger or more widely shared) preferences of others, something that is only possible in a political culture that does not automatically equate such yielding with a loss of status or social capital. The contrast between Zeus' willingness to yield in this way to Hera's demands, on the one hand, and the obstinacy displayed elsewhere in the poem by cardinal figures such as Agamemnon, Achilles, Paris, and Hector, could not be more evident. Secondly, group members must be committed to a decision-making framework governed by the principle of deferred compensation ("das Prinzip der vertagten Gegenleistung"), according to which one party's willingness to accede on the present occasion will be reciprocated in the future by another's.[14] This is the principle enforced by Zeus when he extracts from Hera a commitment to permit the destruction of one of her favorite cities in exchange for the destruction of Troy. Again, the contrast with the politics of the gods' human counterparts could not be clearer: Agamemnon's refusal to balance the present loss of Chryseis against the "three- and four-fold" recompense promised by Achilles in Book 1 (*Il.* 1.127–29) leads directly to the difficulties faced by the Achaeans later in the poem.

The "disposition to yield" and the "principle of deferred compensation" are two of the most important mechanisms by which political actors are able to bridge the gap between divergent preferences and arrive at a more or less universal agreement in favor of one of the available options—at a consensus. Unlike the majoritarian politics of modern democracies (or, for that matter, of ancient ones), such a system recognizes that preferences are of variable intensity and that decision makers ordinarily differ not just in the positions they hold but also in the intensity with which they hold them.[15] In fact, the existence of such differences is the very thing that makes consensus possible, for it is only by comparing intensities that subordinating one's own preference to that of another may come to seem acceptable or desirable.[16]

Flaig's reading of the scene in Book 4 is concept driven: he does not correlate his observations with the specific phraseology of the passage, nor does he comment on Hera's pregnant remark regarding the approval of the gods. But the correlation of her use of the verb *epainein* with the *Iliad*'s widespread and systematically formulaic system for describing the behavior of deliberative groups (analyzed in detail in chapter 1) permits us to read more here than just an underlying conceptual apparatus. Hera is not simply engaged in a deliberative process founded on consensus. She is also reflexively aware of that process and deploys a specialized metalanguage to name its intended result. By declaring that not all gods "approve" Zeus' proposal, she is essentially claiming that Zeus has formulated a proposal for which no consensus is possible—therefore, an impracticable proposal.[17] The self-conscious way in which she, like the narrator, is able to specify the ideal outcome of deliberation entitles us to speak of consensus as a recognized principle of collective decision making in the *Iliad*—at least among those privileged speakers (the narrator and the Olympian gods) who, by virtue of their ability to reflect on the story in progress, share a certain metanarrative awareness of Iliadic conventions.[18] For convenience, we may use the term *epainos*, a noun cognate with the verb *epainein*, to refer to the principle of consensus as constructed and realized within Homeric narrative. Although unattested in Homeric poetry—Simonides (*PMG* 531.3) and Pindar (fr. 181 ed. Snell-Maehler) appear to be the first to use the term, in the sense of "praise"—*epainos* serves as useful shorthand for a complex phenomenon.

Cross-culturally, this phenomenon finds its closest parallels in the decision-making procedures of closely knit groups that enjoy a high degree of face-to-face interaction—procedures often employed, for instance, in small-scale, traditional societies and (to take an example that is perhaps more familiar to some readers of this book) by the many committees that regulate the lives of universities and academic departments.[19] Highly interdependent groups such as these typically recognize that the effective implementation of policy requires the more or less universal support of all stakeholders.[20] Such a context necessarily bestows a considerable amount of power on dissenters, since initiatives can be effectively stymied by even a single dissenting voice. Hera's protest in Book 4 provides a ready illustration of this principle, as does the (failed) *epainos* of Book 23, which persists only until Antilokhos raises an objection. On the other hand, only groups as closely knit as these provide the kind of long-term framework for social interaction that can convince actors of the desirability of the "disposition to yield" and the reliability of the "principle of deferred compensation."

Two comments are in order on the term "consensus" as I am using it here, namely, as a designation for a particular mode of collective support characteristic of certain observable decision-making procedures. Firstly, it should be obvious that this usage must be kept distinct from the way in which political theorists, in a tradition extending back through Mill and Locke all the way to antiquity, speak about "consent" as the foundation of political association and of the authority of the state (as in the notion of "government by consent of the governed").[21] Such speculation about the philosophical grounding of legitimate government represents a separate (though not necessarily unconnected) enterprise from the empirical description of consensus in concrete instances of decision making. "Consensus" in this sense belongs more to the domain of social anthropology than political theory. At the same time, it should be noted that, even in this empirical sense, "consensus" can be more a matter of theory than of practice. That is to say, members of a group may subscribe to consensus as the normative principle of their deliberations and regard their decisions as generally reached by consensus, even when they recognize, in the case of specific decisions, that the rhetoric of consensus has worked to stifle dissent and conceal real differences.[22] Consensus, in other words, can have an ideological dimension.

That is not to say, however, that true consensus is somehow fundamentally opposed to dissent, so that the presence of one necessarily means the absence of the other. A distinction must be drawn between *consensus* and *unanimity*: while consensus does indeed require universal support for a given outcome, it is not the case that all parties to the decision will be "of one mind" on the issue. On the contrary, the mechanisms by which consensus comes about—the "disposition to yield" and the "principle of deferred compensation," both facilitated by the existence of a long-term social context that frames each decision as one in an ongoing series—presuppose that, in any given instance, some participants will experience some degree of dissatisfaction; they will nevertheless acquiesce in the present in order to secure future benefits.[23] Consensus, then, is not so much the elimination of dissent as its recuperation. The two are natural *complements* rather than natural contraries.

An appreciation of this complementarity helps in discerning the place of consensus in the broader thematics of the *Iliad*. The *Iliad* is, by and large, read as a poem of conflict, of scission within the group and skirmishes with those beyond it. Certain well-thumbed scenes of accommodation or rapprochement are regularly trotted out in discussions of the "resolution" of key themes—the "reconciliation" of Achilles and Agamemnon in Book 19, the harmonious distribution of prizes in the funeral games, the ransom of Hector in Book 24. But for the most part we are accustomed to think of the *Iliad* as being primarily interested in modalities of conflict rather than modalities of cooperation.

This has been a highly productive critical position, as evidenced, for example, by Arthur Adkins' classic work on the predominance of competitive over cooperative values, *Merit and Responsibility* (1960). Most recently, Elton Barker has devoted sustained attention to the *Iliad*'s "institutionalization of dissent," reading the poem not only as a celebration of the productive power of dissent and debate but also as an actualization of that power, as it calls on audiences and readers to participate vicariously in the disputes it depicts.[24] Barker is not suggesting, of course, that dissent is an end in itself. He is interested above all in the way that dissenting views are managed, assimilated, and turned to the collective good.[25] But the principal intellectual task of his *Iliad* is to construct a space for dissent; whereas I stress the degree to which the poem presents dissent as the necessary precursor to the imminent formation of consensus. (I say "imminent" because the poem never actually depicts the establishment of this consensus; on this, as on many other points, Barker and I are in substantial agreement.) This is not, I think, to "fetishize" consensus at the expense of dissent but to recognize the intimate bond between them.[26] As consensus and dissent are complementary to each other, so is my study to Barker's, and indeed to those many other works that emphasize (rightly) the centrality of conflict in the *Iliad*'s thematic composition.

CONSENSUS AND "HOMERIC SOCIETY"

At the conclusion of his essay on the divine assembly, Flaig is careful to disclaim the idea of a direct correspondence between the portrayal of consensus in *Iliad* 4 and the forms of political conduct preferred by the *Iliad*'s early audiences.[27] The political cultures of archaic and classical Greece were, in his view, too thoroughly saturated by an ethos of competitive rivalry to have adopted consensus-based procedures as the norm. Elsewhere he remarks on just how unusual is this apparent predilection for agonistic modes of decision making: cross-culturally, comparable societies seem to prefer the enhanced solidarity secured by consensus, as indeed did the Roman senate.[28] Many Greek communities, by contrast, embraced the prospect of deciding matters of collective interest in a more divisive manner, by pitting rival views against each other and submitting them to the zero-sum procedure of majority rule.[29] To be sure, one would not want to overstate the case: consensus-based decision making doubtless informed the process of deliberation in many Greek communities and at a variety of levels. Still, the prominence of *stasis*—of civil discord and the fracturing of the social body—in early Greek political poetry from Alcaeus to Theognis and Solon suggests that the "disposition to yield" had a rather weak hold in archaic communities.

It is therefore difficult to read the mechanisms and principles underlying the gods' deliberations as a straightforward reflection of early Greek political culture(s)—if, that is, one is willing to be constrained by the evidence available for the archaic *poleis* of the late seventh and sixth centuries.[30] (Reconstructions of "Dark Age" communities are another matter, to be considered below.) For

Flaig, the difficulty can be resolved by supposing that it was precisely the frequent experience of paralysis and division resulting from habitually agonistic
modes of political interaction that made consensus an object of interest.[31] Nicole
Loraux makes a similar argument regarding the role of civic unity in the Athenian imagination: "the egalitarian *polis* of consensus . . . exists because actual
cities are divided."[32] When applied to the *Iliad,* however, such an argument runs
up against the even more fundamental difficulty of identifying the society
whose experiences are supposed to anchor the representations of the text, either
as direct reflections or as idealized, imaginary alternatives. The question is not
simply whether we can identify or reconstruct a particular society in which to
situate the Homeric poems but whether we ought even to try, given our present
understanding of the poems' origins and development.

By far the most common approach among writers on Homeric politics is to
correlate the political practices represented in the poems with a hypothetical
society belonging to the period just prior to the emergence of the *polis* as an
identifiable form of social and political organization. The temptation to do so is
strong, since, if the correlation could be securely established, the poems would
then open a unique window on a period of Greek social history for which no
other documentary evidence is available. Perhaps the most prominent and widely
known example of this approach is Moses Finley's *The World of Odysseus* (1954;
rev. ed. 1977), which treats the *Iliad* and *Odyssey* as direct evidence for the structure of Greek society in the "Dark Age" (roughly the eleventh through the ninth
centuries BCE). Finley's work has been extraordinarily influential, and although
there are many who differ on points of greater or lesser significance (the most
important of which, arguably, concerns the presence or absence of the *polis* in
the poems), nevertheless his fundamental methodological assumption—that
the poems can be meaningfully correlated with a historical "Homeric society"—
continues to enjoy widespread acceptance. In a series of writings, Kurt Raaflaub
has presented a forceful defense of this position, arguing that "the 'world' presented by the Homeric epics . . . is consistent enough to reflect a historical society that can be dated and contextualized within the social evolution of early
Greece."[33] Other prominent proponents of this view include Pierre Carlier, Walter Donlan, Ian Morris, and Hans van Wees, and the list could easily be extended.[34] Even Hammer, whose study attempts to decouple Iliadic politics from
the history of institutions, still finds it necessary to situate his arguments in the
historical context of the eighth and seventh centuries.[35]

The argument against this approach is well known. As Anthony Snodgrass
stressed in an article intended largely as a response to Finley, the society depicted

in the Homeric poems is a "composite" that combines elements of disparate social systems and historical epochs, elements that could never have coincided in a single historical society.[36] Although Snodgrass does not direct his attention to deliberative procedures or structures of authority, the implications of his argument are clear: if in the case of such diverse phenomena as marriage customs, burial practices, combat techniques, and material culture the *Iliad* amalgamates features that are fundamentally heterogeneous, what right have we to assume that in the case of political structures the poem has remained faithful to a single, identifiable historical context? In the absence of external evidence of a kind that could prove or disprove the picture we observe in the poems, the reconstruction of a coherent pre-*polis* "Homeric society" inevitably involves a measure of circular reasoning, as analysis of the poems themselves alternately relies on and confirms the assumptions brought to bear on their interpretation.[37] With good reason do some scholars speak of the society represented in the poems as a "fiction."[38]

So far as the internal consistency of the poems is concerned, the arguments on one or the other side of this debate cannot be said to be decisive. No matter how many anachronisms are discovered in the world(s) constructed by the *Iliad* and *Odyssey*, it is always possible to claim that there is a discernible core of consistent practices, corresponding to those the researcher ascribes to a hypothetical historical society.[39] At most it can be said that Snodgrass' skeptical position faces more squarely the methodological difficulties involved in a historicizing reading of the Homeric poems. Commenting on his original essay, however, Snodgrass himself points to a more serious difficulty confronting any effort to correlate the poems with a particular historical period: the recent destabilization of what had been, for most of the twentieth century, a generally accepted view that the poems were fixed as texts in the mid- to late eighth century.[40] In the last two decades especially, a steadily increasing number of scholars, holding widely differing views on the means by which the poems were fixed in writing, have argued in favor of moving the date of fixation forward in time, into the seventh century or even into the sixth.[41] Coupled with this trend is a growing awareness of the degree to which the poems, as the products of oral tradition, have been shaped by, and retain traces of, diverse moments in a long process of reception.[42]

The leading voice in this regard belongs to Gregory Nagy, whose "evolutionary model" for the fixation of the texts, designed to account for attested forms of variation from the archaic through the Hellenistic periods, allows for substantial fluidity through the sixth century (and even some residual fluidity thereafter), with the texts responding at every stage to the influence of their ongoing reception.[43] Nagy's model, of course, is only one of many that have been offered for the way in which the poems acquired their present, written form (although it is, in my view, the one that most convincingly reconciles the attested facts of Homeric tradition with comparative evidence from other cultures). Nevertheless, it exemplifies the mounting pressure not only to extend the formative phase of Homeric poetry into the historical period but also to integrate the feedback of reception into the processes of composition and textualization.[44]

The combined effect of these two tendencies amounts to more than the simple acknowledgment of anachronisms. Such an understanding of the tradition requires not only that the potential range of reference be extended forward in time but also that the dynamic interaction between composition and reception be recognized as applying across this range. On this view, the poems' anachronisms are not merely fossils preserved in the sediment of a generic oral tradition prior to the emergence of the monolithic poems we know but traces of an extended process of shaping and reshaping, in which the narrative traditions that ultimately gave us the *Iliad* and *Odyssey* responded to ever-changing social and material contexts.[45] And this is true even if one believes the poems to have been definitively fixed by the writing or dictation of a master poet: the weight of previous contexts of reception is simply too great to be cast off entirely.[46] Accordingly, it becomes far more difficult to speak of an identifiable "core" of themes determined by a fixed point of reference and surrounded by more or less incidental anachronisms. The influence of reception on the shaping of the tradition is too thoroughgoing. Meanwhile, the tradition's formative period appears now to many Homerists to extend further than was previously thought to be the case.[47]

All this is to say that the diachronic depth of the *Iliad* is distinctly greater than has generally been acknowledged.[48] And it is precisely this depth that poses the greatest challenge to straightforwardly historicizing readings of Iliadic politics, which generally attempt to minimize the interplay between composition and reception by substituting a synchronic for a diachronic perspective. The present study endeavors to confront this challenge directly by reconfiguring the text's diachronic dimension as a central object of interest, rather than an interpretive difficulty to be excused or otherwise disarmed. The chapters that follow lead progressively toward the conclusion that the *Iliad*'s representation of politics is primarily (though by no means exclusively) a reflection of the diachronic shaping of the poem through an ongoing process of reception. This process can be conceptualized as a long-term collective decision-making procedure, by which a series of audiences and performers (and ultimately also scribes, editors, and copyists) comes to determine, by virtue of a consensus that stretches across various times and places, the ultimate shape of our *Iliad* and *Odyssey*. The Iliadic picture of political life—and in particular, the emphasis the poem sets on consensus—is not so much an image of the political practice of Greek society at any particular time, I maintain, as a means by which the Iliadic tradition reflects on the process of its own formation. It is, in essence, an encapsulation of the *Iliad's* own, implicit theory of reception.

In subsequent chapters I will have occasion from time to time to speak of "Achaean society" and its characteristics. The reader should always bear in mind that I do not mean in this way to refer to a real, historical society but to the particular image of social organization constructed by the *Iliad*. This image, in my view, has more to do with the dynamics of poetic tradition than with politics in the strict sense.

This is not to say that the view of decision making that emerges from the poem is entirely disconnected from the political experiences of historical Greek communities or that the poem's treatment of political themes was irrelevant to the way that Greeks of particular times and places imagined and engaged in politics. On the contrary, numerous writers, including all those I have identified with the "historicizing" approach to "Homeric society," have drawn useful connections between the poem's representations and the political realities of particular periods.[49] Likewise, there can be no doubt that, as Greek political thought developed over the course of the archaic and classical periods, the *Iliad's* treatment of consensus proved exceptionally "good to think with," particularly for those individuals and communities struggling to articulate a relationship between collective will and structures of authority in the *polis*.[50] The question is, where did the *Iliad's* distinctive vision of consensus come from? Although I am arguing that this vision encodes a diachronic perspective on the Iliadic tradition, I am not therefore discarding the possibility that it has roots in a synchronically identifiable context. That context, I suggest, is to be found not in the sphere of politics per se but rather in the large regional and Panhellenic festivals, such as the Panionia and the Panathenaia, that provided the premier venue for the rhapsodic performance of Homeric poetry, and arguably for the shaping of the Homeric poems themselves (as suggested by ancient accounts of the "Peisistratean recension").[51] It is here, among the audiences at such festivals—events that were hardly apolitical—that we find a real-life occasion for the assembly of large groups of people with divergent interests, whose collective approval or disapproval notionally converges on a single, unified vision of the epic tradition.

It has become an established tenet of Homeric criticism that the performance of epic at Panhellenic festivals constitutes an essential point of reference for the understanding of many features of Homeric poetics.[52] This is above all true for the "Panhellenism" of the poems themselves, by which is meant the fact that Homeric poetry "synthesizes the diverse local traditions of each major city-state into a unified Panhellenic model that suits most city-states but corresponds exactly to none."[53] That is to say, the Homeric poems—and especially the *Iliad*—represent a negotiation between the competing interests of various Greek communities, whose representatives regularly gathered at Panhellenic religious festivals to witness and judge the recreation of Homeric poetry in performance. In other contexts, the competition between divergent points of view, whether within or between communities, might be likely to take on the zero-sum, strictly agonistic quality that characterized so many aspects of Greek society. But in the context of the Panhellenic presentation of Homeric epic, notwithstanding the zero-sum *agōn* among the rhapsodes themselves, audiences could take part in a genuinely positive-sum, collaborative interaction, in which the goal was not the preservation of one's own interests at all costs but the constructive reconciliation of differences.[54] Crucially, this interaction was also one that foregrounded the diachronic connection to previous occasions, since the performance of traditional poetry is always to a greater or lesser extent the reenactment of previous performances.[55] The experiences of such audiences, I propose, are the most likely model for the *Iliad*'s representation of consensus.

ASSUMPTIONS, METHODS, AND ORGANIZATION

In advancing this argument, I am conscious of the need to observe carefully the limitations on what can be said with confidence about the early history of the Homeric texts.[56] In the wake of Milman Parry's demonstration of the oral and traditional character of Homeric verse, and the work of his student Albert Lord, particularly on the relationship between formula and theme, there is now widespread agreement that the *Iliad* is the product of a highly refined and longstanding oral tradition. But opinions differ as to the manner in which this tradition became fixed in writing, and, consequently, whether the poem as we have it reflects the artistic vision of a single individual (or individuals), or, alternatively, embodies the "corporate" point of view of the tradition as a whole. Most versions of the "dictation theory" stress the former possibility, tying the very creation of the text and/or its ultimate triumph over alternative versions to the artistic superiority of a particular poet or performance. I have already stated my

own preference for Nagy's "evolutionary model" as the most convincing explanation for the emergence of a fixed text out of a tradition of oral performance.[57]
But the conclusions presented in this book are not intended to prove or disprove
one or the other theory regarding the origins of the *Iliad*. To be sure, my ultimate goal is to demonstrate that the poem itself anchors its version of events at
Troy in the collective will of a notional community of audience members, and
this may be taken as an argument in favor of finding in the *Iliad* a "corporate"
point of view—or at least the claim to present one. But there is no reason why a
particular poet, even an exceptionally gifted one, should not seek to ground his
performance in the collective sentiments of the audience he envisions, or foreground the collective authority underwriting any resulting text. A traditional
poet might be positively motivated to do so.[58]

Given the unavailability of external evidence for the early history of the *Iliad*,
the researcher is left with only one secure method for recovering an image of
the workings of the Iliadic tradition: the internal evidence of the poem itself.
This is a method that has been effectively employed by scholars who have
sought to replace the categories and constructs of modern criticism with criteria recoverable from the poem itself, on the grounds that the poem is most truly
measured by its own, implicit standards. Eloquent expositions of this point of
view can be found in books by, among others, Andrew Ford and Oliver Taplin,
both of whom do much to promote an understanding of Homeric poetry on its
own terms.[59] A notable example of this inductive method in action is Richard
Martin's *The Language of Heroes*, which employs the speech act theory of Austin
and Searle to uncover in the narrative of the *Iliad* a system of performative speech
genres, against which the poem itself, as an instance of performative speech,
can then be judged. Martin's book is an important point of reference for my
own study, which likewise seeks to come to terms with the poem's self-
presentation by conceiving of it as a kind of speech act.[60] While Martin, however, directs his attention primarily to the *performers* of speech acts, I focus instead on the other participants in the performative event, the addressees or
audience, whose adequate response, termed by Austin "uptake," is in fact no less
essential to the constitution of the total speech act than the performative utterance itself.[61] My book may therefore be understood as a kind of complement to
Martin's, insofar as it aims to apply the complementary pole of the speech act
model to the problem of the self-definition of Homeric poetry.

The principle that Homeric poetry must be understood on its own terms,
and not according to the criteria of later literature and criticism, found its most
forceful expression in the work of Milman Parry. Parry's writings, and those of

Albert Lord, provide another essential point of reference for the arguments presented in this volume.[62] For Parry, the technique of formulaic composition and the organization of Homeric language into extensive and economical systems of formulaic expressions provide the key to unlocking the meaning of Homeric verse. Although more recent research has shown that the constraints of formulaic diction are not always as rigid as Parry at times seemed to suggest, nevertheless it remains true that the systematic character of Homeric phraseology is thoroughgoing.[63] And this fact permits one to use recurring phraseology as a reliable guide to the themes of Homeric poetry—which Lord showed to be equally traditional and equally systematic—as well as to their development in context.[64] Indeed, as Nagy has demonstrated, from a diachronic perspective it is theme that motivates formula, and not vice versa. Nagy's comments on the methodological and interpretive consequences of this circumstance for his own work are worth quoting in full:

> My reliance on key words in context cannot be dismissed as a reductive and oversimplified method of delving into the thematic complexities of archaic Greek poetry, if indeed the words themselves are functioning elements of an integral formulaic system inherited precisely for the purpose of actively expressing these complexities. The words should not be viewed merely as random vocabulary that passively reflects the themes sought by the poet. The semantic range of a key word in context can be expected to be as subtle and complex as the poetry in which it is encased.[65]

In the pages that follow, I will adhere to a similar method, using the careful observation of repeated words and phrases—above all, instances of the key verb *epainein*—to guide my interpretation of the *Iliad*. While it obviously cannot be claimed that every repeated word in the poem gives voice to some significant theme, nevertheless, in the case of words (like *epainein*) that express the poem's most central themes, every occurrence provides important evidence. And there is also, in light of Lord's work on thematic sequences, a category of negative evidence in addition to this positive one: if a particular phrase, as an expression of a particular theme, can be expected to occur on the basis of patterns observable elsewhere, its substitution by another is significant and in need of explanation.[66]

The case for understanding the *Iliad*'s representation of collective decision making as a mode of reflection on the constitution of the Iliadic tradition itself is a cumulative one. Although the specific arguments in favor of this view are largely confined to the last two chapters of this book, they rest on the conclusions reached in the preceding seven. Many of these conclusions can stand on their own as independent readings of crucial Iliadic scenes, passages, and motifs. Together, however, I hope they amount to a compelling account of the way in which the *Iliad* frames its relationship to, and dependence on, the generations of audiences that witnessed the creation and refinement of this remarkable poem.

The chapters themselves are organized into three parts. Part I, "Frameworks and Paradigms," lays the groundwork for the central chapters by examining the formulaic conventions that govern scenes of collective decision making and observing their use in certain exemplary scenes. Chapter 1 outlines what I have called the "grammar of reception," that is, the system of formulas for describing the responses of audiences in deliberative settings. This grammar sets a premium on the response designated by the verb *epainein*, which I am glossing in terms of "consensus." Chapter 2 seeks to deepen our understanding of what is at stake here by exploring the etymology of this crucial verb and its relation to the larger complex of inherited Indo-European ideas concerning verbal behavior and social order. Chapter 3 demonstrates the way in which the *Iliad* makes collective decision making an issue of central importance right from its opening scene, which can be described as a "state of exception" both politically and in terms of the poem's formulaic grammar. Chapter 4 examines the turmoil that erupts with the Achaeans' rush for their ships in Book 2 as the paradigm for a narrative trajectory that likewise characterizes the poem as a whole: a crisis occasioned by the suspension of political norms leads to the restoration of solidarity, expressed (in Book 2) in terms of the *epainos* of the group.

This paradigm orients all three chapters of part II, "The *Iliad*'s Political Communities," which analyze the development over the course of the poem of political themes, and particularly the *epainos* motif, with respect to each of the *Iliad*'s three political communities: the Achaeans (chapter 5), the Trojans (chapter 6), and the Olympian gods (chapter 7). A number of important conclusions emerge from these chapters. In the first place, the Achaeans never manage to recover in their public discourse the kind of total solidarity that would correspond to the expression of a comprehensive *epainos*. A fully inclusive consensus eludes them to the very end, and so the trajectory outlined by the paradigm of Book 2 remains incomplete. Instead, the climactic expression of *epainos* we expect to find among the Achaeans is displaced to the Trojans, among whom it represents an entirely anomalous moment, another exception to conventional norms playing a crucial role in the poem's narrative economy. This unique Trojan consensus also highlights a tension between innovation and conservatism that often seems to arise in connection with *epainos*—nowhere more clearly than in the deliberations of the gods, who routinely discuss the possibility of some innovative departure from the dictates of "fate," that is, of the traditional narrative.

The metapoetic character of the gods' deliberations leads me, in part III, "Resolutions," to examine the ways in which the *epainos* motif points beyond the fictional world of the poem to the *Iliad's* reception in the here and now of performance. The several closural strategies by which the poem brings to a conclusion its exploration of collective dynamics—the ransoming of Hector's corpse, the trial scene depicted on Achilles' shield, the chariot race at Patroklos' tomb, and the funeral of Hector—form the subject of chapter 8. All of these episodes contribute to the final framing of the poem's central political concerns, but it is above all in the group responses to the performances that conclude the poem, the sung lamentations for Hector at the end of Book 24, that we witness the transferal of collective energies from the political to the poetic domain. The ultimate fulfillment of the poem's implicit demand for the constitution of a truly cohesive collective will can be found in the image of the "boundless people" (δῆμος ἀπείρων, *Il.* 24.776), whose response to Helen's lament brings the poem to a close. This embedded audience is *apeirōn,* "boundless," to the extent that it reflects the existence in the real world of an ever-expanding audience for the poetry of the *Iliad,* an audience on whose sympathetic response the continuity of the tradition absolutely depends.

Chapter 9 assesses more carefully what it means to say that the tradition depends on its audiences; it looks at evidence outside the poem indicating that some ancient readers, at least, saw in the poem's treatment of *epainos* an expression of the critical nexus between the Iliadic tradition and its community of reception. The "exceptional" nature of the poem, which begins with a "state of exception" and never quite arrives at a definitive restoration of norms, takes on special significance in light of the tension between Panhellenic and local, or "epichoric," traditions, since any given rendering of a traditional story is likely to conflict in some respects with one or the other set of traditional norms. This Iliadic "exceptionalism" provides a better way of thinking about what makes the *Iliad* a unique work of art than the outworn opposition between tradition and innovation.

It has long been the custom to look first to the *Odyssey,* with its self-conscious depictions of singers and storytellers, to discover what Homeric poetry has to say about itself as a medium.[67] A short afterword discusses points of connection (and divergence) between the themes I trace in the *Iliad* and those of its companion poem. I will consider myself to have achieved my purpose, however, if I succeed in demonstrating that the *Iliad* has more to say about its nature as a traditional text than has generally been admitted. I will leave it to others to carry the debate forward—for, as over two and a half millennia of criticism have shown, the community of those to whom the Homeric poems speak is truly boundless.

PART I

Frameworks and Paradigms

CHAPTER 1

The Grammar of Reception

This book is fundamentally a study of the *Iliad*'s vision of community. Since this vision is constructed and communicated in language, it is also, in the first instance, a study of the words and formulas employed in the *Iliad* to describe the essential activities of communal life, that is, the activities by which a community constitutes itself as such. One activity in particular—collective decision making—takes pride of place in this regard, for it is by coming together to make decisions on matters of collective importance that a community gives shape to its goals, its guiding principles, and indeed to its very reason for being.

At the center of this investigation of collective decision making stands a single word—the verb *epainein*—a word that plays a crucial role in the language and formulas used in the *Iliad* to describe the process of collective deliberation. This verb, and the associated noun *epainos*, which I will regularly employ as useful shorthand for the general social phenomenon indicated by the verb, are familiar from classical Greek, where they are rough equivalents for the English verb and noun "praise."[1] As Bruno Snell recognized, however, classical usage is an unreliable, even misleading, guide to the meaning of Homeric phraseology.[2]

Although later connotations and denotations, including "praise," are not unrelated to the semantics of the Homeric verb, a proper understanding of its specific significance must be based solely on the facts of Homeric diction and formulaics, supplemented, where appropriate, by the evidence of archaic Greek poetry more generally.[3] Even Snell's own *Lexikon des frühgriechischen Epos*, grounded in his understanding of *Wortfeldforschung*, is somewhat too synthetic to be fully satisfying.[4] There the word is listed and discussed together with the unprefixed form *aineîn*. Analyzing simplex and composite forms together, the entry arrives at the primary meaning "to say 'yes,' assent."[5] This definition is adequate in a general way, but it also obscures an essential restriction on the usage of the form with *epi-*, which is, in all but one instance, used in a deliberative context to designate the response of the assembled group to the proposal of a speaker.[6] The simplex *aineîn*, on the other hand, indicates a more general, more broadly defined kind of "approval": one man's endorsement of a particular goddess (in the *Iliad's* sole reference to the Judgment of Paris, 24.30); collective approval for events that have already taken place (therefore lacking the properly deliberative dimension of *epaineîn*: *Od.* 16.380); the sanction granted by the "*themistes* of Zeus" for a particular course of action (*Od.* 16.403); and so on.[7]

As the above examples show, *aineîn* can take a variety of subjects and a variety of objects, often without any reference to the spoken word as a necessary medium. *Epaineîn*, by contrast, is firmly rooted in the domain of speech. It is usually used absolutely, but on the single occasion on which it takes a direct object, that object is specifically an utterance—a *muthos* (*Il.* 2.335). The connection, in this example, to *muthoi* provides an important indication of the word's proper field of reference. As Richard Martin demonstrated in an exemplary monograph, the archaic Greek notion of *muthos* corresponds to what modern speech act theorists identify as a "performative"—a use of language that aims primarily not to describe but to bring about a certain state of affairs, so that the speech in question is itself an action with a determinable effect on the world.[8] In the case of the *muthos* that occasions the sole use of *epaineîn* with a direct object, the speech act is Odysseus' restoration of order in the Achaean camp after Agamemnon's disastrous "testing" of the troops at the beginning of Book 2, which amounts in fact to a reconstitution of the Achaean body politic (the subject of chapter 4). But it is essential to recognize that Odysseus' performative utterance, his *muthos*, is not in itself sufficient for the successful accomplishment of the speech act. J. L. Austin, whose influential *How to Do Things with Words* laid the foundation for the contemporary theory of speech acts, stressed that the performative utterance is only one component of the speech act as a whole, which requires in addition a number of so-called felicity conditions, many of which are independent of the speaker's actual words, to be met if the act is to be realized.[9]

Among the most important of these conditions is what Austin referred to as "uptake," that is, the successful reception of the utterance by the addressee or audience, who must recognize that the speaker intends to perform a certain act and respond accordingly.[10] It is here, in connection with Austin's "uptake," that we can begin to grasp the true import of the Homeric verb *epainein*. When this word is used to describe the Achaeans' collective approval for Odysseus' *muthos*, we are being told something more than that the Achaeans felt generally well disposed toward the substance of Odysseus' proposal. We are being shown the inner workings of an emerging speech act, the process whereby speaker and audience collaborate in realizing the power of speech to transform reality.

In all other instances, *epainein* is used either absolutely or with only an indirect object (identifying the speaker to whom the audience is responding: this usage occurs only once, at *Il.* 18.312).[11] Yet the word remains just as firmly bound to the production of speech acts as when its relation to *muthoi* is directly stated. This is a straightforward inference from the contextual restriction noted above: with only a single exception, the word refers exclusively to the collective response to a proposal for action in a deliberative setting—that is, to a *muthos* like Odysseus', although the proposal itself may not actually be designated as such.[12] In fact, *epainein* occupies a crucial position in a system of formulas that provides the *Iliad*'s means for describing such responses in all their (limited) variety. This system of formulas—which amounts to a kind of formulaic "grammar of reception," a strictly rulebound way of characterizing collective responses—must provide the starting point for a more detailed exploration of the meaning of *epainein* in Homeric poetry generally, and more particularly its significance for the development of the *Iliad*'s poetic concerns.

THE PHRASEOLOGY OF COLLECTIVE RESPONSE

The nature of Homeric poetry as a largely formulaic medium permits us to ground our understanding of Homeric phraseology in the empirical description of the discrete functions of individual elements within the system of Homeric diction. Milman Parry was the first to formulate as a general principle the "economy" (or "thrift") of this system, by which he meant the tendency of formulas not to duplicate the function of other fixed phrases in equivalent metrical contexts.[13] Although formulaic economy can now be seen not to obtain in so strong a form as Parry initially envisioned, nevertheless it is widely recognized as a serviceable working assumption.[14] As such, it warrants the expectation that the formulas centering on the key verb *epainein* will occupy a unique position in the broader phraseology of reception. By isolating the function of these formulas, we can triangulate their semantics—and the semantics of *epaineîn*—vis-à-vis the functions of contrasting expressions, *without* relying on any undue assumptions based on classical usage or synthetic approaches.

Given the high proportion of direct speech in the *Iliad* and *Odyssey*, it is not surprising that the poems should have evolved an elaborate set of conventions for "framing" the words of characters. There are a variety of "turn-taking" formulas for registering the alternation of speakers in conversation, formulas for introducing and concluding individual speeches, and so on. We are interested here in that subset of framing formulas that pertains to the conclusion of speeches in contexts of collective deliberation. Deliberative contexts are usually indicated by lexical markers like *agorē*, "assembly," or *boulē*, "council." Such explicit labels are not, however, a necessary feature of deliberative scenes. When the gods debate the fate of Hector in Book 22, they are clearly engaged in collective deliberation; in fact, as we will see in chapter 7, the scene hinges on the deployment of the language of *epainos*. But there is no direct indication that their speeches take place in a formal *agorē* or *boulē*. The mere fact that they are engaged collectively in a discussion of a possible course of action that has significant consequences going forward is enough to establish the homology of the exchange with other scenes of collective decision making.

The process of deliberation, oriented as it is toward the prospect of some collective activity or undertaking, almost necessarily focuses attention on the relation between speech and action. In such contexts, the framing formulas that mark the conclusion of speeches take on considerable importance, for, as noted above, they implicitly address the question of "uptake," and so speak to the translation of words into action. The poetry's simplest means of indicating that a deliberative speech act has achieved its intended result is a whole-line formula stating that the speaker's audience "heard and obeyed," as in the case of Priam's pronouncement in the Trojan *agorē* in Book 7:

νῦν μὲν δόρπον ἕλεσθε κατὰ πτόλιν ὡς τὸ πάρος περ,
καὶ φυλακῆς μνήσασθε καὶ ἐγρήγορθε ἕκαστος·
ἠῶθεν δ' Ἰδαῖος ἴτω κοίλας ἐπὶ νῆας . . .

. . . .

ὣς ἔφαθ', οἳ δ' ἄρα τοῦ μάλα μὲν κλύον ἠδ' ἐπίθοντο·
δόρπον ἔπειθ' εἵλοντο κατὰ στρατὸν ἐν τελέεσσιν·
ἠῶθεν δ' Ἰδαῖος ἔβη κοίλας ἐπὶ νῆας·
Il. 7.370–72, 379–81

"For now, take your suppers throughout the city as before,
and be mindful of the watch and keep vigil each of you;

But at dawn let Idaios go to the hollow ships . . ."

. . . .

Thus he spoke, and they heard him and obeyed;
then they took their suppers in companies throughout the host,
and at dawn Idaios went to the hollow ships . . .

This straightforward means of declaring a proposal's efficacy takes for granted its favorable reception on the part of the audience. But in so doing it eclipses the role of collective sentiment in the decision-making process. In this case, the avoidance of a more specific description of the audience's response is telling: when we come to consider this episode more closely, we will find that Priam's proposal is in fact a compromise intended to bridge the gap between two irreconcilable counterproposals and that the apparent readiness with which the Trojans execute it actually conceals deep-seated differences among them as a group.[15]

As an alternative to the simple declaration of a proposal's efficacy, the epic medium has at its disposal a set of formulas that specify the audience's reaction, that is, the concrete manifestation of their disposition toward the speaker's words at the moment of their utterance. Crucially, these response formulas take the place of a direct statement of the transformation of words into action, along the lines of "they heard and obeyed." In fact, explicit notice of a proposal's efficacy becomes redundant once the audience's reaction has been reported. This is a consequence of the strict correlation between audience response and the result of the deliberative process: because successful proposals always meet with one class of responses, unsuccessful ones with another, we can infer from statements of response whether a given proposal will be put into effect.[16] Speech frames are among the most rigorously rulebound elements of Homeric phraseology; this is especially true of the formulas for collective response, where the grammar of reception is not only paradigmatic, governing the range of possible formulas that may be fitted into the response "slot," but also syntagmatic, insofar as it regulates the consequences of any given reaction.[17]

Because they can substitute for a direct statement of efficacy, group response formulas are useful as a means of identifying *ineffective* proposals. The poetry has no means of declaring simply the failure of a proposal, no negative version of "they heard and obeyed"; that function is taken over by certain response formulas that indicate the immediate or eventual failure of a proposal simply by describing the manner of its reception. The system of formulas, moreover, provides a remarkably subtle means of differentiating between speeches and speech contexts that can be, in varying degrees, successful or unsuccessful.

That differences are a matter of degree, and that the responses can, accordingly, be arranged on a scale, endows this system with an expressive utility in addition to its compositional one. The *Iliad*'s poetics of consent develops largely in terms of the contrasts between the various forms of collective response.

Within the *Iliad*, there are five formulaic expressions (with associated variants) for describing the behavior manifested by an audience in response to a deliberative proposal.[18] Each is distinguished by a characteristic verb. Because of the consistent correlation of each of these expressions with the success or failure of the corresponding proposal, we can describe them in terms of an ascending scale of "efficiency." "Efficiency" here means the capacity of a response to bring a proposal into effect—not simply to ratify it, in the sense of establishing the community's support, but to transform it into action. At the bottom end of the scale we find a completely inefficient response, denoting the lack of collective support and de facto the rejection of the proposal; at the top, the fully efficient response of *epainos*, the sign of a robust consensus sufficient to secure results. In between are three intermediate expressions, each indicative of widespread support, but each in some respect falling short of the definitive expression of group will represented by the verb *epainein*.

The five constituent elements of the *Iliad*'s grammar of reception are as follows, listed in order of increasing efficiency according to representative types (variants are appended to each type):

1. ὣς ἔφαθ᾽, οἳ δ᾽ ἄρα πάντες ἀκὴν ἐγένοντο σιωπῇ
Il. 3.95, 7.398, 8.28, 9.29[19]

Thus he spoke, and they were all silent

2. ἔνθ᾽ ἄλλοι μὲν πάντες ἐπευφήμησαν Ἀχαιοί
Il. 1.22, 1.376

Then all the other Achaeans expressed approval

3. ὣς ἔφαθ᾽, οἳ δ᾽ ἄρα πάντες ἐπίαχον υἷες Ἀχαιῶν
Il. 7.403, 9.50

Thus he spoke, and all the sons of the Achaeans shouted in reply

With variant:
ὣς ἔφατ᾽, Ἀργεῖοι δὲ μέγ᾽ ἴαχον (*Il.* 2.333, 2.394)
Thus he spoke, and the Argives shouted loudly

4. ὣς Ἕκτωρ ἀγόρευ᾽, ἐπὶ δὲ Τρῶες κελάδησαν

Il. 8.542, 18.310

Thus Hector spoke, and the Trojans shouted in reply

5. ὣς ἔφαθ᾽, οἳ δ᾽ ἄρα πάντες ἐπήνησαν βασιλῆες

Il. 7.344, 9.710

Thus he spoke, and all the *basilēes* expressed *epainos*

> With variants:
> ὣς ἔφατ᾽ Ἀτρεΐδης, ἐπὶ δ᾽ ἥνεον ἄλλοι Ἀχαιοί (*Il.* 3.461)
> Thus spoke the son of Atreus, and the other Achaeans expressed *epainos*
> ὣς ἔφαθ᾽, οἱ δ᾽ ἄρα πάντες ἐπήνεον ὡς ἐκέλευε (*Il.* 23.539)[20]
> Thus he spoke, and all the others expressed *epainos* for his commands

Significantly, of these five formulas, only the first and the last—the most definitively inefficient and the most definitively efficient response, respectively—are shared by the *Odyssey*.[21] The middle three terms, numbers 2 through 4, are entirely absent from that poem. A comparable grammar for the *Odyssey*, meanwhile, would include several additional phrases not attested in the *Iliad*. We may infer from these facts that the basic needs of the epic medium could be met by a reduced system consisting only of two terms, representing the inefficient and efficient responses, and that these two terms therefore constitute the common core of reception formulas taken over from the tradition at large. To this core each poem adds a set of ancillary expressions that speak to its particular poetic concerns. In the case of the *Odyssey*, for example, the most prominent supplementary response formula sheds particular light on the nature of the Suitors as an autonomous social group.[22] The three intermediate terms of the *Iliad*'s system, on the other hand, all facilitate that poem's exploration of collective will by providing a more finely grained framework for differentiating the political dynamics of various groups in various contexts.

A thorough understanding of this framework, and of the graduated scale of efficiency it encodes, is a necessary prerequisite for any sustained examination of the poem's broader patterns of thematic development. I devote the next several pages to the concise description of each of the five elements in the *Iliad*'s grammar of reception. My aim is to delineate the nuances that assign each to a specific place in the system, for it is by virtue of such distinctions that the unique value of *epainos* can be established.

2. ἔνθ᾽ ἄλλοι μὲν πάντες ἐπευφήμησαν Ἀχαιοί

Then all the other Achaeans expressed approval

The second formula on the scale of efficiency is, in terms of the restrictions on its use, diametrically opposed to the first. It is used only of the Achaeans, and only of the Achaeans in assembly. In fact, it is used only in reference to one particular assembly, the one that opens the action of the poem in Book 1. In both its occurrences, the line refers to the response of the Achaean community—with the notable exception of Agamemnon—to Chryses' request for his daughter's release:

> παῖδα δ᾽ ἐμοὶ λύσαιτε φίλην, τὰ δ᾽ ἄποινα δέχεσθαι,
> ἁζόμενοι Διὸς υἱὸν ἑκηβόλον Ἀπόλλωνα.
> ἔνθ᾽ ἄλλοι μὲν πάντες ἐπευφήμησαν Ἀχαιοὶ
> αἰδεῖσθαί θ᾽ ἱερῆα καὶ ἀγλαὰ δέχθαι ἄποινα·
> ἀλλ᾽ οὐκ Ἀτρεΐδῃ Ἀγαμέμνονι ἥνδανε θυμῷ . . .
> *Il.* 1.20–24 (1.22–24 = 1.376–78)

> "Release to me my dear child, and receive a ransom,
> having reverence for Zeus' son, far-shooting Apollo."
> Then all the other Achaeans expressed approval
> for respecting the priest and receiving the splendid ransom;
> but this did not please the heart of Atreus' son Agamemnon . . .

On the face of it, this response is as inefficient as silence, for the Achaeans' endorsement of Chryses' request fails to win his daughter's release. But it is not immediately obvious why this should be so, since it cannot be said that the audience has not clearly demonstrated its support for the proposal. Evidently, the failure of collective will in this case has to do with the peculiar position of Agamemnon, whose preference appears to trump that of the Achaeans as a whole. Yet it should be noted that Agamemnon soon finds himself compelled to release Chryseis and so to abide by the will of his community.

The fact that this formula has only a single point of reference makes it impossible to generalize about the pragmatic force that can be ascribed to it. In chapter 3, I argue that the indeterminacies surrounding this expression represent a crucial disruption of the poem's formulaic norms, a disruption that sets in motion the subsequent development of central themes. In a certain sense, the *epeuphēmeîn* formula is "ungrammatical": a truly unique utterance, one with a single, nonrepeatable referent, it resists the generalizing process of grammaticalization. And yet it occupies an essential place in the *Iliad*'s system of response formulas, for its own resistance to generalization paradoxically validates the normative force of the other elements of the system.

3. ὣς ἔφαθ', οἳ δ' ἄρα πάντες ἐπίαχον υἷες Ἀχαιῶν
Thus he spoke, and all the sons of the Achaeans shouted in reply

With this third term in the system, we return to a relatively more versatile mode of expression—at least so far as the semantic range of the key verb *epiakhein* is concerned. Like the "silence" formula, this verb can be applied to a variety of contexts quite unrelated to deliberation. It can refer, for instance, to the "acclaim" or simple "cry" of a group on the battlefield, as we see at the end of Book 13, where the Trojans and Greeks respond to an exchange of boasts between Hector and Ajax:

ὣς ἄρα φωνήσας ἡγήσατο· τοὶ δ' ἅμ' ἕποντο
ἠχῇ θεσπεσίῃ, <u>ἐπὶ δ' ἴαχε</u> λαὸς ὄπισθεν.
Ἀργεῖοι δ' ἑτέρωθεν <u>ἐπίαχον</u>, οὐδὲ λάθοντο
ἀλκῆς, ἀλλ' ἔμενον Τρώων ἐπιόντας ἀρίστους.
Il. 13.833–36

Having spoken thus he [Hector] led the way; and they followed with him
with a prodigious shout, and the *laos* behind him <u>cried out</u>.
And the Argives <u>cried out</u> on the other side, nor did they forget
courage, but awaited the attack of the best of the Trojans.

As in the assembly, *epiakhein* here designates the response to a speech, but it does not in this case imply a decision-making process: the speeches in question are mere challenges directed by one hero to another, without any appeal to the community for collective action. Significantly, outside of the deliberative context, the action denoted by *epiakhein* is not restricted to any particular social group; the verb applies to Trojans as well as Achaeans. In the context of the funeral games for Patroklos, it indicates collective cheering, but, again, not collective decision (*Il.* 23.766).[32] Moreover, the word does not appear to have any inherent connection to human social behaviors. The simplex form *iakhein* can designate even inarticulate sound, such as the echoes resounding from the banks of a flooding river (*Il.* 21.10). In short, at its core, *epiakhein* does not seem to indicate a distinctively political action, and it has, accordingly, a wide range of applications.

However, when *epiakhein* is used in the context of a deliberative procedure—that is, when it takes on the role assigned to it by the grammar of reception—the verb exhibits a more limited range. In such contexts, it designates a manner of response that is peculiar to the Achaeans and appears to be characteristic of their political life: neither the Trojans nor the gods ever express their approval in this way when it comes to making decisions. And yet, insofar as the efficiency of the response is concerned, the verb retains an important lack of specificity. Proposals that meet with such a reaction are sometimes put into effect—but not always, as for instance at the beginning of Book 9 (*Il.* 9.50).[33] Furthermore, even when proposals thus received are enacted, we always find some indication of another, more decisive response, which appears to carry the real decision-making force.[34] An instructive case is the response to Odysseus' speech in Book 2 (to which I will return in chapter 4):

ὣς ἔφατ᾽, Ἀργεῖοι δὲ μέγ᾽ ἴαχον, ἀμφὶ δὲ νῆες
σμερδαλέον κονάβησαν ἀϋσάντων ὑπ᾽ Ἀχαιῶν,
μῦθον ἐπαινήσαντες Ὀδυσσῆος θείοιο·
Il. 2.333–35

Thus he spoke, and the Argives shouted greatly, and round about the ships
resounded terribly with the cries of the Achaeans,
who expressed *epainos* for the *muthos* of godlike Odysseus.

We have here a combination of two formulaic responses. The framing formula itself is an adaptation of the *epiakhein* response (although without the preverb *epi-*, which is ordinarily a component of such response formulas). With the participle ἐπαινήσαντες, however, the narrator adds a kind of compressed version or evocation of the response that occupies the top rank on the scale of efficiency. In terms of the system I am describing, this additional qualifier must be understood as the true indicator of an efficient response.

This passage must be kept in mind when, some sixty lines later, we come upon the only instance in which *iakhein* appears to stand alone as an indicator of an efficient response. Agamemnon concludes the sequence of speeches with a brief peroration urging the warriors to prepare for the next day's battle, and he encounters the same response as Odysseus—minus the crucial expression of *epainos*:

ὣς ἔφατ᾽, Ἀργεῖοι δὲ μέγ᾽ ἴαχον ὡς ὅτε κῦμα
ἀκτῇ ἐφ᾽ ὑψηλῇ . . .
Il. 2.394–95

Thus he spoke, and the Argives shouted greatly, like a wave
against a high headland . . .

Agamemnon's speech does include one new proposal that is subsequently acted
upon—he urges the soldiers to prepare a meal in anticipation of the fighting to
come. But his remarks are, substantially, nothing more than a confirmation of
Odysseus' call for the army to remain at Troy. The reaction of the audience is a
transparent indicator of the continuity between these two speeches—and also a
subtle reminder of Agamemnon's deficiencies as a leader.[35] For it is Odysseus'
version of the proposal to remain that receives the definitive response of *epainos*,
while Agamemnon is relegated to a position of secondary importance.

So far as the *(ep)iakhein* response itself is concerned, the picture that emerges
is a mixed one. The reaction signaled by the verb can be correlated with the successful enactment of a proposal, but it is not in itself efficient. It must always be
coupled with some other expression of a decision-making faculty if the speaker's call to action is to be realized. Yet it is a unique characteristic of Achaean
political culture, a distinctively Achaean way of demonstrating collective will,
albeit without fully determining collective action.

4. ὢς Ἕκτωρ ἀγόρευ', ἐπὶ δὲ Τρῶες κελάδησαν
Thus Hector spoke, and the Trojans shouted in reply

The fourth reaction formula is in many ways the Trojan equivalent to the Achaeans' characteristic *epiakhein* response. The key verb *epikeladeîn* occurs only twice
in the poem, both times with reference to the Trojans in assembly. The fact
that the poem uses two distinct, but functionally and semantically parallel, formulas to describe the deliberative activity of Achaeans and Trojans is one of the
clearest signs of a broad strategy aimed at distinguishing the poem's constituent social groups by differentiating their typical modes of political expression.
Like *epiakhein*, *epikeladeîn* is the compound form of a simplex verb (*keladeîn*)
that generally denotes inarticulate noise, such as the tumultuous sound of a
rushing river.[36] Again, the simplex form can indicate nothing more than ap-
plause in the context of an athletic contest—where, incidentally, the verb sheds
its social restrictions and refers to the behavior of the Achaeans (*Il.* 23.869). In
other words, these two verbs are virtually identical in terms of their semantic
range, yet, when applied to collective deliberation, they stand in an exactly complementary distribution.

When it comes to the efficiency of this response, the picture is again mixed. Of its two deliberative occurrences, one is correlated with a more conclusive reaction—namely, the expression of *epainos*, which is on this one occasion only attributed to a Trojan audience (*Il.* 18.310–12). (This extraordinary Trojan consensus, discussed more fully in chapter 6, represents a crucial moment in the *Iliad*'s thematic development.) But it also stands once alone, and on that occasion it appears to carry Hector's words into effect (*Il.* 8.542). On a strict view of these examples, *epikeladeîn* must be said to indicate an efficient response. If that is the case, however, it is interesting in itself that a reaction that should, by analogy with its Achaean counterpart, be less than fully decisive nevertheless suffices for Trojan purposes. At Troy, it seems, collective business can be transacted in a mode that does not on its own meet the requirements of effective deliberation among the Achaeans. It is furthermore significant that these two instances of collective response represent the *only* occasions on which Trojan audiences react openly to a proposal, and they both occur on the battlefield. In the poem's single Trojan civic assembly, we find no indicators of group reaction. This remarkable fact is already suggestive of major political differences between Trojans and Achaeans.[37]

5. ὣς ἔφαθ', οἳ δ' ἄρα πάντες ἐπῄνησαν βασιλῆες
Thus he spoke, and all the basilēes expressed epainos

These differences are nowhere more evident than in the use of the *Iliad*'s fifth and most efficient reception formula, the one that indicates the establishment of a true consensus, signaled by the key verb *epaineîn*. This mode of response is the most contextually restricted element in the *Iliad*'s system, apart from the exceptional *epeuphēmeîn* formula with its single, dedicated application. In the first place, the verb *epaineîn*, like the formula as a whole, can be used only in the context of collective deliberation; whatever kind of action the word denotes, it is something that can only be performed as part of a deliberative process. Secondly, the word is applied only to the deliberations of the Achaeans and the Olympian gods—with one important exception, already alluded to above. In Book 18, at a pivotal moment in the course of the fighting, the Trojans come to a consensus for the first and last time, expressing *epainos* for Hector's proposal to remain camped on the battlefield. The discussion of this episode in chapter 6 will demonstrate that this Trojan consensus is, however, fatally flawed: when the Trojans do at last manage to rise above their characteristically etiolated methods of debate and establish a truly cohesive framework for collective action, they cannot help but get it wrong. As an effective political procedure, *epainos* remains the exclusive prerogative of Achaeans and Olympians. The sense of momentousness that surrounds the Trojan experiment with consensus-based decision making derives from its restriction in general to other social groups.

In the introduction, I pointed out that the poem's narrator, in a rare act of metanarrative commentary, actually articulates the rule that *epainos* should ordinarily result in action:

ὣς ἔφαθ᾽, οἳ δ᾽ ἄρα πάντες ἐπῄνεον ὡς ἐκέλευε.

καί νύ κέ οἱ πόρεν ἵππον, ἐπῄνησαν γὰρ Ἀχαιοί,

εἰ μὴ ἄρ᾽ Ἀντίλοχος μεγαθύμου Νέστορος υἱὸς

Πηλεΐδην Ἀχιλῆα δίκῃ ἠμείψατ᾽ ἀναστάς·

Il. 23.539–42

Thus he spoke, and they were all expressing *epainos* for his command.
And now he would have bestowed the horse, for the Achaeans had expressed
   epainos,
If Antilokhos son of great-hearted Nestor had not
risen and answered Peleus' son Achilles with a claim for justice.

The verb *epainein* therefore designates a *definitively* efficient response. So established is this rule that the *epainein* formula alone indicates, without any further qualification, that a proposal will be enacted. For this reason, the narrator can end the council convened by Agamemnon in Book 7 with a simple statement of the approval of the councilors for Nestor's speech (ὣς ἔφαθ᾽, οἳ δ᾽ ἄρα πάντες ἐπῄνησαν βασιλῆες [Thus he spoke, and all the *basilēes* expressed *epainos*], *Il.* 7.344), and move directly from there to the Trojan *agorē*. The formula itself is an unambiguous signal of the consequence of the Achaeans' discussion, and no further comment is needed, either at the moment of the decision or when Nestor's plan to construct a wall is actually put into action some one hundred lines later.

And yet there are instances in which the expression of *epainos* does not produce the expected result—one of them, in fact, provided by the same passage that elicits the narrator's formulation of the *epainos* rule. Antilokhos' objection to Achilles' proposal (to award second prize in the chariot race to Eumēlos) effectively forestalls its execution. This is in itself instructive, for it highlights those very qualities that permit *epainos* to be described in terms of consensus: a form of agreement that in principle includes all members of the social body, *epainos* obtains only so long as everyone can be understood to participate; at the same time, it falters when confronted with a dissenting voice that cannot be accommodated. But what does Antilokhos' disruption of the decision-making process mean for our understanding of the relationship between *epainos* and action, which the narrator implies is a necessary one?

It is helpful to consider the other two occasions on which the expression of *epainos* fails to bring a proposal to realization. At the end of Book 3, the Achaeans approve Agamemnon's declaration of terms for a negotiated conclusion to the war (ὣς ἔφατ᾽ Ἀτρεΐδης, ἐπὶ δ᾽ ᾔνεον ἄλλοι Ἀχαιοί [Thus spoke the son of Atreus, and the other Achaeans were expressing *epainos*], *Il.* 3.461). The Trojans never have the opportunity to express their own (presumably different) view on the matter; but this is immaterial in light of the fact that the gods intervene, through Pandaros and his bow, to ensure that the negotiations are not permitted to continue. In other words, it is not so much that the *epainos* of the Achaeans is ineffectual as that the broader circumstances, engineered by the gods, have changed, rendering their decision irrelevant. The same thing occurs in Agamemnon's account of how Tydeus and Polyneices once came to Mycenae to ask for aid against Thebes. The Mycenaeans wish to grant their request, but the gods intercede:

οἳ δ᾽ ἔθελον δόμεναι καὶ <u>ἐπῄνεον</u> ὡς ἐκέλευον·
ἀλλὰ Ζεὺς ἔτρεψε παραίσια σήματα φαίνων.
Il. 4.380–81

The people wished to grant assistance and <u>were expressing *epainos*</u> for their request, but Zeus turned them from this course by displaying adverse signs.

Significantly, the Mycenaeans' expression of *epainos* is presumed to be efficient: they would have delivered the requested aid if their decision had not been voided by divine will. In both cases, *epainos* fails to produce results not because of any inherent flaw or deficiency but because of some crucial modification of the context for the decision, tied in each case to the imposition of a framework that supersedes the group's deliberative procedures.

The episode with Antilokhos in Book 23 can be interpreted along similar lines. While there is no divine intervention or appeal to a higher power, Antilokhos' objection does result in an essential adjustment to the framework of the earlier decision. That decision had been made on the assumption that the prizes to be awarded must be limited to those originally designated for the purpose by Achilles. Antilokhos, however, argues that this restricted set of prizes can and should be supplemented from Achilles' store of surplus goods. In essence, he prompts Achilles (successfully) to rescind his earlier system of rewards in favor of another, more flexible one; he thereby changes fundamentally the terms of the debate.

The importance of this change emerges fully into view only when one sets the dispute over prizes in Book 23 against the corresponding distributive crisis of Book 1. The quarrel between Agamemnon and Achilles arises precisely because there is no fund of surplus goods from which to meet Agamemnon's demand for a replacement prize, as Achilles himself points out (*Il.* 1.123–26). When this situation presents itself again in Book 23, Antilokhos is able to alter the very nature of the problem by transforming it from a question of the allocation of limited resources to one of the mere recognition of worth, free of constraints. This momentous shift, which cuts to the core of the *Iliad's* central concerns, understandably voids the prior decision of the Achaeans, for the distributional regime that required the decision in the first place no longer applies.

The point is that when the Achaeans' decision in Book 23 fails to achieve results, this does not mean that the expression of *epainos* is anything less than fully efficient. Rather, a crucial change in circumstances has intervened to render their decision irrelevant. The foundering of their collective will does nothing so much as emphasize just how significant this change is—it can be equated in magnitude with the manifestation of divine power. The simple fact that the narrator can use this occasion to formulate the efficacy of *epainos* as a rule, however, means that the response remains unambiguously decisive. Moreover, there is an important linguistic marker that sets aside all three instances of failed *epainos*, and that thereby preserves the absolute transparency of the *epaineîn* response, that is, the ability of the audience or reader to infer with absolute confidence from the response whether a decision will be put into effect. On all three occasions on which the expression of *epainos* fails to enact a proposal, the key verb *epaineîn* appears in the *imperfect* tense, as though to acknowledge already that the audience's reaction will not arrive at its normal point of completion. By contrast, whenever the verb appears in the aorist tense, it designates an efficient response: viewed as a completed event, the expression of *epainos* implies, as a direct consequence, the translation of a proposal into action. The alternation of tenses is a rulebound feature of the *Iliad's* poetic grammar that, by registering the difference between "complete" and "incomplete" versions of the *epaineîn* response, underscores the normal and, indeed, entirely predictable relationship between *epainos* and action.[38]

This relationship permits us to observe the way in which the grammar of reception is integrated into the poem's architecture at the broadest possible

level. The plot of the *Iliad* is articulated according to narrative units that correspond, roughly, to units of time. The bulk of the story is devoted to events taking place over four days of fighting (with one intervening day devoted to the
burial of the fallen and one crucial night of activity between the second and
third days of battle). Each of these days has its own distinctive narrative sequence, and in each case that sequence is set in motion, programmed, so to
speak, by an expression of *epainos* that commits the poem's actors to the pursuit of a particular course of action. The Achaeans' approval for Odysseus'
speech in Book 2 (*Il.* 2.335) affirms their willingness to enter battle on the first
day; *epainos* for Nestor in Book 7 (*Il.* 7.344) leads to the construction of the burial
mound and defensive wall (and indirectly to the second day's fighting); the consensus in favor of Diomedes' proposal at the conclusion of the Embassy (*Il.*
9.710) assures that the battle will continue on the following day (the third day
of fighting); finally, the Trojans' unique expression of *epainos* binds them to
meet Achilles' onslaught on the fourth day of combat (*Il.* 18.312). Each major
narrative segment is motivated in terms of the implementation of collective will;
each is moreover rendered narratologically necessary in light of the rule that
epainos must be fulfilled in action. In this way what I have described as the syntagmatic dimension of the grammar of reception becomes an organizing narrative principle.

PRELIMINARY OBSERVATIONS

The grammar I have outlined provides the framework for the *Iliad*'s exploration
of political dynamics. The features of this grammar permit a number of general
observations to be made about the terms in which the exploration is conducted. In the first place, the system of response formulas makes a clear distinction between reception as practiced by the Achaeans, on one hand, and by
the Trojans, on the other. The poem has a well-developed vocabulary for describing Achaean deliberations: fully three formulas out of five (numbers 2, 3,
and 5, above), representing three different degrees of efficiency, refer to responses exhibited exclusively, or virtually so, by the Achaeans. This is in keeping with the *Iliad*'s intense interest in the conflicts and social strife that afflict
the Achaeans in particular. The elaboration of a set of responses peculiar to
their discussions allows the poem not only to figure their political culture as
something distinctive but also to take a more nuanced view of their setbacks
and progress as they attempt to resolve the social crisis created by Achilles'
quarrel with Agamemnon.

The existence of a scale of efficiency sets a clear premium on the response that occupies the top position, the response of *epainos,* which represents the most effective form of collective approval that can be mustered. The expression of *epainos* is the only secure guarantee that the policy proposed by a speaker will be enacted and maintained. This emphasis on the need for robust communal support—for consensus—is doubtless true to the experience of many early Greek communities, which must have found the continuing cooperation of group members to be essential to the completion of any collective undertaking. Later chapters will make the case that the value bestowed in the *Iliad* on cooperation and consensus, though obviously comprehensible in terms of the general dynamics of Greek society, has a more specific relevance to the particular community to which the poem addresses itself, namely, the "interpretive community" made up of its many historical audiences and readers.

Finally, the grammaticalization of collective response—by which I mean the organization of response scenes according to regular patterns of phraseology with regularly entailed consequences—highlights by contrast those "ungrammatical" moments at which a unique response or an exception to the prevailing norms escapes from the predictable web of conventional relationships that otherwise characterizes the system. There are two such moments in the poem: the exceptional response of the Achaeans to Chryses' request in Book 1, designated by the verb *epeuphēmeîn,* and the equally exceptional consensus of the Trojans in Book 18, when they adopt a mode of collective approval more typical of the Achaeans, the mode of *epainos.* In subsequent chapters, these two events will emerge as critical points of inflection in the trajectory of the poem's thematic development.

THE LEXICON OF DISSENT

The formulaic system I have described above provides an essential means of indexing the constitution and expression of collective will. Most readers of the *Iliad,* however, are less likely to be struck by these recurring indicators of communal sentiment than by the poem's rich and varied palette for depicting conflict, discord, and dissent, the social frictions that continuously threaten to undermine, rather than reinforce, solidarity. The value set on harmony is implicit in the *Iliad*'s unrelenting portrayal of strife within and between groups, but, on the surface at least, it is much easier to think of the poem as a study in the management of antagonisms than as a celebration of cooperative enterprise.[39] Many, if not most, of the prominent words and themes, including the very first word, μῆνιν ("wrath"), pertain not to positive modes of social interaction but to their opposites. Against this background, the theme that is my primary object of interest—the theme of *epainos*—rises to prominence, precisely because of its contrast with the poem's apparent preoccupations. It is critical, therefore, to explore the language for describing the breakdown of solidarity, in order to construct a more detailed view of the surrounding context in which the unique importance of *epainos* is rooted. The poem's lexicon of dissent is an essential supplement to the grammar of reception: tracing the development of consensus requires attending both to the expression of collective will and to the depiction of tears in the social fabric. Here I provide a highly selective overview of this complementary phraseology of conflict, with special focus on a few key terms that relate directly to the *epainos* motif.

The lexicon of dissent includes both familiar words requiring little or no comment and expressions whose full significance emerges only on closer investigation. A passage from the *Odyssey* that displays a particularly dense collocation of terms relating to the breakdown of social harmony provides a useful indication of the range of the relevant phraseology. During his visit to Pylos, Telemachus hears from Nestor a detailed account of the Achaeans' embarkation from Troy. This narrative—a kind of embedded version of the cyclic *Nostoi*—offers a final glimpse of the Achaeans attempting to make decisions collectively. Accordingly, it comprises a virtual précis of the various themes deployed in the *Iliad* to mark the failure of consensus. Nestor begins by stressing the unity of sentiment he generally enjoyed with Odysseus, which serves as a point of contrast for the subsequent tale:

ἔνθ᾽ ἦ τοι εἷος μὲν ἐγὼ καὶ δῖος Ὀδυσσεὺς
οὔτε ποτ᾽ εἰν ἀγορῇ δίχ᾽ ἐβάζομεν οὔτ᾽ ἐνὶ βουλῇ,
ἀλλ᾽ ἕνα θυμὸν ἔχοντε νόῳ καὶ ἐπίφρονι βουλῇ
φραζόμεθ᾽ Ἀργείοισιν ὅπως ὄχ᾽ ἄριστα γένοιτο.
αὐτὰρ ἐπεὶ Πριάμοιο πόλιν διεπέρσαμεν αἰπήν,
βῆμεν δ᾽ ἐν νήεσσι, θεὸς δ᾽ ἐκέδασσεν Ἀχαιούς,
καὶ τότε δὴ Ζεὺς λυγρὸν ἐνὶ φρεσὶ μήδετο νόστον
Ἀργείοισ᾽, ἐπεὶ οὔ τι νοήμονες οὐδὲ δίκαιοι
πάντες ἔσαν· τῶ σφεων πολέες κακὸν οἶτον ἐπέσπον
<u>μήνιος ἐξ ὀλοῆς</u> γλαυκώπιδος ὀβριμοπάτρης,
ἥ τ᾽ <u>ἔριν</u> Ἀτρεΐδῃσι μετ᾽ ἀμφοτέροισιν ἔθηκε.
τὼ δὲ καλεσσαμένω ἀγορὴν ἐς πάντας Ἀχαιούς,
μάψ, ἀτὰρ <u>οὐ κατὰ κόσμον</u>, ἐς ἠέλιον καταδύντα,—
οἱ δ᾽ ἦλθον οἴνῳ βεβαρηότες υἷες Ἀχαιῶν,—

μῦθον μυθείσθην, τοῦ εἵνεκα λαὸν ἄγειραν.

ἔνθ᾽ ἦ τοι Μενέλαος ἀνώγει πάντας Ἀχαιοὺς

νόστου μιμνήσκεσθαι ἐπ᾽ εὐρέα νῶτα θαλάσσης·

οὐδ᾽ Ἀγαμέμνονι πάμπαν ἑήνδανε· βούλετο γάρ ῥα

λαὸν ἐρυκακέειν ῥέξαι θ᾽ ἱερὰς ἑκατόμβας,

ὡς τὸν Ἀθηναίης δεινὸν χόλον ἐξακέσαιτο,

νήπιος, οὐδὲ τὸ ᾔδη, ὃ οὐ πείσεσθαι ἔμελλεν·

οὐ γάρ τ᾽ αἶψα θεῶν τρέπεται νόος αἰὲν ἐόντων.

ὡς τὼ μὲν χαλεποῖσιν ἀμειβομένω ἐπέεσσιν

ἕστασαν· οἱ δ᾽ ἀνόρουσαν ἐϋκνήμιδες Ἀχαιοὶ

ἠχῇ θεσπεσίῃ, δίχα δέ σφισιν ἥνδανε βουλή.

Od. 3.126–50

For all that time I and glorious Odysseus

never spoke at odds in the assembly or in the council,

but, being of one mind, we offered intelligent and well-meaning counsel

to the Argives as to how things might turn out for the best.

But when we sacked the lofty citadel of Troy,

and took to our ships, and a god scattered the Achaeans,

then indeed did Zeus devise a sorry homecoming

for the Argives, since they were not all thoughtful

or just; for this reason many of them met with an evil fate

on account of the destructive wrath of the grey-eyed one, child of a mighty father,

who set strife among the two sons of Atreus.

These called all the Achaeans to the assembly,

rashly, in no due order, at the setting of the sun—

and the sons of the Achaeans came weighed down by wine—

and they gave an account of their reason for summoning the host.

Then Menelaus bade all the Achaeans

to give thought to their homecoming across the broad back of the sea.

But this did not at all please Agamemnon, for he wished

to restrain the host and offer sacred hecatombs,

so that he might appease the terrible anger of Athena—

the fool, he did not know that he would not persuade her;

for the intention of the eternal gods is not quickly diverted.

So those two stood at odds, exchanging harsh words.

And the well-greaved Achaeans sprang up

with a tremendous roar, and a twofold plan pleased them.[40]

We find here a number of motifs that recall the breakdown of solidarity at the beginning of the *Iliad*. In fact, there is a rather remarkable set of correspondences between Nestor's tale and the *Iliad* proem: both narratives are framed in terms of a *mēnis*, "wrath," and in both cases the *kholos*, "anger," of a divinity leads directly to *eris*, "strife," among two leading figures in the Achaean community.[41] All of these expressions, as well as the mention of a violation of *kosmos*, "order," refer more or less directly to social and relational pathologies that have an obvious bearing on the ability of the community to constitute itself as a harmonious whole.[42] I would like to concentrate for a moment on a lexical signal that has a less transparent relationship to group solidarity but that will nevertheless play a decisive part in the *Iliad*'s exposition of collective dynamics: namely, the curious way in which the verb *handanein* serves to single out a divisive, even counterconsensual, preference.

As Nestor tells the story, Menelaus addresses "all the Achaeans," enjoining them to adopt what will, in the end, turn out to have been the most sensible course of action—to set sail at once on a direct course for Hellas. But this plan "did not please [ἑήνδανε] Agamemnon at all." Nestor deliberately contrasts two different audiences for Menelaus' speech: one that is more or less universal, encompassing "all the Achaeans," and the particularized audience of Agamemnon alone, who seems self-involved to the point of solipsism. There is thus a suggestion that the nature of the preference designated by *handanein* is somehow fundamentally rooted in an individualized perspective that takes no regard for the concerns of the group as a whole. "Pleasure" (or displeasure) is a way of signaling divergence from an otherwise cohesive collective will. The divergence need not always be restricted to individuals acting in isolation: in fact, Agamemnon's dissent prompts a broader splintering of the social body, as a significant subset of the Achaean community opts to remain at Troy. But even when it comes to the collectivized consequences of Agamemnon's personal heterodoxy, *handanein* remains the lexical signal of a preference that divides the community: δίχα δέ σφισιν ἥνδανε βουλή ("and a twofold plan pleased them," *Od.* 3.150).[43]

Once again, Nestor's tale of the end of the Trojan campaign corresponds in a remarkably precise way with the beginning of the *Iliad*. There, too, it is Agamemnon's insistence on his personal preference that fractures the body politic. The divisive problems that plague the Achaean community are set in motion when Chryses presents his appeal for the release of his daughter; the description of the response garnered by his proposal, which I have already had occasion to quote, likewise uses *handanein* to contrast the reactions of two audiences, the Achaeans as a whole and Agamemnon in particular:

ἔνθ' ἄλλοι μὲν πάντες ἐπευφήμησαν Ἀχαιοὶ
αἰδεῖσθαί θ' ἱερῆα καὶ ἀγλαὰ δέχθαι ἄποινα·
ἀλλ' οὐκ Ἀτρεΐδῃ Ἀγαμέμνονι ἥνδανε θυμῷ . . .
Il. 1.22–24

Then all the other Achaeans expressed approval
for respecting the priest and accepting the splendid ransom;
but this did not <u>please</u> the heart of Agamemnon son of Atreus . . .

The nature of this political crisis, which pits Agamemnon's inclination against
the collective will of the community at large, is the subject of chapter 3. For
now, it is sufficient to note that, as in Nestor's account of the return from Troy,
Agamemnon's recalcitrant individualism has broad consequences for the social
life of the group, leading as it does to the withdrawal of Achilles and the sequence of emergencies that follows. In this respect as in others, Nestor's version
of the *Nostoi* revisits fundamental Iliadic themes.[44]

The individualistic overtones that can be detected in these uses of *handanein*
are even further amplified through consideration of the word's deployment in
nondeliberative contexts. Even when it is not a matter of audience response, the
verb is regularly employed to contrast the divergent preference of an isolated
individual with the general practice of a larger group. So, for example, when
Ajax, fighting from the prows, takes up a position of unique prominence during
the battle at the ships, the narrator emphasizes the extent to which his actions
set him apart from the general disposition of the army:

οὐδ' ἄρ' ἔτ' Αἴαντι μεγαλήτορι ἥνδανε θυμῷ
ἑστάμεν ἔνθά περ ἄλλοι ἀφέστασαν υἷες Ἀχαιῶν·
Il. 15.674–75

Then it did not <u>please</u> the *thumos* of great-hearted Ajax
to stand at a distance with the other sons of the Achaeans.

In like fashion, the *Odyssey*'s swineherd Eumaios displays his own version of
Ajax's heroic independence:

ὣς ὁ μὲν ἔνθ' Ὀδυσεὺς κοιμήσατο, τοὶ δὲ παρ' αὐτὸν
ἄνδρες κοιμήσαντο νεηνίαι. οὐδὲ συβώτῃ
ἥνδανεν αὐτόθι κοῖτος, ὑῶν ἄπο κοιμηθῆναι,
ἀλλ' ὅ γ' ἄρ' ἔξω ἰὼν ὁπλίζετο· χαῖρε δ' Ὀδυσσεύς . . .
Od. 14.523–26

So Odysseus lay down there, and beside him
lay the young men. It did not <u>please</u> the swineherd, however,
to make his bed in the same place, apart from the pigs,
but he made ready to go outside; and Odysseus was glad . . .

Instances such as these reveal not just an individualized perspective but a properly separatist impulse, in light of which it becomes easier to understand how the verb *handanein* can serve as an index of divisive, counterconsensual forces.

Handanein is relevant to our inquiry because it is an essential component of the *Iliad*'s decision-making vocabulary. Other items in the lexicon of dissent do not themselves pertain to the deliberative process but nevertheless speak to the more general problem of the utilization of speech to create and maintain a community. I conclude this necessarily brief and selective survey with an examination of two interrelated words that intersect with the theme of *epainos* at the most fundamental level, in connection with the poem's pervasive concern with the establishment of social solidarity through speech. These are the verb *anainesthai*, "deny, refuse," and the adjective *apēnēs*, a word of obscure meaning for which Liddell and Scott offer the glosses "ungentle, rough, hard . . . cruel" (LSJ s.v.). In the next chapter I review the evidence that permits us to connect these two words through their etymological relationship to the root **an-*, which is the same root from which our key verb *epaineîn* ultimately derives. Here, I may simply point out that, on the purely synchronic level of Homeric diction, these two words are functionally and semantically parallel, both signifying the rejection of a mode of speech or utterance that would reinforce solidarity (in Greek, an *ainos*, which also derives from **an-*). More specifically, both are used in reference to an individual who refuses a request or offer, along with the implied social bond.[45] A comparison of structurally similar passages demonstrates the basic equivalence of the two words. During the Embassy of Book 9, Phoenix uses the parable of the *Litai* ("Entreaties" personified) to impress upon Achilles the consequences of refusing an offer of redress:

ὃς δέ κ᾽ <u>ἀνήνηται</u> καί τε στερεῶς ἀποείπῃ,
λίσσονται δ᾽ ἄρα ταί γε Δία Κρονίωνα κιοῦσαι
τῷ ἄτην ἅμ᾽ ἕπεσθαι, ἵνα βλαφθεὶς ἀποτίσῃ.
Il. 9.510–12

Whenever someone <u>refuses</u> and stubbornly rebuffs them,
they go and entreat Zeus, son of Kronos,
to send ruin to attend him, so that he might pay them back with his suffering.

In the *Odyssey*, when Penelope reflects on her duties as hostess vis-à-vis the beggar (her husband in disguise), we find a similarly gnomic pronouncement on the necessity of accepting one's obligations toward those whose social position entitles them to a certain measure of consideration:

ὃς μὲν <u>ἀπηνὴς</u> αὐτὸς ἔῃ καὶ <u>ἀπηνέα</u> εἰδῇ,
τῷ δὲ καταρῶνται πάντες βροτοὶ ἄλγε' ὀπίσσω
ζωῷ, ἀτὰρ τεθνεῶτί γ' ἐφεψιόωνται ἅπαντες·
Od. 19.329–31

Whoever is himself <u>uncaring</u> and knows <u>cruelties</u>,
all men pray for him to suffer
while he lives, and all abuse him when he has died.

In one instance we have the verb *anainesthai*, in another the adjective *apēnēs*, but in both cases what is at stake is the refusal of an implicit or explicit request grounded in the expectations arising from a particular kind of social relationship (*philia*, "friendship," in the case of Achilles, *xenia*, "hospitality," in that of Penelope).[46]

It is typical of this *ainos*-related vocabulary that, in both these passages, it is the social dimension of the transaction that is foregrounded, rather than the verbal one. Where the social consequences of speech are of principal importance, there is a tendency to elide the act of speaking itself. This is especially true of *anainesthai*—in part, no doubt, because the verb's transparent relationship to "speaking" words such as *ainos* and *aineîn* ("make an *ainos*") permits the verbal character of the action to be inferred even if it is not made explicit by the context. So, we repeatedly find *anainesthai* used in reference to the refusal of some socially meaningful action or gesture (a gift, the offer of a seat) with only the barest mention of the speech act that accompanies it, or none at all.[47] The connection between speaking and *apēnēs*, the etymology of which is far more difficult to discern on the basis of surface features, is often even more elliptical. An example like the following, in which the adjective is used to characterize a *muthos*, a speech act, directly, is the exception rather than the rule:

οὕτω γὰρ δή τοι γαιήοχε κυανοχαῖτα
τόνδε φέρω Διὶ μῦθον <u>ἀπηνέα</u> τε κρατερόν τε,
ἦ τι μεταστρέψεις; στρεπταὶ μέν τε φρένες ἐσθλῶν.
Il. 15.201–3

Should I then, dark-haired holder of the earth,

carry to Zeus this *muthos,* so <u>unyielding</u> and formidable,

or will you change it in some way? Noble minds are flexible.

Exceptional as it is, this passage nevertheless provides an important indication of the persistent bond between the semantic sphere governed by the adjective and the domain of speech as a social medium.

Crucially, the parallelism between *anainesthai* and *apēnēs* can be traced in connection with one of the *Iliad*'s most central themes, the motif of the *loigos,* "devastation," that only Achilles (or his substitute) is capable of "warding off" from the Achaeans. Achilles himself is the first to verbalize this theme, when he swears before the heralds who have come for Briseis that he will not intervene to defend the Achaeans in the future:

> τὼ δ᾽ αὐτὼ μάρτυροι ἔστων
> πρός τε θεῶν μακάρων πρός τε θνητῶν ἀνθρώπων
> καὶ πρὸς τοῦ βασιλῆος <u>ἀπηνέος</u> εἴ ποτε δ᾽ αὖτε
> χρειὼ ἐμεῖο γένηται <u>ἀεικέα λοιγὸν ἀμῦναι</u>
> τοῖς ἄλλοις·
> *Il.* 1.338–42

> Let these two be witnesses
> before the blessed gods and mortal men,
> and before the <u>unyielding</u> king, if ever again
> there be need of me <u>to ward off unseemly devastation</u>
> from the others . . .

As Gregory Nagy has shown, the expression λοιγὸν ἀμῦναι, "to ward off devastation," as it is deployed (with variants) throughout the poem, is a succinct recapitulation of the "story about how Achilles' *mēnis* caused grief for the Achaeans."[48] It is, in other words, a metonym for the essential story of the *Iliad.* Here, Achilles implicitly and proleptically identifies as the ultimate cause of that story the behavior of Agamemnon, whom he pointedly characterizes as *apēnēs.* Later in the poem, however, Patroklos lays the same charge against Achilles, as the one whose *apēnēs* behavior has permitted the crisis to unfold:

> τί σευ ἄλλος ὀνήσεται ὀψίγονός περ
> αἴ κε μὴ Ἀργείοισιν <u>ἀεικέα λοιγὸν ἀμύνῃς</u>;
> νηλεές, οὐκ ἄρα σοί γε πατὴρ ἦν ἱππότα Πηλεύς,
> οὐδὲ Θέτις μήτηρ· γλαυκὴ δέ σε τίκτε θάλασσα

πέτραι τ' ἠλίβατοι, ὅτι τοι νόος ἐστὶν <u>ἀπηνής</u>.
Il. 16.31–35

> What benefit will another of a later generation take from you
> if you do not <u>ward off unseemly devastation</u> from the Argives?
> Pitiless one, Peleus the horseman was not your father,
> nor Thetis your mother: the grey sea must have borne you
> and steep cliffs, since your mind is <u>unyielding</u>.

Thetis makes a similar claim in Book 18, when she summarizes the events of the poem up to that point for Hephaistos:

ἔνθ' αὐτὸς μὲν ἔπειτ' <u>ἠναίνετο λοιγὸν ἀμῦναι</u>
Il. 18.450

> Then he <u>refused to ward off devastation</u> himself.

Thetis, however, employs the verb instead of the adjective to characterize Achilles' stubborn refusal to come to the aid of his peers. Apart from simply reinforcing the basic correspondence of these two words, Thetis' use of this more self-evidently speech-related term makes it that much more explicit that at the root of Achilles' alienation and the consequent devastation that faces the Achaeans lies the failure of socially constructive speech, of *ainos*.

The close connection between this vocabulary of verbal rejection (*anainesthai, apēnēs*) and a key metonymic signifier of the Iliadic plot as a whole points meaningfully to the centrality of speech as a social force in the constellation of the poem's most fundamental themes. The repeated characterization of the "devastation" threatening the Achaeans as a failure or denial of *ainos* is the counterpart (or counterpoint) to the motif of collective decision making, which represents the answer to the crisis as a matter of the restoration of solidarity through the assertion of collective support for a constructive speech act (*epainos*). The collective reassertion of *ainos* implicit in the verb *epaineîn* is the corrective for the repudiation of socially constructive speech of which Achilles and Agamemnon are both guilty. The next chapter examines in greater detail the relation between speech and society as encoded in the word *epaineîn* and its cognates. The exploration of the narrative realization of the *Iliad*'s poetics of consent begins in earnest in chapter 3.

CHAPTER 2

Consensus and Kosmos

Speech and the Social World in an Indo-European Perspective

So far I have focused my discussion of the key verb *epaineîn* strictly on the patterns of usage attested by the system of Homeric diction and formulaics. This is an essential first step made necessary by the constraints of formulaic phraseology, which, by virtue of an ecology that assigns to each expression a more or less discrete niche in the overall system, tends to set a premium on the pragmatic significance of words and phrases. It would be a mistake, however, to imagine that Homeric diction is a language unto itself, or that it is so mechanistically determined that its functional ecology effectively erases the range of meanings and connotations associated with word use in ordinary language.[1] The words of Homeric poetry have a prehistory that informs their use in the epics; they can be expected in turn to have had an impact on the contemporaneous and subsequent evolution of the Greek language. So far as the word at the heart of this analysis is concerned, certain connections with broader Greek usage are evident within the Homeric corpus: both the *Iliad* and the *Odyssey* provide examples of *ainos/aineîn* (the simplex form underlying *epaineîn*) used in reference to "praise," a meaning that becomes more and more prominent in the subsequent archaic and Classical development of the *ainos* family of words.[2] The study of Homeric diction thus inevitably compels us to consider that diction not as a self-contained, hermetic system but as a local refinement of an evolving language.

The broader picture obtained when Homeric phraseology is set against the backdrop of larger linguistic and cultural patterns deepens our understanding of the stylizations of formulaic discourse by situating them within the framework of deeply ingrained ways of thinking and speaking. While it is not my intention here to give an exhaustive account of the diachronic development of *ainos* and its cognates, I do wish to sketch the Indo-European background, both sociocultural and linguistic, that underlies and motivates the Homeric elevation of the term *epaineîn* to a position of central importance in the *Iliad*'s thematics. The results will not only lend support to the view that *epainos* in the *Iliad* signifies the consolidation of social and political cohesion—of consensus—but will also cast light on other important uses of the vocabulary of *ainos* in Greek.

THE SOCIOLOGY OF PRAISE

If the notion of "praise" seems to predominate in the later usage of *ainos* and related terms, that notion is already evident in the Homeric corpus.[3] It may even be felt to be implicit in the kind of collective approval we have detected in Iliadic instances of the verb *epaineîn*. There is an obvious continuity between the expression of a collective preference in favor of a particular proposal and the implicit or explicit "praising" of it.[4] And yet, when we consider what Gernet described as the "quasi-juridical efficaciousness" of Homeric *epainos*, mere "praise" is liable to seem but a dim reflection of a much more vital social phenomenon.[5] Here we must be careful not to import the bias of our contemporary societies, which may be inclined to view praise as either a subjective judgment largely devoid of concrete implications or as the rhetorical embellishment (even obfuscation) of preexisting facts. From the perspective of more closely knit, traditional societies, particularly those that assign to the spoken word a position of central importance in the life of the community, praise appears as a social fact of considerable importance in its own right. Adopting such a perspective, we can discern not just a continuity between Homeric usage and *epainos* as "praise" but a fundamental homogeneity rooted in the relation between speech events and the forces that constitute a community as such. Far from being a denatured version of a more efficacious, "quasi-juridical" social process, "praise" in this strong sense—an act of verbal endorsement that creates or reinforces social relationships central to the life of a community—in fact exemplifies precisely the kind of collective significance I am attempting to recover from the Homeric use of *epaineîn*.

An essential guide to the social importance of praise in archaic Indo-European societies can be found in the writings of Georges Dumézil, who, in two important studies, outlines an Indo-European ideology that assigns to authoritative pronouncements on an individual's merits and faults—the dyad of praise and blame—a central role in the constitution of the social body.[6] Dumézil focuses on the evidence provided by the societies of early Rome and India (supplemented by Celtic material in the case of his 1943 book, *Servius et la fortune*), both of which attest a body of legends attached to a primordial king whose efforts to establish civic or cosmic order are mediated in fundamental ways by structures of praise.

At Rome there is Servius Tullius, an "elected" king who consolidates power, in the annalistic tradition represented by Livy and Dionysius of Halicarnassus, through popular affirmation of his virtuous conduct.[7] The principal achievement of Servius' reign—the institution of the *census*—is, in Dumézil's reading, a kind of reciprocal version of the public evaluation of merit that guarantees the king's position: an authoritative judgment on each citizen's worth determines his place in the social order and consequently determines the order of society as a whole. In the Indic context, the accounts in the *Mahābhārata* and the Purāṇas of the mythical king Pṛthu (Pṛthī in the Vedas) transpose to the cosmic level the constitutive power of praise. Pṛthu, the first consecrated king (and hence patron and ritual model of all consecrated monarchs), restores order to the world after the death of his predecessor, Vena.[8] Pṛthu's birth from the corpse of Vena coincides with the birth of two primordial singers of praise, Sūta and Māgadha, forerunners of royal panegyrists. These immediately offer a proleptic encomium of Pṛthu's virtues and future accomplishments, effectively binding the king to fulfill their expectations; in Dumézil's words, "as much and more than *noblesse*, praise *oblige*."[9] Resolved to live up to the praise he has received, Pṛthu proceeds to impose order on a chaotic world and distributes among all classes of beings their appropriate portion of the world's bounty. In both these cases, praise is the essential catalyst for the emergence of order. The affirmation of merit that confirms Servius' rule finds its counterpart in the eulogies that accompany the birth of Pṛthu; praise for the Indic king compels him to construct a new hierarchical harmony in the world, just as Servius redirects the power of public esteem into the constitution of social and civic order.

Dumézil founds his comparison of India and Rome on a basic linguistic fact: the Latin root *cens-* (as in *census, censēre,* and *censor*) is cognate with the Sanskrit root *śaṃs-* "praise," which, from the Vedas on, provides a central component of the vocabulary of official panegyric, especially in connection with rituals of royal consecration. For instance, the Vedic stanzas known as *nārāśaṃsyaḥ* (sg. *nārāśaṃsī*)—literally, "[verses] in praise (*śaṃs-*) of men (*nārā-*)," hymns celebrating the virtues and achievements of kings—are connected in the *Taittirīya Brāhmaṇa* to a consecration ritual explicitly identified with the ritual bestowed by the gods on Pṛthu.[10] The praises pronounced over the newly born Pṛthu are the mythical archetypes for these ritual texts. Latin *cens-* and Sanskrit *śaṃs-* are both reflexes of the Indo-European root **kens-*, to which etymological diction-aries ordinarily assign the meaning "speak solemnly."[11] Dumézil, however, ar-gued for a much more precise definition, hinging on the use of praise (or blame) to put things in their places: "the root implies that the declaration is felt to be true, if it is a matter of fact, just, if it is a matter of evaluation; it implies as well that, morally at least, this declaration will take effect, situating or re-situating in its place in the cosmic or social order the thing that is affirmed or the being that is judged."[12] The emphasis laid here on the consequentiality of the utterance is far from incidental: over and over again, Dumézil stresses that the verbal act designated by reflexes of **kens-* is fundamentally efficacious.[13]

Émile Benveniste counters—rightly perhaps—that Dumézil's definition is colored too much by the specifically Latin treatment of the root. But he too underscores the extent to which the root's core meaning centers on the notion of efficacy: "the Indo-European root **kens-* signifies properly, 'to affirm with authority a truth (that becomes law).' "[14] In spite of the parenthesis, the phrase "that becomes law" is essential: **kens-* designates a use of speech that has con-sequences, that produces obligations based on social or material facts—in a word, a speech act.[15]

Onomastic evidence suggests that the Indo-European verbal root **kens-* remained productive in Mycenaean Greek.[16] In alphabetic Greek, however, it retains only a residual, though important, presence. As early as 1877, Friedrich Froehde proposed that the root is represented in Greek by *kosmos*, a word with a complex set of meanings ranging from "order" to "ornament" and "beauty."[17] Froehde's etymology, accepted by Brugmann and others, has found itself in competition with several other explanations, although it is acknowledged as "the least improbable" in Chantraine's *Dictionnaire étymologique de la langue grecque.*[18]

José Luis García-Ramón, arguing in favor of the derivation from **kens-*, has brought welcome clarity to the situation by offering a convincing rebuttal of the alternatives (García-Ramón 1992a). Proceeding from Dumézil's notion of a "déclaration qualifiante," García-Ramón outlines a semantic development for *kosmos* involving three consecutive stages: originally signifying an "authorita-tive declaration or evaluation," by a process of progressive semantic displace-ment the word comes to mean first "order," then what is "beautiful" or an "or-nament" because it is well ordered (45). The first stage in this development is largely inaccessible to us. Although *kosmos* preserves certain associations with speech, for the most part the notion of an authoritative and efficacious use of the spoken word is bleached from the Greek reflexes of **kens-*.[19] Traces of such an association—but traces only—can be recovered from the *Iliad*, for instance in the so-called *Epipōlēsis* ("Inspection of the Army"), the scene in Book 4 where Agamemnon reviews and galvanizes his troops in preparation for battle. In steeling the resolve of his captains, Agamemnon deploys the complementary tools of praise and blame. The scene is manifestly a continuation of the mustering described in Book 2's Catalogue of Ships, where the orderly marshaling of the various contingents is repeatedly designated by *kosmeîn* or *diakosmeîn*, verbal derivatives of *kosmos*: the *kosmos* of the army is in this way tied directly to Agamemnon's use of authoritative evaluation.[20] But this is only a faint echo of the constitutive social power of evaluative speech described by Dumézil. If we wish to trace the full implications of his studies for Greek material, we must rely on his sociological, rather than linguistic, arguments.

In fact, so far as Greek is concerned, the demonstrative power of Dumézil's work consists not in its use of etymological evidence but in the clarity of its sociological vision.[21] Attempting a kind of "thick description," Dumézil is at pains to situate linguistic data within the context of large-scale social structures and institutions. His avowed purpose is to construct a genealogy of social systems, not linguistic forms. His interest in genetic, rather than typological, comparison requires him to restrict his focus to Indo-European societies, but he readily admits that other cultures would illustrate the same kinds of social forms and forces as well or better.[22] He cites examples from Polynesia and the northwest coast of North America; Jeff Opland has extended the range of comparison to Africa as well, where we likewise find (among the Zulu and Xhosa) specialists in praise and blame standing at the center of vital social networks, serving "to establish and maintain the social order."[23] The same complementarity of praise and blame can be observed among the tribesmen of North Yemen, who readily acknowledge the integral role of praise poetry in cycles of reciprocal exchange.[24] The list of comparanda could doubtless be extended considerably. Dumézil's investigations may be guided by linguistic clues, but it is the widespread relevance of his sociological insights that renders his reconstructions compelling.

One of the most important components of Dumézil's analysis in this regard is the connection he establishes between praise and networks of gift exchange or other distributive mechanisms—what Marcel Mauss calls the "total social fact" of "potlatch," a term he adopts from the Chinooks of North America's Pacific Northwest as a designation for those systematic forms of exchange that embody the very structure of a community.[25] Servius' "election" is founded in large part on his generosity, and the *census* itself amounts to a kind of formalization of economic relationships; Pṛthu, meanwhile, reciprocates his panegyrists' songs of praise in the first instance by bestowing on them lavish gifts, and sub-sequently by ensuring the adequate distribution of the earth's riches to men, gods, and beasts. Praise for the ruler and the relationships of reciprocity that bind together the community are conceived as components of a single, totaliz-ing social framework.

This way of thinking—this ideology of praise in relation to the most funda-mental structures of society—evidently goes back to a remote period in the development of Indo-European cultural forms. Calvert Watkins has stressed the extent to which the poetic systems of various Indo-European societies en-code, at the most fundamental level, the notion of a reciprocal relationship binding the poet, the artisan of praise, with his patron and community.[26] In the traditional classification of the Vedas, for example, the stanzas known as *nārāśaṃsyaḥ*, "praises of men," stand in close relation to, and are often not distin-guished from, those called *dānastutayaḥ*, "praises of gifts."[27] In medieval Irish, the word for "poem," *dúan*, continues the root **dap-*, an essential element of the Indo-European vocabulary for reciprocal exchange.[28] As Benveniste has shown, this root, attested in Latin by *daps*, "(religious) banquet," and in Greek by *dapanē*, "expenditure," and *daptō*, "devour," in fact serves as an index of the Indo-European version of potlatch.[29] Like their counterparts in other Indo-European societies, the medieval Irish poets stood at the center of a network of exchange that con-stituted an integral part of the social fabric.

Within Greek literature, perhaps the most sustained expression of this social and economic system can be traced within the epinician odes of Pindar. The compensatory mechanisms that balance the poet's praise—his *ainos* or *epainos*—against the patron's rewards and the victor's "expenditure" (*dapanē*) of physical, spiritual, and material resources are a running motif in the *epinikia*.[30] Indeed, they form the thematic and ideological core of Pindar's epinician poetics, as Leslie Kurke has demonstrated in her masterful exposition of the social dynam-ics displayed and enacted in the odes.[31] For Kurke, epinician poetry "represents athletics as a kind of potlatch, a competition for prestige based on the lavish expenditure of wealth, physical exertion, and time."[32] The victory ode is only one among many forms of prestige goods caught up in the conspicuous display and consumption of wealth occasioned by an athletic contest. The epinician poet, however, occupies a crucial position in the relay of exchanges surround-ing the athlete's victory, for his song of praise is the instrument by which the potentially divisive forces unleashed by the competition for prestige are subli-mated into an expression of solidarity as the victor is ritually reintegrated into his community.[33]

The tasks of epinician, on Kurke's view, are to manage the tension between aristocratic household and *polis* and to reestablish the social bonds of harmonious communal life. Both the form and the content of such poetry contribute to the achievement of these goals: in the context of choral performance, epinician song unites the voices of community members and instantiates their collective identity; at the same time, many Pindaric themes (*xenia*, "hospitality"; political virtues such as *dikē*, "justice," and *eunomia*, "good governance") actively reinforce the various obligations subtending society.[34] The *epainos* of Pindar's poetry of praise is thus triply engaged in the construction of solidarity: as a token in the network of exchange that unites members of the group, as a ritual of integration, and as a discursive articulation of fundamental principles of social life.

Epinician poetry represents ancient Greek literature's most developed expression of the social function of praise, but many of these themes are present *in nuce* in the Homeric poems—specifically, and not surprisingly, in the section of the corpus that most closely approximates the context for which Pindar composed his odes: the athletic contests in honor of Patroklos in *Iliad* 23.[35] The funeral games mark an important moment in the social life of the Achaeans at Troy. The liberal dispensation of prizes to all contestants (no one goes away empty-handed) rehabilitates a distributive system that has been in disarray ever since the crisis relating to the war-prizes of Agamemnon and Achilles in Book 1. Insofar as it ranks and ties together all members of the community (even, in the case of Patroklos, those no longer living), this system can justifiably be characterized in terms of potlatch.[36] By now, it should come as no surprise that praise holds a recognized place in the compensatory cycle. This comes across clearly in an exchange between Antilokhos, a contestant in the chariot race, and Achilles, organizer of the games, whose generosity underwrites the circulation of valuables. Antilokhos' words point to the role of evaluative speech as a crucial regulatory mechanism in the larger distributive (which is to say, social) system. Objecting to a perceived flaw in the awarding of prizes, Antilokhos urges Achilles to supplement the awards from his own store of goods, "so that the Achaeans may approve/praise [*aineîn*] you" (*Il.* 23.552). Antilokhos, in other words, positions praise as the motor force driving the system and as the ultimate determinant of distributive norms. The promise of this praise, as an adjudication of Achilles' just dispensation, effectively compels him to take action. This is Dumézil's "louange qualifiante," the praise that obligates.[37]

With this last example, we return to the question of the relation between praise—already implicated in the semantics of Homeric *ainos/aineîn*—and the collective dimension we have observed in the Homeric usage of the compound form *epaineîn*. The fundamental kinship of *ainos* as "praise" and *epainos* as "consensus" comes into view when we understand praise not as an isolated evaluative judgment but as an essential social act, one that brings into play the entire structure of a community and in which all community members have a stake. This is praise in the sense of the Indo-European root **kens-*: an authoritative use of speech that plays a vital role in structuring and maintaining the *kosmos*, the social (and indeed cosmic) order.[38]

THE ETYMOLOGY OF CONSENT

I have argued that a more sociologically oriented perspective can bridge the gap between the distinctively Homeric significance of *epaineîn* and later semantic developments, specifically those centered on the notion of "praise." My argument, while guided by the work of Indo-Europeanists on the root **kens-*, has nevertheless relied thus far primarily on typological claims corresponding to the purely sociological side of Dumézil's exposition. This is largely by necessity, since, apart from *kosmos* and its derivatives, **kens-* has receded from view in alphabetic Greek (in contrast to the Mycenaean Greek of the Linear B tablets, in which, as we will shortly see, the root appears to have been better represented). Yet the diminished prominence of this central component of the inherited social lexicon is itself an important part of the story that accounts for Homeric usage. In tracing developments internal to Greek, we find that historical linguistics not only serves as a useful divining rod for identifying comparable social dynamics in other Indo-European cultures but also makes an essential contribution to the explication of Homeric usage on its own terms.

In a series of articles published in the early 1990s, García-Ramón devotes sustained attention to the development of **kens-* in several Indo-European languages, above all Greek.[39] Among the more important results of this work is the demonstration of a productive role for the root in Mycenaean Greek, exhibited especially in onomastic evidence. A whole series of proper names identifiable in the Linear B tablets attests to the ongoing vitality of a Greek reflex in the compositional form **ke(n)s-ti-*, meaning "who makes authoritative declarations to/before" or "who praises / calls upon": in addition to the full forms *ke-sa-do-ro* /*Kessandros*/ and *ke-sa-da-ra* /*Kessandrā*/ ("he/she who speaks authoritatively before" or "who praises men"), as well as *ra-wo-ke-ta* /*Lāwokestās*/ ("who speaks before / praises the *laos*"), we have the so-called Kurzformen *ke-ti-ro* /*Kestilos*/ ("who speaks before / praises the *laos*") and *ke-to* /*Kestōr*/ ("who speaks authoritatively / praises").[40] All of these forms provide evidence for the existence in prealphabetic Greek of a productive verbal paradigm derived from *kens-, in contrast to alphabetic Greek, where vestiges of the Indo-European root are only dimly visible in the nominal form kosmos and its derivatives (in addition, of course, to names built on inherited patterns).

The gradual decline in prominence of *kens- in Greek accounts, in García-Ramón's view, for a twofold process by which these Mycenaean names are either reinterpreted and assimilated to forms with more transparent meanings or replaced by forms that continue their semantics but employ a different verbal root. So, on the one hand, the Mycenaean names /Kessandros/ and /Kessandrā/ merge with the names Κάσσανδρος and Κασσάνδρα, both cognate with Greek κέκασμαι and meaning "he/she who is distinguished among men."[41] Priam's prophetic daughter, then, would have originally been called Kessandrā, signifying her role as one "who makes authoritative pronouncements among men"; when the meaning of the name became unintelligible, it was absorbed into the existing name Kassandrā, likewise appropriate to a woman who "stands out among men."[42]

On the other hand, the semantics of the forms deriving from *kens- are continued, in the first millennium, by a series of names, unattested in Linear B, that are of considerable interest for our purposes, insofar as they belong to the same lexical system as our key verbs aineîn and epaineîn. Alongside /Kessandrā/ we can set Αἰνησιμβρότα (Alc. 1.73), "she who makes pronouncements among [i.e., instructs] / praises men"; beside /Kestilos/, Αἰνεσίλας (IG XII 3, Suppl. 1422) and Αἰνησίλεως (IG XII 7.226, 18), "he who instructs/praises the laos"; and with /Kestōr/ we can compare Αἰνήτωρ (IG XII 1.46, 34, and elsewhere), "he who speaks authoritatively / praises." In fact, on the basis of these onomastic parallels and a broader set of correspondences between the comparative evidence for *kens- and the syntax and semantics of (ep)aineîn, García-Ramón has proposed that "(ἐπ)αινεῖν is the continuator of *kens- in alphabetic Greek by a process of lexical renewal."[43] The importance of this claim should not be underestimated: if correct—and the evidence seems compelling—it would mean that ainos and its cognates are not merely typologically parallel to reflexes of *kens- in other languages but are the true inheritors of the semantics of this root from a diachronic point of view.

How, then, did (ep)aineîn become the bearer of this legacy? Clearly, the replacement of one word or set of words by another is not an arbitrary development but is facilitated by some functional or semantic convergence. The precise nature of the convergence in this case, however, is perhaps less obvious than it might at first seem. The concept of "praise"—the starting point for this discussion—presents an initially promising avenue of approach, but few would follow Werner Jaeger in attempting to derive the many attested meanings of *ainos* (the noun from which the verb *aineîn* is derived) from an original notion of "praise of men and gods."[44] Most experts prefer instead to begin from a more diffuse primary sense centered on speech or narrative, variously inflected in order to emphasize the function of the speech in question.[45]

For Nicholas Richardson, *ainos* originally meant " 'a tale,' and usually one with a message for the hearer"; for Françoise Bader, the message conveyed by *ainos* is specifically an " 'instruction,' into which one must be initiated"; W. J. Verdenius, in a note on a passage in Sophocles' *Philoctetes*, suggests "tale containing an ulterior purpose."[46] Approaching the problem from a different angle, Lowell Edmunds notes that *ainos* itself derives from the verb **ainesthai*, attested in the compound form *anainesthai*, "refuse" (the significance of which for the development of the *Iliad*'s thematic framework I noted at the end of the previous chapter); accordingly, he anchors the meaning of the word in the notions of acceptance, affirmation, and approval, finding confirmation in the epigraphically attested use of *ainos* to designate the legislative decision of a deliberative body.[47] (This usage, obviously relevant to my argument, is discussed further below.) Building in part on Edmunds' observations, Nagy focuses on the relationship between the utterance in question and the social group to which it is addressed, defining *ainos* as "authoritative speech . . . an affirmation, a marked speech act, made by and for a marked social group."[48]

Each of these proposals is at least plausible, but the lack of a clear etymology—in other words, the failure to identify unambiguous cognates in related languages that would enable the secure reconstruction of a common root—has made it difficult to maintain with confidence any particular description of the origin and development of *ainos*. As Alain Blanc has stressed, this difficulty has been compounded by an inability to say with certainty whether **ainesthai* and its derivative *ainos* are to be analyzed as reflecting **ai-nesthai* and **ai-nos* (implying **ai-* or **ain-* as the root) or **an-yesthai* and **an-yos* (implying a root **an-*).[49] Blanc himself charts a possible course out of the impasse, guided by a landmark that has tended to be overlooked. Like Edmunds and Nagy, Blanc notes the derivation from (unattested) **ainesthai*, which should, on the basis of the negative compound *an-ainesthai*, "refuse," mean something like "accept," "approve," "say 'yes.' " But he takes the further step of correlating *anainesthai* with the adjective *apēnēs*, traditionally glossed as "ungentle, rough, hard, . . . cruel" (LSJ s.v.). Comparison of these words in their Homeric contexts reveals that they function as precise equivalents, both serving to designate the refusal of a request. The equivalence is most readily apparent in the juxtaposition of two similarly proverbial passages, one from the *Iliad* and the other from the *Odyssey*:[50]

ὃς δέ κ᾽ <u>ἀνήνηται</u> καί τε στερεῶς ἀποείπῃ,
λίσσονται δ᾽ ἄρα ταί γε Δία Κρονίωνα κιοῦσαι
τῷ ἄτην ἄμ᾽ ἕπεσθαι, ἵνα βλαφθεὶς ἀποτίσῃ.
Il. 9.510–12

Whenever someone <u>refuses</u> and stubbornly rebuffs them,
they go and entreat Zeus, son of Kronos,
to send ruin to attend him, so that he might pay them back with his suffering.

ὃς μὲν <u>ἀπηνὴς</u> αὐτὸς ἔῃ καὶ <u>ἀπηνέα</u> εἰδῇ,
τῷ δὲ καταρῶνται πάντες βροτοὶ ἄλγε᾽ ὀπίσσω
ζωῷ, ἀτὰρ τεθνεῶτί γ᾽ ἐφεψιόωνται ἅπαντες·
Od. 19.329–31

Whoever is himself <u>uncaring</u> and knows <u>cruelties</u>,
all men pray for him to suffer
while he lives, and all abuse him when he has died.

The equation ἀπηνὴς εἶναι = ἀναίνεσθαι makes it possible to explain *apēnēs* as an adjectival derivative of **apainesthai*, a doublet of *anainesthai*, and simultaneously resolves the uncertainty over the analysis of **ainesthai* and *ainos*, since *apēnēs* implies the root **an-* (rather than **ai-* or **ain-*).[51] This **an-* must in turn derive from an Indo-European root **h₂en-* (ἀπηνής < **ἀπ-ᾰν-ής*), which gives, by an entirely regular series of phonological transformations, the long vowel of the adjective, the diphthong of the verb's present stem (**ainesthai* < **an-ye/o-*), and the lengthened vowel of the aorist (ἀν-ήνασθαι < **ἀν-ᾰν-σα-σθαι*).[52]

Once the uncertainty over the Greek root has been resolved, it becomes possible to search for cognates in other languages. As early as 1877, August Fick had proposed correlating Greek *apēnēs* and *prosēnēs* with the family of words in the Germanic dialects deriving from proto-Germanic **unnan*, "permit, grant."[53] Relying simply on semantic proximity, Fick made no attempt to explain the underlying morphology. On the basis of a thorough review of the facts in both Germanic and Greek, however, Blanc is able to provide a morphological and phonological foundation for Fick's proposal.[54] Setting Greek **ainesthai*, "accept," beside proto-Germanic **unnan*, "grant," and noting a difference in meaning comparable to the alternation between "give" and "take" in the Indo-European vocabulary of exchange, Blanc reconstructs the original meaning of IE **h₂en-* as "agree, consent."[55]

Notwithstanding the evidence Blanc supplies in support of his etymology, his proposal must remain tentative.[56] Nevertheless, it represents a plausible hypothesis. More importantly, it accounts both for the Iliadic semantics of *(ep)ainêin* and for the process of lexical renewal by which this word (in the view of García-Ramón) came to replace *kens-* in alphabetic Greek. The notion of "consensus," which we have seen to be at the heart of the *epainos* motif, would, on this hypothesis, be the simple and direct continuation of the semantics of the verbal root at the level of the protolanguage. These semantics, meanwhile, would center on a social mechanism—agreement, consent—that is fundamental to the constitution of social order on a larger scale. In other words, IE *$h_2$en-*, as reconstructed by Blanc, would find a natural place in the semantic sphere to which *kens-*, designating the speech that produces such order, also belongs. We can even imagine a situation in which *$h_2$en-* might designate the response to the authoritative speech act marked by *kens-*, a situation that would leave the former well positioned to take over the semantics of the latter in the subsequent development of Greek.

THE SEMANTICS OF *AINOS* OUTSIDE THE *ILIAD*

Although certain details of the preceding sociological and linguistic accounts must remain speculative, the evidence brought to bear from these two perspectives can be used to delineate a unified field in which the various meanings of *ainos* (and related terms) can comfortably be situated. That field centers on the social dimension of language use, the ability of speech to engender or express relationships that are constitutive of communal life. It is precisely this social dimension that permits the continuity between *epainos* as an expression of consensus and *epainos* as an expression of praise to come into view. Many other *ainos* derivatives exhibit meanings that can similarly be anchored in the social power of speech. Thus *parainein*, for which LSJ suggests the glosses "exhort, recommend, advise . . . propose," designates a verbal act by which a speaker attempts to translate his or her own preferences into action on the part of others, while *katainein*, in the sense of "promise," indicates the speaker's engagement to perform some action on behalf of another or to enter into a particular relationship with another (note the specialized sense "promise in marriage, betroth" [LSJ s.v. 3]). It is the noun *ainos* itself, however, that offers the most interesting range of meanings and therefore the best opportunities to discern the contours of this fundamentally social domain of language use.[57]

According to the *Thesaurus Graecae Linguae*, by far the most common sense of *ainos*—particularly well attested in poetic contexts—is "praise" ("usitatissima omnino est haec significatio" comments the *TGL*). I have already had occasion to stress the social factors that bring this form of public approval into a closer proximity with the "quasi-juridical" aspect of Homeric *epainos* than might at first be evident. More obviously commensurate with Homeric usage is a mode of expression that appears to have been typical of certain Doric communities and that has left sparse, but suggestive, traces in the epigraphical record. In inscriptions from Epidaurus (*IG* IV² 1.71, 4 and 10, 3rd c. BCE) and Delphi (*SIG*³ 672, 15, 2nd c. BCE), we find the expression *kata* (*ton*) *ainon*, "according to [the] *ainos*," used of a decree passed by a deliberative body. *Ainos* in these texts evidently refers—like the Homeric verb *epainein*—to a form of collective approval that transforms proposals into action. Interestingly, the wording of the Delphic inscription (μήτε κατὰ ψάφισμα μήτε κατ᾽ αἶνον) appears to imply a distinction between *ainos* and *psāphisma*, "vote." The force of this distinction is obscure: Dittenberger (ad loc.) suggests that it may reflect the difference between a decision enacted by the council and one enacted by the assembly, respectively, but it is not inconceivable that the terminology also reflects a difference in voting procedure—that is, *ainos* may have referred at some point to a decision passed by acclamation and therefore expressing in a more direct way the collective nature of the will on which it rests.[58] In a manumission tablet from Elatea in Phokis, possibly from the fourth century BCE, the corresponding verb *ainein* denotes the ratification of the act of emancipation by the popular assembly: [ὁ δᾶμ]ος αἰνεῖ, "the *dēmos* approves" (*IG* IX 1.119, 7–8). These traces of a deliberative and even legislative form of *ainos* are significant not only as a correlate for Homeric semantics but also more generally as an indication of an abiding association between the language of *ainos* and the vital mechanisms of communal life.

The last of these examples suggests that, in these Doric polities, *ainos* represents the voice of the community as a whole ("the *dēmos* approves"). In such a context, *ainos* indexes the articulation of collective identity through institutionalized protocols for the exercise of public speech. In other contexts, *ainos* designates an utterance that works in a less formal way to define the membership of a speech community. Poetic diction attests a use of the term *ainos* as a designation for a "fable"—that is, a coded narrative, usually an animal tale, intended to carry some edifying message for its addressee—as in the verse with which the speaker of the *Works and Days* introduces the fable of the hawk and the nightingale:[59]

νῦν δ' αἶνον βασιλεῦσ' ἐρέω, φρονέουσι καὶ αὐτοῖς.
Hesiod, *Works and Days* 202

But now I will tell an *ainos* for the rulers, aware as even they are.

As Nagy has stressed, this coded form of discourse delimits a community of knowledgeable insiders, a privileged audience consisting of those capable of understanding the message.[60] It may even create such a community, by forging a bond of shared knowledge where none has existed before. The emphasis in Hesiod on the understanding that the *basilēes* supposedly share with the speaker ("aware as even they are") takes on considerable importance from this perspective. More than a deferential gesture (as Jacoby supposed), the pregnant attribution of special insight to a group who are elsewhere called "fools" (νήπιοι, 40) suggests that the *ainos* is meant to be a kind of litmus test, a means of determining who qualifies for insider status, perhaps even for the title of *basileus*.[61] The exclusivity of *ainos*—an exclusivity that appears in even starker terms in the derivative forms *ainigma*, "riddle," and *ainissesthai*, "speak in riddles"—thereby serves to construct a community of those "in the know."

Traces of such a community are in fact evident even in the Homeric usage of the term. I have already had occasion to observe the way in which, in both the *Iliad* and the *Odyssey*, a connection to the circulation of wealth indexes the position of *ainos* in a broader social system. A similar point can be made about the way in which speakers regularly highlight the existence of a community of common knowledge, which either lends support to their *ainoi* or renders them superfluous. At the conclusion of the footrace in *Iliad* 23, Antilokhos prefaces an *ainos*—the speech is identified as such by Achilles at *Il.* 23.795—with words that remind one of the introduction to the Hesiodic fable: "friends, I will tell you all, who know . . ." (εἰδόσιν ὔμμ' ἐρέω πᾶσιν φίλοι, *Il.* 23.787).[62] Achilles rewards Antilokhos generously for his words, so that the social dimension of *ainos* is here marked both by the exchange of prestige goods and by the invocation of a common store of knowledge. On other occasions the group's shared knowledge is said to obviate the need for *ainos;* the very correlation of the two, of course, only emphasizes the extent to which they are interdependent. Telemachus configures the Suitors as belonging to an integrated social network when he concludes a eulogy of Penelope with the words, "you yourselves <u>know</u> this, so what need is there for me to <u>praise</u> my mother?" (καὶ δ' αὐτοὶ τόδε ἴστε· τί με χρὴ μητέρος αἴνου;, *Od.* 21.110)—not without some irony, since his addressees in this case are quite far from the *philoi* envisioned by Antilokhos. More sincere is the remark of Odysseus when he is chosen by Diomedes as a companion on a night raid:

Τυδεΐδη μήτ' ἄρ με μάλ' αἴνεε μήτέ τι νείκει·
εἰδόσι γάρ τοι ταῦτα μετ' Ἀργείοις ἀγορεύεις.
Il. 10.249–50

Son of Tydeus, do not praise me overmuch, nor find fault,
for you speak these things among the Argives, who know.

As the two undertake a perilous mission on behalf of the Achaeans as a whole, Odysseus exploits the discourse of *ainos*, and the associated idea of a collective body of knowledge, to underscore the strength of the social bonds uniting their community.

This cursory survey of the varied semantics of *ainos*—the noun, itself derived from **ainesthai*, from which *epainein* derives—provides a useful backdrop against which to set the Homeric vocabulary of collective decision making. *Ainos* exhibits three broad categories of meaning, pertaining (1) to praise, (2) to mechanisms of public deliberation, and (3) to the coded discourse of a privileged in-group. All three of these categories are on display in the Homeric corpus, often in conjunction. We find several instances in which *ainos* or *ainein* designates a speech with a clear laudatory aspect, and several instances in which these same words are correlated with an explicit or implicit appeal to the collective knowledge of the speaker's social group. The deliberative component of the word's semantics, meanwhile, is most clearly represented by the compound verb *epainein*, the word that lies at the center of this study. The point, however, is that these three categories of meaning are not unrelated: each is anchored in an understanding of the power of language either to create or to reinforce *kosmos*, social order. This understanding can be traced from the point of view of Indo-European linguistics and paralleled cross-culturally, with the result that the value attributed to the term *epainein* by the *Iliad*'s grammar of reception becomes more readily comprehensible. The privileged position of *epainos* within the poem's thematics is not the result of the arbitrary selection of one among many possible terms for collective response. It represents instead the specialization of a term that is fundamentally connected to the shaping of social reality through speech—and so is particularly well suited to conveying the notion of consensus. The next step in the analysis is to examine the way in which this term and the notion of consensus are put into play in the *Iliad*'s narrative economy.

CHAPTER 3

Achilles and the Crisis
of the Exception

The *Iliad* begins with a question. After invoking the Muse and stating the overarching themes of Achilles' wrath (*mēnis*) and his strife (*eris*) with Agamemnon, the narrator begins to zero in on a starting point for the narrative by asking, "which of the gods set them on to contend in *eris*?" (*Il.* 1.8). The answer—Apollo—leads the narrator to work backward in time until he can single out a first cause for the god's involvement and the strife it produces. Despite the fact that the proem frames the plot as a matter of divine will (the *Dios boulē*, or "will of Zeus," 1.5), this first cause—Agamemnon's public rejection of Chryses' suit to ransom his daughter—lies solely in the realm of human action.[1] Moreover, it belongs specifically to the field of political action, for Agamemnon's repudiation of Chryses occurs in a context that bears all the hallmarks of collective deliberation: an issue that ultimately impinges on the welfare of the community as a whole is presented publicly, before an audience consisting of the group and its leaders, and all are given the opportunity to express their will regarding the outcome. Certain ambiguities hinder the precise categorization of this scene with respect to some of its most fundamental features. Most importantly, in spite of its formal similarities to the poem's other assemblies, the lack of an unambiguous lexical signal (such as the noun *agorē*, "assembly," as at *Il.* 2.93, or the verb *agorâsthai*, "hold assembly," as at *Il.* 4.1), makes it impossible to determine precisely whether or not this scene is an assembly like the others.[2]

For the time being, it will be sufficient to think of this scene as the poem's first assembly in a general sense—the first occasion on which the community as a whole is called on to give voice to its collective will—even if the applicability of this term in the strict sense must remain uncertain. As the discussion proceeds, this ambiguity, along with others, will emerge as a constitutive feature of a scene that plays a cardinal role in the poem's narrative and thematic economy, in large part *because* of its ambiguities. The *Iliad* takes as its point of origin this assembly and the political tensions it puts on display.

Those tensions center on the problematic relationship between Agamemnon and the community as a whole. Agamemnon's harsh rejection of Chryses' petition in defiance of the express wishes of "all the other Achaeans" (*Il.* 1.22) provides our first view of politics and the exercise of power in the poem. Not surprisingly, this scene has had considerable influence on scholarly interpretations of Iliadic politics, particularly as concerns the prerogatives of Agamemnon's position. One prominent point of view, widespread in the secondary literature, sees Agamemnon's evident disregard for popular sentiment as an indicator of the essential autonomy of his position and, correspondingly, the inability of the social body as a whole either to determine a course of action or to check the leader's resolve. The people in assembly are assigned the passive role of merely listening and expressing their approval, which the leader may or may not take into account. This view has had a number of influential modern proponents beginning with George Grote.[3] Moses Finley offered this general characterization of the political institutions of "the world of Odysseus," citing as evidence the opening scene of the *Iliad:* "The assembly neither voted nor decided. Its function was to mobilize the arguments pro and con, and to show the king or field commander how sentiment lay. The sole measure of opinion was by acclamation, not infrequently in less orderly forms, like the shouting down of an unpopular presentation. The king was free to ignore the expression of sentiment and go his own way."[4] Although there has been no lack of voices offering alternative interpretations,[5] this understanding of Homeric politics has proved extremely persistent. One of its most authoritative representatives, Pierre Carlier, recently penned the following "formula" for the Homeric political system: "the *damos* listens, the elders speak, the king decides."[6]

Carlier's formula, of course, runs counter to the grammar of reception outlined in chapter 1, which assigns to the assembled community not merely an active role in the process of deliberation but a determinative one. It is easy to understand the attractions of the view the formula encapsulates: it permits the ready translation of Agamemnon's position as *anax* into the easily recognizable image of sovereign kingship, where sovereignty is understood as "the power or authority which comprises the attributes of an ultimate arbitral agent . . . entitled to make decisions and settle disputes within a political hierarchy with some degree of finality."[7] And yet, on a broader reading of the poem, it becomes highly doubtful whether sovereign power in this sense can be attributed to Agamemnon; one wonders how Finley might have been compelled to adjust his picture of Odysseus' world were he required to exclude the *Iliad*'s opening scene as evidence. In fact, his "authoritarian" vision of Homeric politics can be criticized from at least two perspectives, the first empirical and the second methodological.

Empirically, crediting Agamemnon with the power to make decisions unilaterally, without regard for the will of the group, ignores the seemingly obvious fact that Agamemnon is unable to maintain his unilateral policy for more than a brief period: it is only some ten days of dramatic time and not even a hundred lines of verse before he is compelled to reverse his position and relinquish his prize. Even in this case, then—the only one in which Agamemnon pursues an agenda that is expressly in conflict with communal preference—the will of the group eventually reasserts itself. Agamemnon may be able to defy collective sentiment in turning away Chryses, but eventually he must release Chryseis, exactly as the Achaeans had wished from the beginning.

It is the methodological objection, however, that is ultimately the more consequential. In seeking to account for Agamemnon's imperiousness within a unified vision of Homeric politics, the authoritarian position as formulated by Finley relies on the assumption that all behaviors depicted in the poem are uniformly unproblematic and that every example bears equal weight as more or less transparent evidence for an underlying system independent of the narrative's poetic concerns. To assert, with Finley, that Agamemnon has the "right" to act as he does, simply because he is able to do so, is to obscure the fundamental distinction between the "facts" of events at Troy and the norms implied by the narrative.[8] Allan and Cairns have recently made an eloquent case for the necessity of this distinction, stressing that, in spite of Agamemnon's de facto unilateralism, issues pertaining to the community are de iure to be decided on the basis of collective will.[9]

Yet there is more at stake here than simply the distinction between what does and what should happen, for the norms of which we are speaking are first and foremost *poetic* norms, pertaining not to an autonomous reality but to a work of art—and, more importantly, to themes at the center of that work's concerns. Leveling the difference between facts and norms risks obscuring the effect that strictly poetic concerns might have on the presentation of these themes in any given instance or the significance that divergence from the norm might have for the development of the theme on the whole. As Donna Wilson has stressed with regard to the motif of compensation (which we will find to be connected in certain ways to the motifs explored in this book), the very focus on a given theme brings with it a measure of distortion.[10] It is especially important to keep this principle in mind in the context of a traditional poem like the *Iliad*, in which it is the play of difference between distinct realizations of traditional elements (formulas, type scenes, etc.) that creates meaning: any given instance is at least as likely to diverge from the norm as to express it. We will find that, as a central concern of the *Iliad*, the politics of collective decision making are virtually never presented straightforwardly or unproblematically.

In the case of the poem's initial assembly, the crucial fact that the rebuff of Chryses violates the most fundamental principle of the poem's grammar of reception—the principle that collective will should be decisive in scenes of collective decision making—must be understood as a strategic act of *beginning* indicative of a particular *intention*, in the rich sense in which both those concepts are explored by Edward Said.[11] A beginning is a point of differentiation and departure, the point at which a given work distinguishes itself from all other works and from the context in which it is produced. In the case of a traditional poem like the *Iliad*, whether we conceive of it in the first instance as a performance or as a text composed according to traditional techniques, arguably the most important component of that context, more present to the minds of listeners than other more or less ephemeral products of the oral tradition, is the repertoire of traditional themes, type scenes, and techniques that make up the content of the tradition. With respect to the motif of collective decision making, we glimpse the contours of this repertoire in the basic set of formulas shared by the *Iliad* and *Odyssey*.[12] The beginning of the *Iliad* acquires its inaugural and intentional significance from the degree and nature of its departure from these traditional norms. The deviation sets up a tension and dynamism as the text works against its traditional context.

It is possible to read the beginning of the *Iliad* this way because the tradition must necessarily exist prior to the traditional text. Even if one wishes to imagine the *Iliad* as a singular text encountered on a singular occasion by a listener or reader who had never before heard the story of Achilles' wrath—even then, such a listener or reader would be called upon to evaluate the poem against the tradition that gave rise to it. Moreover, given the historical reality of the reperformance of the *Iliad* (as, for example, at the Panathenaia), one must also take into consideration the tradition created by the *Iliad* itself: the listener who encounters the *Iliad* on multiple occasions must perceive its inaugural gesture not only against the background of the epic tradition writ large but also in relation to the norms established by the poem itself. For this reason, Barker is right to stress the difficulty of understanding the *Iliad* as a truly originary narrative of political and institutional foundations, as though inscribed on a blank surface.[13] As a traditional poem, intended for repeated performance, it must be read in the manner of a palimpsest, on which the legibility of the characters depends in large part on their disparity with the traces underneath.

POLITICAL NORMS, POETIC NORMS, AND THE STATE OF EXCEPTION

From this point of view, the initial scene of the *Iliad* must be understood as an exception to traditional norms of collective decision making. Were the Achaeans governed by a set of formally instituted laws and procedures, instead of the contested principles to which the poem's political actors routinely appeal, we might speak of this initial situation as a "state of exception" (German *Ausnahmezustand*) in the technical sense: as a situation in which the executive power, represented by Agamemnon, has suspended normal decision-making procedures.[14] Of course, this notion cannot be sensibly applied in the absence of a constitutional framework.[15] As a concept, the state of exception derives its coherence from the existence of a formally constituted set of legal rules and governmental powers. From the Achaeans' point of view, Agamemnon's assertion of autocratic authority may be a deviation from normal practice, but it is not the abrogation of formal rules. From the standpoint of the audience or reader, however, a set of formal rules—those of the grammar of reception—*has* been suspended. These rules are a matter both of the most general principle of collective decision making (namely, that collective will should be decisive), and also of the language used to narrate the scene, for the formula describing the Achaeans' response to Chryses—ἔνθ' ἄλλοι μὲν πάντες ἐπευφήμησαν Ἀχαιοί ("then all the other Achaeans expressed approval," *Il.* 1.22)—is in an important sense exceptional: although this formula occurs twice in the poem, both times it refers to the same, singular event. It therefore falls outside the set of more generally applicable formulas belonging to the grammar of reception.

While only loosely applicable to the political experiences of the Achaean heroes themselves, the notion of the state of exception thus seems eminently appropriate as a description of the suspension of *narrative* protocols in the poem's opening scene. The significance of this initial exception can be understood first of all in terms of the poem's overall narrative trajectory—what Said would call its "intention." The deviation from the norm, as I have suggested, sets in play a certain narrative drive, inaugurating a tension that seeks implicitly to be resolved by the reassertion of the normative. This dynamic is deeply ingrained in Homeric poetics. For Joseph Russo, it is the fundamental "message" expressed at every level of Homeric poetry, from that of the story down to that of the verse (which tends to move from a relatively more flexible opening to a relatively more fixed or predictable close): "The story, like the verse structure, progresses toward what we may call the triumph of the normative over the deviant, of the long-range "proper" resolution over the temporary atypical situation. . . . The epic plot generates its tension, and hence its interest *qua* narrative, in the momentary creation of the atypical or marginal situation and the struggle to re-incorporate this back into the social, political, and cosmic normalities."[16]

Subsequent chapters will reveal in greater detail the extent to which the development of the collective decision-making motif conforms to Russo's description of the epic plot as a progression toward "the triumph of the normative over the deviant." On the most superficial level, the initial state of exception is an obviously necessary first step in this progression. There is a more fundamental sense, however, in which the exception is necessary to the "triumph of the normative." It can be said that it is the exception—the suspension of the norm—that effectively establishes the norm *as a norm,* that is, as a matter of validity, of a force that exceeds mere facticity. Helpful here is Giorgio Agamben's interpretation of the state of exception, and particularly the comparison he constructs between law and language with respect to the dialectic between rules and their application:

Just as linguistic elements subsist in *langue* without any real denotation, which they acquire only in actual discourse, so in the state of exception the norm is in force without any reference to reality. But just as concrete linguistic activity becomes intelligible precisely through the presupposition of something like a language, so is the norm able to refer to the normal situation through the suspension of its application in the state of exception.

It can generally be said that not only language and law but all social institutions have been formed through a process of desemanticization and suspension of concrete praxis in its immediate reference to the real. Just as grammar, in producing a speech without denotation, has isolated something like a language from discourse, and law, in suspending the concrete custom and usage of individuals, has been able to isolate something like a norm, so the patient work of civilization proceeds in every domain by separating human praxis from its concrete exercise and thereby creating that excess of signification over denotation that Lévi-Strauss was the first to recognize.[17]

According to this line of thinking, it is only as a result of a break in the concrete application of a norm that it becomes possible to think of it as a structure independent of facts. The norm does not come into view as such until it ceases to apply; prior to this point, there are only facts. The beginning of the *Iliad* thus has considerable significance over and above any immediate narrative necessity: by suspending a rule of traditional discourse, the poem asserts the rule's general validity, thereby vitalizing a principle that provides a major point of orientation for its narrative trajectory.

Whether as a matter of law or of language—or indeed of any coherent system—the suspension of norms brings about as an immediate consequence a certain crisis of uncertainty. Agamben refers to a "zone of anomie," by which he means to indicate the indeterminacy of facts ungoverned by any rule.[18] The paradox of this "anomie" in his analysis is that the state of exception, by interrupting the relation between facts and norms, calls into question the meaning or classification of facts even as it seems to conjure the norm as such into existence.[19] The paradox can be grasped more concretely in the realm of politics. John Brenkman, elucidating the logic behind Carl Schmitt's famous dictum, "Sovereign is he who decides on the exception," stresses the extent to which the assertion of sovereign power in the state of exception also calls that power into question.[20] That is to say, the normative claim to sovereign power implicit in the declaration of a state of exception necessarily poses the question of the legitimacy of the claim, since political subjects must decide for themselves whether circumstances justify the sovereign's declaration.[21] Brenkman is far more optimistic than Agamben on the issue of decidability and takes Agamben to task for (among other things) casting the crisis as an aporia. Yet both writers make a similar point regarding the consequences of the state of exception: the suspension of norms creates an uncertain environment in which nothing can be taken for granted and the meaning of political action becomes disputable.

The *Iliad*'s opening scenes provide a kind of dramatized symptomatology of the crisis opened up by the state of exception. The clearest manifestation of the crisis is, of course, the quarrel between Agamemnon and Achilles, who attempts to articulate what can be understood, following Brenkman, as the popular response elicited by the decision on the exception.[22] But even before the quarrel erupts, the first symptom of political and social turmoil is the plague. As Apollo's direct response to the dishonor suffered by his priest, the plague is the most immediate result of Agamemnon's unilateralism. It is a concrete expression of the breakdown that threatens the body politic in the wake of

Agamemnon's decision. In suspending the norms that govern communal life, Agamemnon puts in question the very life of the community, in a real as well as a political sense.

In the subsequent assembly, summoned by Achilles in response to the plague, the specifically political consequences of Agamemnon's actions emerge more clearly (*Il.* 1.53 ff.). In responding to the crisis by assembling the social body, Achilles reveals his nature as "the binding force of the Achaean cause," in the words of Dale Sinos.[23] As Sinos has shown, despite Achilles' isolation during most of the poem, he nevertheless embodies the *philotēs*, or social bond, that unites the group.[24] It is as a representative of the collective good that he summons the Achaeans, and as a spokesman for Achaean social norms that he first comes into open conflict with Agamemnon. That conflict concerns material goods rather than political procedure and so does not address directly the initial state of exception. However, the dispute over the distribution of *gera*, "prizes of honor" (singular *geras*), must be understood as a continuation of the exceptional situation imposed by the king, since the distributive crisis is a direct consequence of Agamemnon's refusal to accept *apoina*, "ransom," for Chryseis.[25] Moreover, the dispute over *gera*, like the initial assembly, puts in evidence Agamemnon's belief that his own preference carries greater weight than group decisions: although he presents his demand for a substitute *geras* as a remedy for his own anomalous lack of a prize (*Il.* 1.118–19), it amounts, once again, to the suspension of the order determined by collective will in favor of the privilege asserted by the king. Achilles correctly points out that the reassignment of prizes sought by Agamemnon would require the reversal of an action previously ratified and executed by the community as a whole (1.125–26). When Agamemnon insists that he will impose his will by force if necessary, Achilles goes on to suggest that the Achaeans will not tolerate the leadership of a man so ready to act in defiance of the group:

πῶς τίς τοι πρόφρων ἔπεσιν πείθηται Ἀχαιῶν
ἢ ὁδὸν ἐλθέμεναι ἢ ἀνδράσιν ἶφι μάχεσθαι;
Il. 1.150–51

How will any of the Achaeans willingly obey your commands,
either to go on expedition or to engage in combat?

Appropriately, it is Achilles, the embodiment of sociality, who identifies the essentially political crisis produced by Agamemnon in suspending the normal mechanisms for managing group relations. The state of exception calls into question the fundamental structure of authority in Achaean society.

READING THE STATE OF EXCEPTION

The greater part of the *Iliad* can be understood as an extended exploration of the questions raised by the initial exception. Much of the poem's enduring power derives from the fact that it draws the audience into this process of questioning from the very beginning. It does so by constructing the initial situation in ambiguous terms, which make it difficult for the audience to decide precisely what is supposed to happen.[26] For instance, the narrator tells us that Chryses addresses both the Achaeans as a whole and the two Atreids in particular; Chryses' words conform to this description (*Il.* 1.15–17). We are left to wonder: to whom is he directing his petition, and who is entitled to respond to such a request?[27] If the political crisis of Book 1 arises from the conflict between a personal and a collective decision, that conflict is inherent in the ambivalent formulation of Chryses' appeal. A more important ambivalence concerns the relation of Chryses himself to the Achaeans. As an inhabitant of the Troad whose daughter is a prisoner of war, it may at first seem obvious that Chryses belongs to the Trojan side. But what Trojan or Trojan ally would wish for the Achaeans to sack the city (1.18–19)? Even if we ascribe this wish to Chryses' desire to capture the goodwill of his audience, still we must take account of the fact that Chryseis was taken not from her father's city, Chrysē, but from Ēetion's Thēbē.[28] There is no trace, either in the *Iliad* or in the Epic Cycle, of an attack on Chrysē.[29] Thus Chryses, if he is clearly not an ally of the Achaeans, is not clearly an enemy. The fundamental political question—who is friend and who is foe—is in this important case left open.[30]

These indeterminacies pervade the opening scene, challenging the audience to make a judgment about what is supposed to happen in the context of a situation that seems deliberately to complicate the normal criteria for such a judgment. In this way, we are faced with an interpretive problem that parallels the political problem posed by the state of exception for characters within the narrative. In both cases the inapplicability of normal standards produces a crisis that calls for a response, a crisis that is driven by the fundamental ambiguity of an exceptional situation. Achilles himself has difficulty deciding how to evaluate and react to Agamemnon's actions; he struggles to formulate a response to a situation that has no clear solution. We, for our part, face a number of "challenges of evaluation" arising from the same events, challenges that engage our interest to the extent that they defy definitive determinations.[31]

The greatest such challenge is posed by the very language of the narrative, that is, by the phraseology used to narrate the moment of the exception. Here are the three lines describing Agamemnon's suspension of deliberative norms:

ἔνθ' ἄλλοι μὲν πάντες ἐπευφήμησαν Ἀχαιοὶ
αἰδεῖσθαί θ' ἱερῆα καὶ ἀγλαὰ δέχθαι ἄποινα·
ἀλλ' οὐκ Ἀτρεΐδῃ Ἀγαμέμνονι ἥνδανε θυμῷ . . .
Il. 1.22–24

Then all the other Achaeans expressed approval
for respecting the priest and accepting the splendid ransom;
but this did not please the heart of Agamemnon son of Atreus . . .

I have already indicated that the response formula, with its key verb *epeuphēmeîn*, is highly irregular from the standpoint of the grammar of reception: the exceptional situation requires exceptional language in order to be narrated. This is because of the close bond that exists in a formulaic medium between recurring structures of language and the recurring social actions or events they describe. In the medium of Homeric poetry, the social and political experiences of the heroes, the language in which they interact (that is, the language they use), and the language in which the narrator describes their interactions are all closely intertwined. As a result, the state of exception is at one and the same time an exception to the political regime of the Achaeans at Troy and to the formulaic regime of Iliadic narrative.[32] These two normative systems— more precisely, their respective failures—coincide in the exceptional verb *epeuphēmeîn*.

The difficulty posed by this exceptional expression arises from the pragmatics of formula use, that is, the way the formulas are deployed in the narrative. In the case of every other response formula, the narrative allows us to observe the consequences of each response and so to determine its functional meaning. Silence dismisses a proposal; *epainos* ratifies it. Even the verb *epiakhein*, which has a certain ambiguity as a positive response that is nevertheless not fully efficient, occurs in a wide enough range of circumstances to allow a determination of its social force.[33] Such judgments are possible because there is a clear connection between collective response and the outcome of the decision-making process. But in the case of the initial assembly, that process is interrupted, suspended by Agamemnon's unilateral decision. The imposition of his singular preference, underscored by the verb *handanein*, preempts the decision-making power of the group and therefore prevents the consequences of this particular response from emerging into view.[34] We are never permitted to see what force the response denoted by *epeuphēmeîn* carries—whether it is efficient, like that indicated by *epaineîn*, or inefficient, like *epiakhein*. Agamemnon's short-circuiting of the deliberative process makes such a judgment impossible.

The indeterminacy is all the more acutely felt since *epeuphēmeîn* is in essence *hapax legomenon* ("said once," the term by which classicists designate words that have only a single attestation in a given corpus). It makes little difference that Achilles uses the word again when he explains to Thetis the cause of his anger by renarrating the initial assembly (*Il.* 1.376). This only demonstrates the force of the bond between linguistic and social form: the same, singular language must be used every time the singular event is reported. In fact, reflection on the concept of the *hapax legomenon* suggests that this "twice said" expression is in fact *hapax* in an even truer sense than that in which the term is normally used.

In the context of a textual corpus, the term *hapax legomenon* refers to a word that occurs only once in that corpus. Such a notion, however, is inadequate for the description of texts that originated in a tradition of oral performance. Since the *Iliad* and *Odyssey* were reperformed on countless occasions, no word was ever uttered only once. From the standpoint of the ancient audience, a *hapax* is instead a word that is strictly limited to a particular narrative episode or theme and uttered only when that episode is performed. On the one hand, then, the repetition of *epeuphēmeîn* within the poem in the course of Achilles' "reperformance" of the assembly scene is exactly the same as the repetition of any *hapax* in the course of subsequent performances of the poem. On the other hand, many of our textually defined *hapax legomena* undoubtedly would not qualify as such if we had a more extensive corpus: they only appear to be singular expressions because a relatively small sample of heroic poetry has survived from antiquity.[35] In principle, such apparently unique words could be and could have been used in any number of different contexts. In the case of *epeuphēmeîn*, however, the repetition underscores the close bond between this word and the assembly of *Iliad* 1. Here we have a word that really is bound to a single context: a true *hapax* in the sense in which this term must be applied to a traditional medium.

The resulting difficulty of interpretation can be grasped most easily if we imagine a hypothetical individual familiar with the Greek epic tradition in a general way but encountering the *Iliad* for the first time. (I am not concerned here with the plausibility or historical likelihood of such a scenario but with its value as a thought experiment.) Such a person, familiar with the simple, binary system of responses that seems to have characterized the tradition as a whole (silence on the one hand, *epainos* on the other), would be used to deducing the subsequent course of events from the response expressed by the group. But this particular response would leave the interpreter at a loss, unable to determine on the basis of prior experience how events are likely to proceed. In the same way that political actors find themselves in a "zone of absolute indeterminacy" when legal and political norms have been suspended, so such a listener or reader would be confronted with a basic undecidability in the context of this suspension of formulaic norms.[36] And because the word *epeuphēmeîn* is *hapax* in the sense I have outlined, all subsequent experience of the poem will be of no use: the meaning of the term will remain opaque because its applicability is limited to a single referent, the response of the Achaeans in the poem's opening assembly. In a sense, we cannot even properly speak of "applicability," since this word implies a meaning that is generalizable beyond the specific instance.[37] Rather than conveying a specific meaning, *epeuphēmeîn* can only raise the question of what it is supposed to mean, that is, of what effect the audience's response is in this case supposed to have.

There is, finally, a further layer to the ambivalence of the word *epeuphēmeîn* that is worthy of brief consideration. Apart from its functional meaning, the question arises: what kind of physical response does this word actually denote? In an inscription of the imperial period, *epeuphēmeîn* occurs in a deliberative context that suggests voting by acclamation,[38] but this usage could be modeled on the *Iliad*. Indeed, in the classical period, the uncompounded verb *euphēmeîn* commonly (but by no means exclusively) means "to be silent," and so it is usually interpreted in its sole Homeric occurrence at *Iliad* 9.171.[39] Given that the meaning of the term is otherwise unclear, it is possible that certain audiences might have felt there to be a tension inherent in the word itself between silence—otherwise the marker of an inefficient response—and the kind of vocal approval signified by *epaineîn*.[40] On multiple levels, then, the meaning of the expression πάντες ἐπευφήμησαν Ἀχαιοί is difficult, if not impossible, to determine.

CRISIS AND RESPONSE

The crisis of interpretation that confronts readers and audience members parallels the political crisis encountered by the poem's internal actors. I use the term "crisis" (from Greek *krisis*, "decision, judgment") to emphasize that what is at stake in both cases is a decision: not any longer the decision on the exception but the consequent decision of the community on how to respond. That decision is embodied in Achilles, who is shown confronting in a singularly immediate way both the political and linguistic aspects of the state of exception.

When Agamemnon announces his intention to override the established distribution of prizes by appropriating Achilles' *geras*, Achilles experiences a dilemma involving the most basic political values. He struggles to decide whether to accept

Agamemnon's assertion of privilege, thereby accepting a subordinate position in a political arrangement determined by the king, or on the contrary to reject that arrangement in the most radical way possible—by killing Agamemnon:

ὣς φάτο· Πηλεΐωνι δ' ἄχος γένετ', ἐν δέ οἱ ἦτορ
στήθεσσιν λασίοισι διάνδιχα μερμήριξεν,
ἢ ὅ γε φάσγανον ὀξὺ ἐρυσσάμενος παρὰ μηροῦ
τοὺς μὲν ἀναστήσειεν, ὃ δ' Ἀτρεΐδην ἐναρίζοι,
ἦε χόλον παύσειεν ἐρητύσειέ τε θυμόν.
Il. 1.188–92[41]

Thus he spoke. The son of Peleus felt anguish, and the heart
in his woolly chest was split in deliberation
as to whether, drawing the sword from next to his thigh,
he should push aside the others and slay the son of Atreus,
or put an end to his anger and restrain his heart.

This is a fundamentally political decision, since the integrity of the Achaean community depends on the outcome: the killing of Agamemnon would mean the dispersal of the army. Moreover, insofar as Agamemnon's kingship hangs in the balance, Achilles' dilemma corresponds to the popular response implicit in Schmitt's formula, "Sovereign is he . . ." If the immediate result of Schmitt's sovereign decision is a situation in which the community is called on either to support or to contest the sovereign's right to decide, the *Iliad* collapses that communal imperative onto a single figure, Achilles, who considers how to respond to the exception imposed by the king.

Achilles' deliberation is cast in terms of an established type scene—a hero's weighing of alternatives—but, as though Agamemnon's actions have made it impossible to follow norms of any kind, this particular scene violates a number of conventions.[42] We expect Achilles to act on his second impulse, but in fact he is already drawing his sword when Athena arrives to intervene. Under pressure from her, he opts for a course of action that lies somewhere in between the two alternatives he had previously considered: he resolves neither to retaliate physically nor simply to acquiesce but to continue the quarrel in words.[43] Those words are, specifically, his oath (*Il.* 1.233–44), by which he withdraws from Achaean society and exempts himself from any further obligation to the community. This course of action—or rather, nonaction—is interesting for its ambivalence. Remaining at Troy but as a nonparticipant, Achilles neither fully rejects nor accepts a position in Achaean society. By setting himself apart without completely severing his connection to the group, he comes to occupy an uncertain place that mirrors the uncertainties of Chryses' position and exemplifies yet again the "zone of indistinction" produced by the exceptional situation.[44]

Achilles' pursuit of an ambivalent middle way between acceptance and rejection of Agamemnon's regime is tied to the fact that he alone has direct experience of the linguistic uncertainties resulting from the latter's unilateralism. It is far from insignificant that the single repetition of the exceptional lines narrating Agamemnon's decision and the unique response of the group is spoken by none other than Achilles himself, while explaining to Thetis the cause of his distress. This retelling of events that were narrated only shortly before impresses on us the degree to which Achilles' experience of those events has affected him.[45] More importantly, however, it signals Achilles' special status as a speaker, and the importance of language to his character and identity. Achilles is the only figure in the *Iliad* who is permitted to quote, so to speak, the diegesis. Gods may summarize either future events that are later related by the narrator (*Il.* 8.473 ff., 15.64 ff.) or past events (*Il.* 18.444 ff.), but among human speakers only Achilles doubles the narrative this way, and only he, of gods or humans, quotes the narrator word for word.[46] Moreover, it is not a matter just of one or two verses, but fully eight lines—exactly those lines that encapsulate the irregularities of the opening scene (*Il.* 1.372–79 = 1.13–16, 22–25).

Richard Martin has shown how Achilles' style of verbal performance throughout the poem recalls that of the master narrator himself: "in Achilles we hear the speech of Homer, the heroic narrator."[47] In this particular scene, Achilles adopts not only the verbal patterns of the Homeric narrator but also the formal conventions of Homeric performance, for he begins his retelling with an allusive reference to the conventional invocation of the Muses. Achilles addresses his mother as one who "knows all" (ἰδυίη πάντ', *Il.* 1.365), which is precisely the same way that the Homeric narrator addresses the Muses at the beginning of the Catalogue of Ships (ἴστέ τε πάντα, *Il.* 2.485).[48] By addressing his mother in this way, Achilles not only emphasizes that he relies on her support, as the poet relies on the Muse; he also points out the slight absurdity of his epic performance, which is addressed to a divine auditor who, like the all-knowing Muses, has no need for the mere *kleos*, "aural report," of events. The absurdity, however, is meaningful, since it is the result of Achilles' isolation from human society, an isolation that also finds expression in the physical location of the performance, the antisocial space of the seashore.[49] Having cut himself off from normal social interactions, the master performer is left without an appropriate audience.

The same picture emerges from the next scene in which we encounter Achilles, the Embassy of Book 9, where he is again presented as a performer of epic poetry. When the ambassadors arrive, they find Achilles singing (perhaps in continuation of his "song" from Book 1):

τὸν δ' εὗρον φρένα τερπόμενον φόρμιγγι λιγείῃ . . .

. . . .

τῇ ὅ γε θυμὸν ἔτερπεν, ἄειδε δ' ἄρα κλέα ἀνδρῶν.
Πάτροκλος δέ οἱ οἶος ἐναντίος ἧστο σιωπῇ,
δέγμενος Αἰακίδην ὁπότε λήξειεν ἀείδων.
Il. 9.186, 189–91

They found him delighting his mind with a clear-sounding *phorminx* . . .

. . . .

with this was he delighting his heart, and he was singing of famous exploits.
And Patroklos alone sat opposite him in silence,
waiting until the descendant of Aiakos should cease from singing.

The text emphasizes the solipsism of this performance: no one hears but Patroklos, who is, like Thetis, an intimate associate, while Achilles performs not to please his auditor but only himself.[50] Achilles' solitary performances, in almost complete isolation from social contact, are abnormalities from the standpoint of a culture in which poetry—particularly Homeric poetry—was typically performed at large, public gatherings.[51] In both Book 1 and Book 9, the poem uses the image of Achilles as performer of poetry to index an anomalous situation: the seclusion of Achilles' performances figures the estrangement and isolation of the figure who embodies *philotēs*.

The choice of this image is not gratuitous, for it highlights the fact that the problems confronted by Achilles and by Achaean society more generally are a matter of language. The initial state of exception is, at its core, a failure of language: Chryses' petition fails to achieve its intended result, while the community fails to express effectively its approval for his request (due to the intervention of Agamemnon). As we have seen, this failure of language leaves its mark on the very language of the poem, where there is also a failure of adequate, effective communication. The political crisis created by Agamemnon disrupts poetic language to the point that the ability of the formulaic medium to communicate the meaning of political action is undermined. Achilles, alone among the characters of the epic, has a direct experience of this disruption; so it is not surprising that, for him, poetry becomes a solipsistic exercise. Achilles' performances on the seashore and in the privacy of his tent make manifest the difficult position faced by a profoundly social figure struggling to communicate in a medium that has become dysfunctional.

ACHILLES AND THE FAILURE OF LANGUAGE

The picture of Achilles singing in seclusion is an appropriate introduction to the visit of the embassy in Book 9, since the embassy's mission illustrates the dysfunctional state of language in the Achaean community. True, the negotiations that take place in Achilles' tent focus almost exclusively on the material aspects of the dispute, with Agamemnon offering, through Odysseus, extensive gifts in addition to Briseis in order to induce Achilles to return, while Achilles adamantly refuses to accept any compensation for the dishonor he has suffered. But the simple fact of the embassy—that is, the fact that Agamemnon cannot negotiate directly with Achilles—indicates that communication has become problematic. Important utterances cannot be shared immediately but are subject to a deferral and a transmission that threatens to undermine their transparency. In fact, the two most important utterances that are exchanged in Book 9—Agamemnon's conciliatory offer and Achilles' final response to the entreaties of the ambassadors, that he will not think of battle until his own ships are threatened (*Il.* 9.650–53)—are elided in such a way that their significance is almost totally obscured. Odysseus diplomatically omits from his report of Agamemnon's offer the invidious condition that Achilles acknowledge and accept a subordinate position (*Il.* 9.160–61), and thus he "neatly reverses the import of the speech" as Agamemnon intends it.[52]

This can be construed as a well-intentioned attempt to restore some spirit of conciliation in spite of Agamemnon's heavy-handedness, but it is much harder to understand why Odysseus is again less than fully forthcoming when he reports the results of the embassy back to Agamemnon. He relays only Achilles' initial response (to his own appeal), in which the latter refuses outright to come to the Achaeans' defense, but Odysseus says nothing about the answer Achilles finally gives in concession to Ajax's plea, in which he indicates that he *will* reenter the fighting if Hector threatens his own ships.[53] The failure to report this portion of Achilles' reply, in spite of his explicit injunction to do so (*Il.* 9.649), represents a crucial omission, for it is precisely here that Achilles reveals his susceptibility to claims of *philotēs*.[54] Working on false assumptions, the Achaean leadership make no further attempts to repair relations with Achilles. Odysseus' interference in the process of communication effectively forecloses the possibility of reintegrating Achilles into Achaean society.

Achilles seems to be aware of these difficulties of communication. His first words in response to Odysseus suggest an uncanny intuition of the fact that Odysseus has omitted, and will again omit, important portions of the utterances he is charged with conveying:

διογενὲς Λαερτιάδη πολυμήχαν᾽ Ὀδυσσεῦ
χρὴ μὲν δὴ τὸν μῦθον ἀπηλεγέως ἀποειπεῖν,
ᾗ περ δὴ φρονέω τε καὶ ὡς τετελεσμένον ἔσται,
ὡς μή μοι τρύζητε παρήμενοι ἄλλοθεν ἄλλος.
ἐχθρὸς γάρ μοι κεῖνος ὁμῶς Ἀΐδαο πύλῃσιν
ὅς χ᾽ ἕτερον μὲν κεύθῃ ἐνὶ φρεσίν, ἄλλο δὲ εἴπῃ.
Il. 9.308–13

Zeus-born son of Laertes, Odysseus of many contrivances,
I must tell you forthrightly
how I am minded and how things will come to pass,
so you do not keep coming to sit and whine, now from one side and now from
    another.
Hateful to me as the gates of Hades is the man
who hides one thing in his heart and speaks another.

The reference to "concealment" does more than simply call into question the sincerity of Agamemnon's offer: it points to what Odysseus' version of the offer actually hides by omission.[55] Odysseus conceals by withholding some part of the words entrusted to him. As if to underline this connection, Achilles' comment on the Gates of Hades makes use of the same words as the missing portion of Agamemnon's speech.[56] His remark, however, is multivalent and gains rhetorical force from its multiple layers. As much as it criticizes Odysseus' manipulation of language or Agamemnon's ethical position, it also identifies a positive ideal to which Achilles pledges himself. With these words he declares his intention to speak his mind fully and, more generally, his commitment to maintaining the transparency of language, the fit between words and reality.

Much has been written about the "language of Achilles" ever since Adam Parry published a well-known article by that title.[57] Parry's argument is that Achilles struggles to articulate a point of view at odds with the values of the Homeric world but is frustrated in the attempt by the fact that he has at his disposal no other language than the formulas of Homeric poetry, that is, the language that encodes those values. As a result, he can express himself only by "misusing" that language. Subsequent writers have questioned Parry's argument. The consensus that has emerged holds that Achilles does not "misuse" Homeric language, at least in the way intended by Parry; if anything, he is simply graced with a higher degree of expressivity and flexibility in his selection and use of traditional elements of that language.[58] He is not an abuser but a master of Homeric speech. Nevertheless, Achilles is manifestly at odds with those around him. His actions, as Stephen Nimis notes, remain "inscrutable to others in the poem."[59]

In fact, the root of Achilles' problem and the cause of his alienation are not that he is struggling to say something that cannot be said but that he is committed to a transparent relation between language and reality in a world in which that relation has been broken.[60] Parry is right to focus on the issue of the gap between language and reality and to identify Achilles' comment on the hatefulness of the man "who hides one thing in his heart and speaks another" as the most direct expression of this gap in the poem. But to say that Achilles "does not accept the common language," that he objects to it and seeks to pry it apart, weights the situation wrongly.[61] Achilles is struggling to maintain a language transparent enough to be serviceable to the community and to hold together language and reality in spite of the cleavage between the two that has emerged. When he sees others violating their commitments or misrepresenting social realities by strategic concealment, he stakes out a position that requires him to speak his mind fully and to abide by what he has said. Although the Achaeans may perceive him as mercurial, changing his mind as the mood strikes him, nevertheless in the end he remains bound by his word.[62]

The most traumatic event in the *Iliad,* the death of Patroklos, hinges on Achilles' commitment to fulfilling his word. When Patroklos pleads to be sent into battle, Achilles is already prepared to acknowledge the inevitability of giving up his anger. But he accepts Patroklos' plan because he recognizes that it is the only way to act without contradicting his previous statement to the embassy:

ἀλλὰ τὰ μὲν προτετύχθαι ἐάσομεν· οὐδ᾽ ἄρα πως ἦν
ἀσπερχὲς κεχολῶσθαι ἐνὶ φρεσίν· ἤτοι ἔφην γε
οὐ πρὶν μηνιθμὸν καταπαυσέμεν, ἀλλ᾽ ὁπότ᾽ ἂν δὴ
νῆας ἐμὰς ἀφίκηται ἀϋτή τε πτόλεμός τε.
τύνη δ᾽ ὤμοιιν μὲν ἐμὰ κλυτὰ τεύχεα δῦθι,
ἄρχε δὲ Μυρμιδόνεσσι φιλοπτολέμοισι μάχεσθαι . . .
Il. 16.60–65

But I will let go of what has passed before; nor could I have harbored
an unrelenting anger in my heart, though surely I said that
I would not put an end to my wrath until
the war-cry and battle came to my own ships.
But put my armor on your shoulders
and lead the war-hungry Myrmidons to battle . . .

Because of what he has previously said to Ajax during the Embassy—and
charged the ambassadors with conveying back to Agamemnon—Achilles cannot enter the battle himself; to do so would be to commit just the kind of inconse-
quence he abhors in others. This leaves Patroklos' involvement as the only way to
help the Achaeans. The tragic irony is that Achilles' reasoning is based on a false
premise, namely, that the Achaeans are aware of his statement to Ajax, which
Odysseus never reported. It is impossible to say how things might have turned
out otherwise: if Achilles knew what was actually reported to the Achaeans, he
might have decided against sending Patroklos, on the view that this would appear inconsistent with his refusal to help; while if Nestor knew that Achilles had
shown himself susceptible to persuasion, he might have appealed to him directly, rather than seeking Patroklos as substitute.[63] All this is speculation. The
essential point is that Achilles founds his decision to send Patroklos into battle
on a commitment to keeping his word, but both his word and its relation to his
actions remain invisible to the other Achaeans.

The problems with language, with the relation between word and action, begin with the exceptional language of Book 1. There, as we have seen, the singular
verb *epeuphēmeîn* raises the unanswerable question of what effect the response
denoted by this verb is supposed to have. Under normal circumstances, response
formulas allow the audience to infer the subsequent course of action, but the exceptional expression disrupts the relationship between an utterance and its consequence. It is just this relationship that Achilles seeks to uphold. Achilles' direct
experience of the exception in Book 1 is, if not the immediate cause, at least the
broader context for the position on language he takes up in Book 9.

FROM EXCEPTION TO NORM

The embassy's attempt to reintegrate Achilles into the body politic fails. Achilles cannot countenance the idea of participating in the social life of a group
in which speech itself, the medium of social interaction, has become opaque and
inconsequent. His reintegration requires the establishment (or reestablishment)

of a mode of speech that accurately reflects and predictably shapes social reality. In terms of the conceptual system underlying the Iliadic representation of communal life, this means the restoration of *ainos* as socially constructive speech and of *epainos* as the means by which the community transforms speech into action. The return of Achilles, whose withdrawal results more or less directly from the exceptional political moment with which the poem begins, depends implicitly on the rectification of that exception, that is, on the restoration of *epainos* as the articulation between speech and reality in place of the ambivalent response designated by *epeuphēmeîn*.

The centrality of *ainos* to the story of Achilles' quarrel with Agamemnon is for the most part implied rather than stated directly. Significantly, however, when Achilles seeks a label for the fault to which he attributes the political crisis of Book 1, he chooses a word that makes Agamemnon's delinquencies precisely a matter of his opposition to *ainos*.[64] When Agamemnon's two heralds arrive to take away Briseis, Achilles calls on them to bear witness before gods and men, and above all before the *apēnēs* king:

> τὼ δ᾿ αὐτὼ μάρτυροι ἔστων
> πρός τε θεῶν μακάρων πρός τε θνητῶν ἀνθρώπων
> καὶ πρὸς τοῦ βασιλῆος ἀπηνέος εἴ ποτε δ᾿ αὖτε
> χρειὼ ἐμεῖο γένηται ἀεικέα λοιγὸν ἀμῦναι
> τοῖς ἄλλοις·
> *Il.* 1.338–42

> Let these two be witnesses
> before the blessed gods and mortal men,
> and before the *apēnēs* king, if ever again
> there be need of me to ward off unseemly devastation
> from the others . . .

Traditionally rendered as "hard" or "cruel," *apēnēs* is in fact cognate with *ainos;* its literal meaning is "opposed to" or "negating *ainos*."[65] There is a point to the use of this word here. The taking of Briseis marks the actual, juridically efficacious moment of Achilles' withdrawal. The great oath he had sworn in the assembly (*Il.* 1.233 ff.) constituted a kind of contract whose fulfillment was contingent on Agamemnon's course of action. As Agamemnon has now acted on his threat, Achilles' oath comes into effect, and he demands recognition of that fact by calling the heralds to witness. In other words, this is the moment when the rift that had been manifested verbally in the earlier assembly scene becomes social reality; and at this moment Achilles identifies Agamemnon, the source of that verbal and social rift, as *apēnēs*, as one opposed to socially constructive speech.[66]

Achilles' short speech before the heralds makes *ainos* a central concern by linking it, through its negation, to the key motif of *loigos*, "destruction," a word that, in the *Iliad*, is strictly limited to the calamities resulting from the *mēnis* of a god or hero.[67] Achilles seems to be suggesting that the *loigos* he knows will result from his withdrawal will be the result of Agamemnon's opposition to *ainos*. Elsewhere in the poem, however, this charge is laid against Achilles himself, most poignantly by Patroklos. At the beginning of Book 16, in the speech that convinces Achilles to send him into battle, Patroklos fingers Achilles as the *apēnēs* one:

> τί σευ ἄλλος ὀνήσεται ὀψίγονός περ
> αἴ κε μὴ Ἀργείοισιν ἀεικέα λοιγὸν ἀμύνῃς;
> νηλεές, οὐκ ἄρα σοί γε πατὴρ ἦν ἱππότα Πηλεύς,
> οὐδὲ Θέτις μήτηρ· γλαυκὴ δέ σε τίκτε θάλασσα
> πέτραι τ' ἠλίβατοι, ὅτι τοι νόος ἐστὶν ἀπηνής.
> *Il.* 16.31–35[68]

> What benefit will another of a later generation take from you
> if you do not ward off unseemly devastation from the Argives?
> Pitiless one, Peleus the horseman was not your father,
> nor Thetis your mother: the grey sea must have borne you
> and steep cliffs, since your mind is *apēnēs*.

Just as Achilles and Agamemnon experience *mēnis* reciprocally,[69] so too they can both reciprocally be characterized as preventing *ainos*. Agamemnon, however, is called *apēnēs* in Book 1, while Achilles merits the label only after Book 9, as if to imply that his refusal to accept the embassy's offer was unwarranted and excessive. Indeed, to the extent that Chryses' story can be taken as paradigmatic, Achilles ought to have accepted Agamemnon's reparations, just as the priest eventually accepted his gifts.[70] Moreover, the Chryses narrative actually doubly underscores Achilles' culpability in this episode: if Achilles, by refusing compensation, overturns the positive example set by Chryses, he nevertheless faithfully follows the negative model of Agamemnon in refusing to accept *apoina*—which is the word Agamemnon uses to describe his gifts (*Il.* 9.120).[71] Thus, from one point of view, Achilles' behavior in Book 9 is a repetition of the exceptionalism that set the whole poem in motion. The continuing failure of *apoina* as a social mechanism during the time of the *Iliad's* primary narrative sequence is in fact an important sign of the "state of exception" described by the poem: prior to Chryses' petition and Agamemnon's rebuff, the acceptance of *apoina* was the norm.[72]

The ambassadors avoid the term *apoina*—as "ransom," *apoina* is normally transacted between enemies, and the use of the term would imply an inherently hostile relationship[73]—but one, at least, invokes the broader system of compensation to which the *apoina* mechanism belongs in order to imply that Achilles' behavior violates the norm. Ajax points to the conventions surrounding *poinē*, the correlate of *apoina* among members of the same social group,[74] to demonstrate the abnormality of Achilles' intransigence:

> καὶ μέν τίς τε κασιγνήτοιο φονῆος
> ποινὴν ἢ οὗ παιδὸς ἐδέξατο τεθνηῶτος·
> καί ῥ' ὃ μὲν ἐν δήμῳ μένει αὐτοῦ πόλλ' ἀποτίσας,
> τοῦ δέ τ' ἐρητύεται κραδίη καὶ θυμὸς ἀγήνωρ
> ποινὴν δεξαμένῳ· σοὶ δ' ἄληκτόν τε κακόν τε
> θυμὸν ἐνὶ στήθεσσι θεοὶ θέσαν εἵνεκα κούρης
> οἴης·
>
> *Il.* 9.632–38

> A person accepts *poinē* even from the murderer
> of his brother, or for a child that has died,
> and the murderer remains there in the community after paying a great price,
> while the heart and valorous passion of the other are checked
> when he has received *poinē*. But the gods have set an evil
> and unassuageable passion in your chest, for the sake of a single
> girl.

Ajax emphasizes *poinē* as the means by which social bonds are reestablished in a community. His point is that normally compensation is accepted, and the community is thereby enabled to resume its normal life. Achilles' continued refusal violates the norm of compensation just as much as Agamemnon's exceptional decision not to accept *apoina*. For this reason, after the embassy's offer has been rejected, Achilles merits the designation *apēnēs* just as much as Agamemnon: both have set themselves against the operation of socially constructive speech by contravening the norms of social life.

The logic of the *Iliad* is that the reintegration of Achilles into the body politic means the restoration of the norms of Achaean society. These norms are several, but they are all interconnected. First and foremost is the norm of collective decision making, according to which it is the response of the group, and not the preference of a dominant individual, that determines collective action. Tied to this is the norm of accepting compensation, which is first disrupted by Agamemnon when he suspends the decision-making power of the group in favor of his own determination not to accept *apoina* for Chryseis. This disruption initiates a sequence of rejections of compensation, outstanding among which is Achilles' own rejection of Agamemnon's *apoina* (as Agamemnon puts it), or *poinē* (as Ajax puts it).[75] Finally, on the level of the narrative itself, there is the normative system structuring the language in which these social facts are expressed. In one sense, Achilles' withdrawal from Achaean society is the result of these anomalies, so that his return is contingent on their correction. But in another, perhaps truer, sense, Achilles' absence is itself one of the abnormal circumstances that obtains during the time of the *Iliad*. As the embodiment of *philotēs*, Achilles ought to be part of the group; his participation in social life is one of the norms that, outside the *Iliad*, bind the group together. The *Iliad* describes a struggle to reestablish all of these interconnected norms, with Achilles' withdrawal serving as the most tangible sign of dysfunction. In the chapters that follow I examine the ways in which that struggle plays itself out.

CHAPTER 4

Social Order and Poetic Order

Agamemnon, Thersites, and the Catalogue of Ships

For Joseph Russo, the basic aesthetic impulse of Homeric poetry, from the microlevel of the verse's metrical structure to the macrolevel of the story of the Trojan War, is to reimpose order and regularity after temporarily permitting free play to disorder and abnormality.[1] As a paradigmatic example of this pattern, Russo offers Book 2 of the *Iliad,* in which Agamemnon's ill-conceived attempt to test the morale of his troops leads to the total breakdown of order in the Achaean camp as the soldiers scatter for their ships, ready to sail back home to the Helladic mainland. The possibility of a precipitate departure—a "return home [*nostos*] contrary to destiny," the narrator calls it (2.155)—is put to rest by Odysseus. The response to his speech, which succeeds in producing collective support for the war effort, provides the first occurrence in the poem of the verb *epaineîn* (2.335). "Such an episode," writes Russo, "represents the momentary outbreak of the eccentric, of the deviant action, which is finally subdued as the eccentricity is brought back into line with what is proper and normative in the social, military, and political order."[2] Here, "what is proper and normative" is, in the first instance, simply the preservation of the Achaean confederacy. But it is also the continued progress of events toward their destined, that is to say, traditional, outcome, since the dissolution of the confederacy means a "*nostos* contrary to destiny."[3] In the context of the present inquiry, what is most interesting about this episode is that the community's expression of collective will in the form of *epainos* coincides not only with the restoration of sociopolitical order but also, in an important sense, with the restoration of *poetic* order: Odysseus' speech and the response it receives prevent the plot from turning in a direction not sanctioned by tradition.

The last chapter explored the way in which *epainos* is implicated in the set of irregularities that characterizes the poem's beginning. Those irregularities are a matter of the norms governing Achaean society and the language that describes that society. The appearance of *epainos* in Book 2 after its marked absence in Book 1 does not bring with it the complete restoration of those norms. After all, Achilles remains withdrawn. Nevertheless, Book 2 reveals the link between *epainos* and the normative framework of the poem on the broadest possible level, that of the shape of the poem as determined by tradition. At the same time, the book functions as a kind of paradigm for the exploration of political themes in the poem as a whole.

The book begins with Zeus' plan for fulfilling his promise to bring honor to Achilles. He resolves to send a false, "destructive" (οὖλον, *Il.* 2.6) dream to Agamemnon, which, with the message that he will "now" (νῦν, 2.12) take Troy, will prompt the king to engage the Trojans in battle. The dream is false but not because it suggests the immediate downfall of Troy—in the context of a war that has already lasted nine years, *nun*, "now," need not mean the very next day, and the narrator signals that Agamemnon is foolish to make this inference (*Il.* 2.37–38). The crucial falsehood is rather the assertion that the divine community has at last reached a consensus about the fate of Troy:

οὐ γὰρ ἔτ' ἀμφὶς Ὀλύμπια δώματ' ἔχοντες
ἀθάνατοι φράζονται· ἐπέγναμψεν γὰρ ἅπαντας
Ἥρη λισσομένη, Τρώεσσι δὲ κήδε' ἐφῆπται.
Il. 2.13–15

The immortals who dwell on Olympus are no longer
divided in their counsels: for Hera has bent all into conformity
by her pleading, and sorrows impend for the Trojans.

In fact, the end of Book 1 has just offered a vivid demonstration of the differences that still divide Olympus and will continue to do so throughout the poem, and the audience has just witnessed Hera "bending into conformity" not the other gods but her own rebellious will (ἐπιγνάμψασα φίλον κῆρ, *Il.* 1.569). The dream's false message presupposes that the sack of Troy depends upon political circumstances—specifically, that it requires the collective support of the divine community as a whole. In this way, the long-term outcome of the story of the Trojan War is already brought into relation with the political life of the interested groups at the outset of the book.

Acting on the assumption that the new day will bring him a long-awaited victory, Agamemnon summons the Achaeans as a whole to a general assembly and then holds a separate meeting with the council (boulē) of elders beside Nestor's ship (Il. 2.50–54). This is the first of several indications in Book 2 of an articulation of the Achaean social body into two distinct groups, the laoi, or general soldiery, on one hand, and on the other their leaders, called either gerontes, "elders," as here, or basilēes, "kings."[4] In the boulē, Agamemnon lays out a plan for mustering the troops, resolving to "test" them (πειρήσομαι, Il. 2.73) by bidding them first to abandon the war; he calls on those present in the council, for their part, to prevent the troops from actually doing so. The fact that Agamemnon feels obliged to test the troops, as well as the provisional way in which he speaks of their readiness for action (αἴ κέν πως θωρήξομεν, 2.72), echoed by Nestor (2.83), indicates that he recognizes certain difficulties impeding the mobilization of the army.

The text does not specify what those impediments might be. An audience might reasonably have inferred, however, that Agamemnon's wariness reflects the events of the previous nine years of the war; Wolfgang Kullmann points specifically to the crisis of morale narrated toward the end of the Cypria, the poem that immediately precedes the Iliad in the sequence of the so-called Epic Cycle.[5] As Kullmann himself stresses, while the poems of the Cycle may well have been fixed at a later date than the Iliad, nevertheless they can be supposed to represent genuinely archaic traditions.[6] According to Proclus, the Cypria told of how, after laying siege to Troy and sacking certain surrounding cities, the Achaean host attempted to abandon the war and return home but was prevented from doing so by Achilles.[7] This apparent mutiny appears to have been the consequence of the famine described in the scholia to Lycophron (and attributed to the poet of the Cypria, among others).[8] The story is relevant to Book 2 of the Iliad for two reasons. Firstly, it explains why Agamemnon should be less than fully confident about his troops' willingness to arm for battle. Ancient audiences familiar with broader Cyclic traditions would have recalled that at least once before the army had refused to carry on the fight. Secondly, and perhaps more importantly, the episode in the Cypria provides a clear parallel for the action of Iliad Book 2: in both cases, a sudden and premature departure is prevented by the intervention of one of the tradition's central heroes. The parallel has the effect of providing a background against which to understand the significance of the

Iliad's narrative. The background enriches our understanding of the crisis provoked by Agamemnon's test to the extent that it highlights the absence of Achilles, whose role as established by the *Cypria* is now taken over by Odysseus.

Of course, even without the context provided by the Cycle, Agamemnon's
doubts about the readiness of his troops are more than justified by the plague
and political crisis of Book 1. A test—which he claims is *themis,* an established
rule or custom (*Il.* 2.73)—is therefore in order.[9] The stratagem he proposes,
however, seems peculiarly ill suited for meeting the difficulties he foresees. If
his goal is to ascertain which of his soldiers are ready to fight and which are not,
that purpose is much better served by the plan Nestor proposes in the assembly
after Odysseus has restored order:

κρῖν' ἄνδρας κατὰ φῦλα κατὰ φρήτρας Ἀγάμεμνον,
ὡς φρήτρη φρήτρηφιν ἀρήγῃ, φῦλα δὲ φύλοις.
εἰ δέ κεν ὣς ἔρξῃς καί τοι πείθωνται Ἀχαιοί,
γνώσῃ ἔπειθ' ὅς θ' ἡγεμόνων κακὸς ὅς τέ νυ λαῶν
ἠδ' ὅς κ' ἐσθλὸς ἔῃσι· κατὰ σφέας γὰρ μαχέονται.
γνώσεαι δ' εἰ καὶ θεσπεσίῃ πόλιν οὐκ ἀλαπάξεις,
ἦ ἀνδρῶν κακότητι καὶ ἀφραδίῃ πολέμοιο.
Il. 2.362–68

Divide the men by tribe and by clan, Agamemnon,
that clan may bring aid to clan and tribe to tribe.
If you do thus and the Achaeans obey,
then will you know which of the leaders and which of the men are cowards,
and which are valiant: for they will fight alongside their own.
And you will know whether your failure to take the city is by divine decree,
or on account of the cowardice of the men and their folly in war.

Nestor's advice on how best to detect (his word is *gignōskein,* "know") the merits
and faults of the men seems to answer directly Agamemnon's desire for a test,
creating the impression of a dialogue between this passage and the *boulē* at the
beginning of the book.[10] Nestor, who initially avoids expressing an opinion on
the merits of Agamemnon's plan, now corrects it, after it has proven to be a
failure.[11] On the other hand, if Agamemnon's aim is to counter the general reluctance of his army and motivate it for battle, he would do better to adopt the
method used by Achilles in Book 16. When he musters the Myrmidons, Achilles refers even more directly than Agamemnon to his troops' desire to return
home (*Il.* 16.205–6), but he does so in order to consign that desire rhetorically to

the past, as he calls on his soldiers to remember their former declarations of eagerness for the fray. Odysseus pursues the same strategy when he tries to restore order: in the speech that receives the *epainos* of the assembled army, he acknowledges the desire to return home but also reminds the soldiers of their former "promise" to return only after sacking Troy (*Il.* 2.284–300). In short, among a range of comparable examples, Agamemnon's remarks stand out for the degree to which they seem calculated not to prevent but to provoke disorder.[12]

Moreover, Agamemnon's strategy as a whole betrays the same indifference toward the principles that undergird political stability as we saw in Book 1. He does not wish the Achaeans to decamp, but he nevertheless exhorts them to do so. He appears even to expect that the soldiers will approve his proposal, since he instructs his commanders to "restrain" them (*Il.* 2.75). His proposal of a plan that he does not want to be put into effect exposes an attitude toward the political process that is at odds with the normative structures of Achaean social life, for it implies the understanding that the approval of the audience will not have the force of a ratification. Agamemnon once again reveals his disregard for the mechanisms of collective decision making by presupposing that popular support for his proposal can be overridden or checked by the intervention of the *basilēes*. There could be no clearer indication that Agamemnon's mindset is antithetical to the principles of consensus-based governance.

The "restraint" Agamemnon directs his commanders to enforce deserves some comment, since efforts to impose such "restraint" (designated by forms of the verb *erētuein*) punctuate the subsequent narrative. Agamemnon does not necessarily envision the need to prevent the soldiers from leaving the assembly (as they in fact do). The task he assigns to the *basilēes* seems intended rather to curb verbal reactions from the troops. When the army assembles, we see clearly that "to restrain" the troops means simply to quiet them, so that speakers may be heard:

τετρήχει δ' ἀγορή, ὑπὸ δὲ στεναχίζετο γαῖα
λαῶν ἱζόντων, ὅμαδος δ' ἦν· ἐννέα δέ σφεας
κήρυκες βοόωντες ἐρήτυον, εἴ ποτ' ἀϋτῆς
σχοίατ', ἀκούσειαν δὲ διοτρεφέων βασιλήων.
σπουδῇ δ' ἕζετο λαός, ἐρήτυθεν δὲ καθ' ἕδρας
παυσάμενοι κλαγγῆς· ἀνὰ δὲ κρείων Ἀγαμέμνων
ἔστη σκῆπτρον ἔχων τὸ μὲν Ἥφαιστος κάμε τεύχων.
Il. 2.95–101

A confused assembly gathered, and the earth groaned beneath
the people as they sat down, and a great noise arose; <u>nine</u>
<u>shouting heralds restrained them, calling on them to hold back</u>
<u>their cries and listen to the Zeus-nurtured kings.</u>
The people eagerly sat down, and <u>restrained themselves in seated rows,</u>
<u>ceasing from shouting.</u> And lord Agamemnon stood up
holding a scepter that Hephaistos had fashioned.

This kind of restraint, then, can be understood as a prerequisite for deliberation. It is part of the framework that makes deliberation possible.[13] Agamemnon's plan seems to be to forestall the immediate approval of his proposal by
suppressing any vocal reaction on the part of the audience, in effect leaving the
floor open for counterproposals and further debate. We can surmise that, if his
plan were successful, the scene would unfold like the assembly at the beginning
of Book 9, where Agamemnon's proposal—again, to flee Troy—meets with silence and is then followed by the proposals of Diomedes and Nestor. (The irony,
of course, is that Agamemnon is no longer testing the troops in Book 9 but sincerely advocates for withdrawal.)

The plan, however, is a failure. Given Agamemnon's willingness to dismiss
or suppress expressions of collective will, it comes as no surprise that his speech
has an immediately disintegrating, even atomizing, effect on his audience. This
effect can be observed in the phraseology of reception. Agamemnon "stirs the
thumos" of his hearers:

ὣς φάτο, τοῖσι δὲ θυμὸν ἐνὶ στήθεσσιν ὄρινε . . .
Il. 2.142

Thus he spoke, and he stirred the *thumos* in their chests . . .

This verse represents a unique adaptation to a group context of a formula that is
elsewhere used only of the reaction *of an individual* to a request or command:

ὣς φάτο, τῷ δ' ἄρα θυμὸν ἐνὶ στήθεσσιν ὄρινε
Il. 4.208, 11.804, etc.

Thus he spoke, and he stirred the *thumos* in his chest.

Pragmatically, this verse always precedes the departure of the affected individual for some new destination in accordance with the terms of the request,
a pattern that is maintained here when the soldiers immediately scatter for
their ships.[14] The use of phraseology that is elsewhere applied to individuals

emphasizes that the soldiers do so separately, and by implication chaotically. Each soldier experiences a particular, not a general, impulse to flee. Even though every soldier individually supports his proposal, Agamemnon seems unable to elicit a collective response. He cannot appeal to the army as a group but only as a conglomeration of individuals, just as he sees himself as an individual whose actions are not constrained by the group. The response to his speech reflects his own dismissive attitude toward the collective will.

Atomized by Agamemnon's test, the army abruptly rises from the assembly. Chaotically and without any sense of overarching order—like waves on the open sea (*Il.* 2.144–46, an image to which I return below)—the soldiers make for their ships. The threat of a deviation from the traditional outlines of the Troy story causes the divine apparatus to spring into action. The poet declares that the Achaeans would have had a *nostos* "contrary to destiny" if Hera had not instructed Athena to intervene.[15] Already on an earlier occasion Athena has acted at Hera's behest in order to forestall an undesirable turn of events. In Book 1, as Achilles contemplates murdering Agamemnon, she is sent by Hera to stay his hand. On that occasion, the narrator cites Hera's concern for both Agamemnon and Achilles as the reason for her involvement (*Il.* 1.195–96); similarly, in Book 2 Hera voices a concern not for the potential violation of "destiny" but for the fact that a premature return would bring dishonor on the Achaeans. These explicit justifications, however, should not obscure the basic similarity of the two interventions: in both cases the goddesses are reacting to a situation that threatens to undermine the "destined," that is, traditional, course of events. As much as a premature return, the killing of Agamemnon would render the traditional outcome of the story impossible.[16] In both of these cases, Athena functions as the divine agent who returns the action to its normative course when it is in danger of veering in an undesirable or unsanctioned direction. This is a role that she will reprise elsewhere in the poem.[17]

Athena descends from Olympus to find Odysseus, whom she enlists in the task of "restraining" (ἐρήτυε, *Il.* 2.180) the Achaeans in their headlong flight. The repetition of this verb emphasizes that the restraint required has changed dramatically from what Agamemnon at first envisioned. Odysseus, taking control of the situation by taking in hand Agamemnon's scepter, begins "restraining with gentle words" (ἀγανοῖς ἐπέεσσιν ἐρητύσασκε, 2.189) those of the *basilēes* he finds on their way to the ships.[18] The rank and file—the "men of the *dēmos*" (2.198)—are treated far less considerately. Odysseus "drives" them (the verb, *elaunein,* generally refers to the striking of horses) with the scepter and calls to them not with the "gentle words" he had used with his peers but with a *muthos,* a word of command (2.199).[19] For the second time we find an indication of a hierarchical articulation of the Achaean social body into two groups, which appear to differ as much in the character of their political experiences as they do in status and titles.[20] Among the basilées, persuasion is evidently the rule, while the dēmos is subject to the commands of an authority backed by force.

This difference points to the need for nuance in assessing the nature of the Achaean political community. The central thesis of this book is that the poem assigns to the community as a whole the power to determine the course of collective action. The "community as a whole," however, is not a homogenous, undifferentiated entity, nor is collective action as egalitarian an enterprise as this formulation might be thought to imply. Although epainos implies the cohesion of the group, this cohesion is a matter of both horizontal and vertical, that is, hierarchical, relationships. In the context of such a hierarchy, there is a place for a certain amount of compulsion. The consensus signaled by epainos is not the same as unanimity, understood as the coincidence of independent wills. It is, rather, the coordination of wills in and by a social structure, which in most cases will include a certain number of hierarchical and potentially coercive relationships.

THERSITES AND THE CONDITIONS FOR CONSENSUS

That coercion can and occasionally must play a role in the establishment of conditions conducive to epainos is nowhere more in evidence than in the episode centering on Thersites, who presents the last major obstacle as Odysseus alternately persuades and compels the Achaeans to return to the assembly. When all the others have been "restrained in seated rows" (ἐρήτυθεν δὲ καθ' ἕδρας, Il. 2.211), Thersites alone (μοῦνος—the text emphasizes his isolation) continues to be disruptive. He launches a vitriolic attack on Agamemnon, echoing many of the remarks made by Achilles in the assembly of Book 1. Agitating in favor of returning (2.235–37), Thersites now comes to embody the threat of a premature nostos. Odysseus responds with a stern rebuke (a muthos, 2.245) and a severe beating that effectively silences this last disorderly holdout.

The figure of Thersites raises a number of questions, not the least of which is where he belongs in terms of the hierarchical distinction between basilées and dēmos.[21] A widespread opinion, based on the unflattering description of him and the harsh treatment he receives, holds that Thersites belongs to the plēthus, the common mass of soldiers.[22] Others prefer to see in him a basileus, albeit one of relatively low status, noting that he speaks of himself as taking prisoners (Il. 2.231) and that, outside the Iliad, he is assigned a noble lineage.[23] Within the poem, however, he is subject to a violence that seems otherwise reserved for the *dēmos*. This is not necessarily decisive: according to one tradition, Thersites suffered crippling violence at the hands of Meleager during the hunt for the Calydonian boar, even though his very presence at the hunt indicates that he numbered among "the best men of Hellas."[24] Nevertheless, immediately prior to his appearance in the *Iliad*, the poem has sketched an opposition between force and persuasion, limiting the former to the exercise of authority over the *dēmos*. There is at least a strong suggestion that this is the class to which Thersites belongs, a suggestion that is perhaps indicative of an effort on the part of Iliadic tradition to reconfigure his role or persona.[25]

Thersites' precise position in the Achaean social hierarchy remains vague. If this vagueness represents a divergence from non-Homeric traditions, where he belongs unambiguously to the nobility, all the same the *Iliad* maintains important continuities with these traditions. The consistent features of the Thersites figure do more to explain his role in the poem—and the necessity of silencing him—than his ambiguous social status. Everywhere we encounter Thersites he represents a disruptive force that must be expelled or neutralized regardless of his status. Apollodorus relates the story of Thersites' involvement in a struggle to seize the royal power of Calydon (1.8.5–6): as one of the sons of Agrios, he worked with his brothers to depose the rightful ruler, his uncle Oineus.[26] Since Tydeus had already perished in the attack on Thebes, it was left to Oineus' grandson, Diomedes, to return the rule to the Oineidai.[27] Diomedes killed all the sons of Agrios, with the exception of Onkhēstos and Thersites, who fled to Arcadia. Thersites and the other sons of Agrios also took part in the hunt for the Calydonian boar, after which they provoked the quarrel that resulted in the war with the Kourētes (in one version) and the death of Meleager.[28] Even in death Thersites retains the power to destabilize the community: in the *Aithiopis*, which followed the *Iliad* in the Epic Cycle, his killing at the hands of Achilles causes *stasis*, "strife," among the Achaeans.[29] According to Quintus of Smyrna, who is probably following the story as told in the *Aithiopis*, this *stasis* consisted in a dispute between Achilles and Diomedes, who sought to avenge his estranged cousin's death.[30]

Outside the *Iliad*, then, Thersites consistently represents a threat to the established order. The same is true in the *Iliad*, where Thersites' critique of royal authority introduces the threat not just of political instability (the dissolution of the army) but also of poetic chaos, in the first place through the premature and untraditional departure of the Achaeans from Troy. Furthermore, as Gregory Nagy has argued, Thersites' speech threatens to undermine the generic integrity of the poetry in which it is embedded, by introducing the poetry of blame into a medium that identifies itself with praise.[31] Thersites even includes in his speech of blame a direct contradiction of the fundamental premise of the *Iliad* when he characterizes Achilles as indifferent to Agamemnon's abuses:

ἀλλὰ μάλ᾿ οὐκ Ἀχιλῆϊ χόλος φρεσίν, ἀλλὰ μεθήμων·
ἦ γὰρ ἂν Ἀτρεΐδη νῦν ὕστατα λωβήσαιο·
Il. 2.241–42

Achilles harbors no anger in his mind, but is showing his indifference—
otherwise the son of Atreus would now have committed his last outrage.

This denial of Achilles' anger amounts to a negation of the thematic cornerstone of the poem.[32] The danger posed by Thersites, therefore, is not just that he will undermine the stability of the Achaean confederacy but that he will undermine the poetic conventions that support the narrative of their expedition against Troy. The poem points to this convergence of social and poetic or verbal order by twice opposing his speech to *kosmos:*

Θερσίτης δ᾿ ἔτι μοῦνος ἀμετροεπὴς ἐκολῴα,
ὃς ἔπεα φρεσὶν ᾗσιν <u>ἄκοσμά</u> τε πολλά τε ᾔδη
μάψ, ἀτὰρ <u>οὐ κατὰ κόσμον</u>, ἐριζέμεναι βασιλεῦσιν . . .
Il. 2.212–14

Thersites alone still bellowed with a measureless torrent of words,
one whose mind was filled with many <u>disorderly</u> words
for quarreling with kings to no point, and certainly <u>without order</u> . . .

These lines characterize Thersites' speech as opposed to *kosmos* both in itself and in its application. We have seen that *kosmos* designates the overlapping verbal and social order at which *ainos* aims (and that it derives from the root, **kens-*, that *(ep)aineîn* replaces in alphabetic Greek).[33] Such speech represents an irreducible obstacle to Odysseus' project of restoring order (to say nothing of Athena's project of returning events to a course sanctioned by "destiny," that is, tradition), since that project requires the recuperation of socially constructive speech. If *epainos* is to be achieved, Thersites must be silenced.

It might be tempting to suppose that Thersites' voice is brutally suppressed because it is a voice of dissent, of criticism against an authority that does not tolerate censure.[34] However, where political outcomes are determined by *epainos*, we find that dissenting voices (like that of Antilokhos in Book 23) are not automatically subject to the kind of violence directed against Thersites, even when they block the formation of a consensus. Rather than being forcefully repressed, such voices are typically integrated into the project of consensus building through attempts to discover mutually satisfactory arrangements.[35] Thersites, therefore, presents something of a problem. One way out would be to suppose that dissent is the exclusive privilege of the *basilées* and to exclude Thersites from that class; but this, as we have seen, would be to prejudge an issue that the *Iliad* leaves vague. A better solution is found in a distinction between political speech proper, which happens in an explicitly political context and includes legitimate dissent, and the speech that surrounds that context, which appears as noise from the perspective of those engaged in properly political debate. This kind of speech, regardless of its content, must be silenced before politics can begin.

Bruce Lincoln's reflections on the conditions that make the exercise of authority possible usefully foreground what is at stake: "When an authorized speaker advances to an authorized and authorizing place, the audience falls quiet. This silence ought not to be taken for granted but ought to prompt a prolonged inquiry. How does this silence come to be? How is it maintained or enforced, and how fully? What does this absence of speech signify? More pointedly, one might ask if it is the speaker (or the speaker's henchmen) who silences an audience, or if an audience silences itself in order that the speaker might speak?"[36] The Thersites episode might productively be considered just the kind of inquiry that Lincoln calls for. It is an exploration of the tensions surrounding the emergence of political speech from surrounding noise.

We have seen that the *Iliad* refers to the quieting of that noise in terms of "restraint" imposed by heralds. The lines introducing Thersites portray his speech as the last remaining obstacle to this restraint, the last trace of the sealike noise with which the Achaeans reconverge on the place of assembly:

> οἳ δ᾽ ἀγορὴν δὲ
> αὖτις ἐπεσσεύοντο νεῶν ἄπο καὶ κλισιάων
> ἠχῇ, ὡς ὅτε κῦμα πολυφλοίσβοιο θαλάσσης
> αἰγιαλῷ μεγάλῳ βρέμεται, σμαραγεῖ δέ τε πόντος.
> ἄλλοι μέν ῥ᾽ ἕζοντο, ἐρήτυθεν δὲ καθ᾽ ἕδρας·
> Θερσίτης δ᾽ ἔτι μοῦνος ἀμετροεπὴς ἐκολῴα . . .
>
> *Il.* 2.207–12

> The men rushed back
> to the place of assembly from their ships and tents
> with a roar, as when a wave of the loud-sounding sea
> crashes on a great beach, and the sea thunders.

The others took their seats, and restrained themselves in seated rows,
but Thersites alone still bellowed with a measureless torrent of words . . .

His chaotic speech "without measure" disregards the constraints on which genuine debate depends. The poem represents it as a species of the *klangē*, or indiscriminate noise, from which the Achaeans must cease in order to open up a space for properly political speech (*Il.* 2.100; cf. κεκλήγων, 2.222). The violence directed against him by Odysseus is, by the same token, an intensified form of the pressure customarily brought to bear by the heralds in "restraining" the people prior to an assembly.[37] The instrument of violence, the *skēptron*, stands not so much for a royal power that mercilessly crushes its critics as for the authority of the heralds, who enable discussion (and dissent) by enforcing silence.[38] That the brutal force wielded by Odysseus is an exercise of the heraldic function is underscored by the role played by Athena—whom Hera had sent precisely to "restrain" the people (*Il.* 2.164)—in the immediate sequel to the beating:

> ἀνὰ δ' ὁ πτολίπορθος Ὀδυσσεὺς
> ἔστη σκῆπτρον ἔχων· παρὰ δὲ γλαυκῶπις Ἀθήνη
> εἰδομένη κήρυκι σιωπᾶν λαὸν ἀνώγει,
> ὡς ἅμα θ' οἱ πρῶτοί τε καὶ ὕστατοι υἷες Ἀχαιῶν
> μῦθον ἀκούσειαν καὶ ἐπιφρασσαίατο βουλήν·
> *Il.* 2.278–82

> Odysseus the sacker of cities stood up
> holding the scepter, and beside him grey-eyed Athena,
> in the guise of a herald, commanded the people to be silent,
> so that the sons of the Achaeans, first and last,
> could hear his speech and mark his counsel.

In bringing the Thersites episode to a close, these lines lay stress on the fact that his outburst was an obstruction to deliberation; now that he has been silenced, all of the Achaeans have equal access to the decision-making process. He encounters violence not because he speaks out against Agamemnon but because he prevents properly political speech from being heard. His violent exclusion is justified to the extent that it allows the inclusion of everyone in the deliberative process. Far from representing it as the suppression of a dissident voice, the poem constructs this exclusion as the application of a force that is necessary in order for a variety of voices (including, in principle, dissident ones) to be heard.[39]

ODYSSEUS AND POETIC DESTINY

The removal of Thersites establishes the necessary framework for collective consideration of properly political speech. With Athena now serving as herald and quieting the *laos*, Odysseus shifts into the role of speaker. He begins by addressing Agamemnon—"Son of Atreus, now indeed the Achaeans wish to make you most worthy of reproach among mortal men" (*Il.* 2.284–85)—but soon switches to the audience that really matters, the Achaeans themselves, whom he enjoins to stay at Troy until they discover whether Kalkhas has interpreted the omen at Aulis correctly:

> τλῆτε φίλοι, καὶ μείνατ᾽ ἐπὶ χρόνον ὄφρα δαῶμεν
> ἢ ἐτεὸν Κάλχας μαντεύεται ἦε καὶ οὐκί.
>
> *Il.* 2.299–300
>
> Endure, my friends, and remain for a time, until we learn
> whether Kalkhas prophesies truly or not.

Odysseus himself seems not to have any doubts about the truth of the prophecy. When he describes the omen of the serpent and the sparrows, he states as a matter of fact that Zeus sent the serpent and that Zeus turned it to stone as a sign for the Achaeans (*Il.* 2.309, 319). His purpose in recalling the omen seems to be to remind (or convince) the assembled soldiers of the destiny that awaits them, the destiny that their flight threatened to undermine but that nevertheless remains fixed as if in stone. As a character within the narrative, Odysseus cannot refer directly to the future, as the narrator did with the reference to a "*nostos* contrary to destiny," but he can refer to a past figuration of that future. Past figuration and destined future converge, however, as doubles for poetic tradition: Kalkhas, quoted by Odysseus, declares the omen to be a "great portent, late of import and fulfillment, whose fame [*kleos*] will never perish" (*Il.* 2.324–25). Kalkhas' language indicates that the omen, along with the events it foreshadows, will become enshrined in the tradition that will culminate in the *Iliad* and the Epic Cycle.[40]

Odysseus' proposal to stay at Troy and the vision he has presented of future epic glory are approved with a resounding expression of *epainos:*

> ὣς ἔφατ᾽, Ἀργεῖοι δὲ μέγ᾽ ἴαχον, ἀμφὶ δὲ νῆες
> σμερδαλέον κονάβησαν ἀϋσάντων ὑπ᾽ Ἀχαιῶν,
> μῦθον ἐπαινήσαντες Ὀδυσσῆος θείοιο·
>
> *Il.* 2.333–35

> Thus he spoke, and the Argives gave a great shout, and round about
> the ships resounded terribly with the cries of the Achaeans,
> who expressed *epainos* for the *muthos* of godlike Odysseus.

Since Odysseus' *muthos* includes both the proposal to remain and a description of a future identified as the subject of epic tradition, the *epainos* of the audience ratifies simultaneously both the proposed course of action and the tradition to which it belongs.[41] In this way, the conjoined threats of an undesired *nostos* and a violation of "destiny" are put to rest. At the same time, social cohesion is restored as the atomized reaction produced by Agamemnon's flawed proposal modulates into *epainos*, a response that integrates members of the group into a collective entity. Order prevails over chaos, and an exercise of collective will brings the momentary excrescence of the "eccentric" (in Russo's terms) back into line with the broad norms of epic tradition.

There is a certain irony in the fact that Odysseus advocates *against nostos*, and that he alone is explicitly presented as being reluctant to take advantage of the opportunity to return.[42] If the "return contrary to destiny" represents an unlicensed deviation of the story, it is at least a deviation in a direction in which Odysseus could be expected to display his particular virtue. Even within the *Iliad* he is associated with *nostos:* Diomedes chooses him as his companion in the night mission because he judges him to be especially skilled at securing a return (*Il.* 10.246–47).[43] When he stands to deliver his speech, the narrator does identify him as ὁ πτολίπορθος Ὀδυσσεὺς, "Odysseus the sacker of cities," as if to emphasize that, by preventing a premature *nostos*, Odysseus ensures his own ultimate epic fame as the one who contrives the destruction of Troy.[44] Nevertheless, in the choice between *nostos* and continued fighting at Troy, one senses an implicit contrast of Odyssean and Iliadic traditions. In an arresting twist on that contrast, Odysseus argues for the continuation of an Iliadic narrative—a narrative that features Achilles—over a narrative of return in which he would doubtless play the central role.[45]

As I noted above, Achilles is the one who prevents the flight of the Achaeans in the very similar scene from the Cyclic *Cypria*. The surprise and irony of Odysseus' appearance in a role far more suited to Achilles emphasizes the latter's absence in the aftermath of Book 1: the part falls to an actor whose performance, though successful, nevertheless rings hollow.[46] The presentation of Thersites produces a similar effect. Many have noted that his diatribe echoes the complaints lodged against Agamemnon by Achilles himself in Book 1, and even quotes Achilles' words.[47] Thus Achilles, the embodiment of sociality, who ought to be the one to keep the host together, is instead identified through verbal echoes with the obstacle to social unity.[48] The alignment of Achilles with Thersites underscores how topsy-turvy the Achaean social world has become without him. Even Agamemnon seems struck by Achilles' absence in Book 2. Praising the advice that Nestor offers as a follow-up to Odysseus' speech, he laments the fact that his quarrel with Achilles has deprived him of one of his most valuable counselors (Il. 2.371–80). The shadow of the withdrawn hero hangs over the book, reminding us that, even if order has been restored, the new normality is still an attenuated one, marred by the absence of Achilles.

RESTORING THE *KOSMOS* OF TROOPS AND TRADITION

The reception of Odysseus' speech marks the restoration of social order and integrity to the greatest extent possible without Achilles. The two speeches that close out the assembly contribute nothing further in this regard. Nestor begins with an address to the army as a whole but soon directs himself to Agamemnon alone (thus reversing the pattern of Odysseus' speech, which was addressed first to Agamemnon and then to the army). His recommendations, offered solely to the king, present no opportunity for collective decision or action. Agamemnon concludes the assembly by directing the soldiers to fortify themselves with a meal and prepare for battle. It is a striking indication of Agamemnon's general antipathy toward the dynamics of collective decision making that even here, where he offers nothing more than a refinement of a plan that has already been approved, he elicits only shouting, and not the fully efficient response of *epainos* (Il. 2.394).[49]

The reaction to Agamemnon's speech may fall short of the response Odysseus received, but the simile describing that reaction provides a striking indication of the fact that the army, once on the brink of disintegration, has been restored to unity. The narrator compares the soldiers' shouting to the noise of waves crashing against a headland:

ὣς ἔφατ', Ἀργεῖοι δὲ μέγ' ἴαχον ὡς ὅτε κῦμα
ἀκτῇ ἐφ' ὑψηλῇ, ὅτε κινήσῃ Νότος ἐλθών,
προβλῆτι σκοπέλῳ· τὸν δ' οὔ ποτε κύματα λείπει
παντοίων ἀνέμων, ὅτ' ἂν ἔνθ' ἢ ἔνθα γένωνται.

Il. 2.394–97

Thus he spoke, and the Argives roared with a great shout, like a wave
against a steep shoreline, when the South wind comes and stirs the sea—

a jutting headland, which is always buffeted by waves
in all winds, whenever they blow from one direction or another.

As Seth Benardete has observed, this simile must be read against the simile
that describes the army's reaction to Agamemnon's first speech:[50]

κινήθη δ' ἀγορὴ φὴ κύματα μακρὰ θαλάσσης
πόντου Ἰκαρίοιο, τὰ μέν τ' Εὖρός τε Νότος τε
ὦρορ' ἐπαΐξας πατρὸς Διὸς ἐκ νεφελάων.
Il. 2.144–46

The assembly was stirred like the great waves of the sea—
the Icarian sea—waves which the East and South winds
propel as they rush down from the clouds of father Zeus.

The soldiers' disorganized and centrifugal movements are here compared to
waves on the open sea, driven by a combination of winds.[51] After passing through
the crucible of Odysseus' efforts at reintegration, the army shows a more unified
response: their reaction is still likened to the motion of the sea, but the waves are
now driven by a single wind, and their action is organized around a single point
of reference, the jutting headland that seems to figure Agamemnon as the focus
of the army's attention.

This progression of similes is one of several markers of emerging cohesiveness that lead up to the poem's definitive statement of social and poetic order,
the so-called Catalogue of Ships. The "*tis*-speech" encapsulating the reaction
of the army as a whole to Odysseus' forceful silencing of Thersites already signified the reestablishment of a group identity (*Il.* 2.271–77).[52] The sacrificial
meal that immediately follows Agamemnon's speech similarly expresses the
solidarity of the community.[53] When Agamemnon marshals the troops after
the meal, a series of four similes describes the gathering soldiers. The first
compares the flash of bronze to fire on a mountaintop (*Il.* 2.455–58), the second and third compare the swarming soldiers to undifferentiated masses of
birds (2.459–65) or swarming insects (2.469–73). The fourth continues to figure the soldiers as a group of animals but focuses now on the order imposed
when the group is divided into its component parts, likening the leaders to
goatherds separating out their individual flocks when they have mingled in a
pasture:

τοὺς δ' ὥς τ' αἰπόλια πλατέ' αἰγῶν αἰπόλοι ἄνδρες
ῥεῖα διακρίνωσιν ἐπεί κε νομῷ μιγέωσιν,

ὡς τοὺς ἡγεμόνες διεκόσμεον ἔνθα καὶ ἔνθα
ὑσμίνην δ᾽ ἰέναι . . .

Il. 2.474–77

Just as goatherds easily divide their broad herds of goats
when they have mingled in the pasture,
so the leaders arranged their men here and there
to be ready to go to battle . . .

The progression from indiscriminate collections of animals to a body sorted into distinct subgroups suggests a transition from a state of relative disorder to one of organized coordination. The dynamics of marshaling the troops parallel in this regard the dynamics of assembling them in the *agorē*. The leaders at the muster correspond to the heralds in the assembly: both work to bring order.[54]

The poem uses the word *diakosmeîn*, "arrange, put in order," to refer to the activity of organizing the army. This denominative verb is formed from the noun *kosmos* and the preverb *dia-*, which signifies the idea of separation, on which the resulting order depends (cf. δια-κρίνωσιν, "divide," in the previous line).[55] Like the simplex verb *kosmeîn*, a standard term for marshaling troops, *diakosmeîn* in this context indicates that the order imposed by military leaders on their troops is a species of *kosmos*, of social order more generally.[56] The ultimate emblem of that order is the Catalogue of Ships, which, following on the goatherd simile, appears to describe not just the various components of Agamemnon's fleet when he sailed for Troy but also the units into which the leaders divide the army on the present occasion.[57]

The Catalogue is also a poetic tour de force, marked as such by the special invocation to the Muses with which it begins. The invocation emphasizes the superhuman effort required to name all the Achaeans who came to Troy. Even if the narrator finally settles for the more limited task of naming only the leaders—a choice that reflects the implicit logic linking the Catalogue to the activity of the leaders in the muster—he nevertheless requires and calls on the Muses to help in this feat of memory.[58] The Catalogue demonstrates the narrator's divinely assisted mastery of a vast body of traditional material that would be simply too unwieldy for an ordinary human. Thus, while it figures the social and martial order achieved by the leaders under the auspices of Agamemnon, the Catalogue also exhibits the poetic order imposed by the narrator with the help of the Muses. The *kosmos* exemplified by the Catalogue includes both the order of the army and the order of the poem that describes it. If Agamemnon and Menelaus can be described as κοσμήτορε λαῶν, "arrangers of hosts," because of their ability to assemble and bring to order large groups of fighting men, Homer himself earns the title "arranger of heroes" (ἀνδρῶν ἡρώων κοσμήτορα) because Homeric poetry brings together and organizes in its narrative the heroes who fought at Troy.[59]

Social order and poetic order converge in the Catalogue in a way that is consistent with the historical meaning of the word *kosmos*. We saw in chapter 2 that the root from which this word derives, **kens-*, refers to a verbal act, often by a verbal specialist or poet, that brings order to the social world. On the level of the performance of the *Iliad*, the Catalogue is just such an act. It literally organizes the Achaean community. Moreover, by virtue of the connections felt by real-life audiences to the communities and individuals named in the Catalogue, this particular performative act contributes to a perception shared by performer and audience of an overarching structure uniting the Hellenic community as a whole.[60] However, within the poem, the *kosmos* of the Catalogue is merely the endpoint of the process of restoring order after Agamemnon's failed attempt to test the resolve of his troops. The crucial verbal act in this process is marked not by the term *kosmos* but by the word that has more or less replaced it in alphabetic Greek, *ainos:* Odysseus' speech and the *epainos* it receives represent the total speech act on which the order of the Achaean social body depends.

With the community's expression of *epainos*, the threat to tradition initiated by Agamemnon's test—the *"nostos* contrary to destiny"—is resolved. The subsequent events of Book 2 are only so many reiterated manifestations of the community's will to reconstitute itself after nearly falling apart. The Catalogue occupies a privileged position as the last and most conspicuous of these statements of unity. As a masterful compilation of traditional information about the Trojan expedition, uttered with the support of the Muses themselves, it also represents a confirmation of the tradition challenged at the beginning of the book. This authoritative demonstration in performance of the power of tradition to transmit knowledge about the past puts to rest any lingering fears that the overarching norms of tradition might give way to the eccentric or atypical. The performance of the Catalogue displays the power of tradition to overcome tremendous pressures, including even the physical limitations of the human bearers of tradition. Yet this power does not derive solely from the Muses, independently of the community to which the tradition belongs. The central role of *epainos* in Book 2's drama of norm and deviation reveals that the community itself bears a large proportion of the power—and responsibility—to maintain traditional norms.

Significantly, the collective response to Odysseus' speech in Book 2 is the only occasion on which the Achaeans achieve the total solidarity of community-wide *epainos.* This uniquely cohesive moment is embedded within a largely self-contained narrative of social crisis and reconsolidation, culminating in a monumental statement of poetic, as well as social, order. The narrative of Book 2 describes a kind of paradigmatic trajectory against which can be measured the political progress (or lack thereof) of the various communities depicted in the poem. These communities are the subject of the next section. In no case does anything like the comprehensive consensus achieved by Odysseus in Book 2 occur; but behind these variously flawed or incomplete narratives we can glimpse the prospect of a broader realization of the *epainos* ideal on the level of the tradition as a whole. This consensus—the consensus of real-world audiences that authorizes the Iliadic tradition—is implied as the fulfillment of the poem's political dynamics, in much the same way as the narrator's definitive formulation of the tradition brings to a conclusion the paradigmatic narrative of Book 2.

PART II

The *Iliad*'s Political Communities

CHAPTER 5

In Search of Epainos

Collective Decision Making among the Achaeans

In the previous chapter, Book 2 emerged as a paradigmatic instance of the *Iliad*'s overarching drive to move from the free play of eccentricity to the reassertion of the normative. The key to this movement is the *epainos* achieved by Odysseus' speech to the assembled troops, the exemplary value of which is underscored by the fact that this is the first instance of *epainos* in the poem. The community's expression of approval for Odysseus' proposal to remain at Troy marks the return of order, eliminates the threat of an untraditional outcome to the story, and leads to the definitive statement of Iliadic tradition with which the book ends, the Catalogue of Ships.

The same drive to reestablish normative order shapes the *Iliad* as a whole. However, while Book 2 draws the arc to its completion, showing both the restoration of consensus and its relation to poetic tradition, the larger narrative of the wrath of Achilles and its consequences is more open-ended. The poem presents a number of other scenes in which *epainos* is negotiated or achieved among the Achaeans; as I pointed out in chapter 1, such scenes articulate the plot. Yet *epainos* on these occasions is never as global or as effective as it is in Book 2. It is either reduced in scope, applying only to the *basilēes* in the *boulē* rather than the army as a whole, or else rendered moot by some decisive change in circumstances, as in the case of the chariot race in Book 23 (discussed in chapter 1). Crucially, the integrative force of *epainos* is never brought to bear on the most important problem facing Achaean society—the alienation of Achilles—even when Achilles himself summons an assembly to address the issue head-on

(Book 19). This avoidance of a central theme at the moment of its greatest relevance is one of the more fascinating and challenging aspects of the *Iliad*'s structure. It will lead me eventually to consider the way the poem's internal audiences point outward, toward the real-world audiences that provided the context for the performance and reception of the *Iliad* itself. For the time being, however, I will stay within the confines of the poem. In this chapter I examine the remaining instances of *epainos* among the Achaeans, as well as the curious absence of *epainos* from the climactic assembly that marks Achilles' return to battle. My discussion aims to provide a broad outline of the trajectory plotted by the Achaeans' attempts to restore solidarity, a trajectory that will lead naturally to an investigation of the *Iliad*'s other political communities.

AGAMEMNON AND *EPAINOS*

The sense of order established in the course of Book 2 and encapsulated in the Catalogue of Ships extends into the subsequent narrative. Book 3 takes as its starting point the *kosmos* of both armies, which has just been realized poetically in the Greek and Trojan catalogues (αὐτὰρ ἐπεὶ κόσμηθεν ἅμ᾽ ἡγεμόνεσσιν ἕκαστοι ["but when the companies were set in order, each with its leader"], *Il.* 3.1). Both sides take the field, and although the contrast between the silence of the Greeks and the clamor (*klangē*) of the Trojans, which is compared to the noise of birds fleeing the onset of winter, suggests that *kosmos* comes in varying degrees, nevertheless the book quickly raises the hope that order may prevail over chaos.[1] Paris, at Hector's prompting, proposes to settle the conflict by single combat with Menelaus, thus avoiding a general mêlée. The proposal emphasizes that both the risks and the rewards of this combat fall to Paris and Menelaus alone:

> ὁππότερος δέ κε νικήσῃ κρείσσων τε γένηται
> κτήμαθ᾽ ἑλὼν εὖ πάντα γυναῖκά τε οἴκαδ᾽ ἀγέσθω·
> οἱ δ᾽ ἄλλοι φιλότητα καὶ ὅρκια πιστὰ τάμωμεν.
> *Il.* 3.92–94

> Whichever should be victorious and should prove the stronger,
> let him take all the goods and the woman and carry them to his home;
> but let the rest of us make peace and trustworthy oath-sacrifices.

Menelaus agrees, on condition that Priam himself swear an oath to abide by the terms of the duel, and for a moment it looks as though the war may be resolved by an organized, rulebound contest between the two principal parties to the dispute. The reaction to Menelaus' speech indicates that both sides welcome this opportunity to avoid a large-scale conflict:

ὣς ἔφαθ', οἳ δ' ἐχάρησαν Ἀχαιοί τε Τρῶές τε
ἐλπόμενοι παύσασθαι ὀϊζυροῦ πολέμοιο.
Il. 3.111–12

Thus he spoke, and the Achaeans and Trojans felt joy
in the expectation of relief from painful war.

This expression of a collective reaction falls outside the system of formulas I outlined in chapter 1, which draws attention to the fact that what Paris and Menelaus are proposing is not a matter of group action. Trojans and Achaeans are rather being called on to surrender their active roles—indeed, to surrender even the collective mode of open warfare—and allow the conflict to revert to the purely private form of a quarrel between two individuals. Also underlying the variant phraseology is the unusual circumstance that the response in this case includes two distinct social groups, a rare instance of Greek and Trojan harmony.[2]

The possibility of a peaceful resolution presents yet another instance of the recurring anxiety that events might turn out otherwise than as tradition requires.[3] On the basis of the paradigm established by Book 2, in which *epainos* prevented a premature ending to the war, we should expect the political will of the community to play a role in suppressing the potential deviation. In the event, collective sentiment does come into play—but not in the way we might anticipate. When Paris is saved from imminent death by the intervention of Aphrodite and the duel is terminated by his sudden disappearance, Agamemnon judges Menelaus the winner and demands from the Trojans immediate payment of the terms:

κέκλυτέ μευ Τρῶες καὶ Δάρδανοι ἠδ' ἐπίκουροι·
νίκη μὲν δὴ φαίνετ' ἀρηϊφίλου Μενελάου,
ὑμεῖς δ' Ἀργείην Ἑλένην καὶ κτήμαθ' ἅμ' αὐτῇ
ἔκδοτε, καὶ τιμὴν ἀποτινέμεν ἥν τιν' ἔοικεν,
ἥ τε καὶ ἐσσομένοισι μετ' ἀνθρώποισι πέληται.
Il. 3.456–60

Hear me, Trojans, Dardanians, and allies:
the victory of Menelaus dear to Ares is evident:

surrender Argive Helen and with her the property,

and pay a fitting penalty,

which will be remembered even among men of later generations.

Aside from being a tendentious interpretation of a situation not explicitly fore-seen by the original agreement—the judgment about who "is victorious and proves the stronger" remains open to question in the absence of a corpse[4]—Agamemnon's declaration involves a crucial addition to the terms as initially formulated by Paris: the penalty "which will be remembered even among men of later generations." This additional stipulation was introduced already in the oath pronounced by Agamemnon (*Il.* 3.286–87), in which he crucially reframed the essentially private transaction agreed to by Menelaus and Paris in terms of the collective obligation of *Trojans* vis-à-vis *Argives:*

εἰ δέ κ' Ἀλέξανδρον κτείνῃ ξανθὸς Μενέλαος,

Τρῶας ἔπειθ' Ἑλένην καὶ κτήματα πάντ' ἀποδοῦναι,

τιμὴν δ' Ἀργείοις ἀποτινέμεν ἥν τιν' ἔοικεν,

ἥ τε καὶ ἐσσομένοισι μετ' ἀνθρώποισι πέληται.

Il. 3.284–87

But if tawny-haired Menelaus slays Alexander,

the Trojans are to return Helen and all the property,

and pay to the Argives a fitting penalty,

which will be remembered even among men of future generations.

Agamemnon thus broadens the significance of the duel, so that it is no longer simply a private affair. The stakes now entail direct consequences for the com-munities to which the dueling parties belong.[5] The response to Agamemnon's pronouncement of victory is consonant with the collective nature of its claims. While Menelaus prompted only *kharis* in his hearers, Agamemnon elicits *epainos* from at least one of the concerned groups:

ὣς ἔφατ' Ἀτρεΐδης, ἐπὶ δ' ᾔνεον ἄλλοι Ἀχαιοί.

Il. 3.461

Thus spoke the son of Atreus, and the other Achaeans were expressing *epainos*.

This is the only occasion in the *Iliad* on which any utterance of Agamemnon generates *epainos* from his audience. It deserves careful scrutiny.

We may begin by noting that the imperfect tense of the verb marks the ap-proval of the audience as provisional and ultimately ineffective.[6] Agamemnon's problematic relationship to collective will emerges even in the way that will is expressed. The grammatical flagging of a flawed consensus, however, is only the surface manifestation of a deeper dysfunction. The situation as a whole is inherently problematic. At issue is the collective action of the Trojans, not the Achaeans, yet it is the Achaeans whose reaction is specified. We never have the opportunity to learn what response, if any, the Trojans themselves make: Book 3 ends with line 461, and the scene immediately switches to Olympus, where the gods decide to incite the Trojans, through Pandaros, to break the truce. Pandaros' bowshot thus takes the place of a direct response to Agamemnon's injunction.

The relationship of the divine apparatus to the truce and its aftermath is explored more fully in chapter 7. For now, I note that the abrupt transition to another scene of action leaves in question the possible force of consensus among the Achaeans in this context. When a group assembles to discuss its own affairs, *epainos* always results in action. Does the same hold true when a group expresses *epainos* for a proposal about the affairs of others? Can consensus among Agamemnon's army produce effects beyond the limits of the Achaean community? This is a point on which the poem provides no answer. The sudden shift to Olympus, where the knot will be cut by divine intervention, and the lack of any direct indication of the relationship between the political will of the Trojans and Achaean *epainos* allow the question of the force of this collective response to remain suspended, permanently deferred. The effect is remarkably similar to the result of the first assembly in the poem, in which Agamemnon's intervention prevents the force of an exceptional group response from ever being realized. A persistent pattern emerges: Agamemnon's involvement in deliberative procedures does not settle any issues but rather calls into question the meaning and force of the will of the group.

As we have seen, Agamemnon's public pronouncements also tend to run counter to the traditional course of the Trojan story. As in Book 2, where he advocates a return that is "contrary to destiny," here he proposes a solution to the conflict that would vitiate much of the Trojan War tradition.[7] What is remarkable about this scene, in contrast to Book 2, is that a part of the audience actually approves his proposal. In the earlier episode, *epainos* was crucial to the restoration of the order of events prescribed by tradition. Now *epainos*—albeit expressed by only a part of those concerned—threatens to undermine that same order in a different way. The gods predictably take steps to keep things on track, but the audience is left with an even stronger impression that Agamemnon's participation in the political process produces confusion and uncertainty in place of results.

The failure of *epainos* in this case is yet another symptom of Agamemnon's political incompetence. Just a short while later, however, he makes a remark suggesting that, from his point of view, there is nothing unusual about this failure. Immediately after Pandaros violates the truce, Agamemnon makes a tour of his regiments, alternately praising and rebuking his captains in order to stir their fighting spirit. When he comes to Diomedes, he faults him for hanging back from battle out of cowardice, contrasting his behavior with the courage of his father Tydeus, which he illustrates with a brief narrative about the preparation of the Argive expedition against Thebes. This narrative begins with an assembly scene that reveals a great deal about Agamemnon's understanding of *epainos,* or at least about the way he wishes it to be understood:

ἤτοι μὲν γὰρ ἄτερ πολέμου εἰσῆλθε Μυκήνας
ξεῖνος ἅμ᾽ ἀντιθέῳ Πολυνείκεϊ λαὸν ἀγείρων·
οἳ δὲ τότ᾽ ἐστρατόωνθ᾽ ἱερὰ πρὸς τείχεα Θήβης,
καί ῥα μάλα λίσσοντο δόμεν κλειτοὺς ἐπικούρους·
οἳ δ᾽ ἔθελον δόμεναι καὶ ἐπήνεον ὡς ἐκέλευον·
ἀλλὰ Ζεὺς ἔτρεψε παραίσια σήματα φαίνων.
Il. 4.376–81

For he came to Mycenae—not as an enemy,
but as a guest, assembling an army with godlike Polyneices.
They were then marching against the sacred walls of Thebes,
and they were pleading forcefully [for us] to furnish renowned allies.
The Mycenaeans wished to furnish them, and they expressed *epainos* for the request,
but Zeus turned them from this course by displaying adverse signs.

Agamemnon goes on to recount Tydeus' exploits as Argive ambassador to Thebes, but this, the first episode of the story, seems particularly relevant to his own recent experience. It introduces an apologetic subtext into a speech primarily intended to criticize a subordinate: the story of Tydeus, which models the kind of behavior enjoined upon Diomedes, also provides an explanation for Agamemnon's failure to achieve his goal in the assembly. At Mycenae, too, the story goes, the community expressed *epainos* for the proposal of a prestigious speaker, but nevertheless the proposal could not be carried into effect. (Note the same "provisional" imperfect as at *Il.* 3.461.) And if Tydeus, put forward as an example of excellence, was unable to transform *epainos* into action, how can Agamemnon be faulted for suffering the same reverse? It is a neat touch of irony that Agamemnon attributes the failure of Mycenaean consensus to divine interference.[8] He cannot know it, but he has in fact hit on a fairly precise explanatory parallel for the situation at Troy. The detail that Zeus expressed his will by "displaying adverse signs"—which recalls Athena's manifestation as a shooting star as she descends to earth to subvert the truce (*Il.* 4.75–78)—may suggest that Agamemnon has some intuition of the truth. In any case, it lends weight to the anecdote as an exculpatory precedent for Agamemnon's own recent failure.

On the whole, however, Agamemnon's use of this anecdote doesn't so much excuse him for failing to achieve *epainos* as it does align him with a mentality that denies any necessary link between *epainos* and action. This is the last in a series of signs (including the exceptionalism of Book 1 and the nearly disastrous assembly of Book 2) that Agamemnon is fundamentally at odds with the normative structures of collective decision making. It provides a kind of final gloss, spoken in Agamemnon's own voice, on the accumulated failures of the preceding books. His remarks reveal more starkly than ever the breadth of the gap that separates him from the life of the community.

COUNCIL AND ASSEMBLY

Other speakers appear to be more in tune with group dynamics. However, apart from Odysseus, whose success in engaging the support of the Achaeans as a whole I examined in the last chapter, the ability of these other speakers to forge an operational consensus is confined to the more restricted group of the Achaean élites, the *basilées*. In fact, for the remainder of the poem, *epainos* will only be achieved in the councils of the leaders—although their decisions naturally have consequences for the community at large. The next occasion on which the group is called to decide on a collective undertaking comes at the end of the first day of battle. Following an indecisive duel between Ajax and Hector, the *basilées* retire to Agamemnon's tent for a common meal, after which Nestor proposes that the Achaeans construct a funeral mound for their dead and fortification walls around the ships. The response formula that caps Nestor's speech indicates the *epainos* of the assembled princes (ὣς ἔφαθ᾽, οἳ δ᾽ ἄρα πάντες ἐπήνησαν βασιλῆες ["thus he spoke, and all the *basilées* expressed *epainos*"], *Il.* 7.344).

The plan ratified by the *basilées* calls for action on the part of the entire Achaean army.[9] Nevertheless, the manner in which this decision is reached—by the deliberation of a select group in the private setting of Agamemnon's tent— stands in contrast to preceding scenes of deliberation, which have involved both leaders and common soldiers gathered in assembly. If consensus is possible, it is only in the restricted setting of the leaders' council.

This circumstance is underscored by the failure to achieve *epainos* in the full assembly that follows shortly thereafter, when the Trojan herald Idaios enters the Greek camp in order to offer a settlement on behalf of Paris (the return of all the valuables taken from Sparta, with the exception of Helen, as well as additional compensation from Paris' own property)—or, failing that, to seek a temporary truce for the burial of the dead. Several features of this scene recall the end of Book 3, including the proposal of a settlement, the conclusion of a truce, and the use of oaths to solemnify it. In Book 3, however, this sequence of motifs culminates, as we have seen, with the *epainos* of the Achaeans; the result here is very different. Idaios' speech meets first with a dismissive silence. This silence is broken when Diomedes makes a short, defiant speech forbidding any-one even to think of accepting compensation. Acclamation now replaces silence as the Achaeans express approval for Diomedes' words, but this approval, sig-naled by the word *epiakhein*, falls short of *epainos*. Agamemnon then gives a formal reply that betokens the limited ability of the larger community to consti-tute itself as a fully cohesive entity:

ὣς ἔφαθ', οἳ δ' ἄρα πάντες ἀκὴν ἐγένοντο σιωπῇ·
ὀψὲ δὲ δὴ μετέειπε βοὴν ἀγαθὸς Διομήδης·
μήτ' ἄρ τις νῦν κτήματ' Ἀλεξάνδροιο δεχέσθω
μήθ' Ἑλένην· γνωτὸν δὲ καὶ ὃς μάλα νήπιός ἐστιν
ὡς ἤδη Τρώεσσιν ὀλέθρου πείρατ' ἐφῆπται.
ὣς ἔφαθ', οἳ δ' ἄρα πάντες ἐπίαχον υἷες Ἀχαιῶν
μῦθον ἀγασσάμενοι Διομήδεος ἱπποδάμοιο·
καὶ τότ' ἄρ' Ἰδαῖον προσέφη κρείων Ἀγαμέμνων·
Ἰδαῖ' ἤτοι μῦθον Ἀχαιῶν αὐτὸς ἀκούεις
ὥς τοι ὑποκρίνονται· ἐμοὶ δ' ἐπιανδάνει οὕτως.
ἀμφὶ δὲ νεκροῖσιν κατακαιέμεν οὔ τι μεγαίρω·
Il. 7.398–408

Thus he spoke, and they were all silent.
Then at length Diomedes, accomplished in the war-cry, spoke among them:
"Let no one now accept Alexander's goods,
nor even Helen: it is evident, even to one who is especially foolish,
that the snares of destruction have been fastened upon the Trojans."
Thus he spoke, and all the sons of the Achaeans shouted in reply
out of admiration for the *muthos* of horse-taming Diomedes.

And then lordly Agamemnon addressed Idaios:

"Idaios, you yourself hear the *muthos* of the Achaeans,

their answer to you; <u>and so it pleases me as well</u>.

But as for the corpses, I do not in any way begrudge you the burning of them.

There is an unmistakable echo of the exceptional assembly of Book 1 in Agamemnon's use of the verb *epi-handanein* (*Il.* 7.407), which recalls the narrator's use of unprefixed *handanein* to designate Agamemnon's divisive preference on that earlier occasion.[10] The prefix *epi-*, which indicates the coordination of Agamemnon's will with that of the community, may suggest that some progress has been made since then. Nevertheless, Agamemnon's singling out of his own point of view—implying as it does that his own preference is decisive—is itself a sign of the internal divisions that still prevent the formation of a truly cohesive collective will among the Achaeans as a whole. The contrast with the solidarity exhibited by the *basilēes* could not be made more forcefully, especially since the outcome of this scene is essentially the actualization of the plan proposed by Nestor.[11]

The echo of Book 1 in Agamemnon's words is not merely a reminder of the responsibility he bears for the difficulties facing the Achaean community. By evoking the ultimate cause of the quarrel with Achilles, it also points to the absence of the latter as the principal reason why a global consensus is simply not possible for the Achaeans at this time. Without Achilles, the embodiment of *philotēs*, the Achaeans can enjoy only a truncated solidarity, evident in the contrast between the *epainos* realized in the restricted environment of the council and the more splintered dynamics of the full assembly.

Achilles' withdrawal determines not just the scope of *epainos* in Book 7 but also the object toward which it is directed: the plan to construct a defensive wall manifestly represents a stopgap measure intended to compensate for the absence of the only man able to protect the Achaeans from Hector's onslaught. The narrator explicitly correlates the wall with the period of Achilles' wrath at the beginning of Book 12:

τὸ καὶ οὔ τι πολὺν χρόνον ἔμπεδον ἦεν.

ὄφρα μὲν Ἕκτωρ ζωὸς ἔην καὶ μήνι᾽ Ἀχιλλεὺς

καὶ Πριάμοιο ἄνακτος ἀπόρθητος πόλις ἔπλεν,

τόφρα δὲ καὶ μέγα τεῖχος Ἀχαιῶν ἔμπεδον ἦεν.

Il. 12.9–12

And it [the wall] did not remain standing for any long period of time.

As long as Hector was alive and Achilles was wrathful

and the city of lord Priam was still unravaged,
only so long did the Achaeans' wall remain standing.

Although the narrator assigns to the wall a lifespan that extends beyond the limits of the poem, until the sack of Troy, nevertheless the thrust of this formulation is to equate the wall with the period of time covered by the *Iliad*, understood as the poem of Achilles' wrath.[12] The conjunction of three parallel circumstances delimiting the wall's existence—the return of Achilles to battle, the death of Hector, and the destruction of Troy—resonates with the way the poem generally represents the fall of Troy as the inevitable consequence of the events it relates.[13] The implication is that the wall is literally rooted (*empedos* means "fixed in the earth") in the events narrated by the *Iliad*, and more precisely in the necessity created by Achilles' absence. It is a device or artifice, a *mētis* (so the narrator describes Nestor's proposal at *Il.* 7.324) that substitutes for the physical might (*biē*) of Achilles.[14] It is necessary only so long as that might is withheld, and it fades from view (and ultimately from existence) as soon as Achilles returns.

The deliberation in Agamemnon's tent and the restricted consensus it produces thus participate in a broader complex of motifs that serves precisely to highlight the consequences, both political and strategic, of Achilles' withdrawal. The same textual strategy determines the way the *epainos* theme is handled in its next occurrence, in Book 9. By the end of the second day of battle, narrated in Book 8, Hector has routed the Achaeans and penned them within their wall. With the Trojans camped on the other side, ready to press their advantage in renewed combat the next morning, there is a palpable danger that the *mētis* devised in Book 7 will prove insufficient to save the Greeks from disaster. Book 9 describes their efforts, in the assembly, the council, and in direct negotiation with Achilles, to cope with the emergency. As though to emphasize that the present crisis is merely a continuation of the difficulties faced in the earlier council sequence, the presentation of these efforts bears a number of striking similarities to the deliberations described in Book 7. Continuity of thematic and structural elements—including the contrasting of assembly and council, the contrapuntal arrangement of speeches by Diomedes and Nestor, and emphasis on *mētis* as the only available resource—underscores the persistence of the problems created by Achilles' withdrawal.

The ninth book begins with an assembly that, like the assembly concluding Book 7, accentuates the impossibility of establishing *epainos* among the community at large. Once again, this picture emerges from the contrast with previous assemblies, particularly, in this case, the assembly of Book 2. The scene is in many ways the same: Agamemnon summons the army to the *agorē* in order to propose abandoning the war (*Il.* 9.26–28 = 2.139–41). Now, however, he is not merely testing his soldiers' resolve but sincerely advocating for an inglorious retreat. The simile that opens the book likewise evokes the earlier episode. The first time that Agamemnon proposed decampment, the resulting turmoil among the men was compared to the chaotic action of sea waves buffeted by discordant winds (Euros and Notos, *Il.* 2.144–46). Now a comparable state of confusion, evident even before Agamemnon speaks, is conveyed by the same metaphorical image:[15]

ὡς δ' ἄνεμοι δύο πόντον ὀρίνετον ἰχθυόεντα
Βορέης καὶ Ζέφυρος, τώ τε Θρήκηθεν ἄητον
ἐλθόντ' ἐξαπίνης· ἄμυδις δέ τε κῦμα κελαινὸν
κορθύεται, πολλὸν δὲ παρὲξ ἅλα φῦκος ἔχευεν·
ὣς ἐδαΐζετο θυμὸς ἐνὶ στήθεσσιν Ἀχαιῶν.
Il. 9.4–8

As when two winds stir up the fishy sea,
Boreas and Zephuros, which blow from Thrace,
and they come on all of a sudden; and at once a dark wave
towers up, and tosses much seaweed out from the sea:
thus was the *thumos* of the Achaeans torn apart in their chests.

The army responds to Agamemnon's address with silence rather than the immediate flight of Book 2 (*Il.* 9.29). Nevertheless, as before, the situation requires an additional speaker to step forward and assert a commitment to continue fighting. That role is filled by Diomedes, who declares himself and Sthenelos willing to fight on alone if need be, and to prosecute the war to the end even if Agamemnon and the rest of the host should return to Hellas.[16] The assembled Achaeans acclaim his words, thereby reaffirming their own intention to stay and fight (9.50–51). There is, however, a signal difference between this reaction and the one that caps the corresponding speech of Odysseus in Book 2. While Odysseus' address generates an *epainos* that restores the solidarity of the group, Diomedes falls distinctly short of that goal: the cheering that concludes his words is expressed by the inefficient response verb *epiakhein* (9.50). As in Book 7, the discrepancy from a pattern established by a previous, parallel assembly scene draws attention to the fact that the social body now faces limitations on its ability to achieve consensus.

Nestor himself points to these limitations in a speech that follows the soldiers' acclamation, declaring that, though he has spoken well, Diomedes has not yet reached the "*telos* of *muthoi*" (ἀτὰρ οὐ τέλος ἵκεο μύθων, *Il.* 9.56). The meaning of this phrase is far from transparent—*telos* may signify either a "goal" or a simple "conclusion," and the force of the plural *muthoi* is difficult to assess—but the range of meanings it accommodates may be central to the message.[17] Nestor's criticism appears to assign responsibility for the limited success of Diomedes' remarks to his own performance as speaker; at the same time, however, it points beyond Diomedes' individual faults to the community's broader problem. The respects in which Diomedes goes wrong are therefore interesting not only in themselves but also as indices of the more general crisis.

From an illocutionary standpoint, Diomedes' speech seems to sit uneasily in the deliberative context in which it is situated. That is to say, the deliberative context calls for a particular kind of speech act—a proposal—while Diomedes' speech appears to be anything but. It includes no direct address to the army as a whole, no hortatory subjunctive or plural imperative expressing an executable call to action.[18] Its language and rhetoric place it rather in the sphere of blame-speech or invective, a speech genre that Diomedes himself invokes with his use of the verb *oneidizein*, "reproach" (*Il.* 9.34).[19] Moreover, in place of a proper proposal, Diomedes offers only a declaration of his own intention. Most crucially, that intention is expressed in terms of a remarkably bald indifference to the sentiments of the group as a whole: "Let the others flee with their ships to their dear homeland, but Sthenelos and I will fight until we put an end to Troy" (9.46–49).[20] Far from countering Agamemnon's call for retreat by reinforcing the solidarity of the group—the strategy that produces *epainos* in Book 2—Diomedes seems actually to dismiss the importance of coordinated effort. This repudiation of collective action not only runs counter to the general tenor of public debate in the *Iliad*; it represents a threat to the social values political speech should ideally endorse.

The deficiencies of Diomedes' speech are thus clear. Diomedes can be said not to have reached the *telos*—the customary "endpoint"—of *muthoi* insofar as he has not organized his address around a practical proposal that would muster a collective resolve for coordinated, group action. Nestor's remarks, however, have an additional implication, one that involves a more precise understanding of the specific course of action called for by the present circumstances. The persistent theme of this section of the poem is the need to find some way of dealing with Achilles' self-segregation from the Achaean community. In this context, the optimal form of political action will not merely validate the cohesiveness of the community as it is but will strive to restore the group to total solidarity, by rein-corporating Achilles. All of the subsequent action of Book 9—action consisting largely of exchanges of *muthoi*—will be directed toward this end, under Nestor's supervision. Diomedes has not reached the "*telos* of *muthoi*" because he has not broached this, the central problem confronting Achaean society.

As a first step in moving toward a more comprehensive solution, Nestor makes a set of concrete proposals, including provisions for a collective meal (*dais*) and a council of the *gerontes* in Agamemnon's quarters (*Il.* 9.65–75). The emphasis on the *dais* motif provides the affirmation of community that was missing from Diomedes' speech. Once the council convenes, Nestor opens the discussion:

τοῖς ὁ γέρων πάμπρωτος ὑφαίνειν ἤρχετο μῆτιν
Νέστωρ, οὗ καὶ πρόσθεν ἀρίστη φαίνετο βουλή·

Il. 9.93–94 = 7.324–25

Aged Nestor first of all began to weave a *mētis* among them,
Nestor, whose counsel had appeared to be the best on previous occasions as well.

These lines, identical to those that introduced the proposal to construct the wall in Book 7, indicate that the Achaeans are still searching for a *mētis* to resolve the problem of Achilles' withdrawal. The contrivance they are after now, however, is not one that will substitute for Achilles' might—that course of action has already been tried—but one that will reappropriate it. Nestor proposes that they devise a way to persuade Achilles to return to battle "with pleasing gifts and soothing words" (*Il.* 9.113). Agamemnon accordingly outlines the riches he will bestow on Achilles if he should relent—although the extent to which his offer is calculated to be either pleasing or soothing is questionable.[21] Nestor then suggests that a delegation consisting of Phoenix, Ajax, and Odysseus, accompanied by two heralds, convey these terms to Achilles, a proposal with which the rest of the elders are in agreement. Their support for Nestor's plan is signaled by an unusual expression, one that does not belong to the regular set of response formulas:

ὣς φάτο, τοῖσι δὲ πᾶσιν ἑαδότα μῦθον ἔειπεν.

Il. 9.173

Thus he spoke, and his *muthos* was pleasing to them all.

After this striking statement of group sentiment, the council concludes and the embassy departs.

The singular way in which the agreement of the elders is expressed has an important function in terms of the architecture of the book as a whole. The narrator specifies that Nestor was the "first" to begin "weaving" a *mētis*, a formulation that suggests that his speech is part of a sequence.[22] Most immediately, that sequence includes the exchange of speeches between Nestor and Agamemnon in the council, in which the two of them collaborate in constructing a plan for approaching Achilles with gifts. But there is also a broader sequence of speeches extending throughout Book 9 and concluding with the council session that marks the return of the embassy from Achilles' tent. This broader sequence follows a trajectory leading from an initially inchoate collective will (established by the inconclusive reaction of the audience in the assembly and the failure of Diomedes to "reach the *telos* of *muthoi*") to a conclusive consensus reached only in the final council session. The unique language with which the narrator formulates the elders' approval of the embassy plan—and specifically the use of the verb *handanein*, of which ἑαδότα is a perfect participle—situates this council scene at a specific, medial point on the trajectory.

The agreement of the elders appears to be both universal ("pleasing to all") and efficient, insofar as it enables Nestor's plan to be put into action. Nevertheless, it is not designated by either of the expressions normally signifying successful "uptake"—that is, neither by the "they heard and obeyed" formula nor with reference to *epainos*—but in terms of a verb that we have seen not only to be linked to individual as opposed to group preference but also to have a decidedly counterconsensual force. One reason for this unexpected usage is easily discernible: the plan to mollify Achilles with gifts will ultimately fail. Since Nestor's proposal will not achieve the goal toward which it is directed, the language of *epainos* is plainly inappropriate. Moreover, its avoidance can be understood as a signal of the futility of the attempt. But there is more than a strategy of avoidance at work here.

The specific semantics of *handanein*, especially its association with an individualized point of view, have a particular relevance. The verb makes the agreement of the elders a matter of the coincidence of multiple individual interests, unassimilated into the larger social framework signaled by the verb *epainein*. In other words, while the approval of the *gerontes* may be unanimous, it is nevertheless represented as something categorically distinct from consensus. The latter, we recall, exceeds mere unanimity: it is grounded in a particular kind of social cohesion that presupposes long-term relationships and a persistent basis for comparing past, present, and future transactions. The possibility of such cohesion, however, is precisely what is in question as the embassy sets out for

Achilles' tent. Their purpose is to see whether or not the relationship most crucial to the community can be restored; that community's very future is felt to
depend on the result of their efforts (thus Nestor's anxious declaration, "this
night will either destroy the army or save it," *Il.* 9.78). That their enterprise
proceeds from a group decision based not on an integrated collective will but
on the discrete preferences of individuals points up the fact that the social
body remains painfully fragmented, even existentially at risk, so long as Achilles' relation to the group is uncertain. The use of *handanein* to describe the reaction of the council members is thus of a piece with the inconclusive result of
the book's initial assembly. Although the council marks a step forward to the
extent that it produces an executable plan, it still falls short of comprehensive
solidarity, its limitations bound to the fact that Achilles' status remains in
doubt.

Under the leadership of Odysseus, who receives special instructions from
Nestor (*Il.* 9.180), the embassy attempts to resolve the uncertainty by convincing
Achilles to rejoin the community. Each of the ambassadors eventually makes a
separate appeal, but it is Odysseus, the "man of many devices" (*polumētis*), who
begins the negotiations. His prominence is a reminder of the fact that the
Achaeans are seeking to discover a solution through *mētis*. True to his traditional epithet, Odysseus displays his mastery of artifice in his presentation of
Agamemnon's terms, deliberately disguising the overtly hostile components
of the offer. Achilles, however, forcefully rejects any kind of reconciliation and
goes on to deplore the inadequacy of the Achaeans' strategy of *mētis* as a substitute for his own *biē:*

ἀλλ' ὑμεῖς μὲν ἰόντες ἀριστήεσσιν Ἀχαιῶν
ἀγγελίην ἀπόφασθε· τὸ γὰρ γέρας ἐστὶ γερόντων·
ὄφρ' ἄλλην φράζωνται ἐνὶ φρεσὶ μῆτιν ἀμείνω,
ἥ κέ σφιν νῆάς τε σαῷ καὶ λαὸν Ἀχαιῶν
νηυσὶν ἔπι γλαφυρῆς, ἐπεὶ οὔ σφισιν ἥδέ γ' ἑτοίμη
ἦν νῦν ἐφράσσαντο ἐμεῦ ἀπομηνίσαντος·

Il. 9.421–26

But you go and declare this message to the best of the Achaeans—
for that is the privilege of elders—
so that they may devise in their minds another, better *mētis,*
which will save both their ships and the Achaean army
at the hollow ships, since this one has not proved useful to them,
the one they devised while I have been wrathful.

Phrased ambiguously, this declaration of the failure of *mētis* covers both the wall and Nestor's most recent contrivance, the embassy itself.[23]

Achilles has stated his intention to sail for Phthia in the morning (*Il.* 9.356–63). With the strategy of Odyssean *mētis* laid bare, Phoenix makes a much more direct appeal, based largely on his own, personal connection to Achilles as foster-father to foster-son (9.485–95).[24] This appeal is more direct, in that it speaks openly about the imperative to respect the social bonds represented by *ainos*, the socially constructive speech that is the foundation of *epainos*. Phoenix twice presses Achilles not to "refuse/deny *ainos*" (*anainesthai*), first in the parable of the *Litai* (9.510) and then through the exemplum of Meleager (9.585). His language picks up on a recurring motif in Book 9. In the council preceding the embassy, Agamemnon "does not deny the *ainos*" that the quarrel with Achilles arose through his own fault (οὐδ᾽ αὐτὸς ἀναίνομαι, *Il.* 9.116); this amounts to a cautious openness to the possible restoration of the social bond signaled by *ainos*. When the embassy returns, however, Odysseus reports that Achilles "refuses the *ainos*" with respect to Agamemnon and his gifts (ἀναίνεται, 9.679).[25]

Phoenix thus presents his entreaty in terms of a central concern of the episode as a whole—but with only a marginally better result. Although Achilles softens his position somewhat, asserting now not that he will sail in the morning but that he will consider then whether to sail or to stay at Troy (*Il.* 9.618–19), he nevertheless remains staunchly opposed to any reconciliation with Agamemnon.[26] The ambassadors conclude their mission when Ajax, recognizing that Achilles will make no concession to any claim of obligation to the group, declares that their project of restoring solidarity will not succeed:

διογενὲς Λαερτιάδη πολυμήχαν᾽ Ὀδυσσεῦ
ἴομεν· οὐ γάρ μοι δοκέει μύθοιο τελευτὴ
τῇδέ γ᾽ ὁδῷ κρανέεσθαι· ἀπαγγεῖλαι δὲ τάχιστα
χρὴ μῦθον Δαναοῖσι καὶ οὐκ ἀγαθόν περ ἐόντα . . .
Il. 9.624–27

Odysseus of many contrivances, Zeus-born son of Laertes,
let us go: for it seems to me that no fulfillment [*teleutē*] of *muthos*
is to be accomplished by this road. As swiftly as possible we must report
the *muthos* to the Danaans, even though it is not a good one.

His language (μύθοιο τελευτή, "a fulfillment of *muthos*") recalls the expression by which Nestor had pointed to the deficiencies of the initial assembly (τέλος . . . μύθων). The *telos* that was there implicitly wanted—the rehabilitation of the community as a whole through the reintegration of Achilles—has now been explicitly attempted, but without success. Worse still, the embassy, meant to be an assertion of solidarity, has itself become fragmented in the process: when the others depart to report the outcome of the negotiations, Phoenix stays behind with Achilles.

Back in Agamemnon's tent, the remaining ambassadors find the council awaiting their return. Odysseus relates Achilles' most intransigent reply (the reply he had made to Odysseus' own appeal): he will not accept Agamemnon's gifts nor intervene to save the Achaeans and their ships; he intends to sail in the morning, and he advises the rest of the army to do the same, since the "end of lofty Troy" is no longer in sight (*Il.* 9.677–87). With this reiteration of the call to abandon the war, the scene reverts to the pattern of the book's initial assembly, but Achilles now plays the part of Agamemnon.[27] The silence of the council in response to Odysseus' report replicates the silence that greeted Agamemnon in the assembly. Diomedes too reprises his earlier role, delivering a speech more or less the same in tenor ("stay the course") but noticeably different in form and rhetoric:

Ἀτρεΐδη κύδιστε ἄναξ ἀνδρῶν Ἀγάμεμνον
μὴ ὄφελες λίσσεσθαι ἀμύμονα Πηλεΐωνα
μυρία δῶρα διδούς· ὃ δ᾽ ἀγήνωρ ἐστὶ καὶ ἄλλως·
νῦν αὖ μιν πολὺ μᾶλλον ἀγηνορίῃσιν ἐνῆκας.
ἀλλ᾽ ἤτοι κεῖνον μὲν ἐάσομεν ἤ κεν ἴῃσιν
ἤ κε μένῃ· τότε δ᾽ αὖτε μαχήσεται ὁππότε κέν μιν
θυμὸς ἐνὶ στήθεσσιν ἀνώγῃ καὶ θεὸς ὄρσῃ.
ἀλλ᾽ ἄγεθ᾽ ὡς ἂν ἐγὼ εἴπω πειθώμεθα πάντες·
νῦν μὲν κοιμήσασθε τεταρπόμενοι φίλον ἦτορ
σίτου καὶ οἴνοιο· τὸ γὰρ μένος ἐστὶ καὶ ἀλκή·
αὐτὰρ ἐπεί κε φανῇ καλὴ ῥοδοδάκτυλος Ἠώς,
καρπαλίμως πρὸ νεῶν ἐχέμεν λαόν τε καὶ ἵππους
ὀτρύνων, καὶ δ᾽ αὐτὸς ἐνὶ πρώτοισι μάχεσθαι.
Il. 9.697–709

Son of Atreus, supreme lord of men, Agamemnon,
you ought not to have entreated the blameless son of Peleus
by offering countless gifts: he is high-minded even otherwise,
but now you have sent him on to even greater heights of pride.
But let us leave him be, either to go
or to stay; he will fight again when

the *thumos* in his chest bids him, and the god stirs him.

But come, let us all follow my proposal:

now take your rest, after satisfying your hearts

with food and drink—for these bring strength and courage—

but when lovely, rosy-fingered Dawn appears,

you [Agamemnon] muster the army and the horses before the ships,

encouraging them, and yourself fight among the first ranks.

Gone are the abusive tone and, more importantly, the egotistical indifference to cooperative effort. Instead we find an explicit appeal for collective action that stresses the value of both the communal rituals of food and drink and of the hierarchical structure of the Achaeans' martial society (represented by Agamemnon's function as commander-in-chief). Moreover, Diomedes now directly addresses the problem of Achilles' absence, albeit to bracket it as immaterial to the question of an immediate course of action. Thus, while acknowledging that the broader *telos* of Achilles' reintegration is for the time being out of reach, he corrects every one of the infelicities that prevented him from reaching the "*telos* of *muthoi*" in his earlier performance.

Diomedes' success at producing a speech that fosters social cohesion (to the extent possible under the circumstances) is reflected by the response of his audience:

ὣς ἔφαθ', οἳ δ' ἄρα πάντες ἐπήνησαν βασιλῆες
μῦθον ἀγασσάμενοι Διομήδεος ἱπποδάμοιο.
Il. 9.710–11

Thus he spoke, and all the *basilēes* expressed *epainos*,
out of admiration for the *muthos* of horse-taming Diomedes.

Book 9 ends with this *epainos* of the *basilēes*. So too does the trajectory plotted by the book's consecutive scenes of collective decision making, a trajectory leading from the inconclusive outcome of the initial assembly to a decision based on the (unintegrated) coordination of individual preferences, and on to a final consensus. This consensus, however, is a limited one, representing only the collective will of the council of elders. The fact that it emerges in a scene that replays the opening assembly underscores the relative narrowness of its scope.

The link between the reduced ambit of group solidarity and the situation of Achilles is transparent, and it becomes more so through the embassy's experience of social fracture in the form of the loss of Phoenix. Achilles' continued resistance to the demands of the Achaean community splinters the group that

represents that community, reproducing on a small scale the constricted potential for collective action that afflicts Achaean society as a whole. In other words,
the reduction of the embassy from three members to two—a reduction mediated by Achilles—mirrors the relationship between the full assembly that opens
the book and the restricted council with which it concludes.[28] If Achilles is the
force that fragments the group, the implication is that the restoration of total
solidarity depends upon his reintegration. Barring that, the effective formulation of collective will at the level of the group as a whole—that is, as manifested
by consensus in the assembly—would appear to be out of reach.

In establishing the contrast between an ideal but unachievable consensus and
the more limited *epainos* on which the Achaeans must rely during the period of
Achilles' wrath, Book 9 makes use of many of the same elements as Book 7. In
Book 7, however, there is no trace of the kind of teleological development we observe in Book 9. In the latter, the arrangement of assembly and council scenes,
the interplay of speeches by Nestor and Diomedes, and the reactions they garner
from their audiences all describe a clear progression tending toward an implied
fulfillment. This progression reproduces the general movement of the poem as a
whole: after an initial, flawed assembly that appears to threaten the integrity of
the group, the narrative proceeds by stages toward the restoration of the mechanisms regulating communal life. In Book 9 the thematic sequence never reaches
its implicit endpoint, obviously because Achilles remains in isolation. The *Iliad*,
on the other hand, offers the possibility of drawing the arc to its conclusion,
since it narrates the return of Achilles to the battlefield. And yet, one of the most
curious features of the *Iliad*'s structure is that it does not arrive at this implicit
telos. The promise of renewed solidarity at a global level remains unfulfilled even
after Achilles renounces his *mēnis*. The abbreviated teleology of Book 9 turns out
to be the result not of its position within the narrative but of a precise analogical
relationship with the poem as a whole.

FRUSTRATED EXPECTATIONS

If the *Iliad* were to present the total rehabilitation of the social body, we would
expect to find it in the final Achaean assembly of the poem, narrated in Book 19,
at the start of the fourth day of fighting. Not only does this assembly mark Achilles' return to battle; structurally, some statement of *epainos* is called for as a
prelude to the renewal of combat.[29] At Thetis' prompting, Achilles summons
the entire host to the *agorē*, with the express purpose of forswearing his wrath
as a necessary prelude to leading the Achaeans into battle. Climactic by virtue

of its position in the plot, this assembly provides the last opportunity to observe the political life of the community.[30] It is represented as a maximally inclusive event that brings together every member of the body politic in a grand expression of unity after a prolonged period of social fragmentation:[31]

αὐτὰρ ὃ βῆ παρὰ θῖνα θαλάσσης δῖος Ἀχιλλεὺς
σμερδαλέα ἰάχων, ὦρσεν δ᾽ ἥρωας Ἀχαιούς.
καί ῥ᾽ οἵ περ τὸ πάρος γε νεῶν ἐν ἀγῶνι μένεσκον
οἵ τε κυβερνῆται καὶ ἔχον οἰήϊα νηῶν
καὶ ταμίαι παρὰ νηυσὶν ἔσαν σίτοιο δοτῆρες,
καὶ μὴν οἳ τότε γ᾽ εἰς ἀγορὴν ἴσαν, οὕνεκ᾽ Ἀχιλλεὺς
ἐξεφάνη, δηρὸν δὲ μάχης ἐπέπαυτ᾽ ἀλεγεινῆς.
Il. 19.40–46

But glorious Achilles went along the seashore
shouting terribly, and he stirred the Achaean heroes.
And even those who before used to remain among the ships [i.e., instead of
    participating in the fighting],
those who were steersmen and handled the ships' rudders,
and who were stewards among the ships, distributors of food,
even these came on that occasion to the assembly, since Achilles
had appeared, though he had long refrained from painful battle.

This gathering of every stakeholder in the community provides the natural setting for the renewal of a comprehensive collective will, and the logical point of conclusion for the poem's thematics of consensus. Here, if anywhere, one expects to find a decisive *epainos* that would make manifest the solidarity of the group and restore in full the connection between communal will and collective action.

This expectation is frustrated, however, for the simple reason that the community is never directly called on to express its will. In spite of the fact that the social body has assembled in its entirety to attend to a matter of direct political and practical relevance, no proposal is put before the group as a whole. Everything happens as though Achilles' *mēnis* were strictly a matter of a private dispute with Agamemnon. Achilles speaks first, directing his words specifically to Agamemnon (and not to the assembly): he expresses regret at the fact that a quarrel over a woman has produced so much destruction to the benefit of the Trojans, announces his intention to put his anger behind him, and concludes by directing Agamemnon to "rouse the long-haired Achaeans for war" (ὄτρυνον πόλεμον δὲ κάρη κομόωντας Ἀχαιούς, *Il.* 19.69). Replying, Agamemnon begins with a short preamble addressed to the audience at large, but the fact that he speaks without "standing in the middle" (οὐδ' ἐν μέσσοισιν ἀναστάς, 19.77) indicates that he intends his words primarily as a private communication to Achilles.[32] He says as much when he shifts to the substance of his speech: "I will declare myself [ἐνδείξομαι] to the son of Peleus; but you other Achaeans attend, and mark well my speech, each one" (19.83–84). After a lengthy narrative about the birth of Heracles, designed to assign the blame for his error to divine *Atē*, Agamemnon states his desire to bestow on Achilles the gifts promised by the embassy and concludes, like Achilles, not with a proposal for collective action but with an imperative addressed to Achilles himself: "stir yourself for war, and stir the other fighting men" (ἀλλ' ὄρσευ πόλεμον δὲ καὶ ἄλλους ὄρνυθι λαούς, 19.139). The tensions that remain between the two princes are evident in this exchange of reciprocal imperatives: each seems determined to have the last word in commanding the other.

Throughout this assembly scene, there is but a single statement concerning the reactions of the gathered troops. Following immediately on the conclusion of Achilles' speech, it marks the impact he has made on the Achaeans as a whole:

ὣς ἔφαθ', οἳ δ' ἐχάρησαν ἐϋκνήμιδες Ἀχαιοὶ
μῆνιν ἀπειπόντος μεγαθύμου Πηλεΐωνος.
Il. 19.74–75

Thus he spoke, and the well-greaved Achaeans felt joy,
since the great-hearted son of Peleus was forswearing his *mēnis*.

The language recalls the reaction of Greeks and Trojans in Book 3 to the proposition of a duel between Menelaus and Paris (the example with which this chapter began). In neither case are we dealing with a "response formula" in the strict sense: the narrator describes an affective rather than expressive response; there is no direct manifestation of collective will.[33] As in Book 3, the specification of a purely internal reaction provides an indication that, although the matter at hand is of interest to the group, it does not depend in any substantive way on its support or determination. The absence, however, of any mention of *epainos* in a context so overdetermined as a display of social cohesion is striking. The "joy" of the Achaeans seems like a placeholder for a more substantive demonstration of communal integrity—a demonstration that ultimately never occurs.

The connections between Achilles' "reconciliation" with Agamemnon and the *entente* of Book 3 extend beyond the parallel reactions of the groups involved.

Both scenes focus on the attempt to resolve a private quarrel resulting from the abduction of a woman. And on both occasions, the actors have recourse to oath-sacrifices (*horkia*) as a means of exerting control over the terms of the dispute (*Il.* 3.268–94; 19.249–68).[34] In one case, the disputants belong to distinct, hostile communities, while in the other they are (or should be) members of the same social group. Nevertheless, the effect of these multiple convergences is to cast the reconciliation in the mold of the duel and thus to encourage us to question the extent to which Achilles and Agamemnon *can* be thought of as confederates. In fact, resonances with the earlier scene suggest that Achilles remains as alien to the Achaean community as Paris or another Trojan. The image of Achilles as a hostile outsider is reinforced by Agamemnon himself, who insists on referring to the gifts he offers as *apoina* (as he did in Book 9). As "ransom"— typically for someone captured on the battlefield or otherwise during time of war—the transaction of *apoina* is virtually by definition limited to individuals enjoying no social bond other than their enmity.[35] The apparent reconciliation thus simultaneously implies the persistent isolation of Achilles. It is worth remembering, too, that the assembly of Book 3 is unusual in recording the collective response of both Achaeans and Trojans—that is, members of two distinct social entities. The echo of that strange Greco-Trojan accord in the reconciliation scene may suggest lingering fractures that extend throughout the community.

Achilles expresses indifference to Agamemnon's gifts (*Il.* 19.146–48). Odysseus seems to sense the inadequacy of the situation with respect to both private and collective relationships; he takes up his now familiar role as promoter of social cohesion, urging Achilles not to enter battle immediately but first to bid the Achaeans to take their morning meal (*deipnon:* 19.171–72). His insistence that provisions be made for the *deipnon* serves at least two purposes. In the first place, it creates an opportunity for Agamemnon's gifts (as in the Embassy, Odysseus studiously avoids calling them *apoina*) to be formally presented in the presence of the army. More importantly, however, it represents an attempt to collectivize the event: as one of the prime Homeric expressions of solidarity, a common meal would reconfigure the reconciliation as a true renewal of the community as a whole.[36]

Achilles at first demurs, claiming he has no interest in eating while Patroklos lies dead; significantly, he avoids the loaded term *deipnon,* thereby reducing the subject of discussion from a (socially meaningful) meal to mere "food" (βρωτύν, *Il.* 19.205; βρῶσις, 19.210).[37] He eventually relents, however, and allows Agamemnon to present his gifts, including Briseis, and to swear an oath that he never slept with the woman. Achilles concludes a brief speech of acknowledgment by enjoining the army to take its meal, as Odysseus had suggested (νῦν δ' ἔρχεσθ' ἐπὶ δεῖπνον, ἵνα ξυνάγωμεν Ἄρηα ["now go to your meal, so that we may join battle"], 19.275). This—the first time Achilles has addressed the community at large since Book 1—offers a genuine opportunity for a collective response, an expression of the will of the group to constitute itself as a community through the symbolism of the *deipnon* and to muster for battle. But the text immediately forestalls any such significance, describing the result of Achilles' words not in terms of the audience's response but solely with reference to Achilles' own agency: "So he spoke, and he hastily dismissed the assembly" (ὣς ἄρ' ἐφώνησεν, λῦσεν δ' ἀγορὴν αἰψηρήν, 19.276). Once again, the absence of an *epainos* that is sorely wanted, even expected, makes itself felt.

The assembled warriors disperse to their ships, but, crucially, there is no mention of the fact that they presumably dine there, to say nothing of the kind of elaborate description of a *deipnon* that capped the assembly of Book 2 as the climactic sign of a reconstituted community. There is no mention of a *deipnon* at all until the Achaean elders, attending Achilles in his tent, beg him to take some food—"but he refused, groaning" (*Il.* 19.304). Achilles' fasting, foregrounded by the remarkable detail that he receives sustenance from the gods (19.340–56), manifests concretely his continuing isolation from the society of his peers.[38] Achilles remains unintegrated into the group, and, as a result, the group remains less than whole.

Not until his meal with Priam in Book 24 will Achilles participate in the typical rituals of human social life. That episode (discussed in chapter 8) resolves to an extent his marginal situation. But it does not in any way constitute a reintegration of Achilles into Achaean society. Even in the funeral games for Patroklos, Achilles remains aloof. His return to full standing as a member of the social body—a return that would make the community complete and whole for the first time in the poem—is permanently deferred. This abiding lack of resolution is emblematized on Achilles' famous shield, which he handles for the first time at the start of Book 19. One of the central images on the shield, as described at the end of Book 18, depicts a legal dispute over the payment of blood-price (*poinē*, *Il.* 18.498) for a man who has died. Insofar as this quarrel (*neikos*, 18.497) revolves around compensation, it clearly encapsulates the central themes of Achilles' story. Like that story, the trial scene, too, is frozen in a permanent state of non-resolution. Not only does the litigant who corresponds most obviously to Achilles "refuse to accept anything" (ὃ δ' ἀναίνετο μηδὲν ἑλέσθαι, *Il.* 18.500)—the verb *anainesthai* casts this refusal as a denial of *ainos,* and thus a denial of a social bond—but, as Leonard Muellner has shown, the distinctive syntax of this formulation indicates that he will *never* accept any compensation.[39] The quarrel is as unresolvable and static as the metalwork in which it is figured. So too, it seems, is the situation of Achilles with respect to the Achaean community.[40]

In his illuminating study of the *Iliad,* James Redfield argues that Achilles' irreducible isolation is the result of a contradiction inherent in the culture to which he belongs, a culture that predicates the very existence of the community on the willingness of certain of its members, warriors like Achilles, to inhabit a domain that is, in some sense, a negation of community. The failure of the various rituals of reintegration—Agamemnon's oath, the Achaeans' *deipnon,* even the meal Achilles shares with Priam—to reincorporate Achilles into the group is simply an expression of the inadequacy of ceremony, as a cultural procedure, to resolve contradictions that are themselves produced by culture. Such contradictions, in Redfield's view, can be resolved only in art, and only formally, by the imposition of aesthetic closure on what remains an irremediable contradiction.[41] And yet, with regard to the *epainos* motif, even this formal closure is lacking: the paradigm established by Book 2, according to which the solidarity of the group is restored by the expression of *epainos,* remains unfulfilled in the poem as a whole. The lack of closure, I submit, points a way out of the formal cul-de-sac described by Redfield. By creating an implicit demand for resolution, the poem leads back, in a way not foreseen by Redfield, from the domain of aesthetics to that of ceremony—more precisely, to the domain of performance as the ceremonial enactment of the work of art. In performance, an artwork that in itself imposes a merely formal resolution on the problem of belonging can resolve its contradictions at a deeper level by becoming the vehicle for the expression of collective solidarity. Achilles may be unassimilable by his own community, but his story can provide the foundation for a community of another order, a community constituted through the performance of epic poetry. And the *epainos* that is missing from Achilles' story can be realized among the audience for whom the story is performed.

Before moving on to consider this broader, extra-Iliadic community, however, more remains to be said about the communities depicted within the poem. As a consequence of the deferral of Achaean consensus, we observe a striking displacement of the *epainos* that the poem's architecture requires. As I noted in chapter 1, the *Iliad* is articulated in terms of temporal and narrative units punctuated by expressions of *epainos.* Each day's activity is determined by a collective will to pursue a particular course of action (either engagement in combat or the performance of burial rites). In the case of the first three days of battle, it is the collective will of the Achaeans that plays this pivotal role. But on the cusp of the fourth and final day of combat, the day initiated by the climactic assembly of Book 19, the determinative exhibition of *epainos* is displaced to—or usurped by—the Trojans. This, the sole instance of Trojan consensus in the poem, and the thematic progression leading up to it, are the subjects of the next chapter.

CHAPTER 6

A Consensus of Fools

The Trojans' Exceptional *Epainos*

At the close of the *Iliad*'s third day of battle, the Trojans hastily convene a battle-field assembly. Achilles has just appeared at the Achaean fortifications, scattering the Trojan charge with a powerful war-cry and thereby creating an opportunity for the rescue of Patroklos' corpse. The Trojans gather to discuss whether they should camp on the battlefield (as they had the night before) or return to the city. Pouludamas, who repeatedly plays the part of the Trojans' wise counselor, advises the latter course of action, but Hector vehemently opposes him, arguing that the Trojans should stay where they are, the better to renew the fight in the morning.[1] Although the narrator himself judges Hector's proposal to be ill conceived, nevertheless the Trojans express *epainos* for it (Ἕκτορι μὲν γὰρ ἐπῄνησαν κακὰ μητιόωντι ["they expressed *epainos* for Hector, though his plan was a bad one"], *Il.* 18.312). This is the only instance of Trojan *epainos* in the poem.

The Trojan consensus surprises not only because it appears to be a unique event in the political life of Priam's people. It also usurps an important structural function that has, up to this point, belonged to the Achaeans. The organizational principles observed throughout the *Iliad* call for some expression of *epainos* to mark the boundaries between the poem's primary narrative units, the successive days of battle that constitute the bulk of the narration. As a rule, this task is fulfilled by the Achaeans, whose collective will—usually formalized in an evening council scene—commits them to a course of action that sets in motion the events of the following day.[2] Here, however, it is the Trojans whose resolve to continue fighting at the ships, regardless of the fact that Achilles has

at last appeared, determines the inevitability of the climactic battle. The expected Achaean deliberation is postponed until the next morning, when
Achilles summons the entire army to the assembly; their anticipated *epainos*
is postponed indefinitely. Hector, who has already donned the armor of Achilles "in violation of order" (οὐ κατὰ κόσμον, *Il.* 17.205), seems likewise to rob
Achilles of a role that is rightfully his: the consensus that the Achaean hero
ought to produce in the assembly of Book 19 is preempted by Hector's performance among the Trojans. This too is in violation of *kosmos*, in the sense of
"poetic order."[3]

The Trojan consensus of Book 18 is thus an unexpected, not to say startling,
occurrence. The full measure of what makes it so unusual, however, can be
taken only after consideration of the political culture of the Trojans more generally. For in deciding through *epainos,* the Trojans make use of a deliberative
mode from which they are in general excluded. The Iliadic narrator is careful to
distinguish Trojan political behaviors from those of the Greeks—and not just
through the use of distinctive response formulas, a technique noted in chapter 1.
A favorite strategy, on display in the juxtaposition of the assemblies of Books 18
and 19, is to arrange deliberative scenes in contrasting pairs, so as to highlight
the differences in the ways the two groups arrive at decisions.[4] The comparison
usually works to the Achaeans' advantage; the pairing of Books 18 and 19, which
highlights the apparent success of the Trojan assembly, is, superficially at least,
exceptional in this regard. The clearest example of the method occurs at the transition in Book 7 from the Achaean *boulē,* in which the *basilēes* ratify Nestor's
proposal for the construction of the wall, to the Trojan *agorē:*[5]

ὣς ἔφαθ᾽, οἳ δ᾽ ἄρα πάντες ἐπήνησαν βασιλῆες.
Τρώων αὖτ᾽ ἀγορὴ γένετ᾽ Ἰλίου ἐν πόλει ἄκρῃ
δεινὴ τετρηχυῖα, παρὰ Πριάμοιο θύρῃσι·
Il. 7.344–46

Thus he spoke, and all the *basilēes* expressed *epainos* in response.
But now the Trojans held an assembly on the acropolis of Ilion,
one angry and full of discord, beside Priam's palace doors.

The "discord" of the Trojan assembly contrasts sharply with the harmony of the
Argive captains. Even though at this point in the narrative the Achaean community is experiencing severe limitations on its ability to forge consensus, nevertheless it is represented as enjoying relative solidarity by comparison with the
fractured and fractious *agorē* of the Trojans.

The deficiencies of the Trojans' deliberative procedures are adumbrated already from their earliest appearance in the poem as political actors. The first Trojan assembly occurs in Book 2, immediately after the Catalogue of Ships, the definitive statement of Achaean social order. Functionally, it is parallel to the Achaean *agorē* that opens the book, since it leads directly to the marshaling of Hector's troops and the corresponding catalogue of Trojans and allies. The parallelism, however, underscores a divergence along the same lines as the highly compressed contrast evident in the articulation of Book 7. While the Greek Catalogue is the immediate result of an *epainos* expressing a collective commitment to the war, the Trojans show no sign of being able to arrive collectively at a truly corporate decision. In fact, *indecision* is singled out as the salient characteristic of Trojan deliberation by the scene's first speaker, the goddess Iris, who enters the *agorē* and addresses Priam in the guise of his son, Politēs:

ὦ γέρον αἰεί τοι μῦθοι φίλοι ἄκριτοί εἰσιν . . .

Il. 2.796

Old man, dear to you always are speeches that do not arrive at a result . . .[6]

Our initial impressions of the Trojans as a political community are shaped by this evaluation, which, notwithstanding any possible rhetorical motivation in context, carries a measure of objectivity and authority by virtue of its divine (from the point of view of the audience) source. The Trojans are thus introduced with an appended commentary characterizing their deliberations as habitually unable to produce a *krisis*, a "decision."[7] Iris/Politēs goes on to describe the mustering of the Achaean army and directs Hector to summon his own warriors to the battlefield. In doing so, she highlights another distinctive feature of the Trojan situation, one that has a direct bearing on the Trojans' ability to consolidate themselves into a cohesive group—namely, their linguistic diversity:

Ἕκτορ σοὶ δὲ μάλιστ᾽ ἐπιτέλλομαι, ὧδε δὲ ῥέξαι·
πολλοὶ γὰρ κατὰ ἄστυ μέγα Πριάμου ἐπίκουροι,
ἄλλη δ᾽ ἄλλων γλῶσσα πολυσπερέων ἀνθρώπων·
τοῖσιν ἕκαστος ἀνὴρ σημαινέτω οἷσί περ ἄρχει,
τῶν δ᾽ ἐξηγείσθω κοσμησάμενος πολιήτας.
Il. 2.802–6

I entrust this charge especially to you, Hector—make it so—
for there are many allies in Priam's great city,
but tongues differ among men of diverse origin.

Let each man give the order to those whom he commands,
and lead them out when he has put his fellow townsmen in order.

The fact that the Trojans have assembled their forces from many different communities lacking a common language makes true collective action a practical
impossibility: group efforts can be, at best, only a matter of the coordination of
independent units. Of course, Agamemnon's army is likewise a composite of
contingents of diverse origin; but the Achaeans nevertheless share a language,
thanks to which they are able to participate in the *agorē* and respond to proposals
as a group. Without a lingua franca, it is difficult to imagine how any Trojan
speaker could compose an utterance sufficiently pentecostal to address the greater
Trojan community as a whole.[8] And without such a universally intelligible utterance, the catalyst for *epainos* as the basis for collective action is missing.

It is telling that, although Iris/Politēs arrives in the midst of an ongoing assembly (ἀγορὰς ἀγόρευον ["they were holding an assembly"], *Il.* 2.788), the scene develops without any direct reference to the typical mechanics of public deliberation.
There is no address to the group and no indication of the group's reaction to the
news of the warriors now flooding onto the plain. The goddess directs her remarks
to individuals, first to Priam and then to Hector. The only reaction recorded is
that of Hector himself, who responds to Iris' speech by summarily dismissing the
assembly, as though it were nothing more than an impediment to effective action:

ὣς ἔφαθ᾽, Ἕκτωρ δ᾽ οὔ τι θεᾶς ἔπος ἠγνοίησεν,
αἶψα δ᾽ ἔλυσ᾽ ἀγορήν· ἐπὶ τεύχεα δ᾽ ἐσσεύοντο·
Il. 2.807–8

Thus she spoke, and Hector did not fail to recognize the word of a goddess;
he quickly dismissed the assembly, and they hurried to their arms.

This curiously ineffectual *agorē* seems to have been convened only so that it could
provide an object for Hector's initiative. By contrast with the kind of collective
decision making practiced by the Achaeans, the Trojan community plays no
discernible role in the transformation of speech into action. Hector's assertive-
ness effectively confirms Iris' initial judgment, since it highlights the inability
of the assembly to come to a *krisis* on its own terms.

A similar impression emerges from the "discordant" assembly of Book 7.
The speakers—Antēnōr, Paris, and Priam—make superficial attempts to include
the community in the decision-making process, addressing their words to the assembled "Trojans, Dardanians, and allies" (*Il.* 7.348 = 368). But the audience has
no part in actually deciding the outcome of the discussion; the scene lacks any

indication of audience response, as though the social dynamics of reception were totally nonfunctional at Troy.[9] Antēnōr, singled out as a skilled and constructive speaker by the epithet *pepnumenos* ("prudent," *Il.* 7.347), begins the debate with an apparently genuine attempt to move the community as a whole to action, calling for the return of Helen and the other property Paris took from Sparta—that is, essentially the fulfillment of the terms of the failed duel between Paris and Menelaus.[10] He speaks in the first- and second-person plural, as if this act of restitution were a matter of communal responsibility.[11] But in a kind of reversal of the rhetorical procedure by which Agamemnon had transformed the terms of the duel from a set of strictly private to collective obligations, Paris immediately personalizes the matter and refuses outright to give up Helen:

Ἀντῆνορ σὺ μὲν οὐκέτ᾽ ἐμοὶ φίλα ταῦτ᾽ ἀγορεύεις·
οἶσθα καὶ ἄλλον μῦθον ἀμείνονα τοῦδε νοῆσαι.
εἰ δ᾽ ἐτεὸν δὴ τοῦτον ἀπὸ σπουδῆς ἀγορεύεις,
ἐξ ἄρα δή τοι ἔπειτα θεοὶ φρένας ὤλεσαν αὐτοί.
αὐτὰρ ἐγὼ Τρώεσσι μεθ᾽ ἱπποδάμοις ἀγορεύσω·
ἀντικρὺ δ᾽ ἀπόφημι γυναῖκα μὲν οὐκ ἀποδώσω·
κτήματα δ᾽ ὅσσ᾽ ἀγόμην ἐξ Ἄργεος ἡμέτερον δῶ
πάντ᾽ ἐθέλω δόμεναι καὶ οἴκοθεν ἄλλ᾽ ἐπιθεῖναι.

Il. 7.357–64

Antēnōr, these things you say are no longer dear to me:
you know how to conceive another *muthos* better than this.
But if you truly say this in earnest,
then the gods themselves have taken away your *phrenes*.
But I will make this pronouncement among the horse-taming Trojans:
I refuse outright to give back the woman;
but whatever valuables I brought from Argos to our house,
all these I am willing to give back and to add more from my household.

Paris' address to "the horse-taming Trojans" is hardly more than an acknowledgment of the presence of the assembled group; it certainly does not ascribe to them any agency in the matter. On the contrary, it asserts a personal right to decide without regard for the will of the group. In this way, whatever collective procedure Antēnōr might have set in motion is immediately undercut.

It falls to Priam to resolve the impasse. His speech, addressed again to the "Trojans, Dardanians, and allies," seems to be an attempt to balance Paris' claim of private interest with a collective mode of action. He calls for an evening meal and the posting of guards, and he proposes that the herald Idaios should convey Paris' offer to the Achaeans in the morning. All of these provisions would seem to involve the broader community. He stresses, however, that the offer itself is a more or less private transaction: Idaios is to speak to Agamemnon and Menelaus in particular, and Paris is identified as "the one on account of whom this quarrel has arisen" (*Il.* 7.373–74).[12] Even so, Priam appears to have little confidence that the Achaeans will settle now for this sort of private resolution, for he directs Idaios also to ask for a temporary cessation of hostilities so that the dead may be buried and to declare the Trojans' willingness to continue fighting thereafter, "until a *daimōn* parts [*diakrinein*] us and gives victory to one or the other side" (7.377–78). The divinely mediated "parting" envisioned by Priam would be the ultimate decision on the question of how to resolve the quarrel. Priam thus concludes his speech by delegating to the gods the task of arriving at a *krisis* (the noun is a derivative of the verb *krinein,* as in *dia-krinein*), a tacit admission of the truth of Iris' earlier statement criticizing the Trojan fondness for speeches that are "without *krisis*" themselves.

The discussion about the return of Helen creates the impression that, at Troy, Priam's family has the last word. It also establishes a pattern according to which a wise counselor's sound advice is unceremoniously rebuffed by a representative of that family. In Book 12, Pouludamas claims to have often played the part of Antēnōr to Hector's Paris in other stagings of this scene, prefacing a warning not to press the attack with the complaint, "Hector, you are always rebuking me in assemblies, though I advise good things" (*Il.* 12.211–12). His allegations are, in fact, confirmed by Hector's dismissive reply, which, by repeating the initial verses of Paris' speech, contributes to the impression that we are witnessing the repetition of a common pattern (*Il.* 12.231–34 = 7.357–60; cf. 18.285).

In truth, Hector does not always reject Pouludamas' advice. In two instances he acts on it. Both times, however, the narrator emphasizes the predominance of Hector's own preference over any other concern; he listens to Pouludamas because the latter's counsel "pleases" him:

ὣς φάτο Πουλυδάμας, ἅδε δ' Ἕκτορι μῦθος ἀπήμων
Il. 12.80 = 13.748

Thus spoke Pouludamas, and his profitable [literally, "causing no pain"] *muthos* pleased [*handanein*] Hector.

Pouludamas' proposals always concern some recommended collective action: on the first occasion he advises the Trojans to storm the Achaean fortifications on foot, leaving their chariots behind, and on the second, he counsels a strategic retreat and regrouping. In the former case, he even addresses his speech to "Hector and the other leaders of Trojans and allies" (*Il.* 12.61). Nevertheless, in spite of the obviously collective import of his recommendations, the decision to act is made solely by Hector, in accordance with his own inclinations.[13] This grounding of decisions in personal preference, signaled by the verb *handanein*, aligns Hector with the behavior of Agamemnon in Book 1. A manner of decision making that is altogether exceptional by Achaean standards seems rather to be the norm among the Trojans.

That is not to say that the Trojans are entirely unfamiliar with the procedures of collective decision making. At the end of Book 8, in an assembly that is structurally paired with the Achaean *agorē* (and subsequent council scenes) of Book 9, Hector gathers his warriors on the battlefield to discuss dispositions for a night encampment. The scene clearly prefigures the battlefield assembly of Book 18, with Hector proposing that the Trojans camp where they are, rather than return to the city, so that they can press the attack in the morning. He does so in terms that seem to presuppose a genuine process of deliberation: he speaks to the "Trojans, Dardanians, and allies" as a whole (*Il.* 8.497), and the use of a combination of imperatives and more inclusive first-person hortatory subjunctives allows him to strike a tone somewhere between command and exhortation. Hector thus observes certain deliberative protocols, and his audience responds in kind— deliberatively—with an unmistakable expression of support:

ὣς ῞Εκτωρ ἀγόρευ᾽, ἐπὶ δὲ Τρῶες κελάδησαν.
Il. 8.542

Thus Hector spoke, and the Trojans shouted in reply.

This response formula—as distinctive of the Trojans as the *epiakhein* formula is of the Achaeans, and apparently a kind of variant of the latter—is clearly meant to designate the expression of the Trojans' collective will to execute Hector's plan.[14] It is therefore an exaggeration to claim that Hector issues simple military orders that are "carried out at once, without any reply."[15] By the same token, however, it would be an exaggeration to say that this Trojan assembly conforms fully to the ideal Achaean form of decision making through consensus. Hector's authoritarian streak is still very much in evidence. The scholia record an ancient assessment of Hector's summary remark, "Let it be as I say, great-hearted Trojans" (*Il.* 8.523), which nicely encapsulates the tone: "he speaks in the fashion of a tyrant, not of a king."[16] Moreover, the simple fact that the Trojan mode of collective expression is distinguished lexically from Achaean behaviors makes it difficult to assess the force of the Trojans' response. It appears to be efficient, insofar as Hector's orders are put into effect, but can we really infer that the shouts of the group actually determine the outcome of the assembly, considering that elsewhere action is unambiguously determined by Hector's will alone? There is a palpable ambivalence in this scene; it conveys the impression of an uneasy balance between the kind of heavy-handed autocracy that seems generally to characterize the Trojans' political life and a more collective manner of decision making.

This ambivalence is intensified into an outright contradiction in the climactic assembly of Book 18, which we are now in a much better position to appreciate after this survey of Trojan politics in action. The final Trojan *agorē* makes use of a number of motifs familiar from previous episodes. The matter under consideration—whether to return to the city or to pass the night beneath the Achaean fortifications—is the same as that in Book 8. Dramatically, however, the discussion develops according to the pattern of the confrontational exchanges between Antēnōr and Paris and, more directly, Pouludamas and Hector in Book 12. Pouludamas, identified as a gifted speaker by the epithet *pepnumenos* (which he shares with Antēnōr) and the notice that "he alone looked both before him and behind" (*Il.* 18.249–50), advocates a strategic withdrawal, arguing that Achilles is sure to enter the battle in the morning.[17] Hector angrily rebuffs him, with echoes of earlier confrontations as well as acid allusions to Pouludamas' own words, and accuses him of being a "fool" (*nēpios*, 18.295) for urging retreat at the very moment when Zeus has offered victory.[18] Furthermore, giving free rein to the tyrannical tendency exhibited already in Book 8, he not only commands Pouludamas to be silent but even threatens to prevent any group response to his proposal:[19]

νήπιε μηκέτι ταῦτα νοήματα φαῖν' ἐνὶ δήμῳ·
οὐ γάρ τις Τρώων ἐπιπείσεται· οὐ γὰρ ἐάσω.

Il. 18.295–96

Fool, do not declare these sentiments any longer among the people,
for no Trojan will obey—for I will not allow it.

This is nothing less than an attempt to disable the social mechanisms that would produce a decision based on group will. Nevertheless, in spite of, or perhaps precisely because of, Hector's effort to direct the outcome of the assembly on his own terms, the assembled Trojans do express their collective will—in favor of Hector's plan to camp on the plain. They thereby demonstrate that they, and not Pouludamas, are the ones who are *nēpioi*:

ὣς Ἕκτωρ ἀγόρευ', ἐπὶ δὲ Τρῶες κελάδησαν
νήπιοι· ἐκ γάρ σφεων φρένας εἵλετο Παλλὰς Ἀθήνη.
Ἕκτορι μὲν γὰρ ἐπήνησαν κακὰ μητιόωντι,
Πουλυδάμαντι δ' ἄρ' οὔ τις ὃς ἐσθλὴν φράζετο βουλήν.
Il. 18.310–13

Thus Hector spoke, and the Trojans shouted in reply—
fools: for Pallas Athena took away their *phrenes*.
For they expressed *epainos* for Hector, though his plan was a bad one,
but no one did so for Pouludamas, who advised good counsel.

The same shouting that greeted the proposal to remain on the battlefield in Book 8 is now additionally characterized as an expression of *epainos*—albeit an *epainos* of fools. Paradoxically, Hector's most candid declaration of indifference to public opinion freely expressed is matched by the most cohesive manifestation of solidarity allotted to the Trojans in the poem.

The contradiction at the heart of Hector's ambivalence toward collective action is laid bare by this confrontation of seeming incompatibles, authoritarianism and consensus. Like contrasting colors, each serves to set off the other, but the overall effect is to portray the *epainos* of a Trojan audience as, fundamentally, a contradiction in terms. If the Trojans are able to achieve *epainos* at all, it is only through the intervention of a god (Athena). Even so the occasion is marred by numerous indicators that something is amiss, including, first of all, the qualification of those expressing their will as *nēpioi:* as Susan Edmunds has shown, central to the meaning of this term is the notion of a social "disconnection," an estrangement from one's community that makes the idea of a consensus of *nēpioi* a virtual oxymoron.[20]

The text also stresses that the audience does not adopt the seated position typical of orderly proceedings but instead remains standing, out of fear at Achilles' sudden appearance (*Il.* 18.246–48).[21] Moreover, even the syntax of *epainos* takes an irregular form, suggesting a fundamental difference in modality between this Trojan consensus and its Achaean counterparts. As a rule, *epainein* is used absolutely in the Homeric poems, on one occasion only taking an accusative object designating the utterance that has produced the response (*Il.* 2.335). This normal usage emphasizes the absolute quality of the action as a total social phenomenon that extends throughout society and is, in principle, free of restriction temporal or otherwise. Here, however, we find the verb construed, exceptionally, with a dative object indicating the speaker. By linking Trojan solidarity directly to the person of Hector, this construction provides an ominous indication of the limit imposed on Trojan consensus by Hector's imminent death.[22] For even when *epainein* takes as its object an utterance, the consensus that transforms the utterance into a total speech act may outlive the speaker. But a solidarity centered on an individual, rather than his words, becomes meaningless when that individual is no longer present. This is the consequence of Hector's curious melding of authoritarianism and collective decision making: the cohesion of Trojan society is inseparable from the talismanic authority embodied in Hector himself. The bond that unites the Trojan community proves ultimately to be a cult of personality.

Ironically, this extraordinarily personalized consensus seems to ratify the destruction of the figure that grounds it. After laying out his orders for the night, Hector concludes his speech by stating his own resolve to face Achilles, if he should encounter him on the battlefield:

εἰ δ᾽ ἐτεὸν παρὰ ναῦφιν ἀνέστη δῖος Ἀχιλλεύς,
ἄλγιον αἴ κ᾽ ἐθέλῃσι τῷ ἔσσεται· οὔ μιν ἔγωγε
φεύξομαι ἐκ πολέμοιο δυσηχέος, ἀλλὰ μάλ᾽ ἄντην
στήσομαι, ἤ κε φέρῃσι μέγα κράτος, ἤ κε φεροίμην.
ξυνὸς Ἐνυάλιος, καί τε κτανέοντα κατέκτα.
ὣς Ἕκτωρ ἀγόρευ᾽, ἐπὶ δὲ Τρῶες κελάδησαν . . .
Il. 18.305–10

"But if glorious Achilles has truly roused himself by the ships,
the worse will it be for him if he so wishes: I will not flee
before him, away from the din of battle, but will take my stand
directly opposite him, whether he should take the victory, or I.
Enualios is impartial, and he slays the slayer."
Thus Hector spoke, and the Trojans shouted in reply.

As Hector himself later recognizes (*Il.* 22.99–110), these words bind him to confront Achilles—and ultimately to die at his hands. Hector formulates the necessity that compels him in terms of the reproach he would incur from Pouludamas and the Trojans were he not to stand his ground. In terms of the *Iliad*'s poetic logic, however, it is the *epainos* of the Trojans that constitutes the real constraint. If Hector had fully disabled the mechanisms of collective deliberation, he might have preserved for himself some freedom of action. As it is, he secures the ratification of his own demise, for the group's response transforms his words into a true speech act, an utterance that shapes reality, and the poem's formulaic grammar requires that subsequent events conform.

In ensuring Hector's fatal encounter with Achilles, the *epainos* of the Trojans also serves the important function of guaranteeing that the poem does not diverge from its traditional plot. To a certain extent this can be said of almost every instance of *epainos*, since collective will regularly plays an important part in moving the poem's action forward toward its conclusion.[23] But the involvement of Athena lends this occasion special significance, marking it as a moment of crucial importance for the progress of the poem's thematic development. It is Athena who intervenes in Book 2 to prevent an untraditional return of the Achaean fleet; as we shall see, she descends more than once from Olympus to put things back on track.[24] She is the customary agent of recalibration whenever the poem confronts the possibility of some event that would run counter to poetic "destiny," and her actions are typically correlated with the *epainos* of one of the concerned groups. (Here, she actively facilitates *epainos* by "taking away the *phrenes*" of the Trojans.)[25] In the case of this intervention, there is no overt marker of the potential for an unwarranted outcome, no "reversal passage" delineating the boundaries of tradition, as in Book 2. But the threat to the traditional plot is no less strongly felt, as ancient commentators emphasized: as the scholia put it, "if the Trojans followed Pouludamas' advice, the rest of the *Iliad* would be disqualified (ἐξαγώνιον)."[26]

Although the narrator does not remark directly on the prevention of an untraditional turn of events, the text is structured in such a way as to suggest unmistakably that the *epainos* of the Trojan assembly settles the poem's most pressing uncertainty. Since Book 1, the greatest source of tension in the unfolding narrative of the Achaeans' struggle at Troy has been the question of whether Achilles will return to the battlefield or whether he will abandon his part in the Trojan story and the *kleos* it promises for him. In his masterly speech to Odysseus during the Embassy, Achilles himself formulates these alternatives in terms of the "two-fold dooms" (διχθαδίας κῆρας, *Il.* 9.411) that lie before him, either to die at Troy or to live a long life without *kleos*. But now, as though the Trojans' *epainos* resolves not a strategic question but this most central dichotomy, the narrative cuts immediately from the Trojan *agorē* to Achilles, who, lamenting over the corpse of Patroklos, acknowledges for the first time the inevitability of his fate:

ἄμφω γὰρ πέπρωται ὁμοίην γαῖαν ἐρεῦσαι
αὐτοῦ ἐνὶ Τροίῃ, ἐπεὶ οὐδ' ἐμὲ νοστήσαντα

δέξεται ἐν μεγάροισι γέρων ἱππηλάτα Πηλεὺς
οὐδὲ Θέτις μήτηρ, ἀλλ' αὐτοῦ γαῖα καθέξει.
Il. 18.329–32

For we are both fated to stain red the same earth
here in Troy, since neither will the aged horseman Peleus
receive me on my return to his halls,
nor Thetis my mother, but the earth will hold me here.

No longer is there any sense of an alternative future for Achilles. His "two-fold dooms" have been narrowed to a single destiny, which is as inescapable for him as it is necessary to the story of Troy's destruction. Achilles has already been told that his own death must follow soon after that of Hector (*Il.* 18.96). The logic is clear: by compelling Hector to face Achilles in battle, the *epainos* of the Trojans ensures the demise of them both, and ultimately the obliteration of Troy itself.

In this way, the single instance of Trojan consensus serves the same function of confirming the traditional Iliadic narrative as the paradigmatic *epainos* of the Achaeans in Book 2. At the same time, it renders the expression of *epainos* in the subsequent Achaean assembly unnecessary. The Trojans now come to the fore as the group whose will determines the course of events. They become thereby a kind of substitute or double for the Achaean community, just as Hector becomes a double for Achilles when he dons the latter's armor. Moreover, their self-assertion in usurping the structural role of licensing the action of the next narrative unit, a role elsewhere assigned to the Achaeans, corresponds to the abandonment of the defensive tactics that seem generally to characterize the Trojan way of war in favor of an aggressive strategy more appropriate to the Achaeans as besiegers. For the Trojan ethos, at least so far as it is embodied in Hector, favors a defensive mode of action: Hector's very name designates him as "the protector," the proponent of a strategy of defense implicit also in the name of his son, Astyanax.[27] In Book 8, when Hector first proposed the aggressive measure of remaining on the battlefield until morning, he nevertheless remained true to this identity by including in his proposal several provisions for the protection of the city against the threat of a nocturnal assault. Now, however, he seems to forget entirely about the city's security; he has become entirely fixated on pressing the attack. The Trojans, for their part, forget themselves when they approve his plan. The disconnection signaled by their designation as *nēpioi* is ultimately a disconnection from their own identity as a people of resistance rather than conquest. Indeed, Athena must intervene to produce among the Trojans a collective will that runs counter to their better instincts, by taking away their *phrenes* (*Il.* 18.311).

From this perspective, the greatest flaw in the Trojans' experience of consensus is that it involves a denial of the community's identity rather than an affirmation of it. This is true to the precise extent that the Trojan *epainos* brings about a departure from an established pattern of behavior.[28] That is to say, this is a consensus for an *innovative* course of action. The significance of this fact as an indication of the difference between Trojan political practice and that of the Achaeans should not be underestimated. As a rule, among the Achaeans, and (as we shall see) among the gods as well, *epainos* is an essentially conservative phenomenon. It is directed not toward the authorization of some radical new departure but toward the consolidation of the status quo. The successful proposals of Odysseus in Book 2 and of Diomedes in Book 9 do not outline any novel objectives; they simply confirm a commitment to a project that has come under threat. It is telling that the few examples of *epainos* for innovative proposals are generally overruled by higher powers: the Achaeans' ratification of Agamemnon's judgment regarding the duel is prevented from taking effect by the gods, as is the Mycenaeans' approval of a proposed expedition to Thebes in Agamemnon's tale.[29]

The only true exception to this rule—the *epainos* of the Achaean *basilēes* for Nestor's plan to construct a defensive wall, which is arguably as much of a departure from the norm as the Trojans' decision to pursue an aggressive policy—is in fact marked as such. Poseidon protests vigorously against this development as an affront to cosmic order, and Zeus reassures him that the wall is not destined to last long (*Il.* 7.443–64), while the narrator assures us of the same thing (*Il.* 12.9–33). That is to say, this is an *epainos* with a "sunset clause," a remarkable qualification that seems designed both to alert us to the fact that something unusual is in progress and to attenuate the significance of a collective will to pursue an unforeseen purpose. I examine the metapoetic significance of this unusually innovative consensus in chapter 9. For now, I would like to stress that, while it would be reductive to interpret this portrayal of consensus and its objects simply in terms of an ideological commitment to conservatism, nevertheless the Iliadic image of collective decision making clearly privileges the community not as an engine of change but, on the contrary, as a curb on innovation. As in so many other respects, the Trojans fall short of the ideal.

The Trojan assembly of Book 18 provides the last opportunity to observe the forging of a working consensus and the enactment of its consequences. Those consequences are radically innovative from the Trojan point of view; paradoxically, however, it is precisely this innovation that propels the poem inexorably toward the conclusion sanctioned by the broader Trojan tradition. *Epainos* finally seals the fate of Priam's city and ensures that the *Iliad* will conclude as the Troy story demands it must—but it is an *epainos* that is deeply flawed, irregular in virtually all respects, not least because it expresses the collective will of a people whose political practice seems fundamentally opposed to consensus. Yet the Achaeans never have the opportunity to reassert *epainos* in a more normative form. If there is to be a corrective antidote to the imperfect vision of consensus with which the poem ends, a restoration of the norm, it is not to be found at the level of the poem's explicit narration. However, in the collective decisions of the gods, the last of the political communities to be considered in part II, we find indications of another level at which consensus may be established.

CHAPTER 7

The View from Olympus

Divine Politics and Metapoetics

The practice of politics is not a solely human activity in the *Iliad*. The gods, too, are subject to the political imperatives of collective decision making. No less than their human protégés, they must make accommodations and negotiate conflicting preferences in pursuit of a common basis for group action. To be sure, divine actors may pursue their own interests in defiance of the will of their peers. As in the case of Agamemnon, however, this apparent autonomy masks a more fundamental dependency on communal support, a subordination of individual action to the will of the group if actions are to achieve results. Agamemnon must ultimately submit to the Achaeans' collective will and return Chryseis to her father. So, too, as we will see, even Zeus, the mightiest of gods, finds himself hobbled by dissenting voices on Olympus. Consensus constrains divine as well as human power.[1]

The gods are, so to speak, political cousins of the Achaeans. In spite of Zeus' occasionally tyrannical reliance on brute force, in a manner reminiscent of Hector, the politics of Olympus still appear to be founded on *epainos*. Hera can force Zeus' hand by speaking threateningly of a lack of consensus (*Il.* 4.29; cf. 16.443, 22.181: I discuss all these passages in detail below); to the extent that both she and her consort acknowledge *epainos* as a value, they adhere more closely to the Achaean ideal of political life than to the Trojan. Moreover, even infringements of this ideal can be understood as reflections of or reactions to the political situation among the Achaeans. So, for instance, our first view of the divine community, as the gods assemble at the palace of Zeus at the end of Book 1, corresponds in important ways with the poem's initial Achaean assembly. In each case, the leader of the community formulates an intention that is expressly at odds with, or at least indifferent to, the will of the group; in each case he is motivated to do so by the value he attaches to a particular female.[2] As an essentially private decision, Zeus' plan to fulfill Thetis' request parallels Agamemnon's decision to keep Chryseis for himself, while his dismissal of Hera's concerns includes verbal echoes of Agamemnon's treatment of Chryses, underscoring the parallel.[3] The plan to bring honor to Achilles, implemented over the objections and resistance of Hera and others, is thus a kind of divine extension of the initial state of exception among the Achaeans.

The first scene of proper deliberation among the gods stands in a similar relation to political developments on the human plane. When the duel between Paris and Menelaus results in an impasse, the scene shifts suddenly to Olympus, where the gods take up the question of whether the warring parties ought to be able to resolve the conflict peaceably (*Il.* 4.1–72).[4] Zeus opens the discussion with a speech that, according to the narrator, is intended to "provoke" Hera:

αὐτίκ' ἐπειρᾶτο Κρονίδης ἐρεθιζέμεν "Ηρην
κερτομίοις ἐπέεσσι παραβλήδην ἀγορεύων·
δοιαὶ μὲν Μενελάῳ ἀρηγόνες εἰσὶ θεάων
"Ηρη τ' Ἀργείη καὶ Ἀλαλκομενηῒς Ἀθήνη.
ἀλλ' ἤτοι ταὶ νόσφι καθήμεναι εἰσορόωσαι
τέρπεσθον· τῷ δ' αὖτε φιλομειδὴς Ἀφροδίτη
αἰεὶ παρμέμβλωκε καὶ αὐτοῦ κῆρας ἀμύνει·
καὶ νῦν ἐξεσάωσεν ὀϊόμενον θανέεσθαι.
ἀλλ' ἤτοι νίκη μὲν ἀρηϊφίλου Μενελάου·
ἡμεῖς δὲ φραζώμεθ' ὅπως ἔσται τάδε ἔργα,
ἤ ῥ' αὖτις πόλεμόν τε κακὸν καὶ φύλοπιν αἰνὴν
ὄρσομεν, ἦ φιλότητα μετ' ἀμφοτέροισι βάλωμεν.
εἰ δ' αὖ πως τόδε πᾶσι φίλον καὶ ἡδὺ γένοιτο,
ἤτοι μὲν οἰκέοιτο πόλις Πριάμοιο ἄνακτος,
αὖτις δ' Ἀργείην Ἑλένην Μενέλαος ἄγοιτο.

Il. 4.5–19

Straightaway the son of Kronos tried to provoke a quarrel with Hera,
speaking mischievously with taunting words:
"Menelaus has two goddesses as his helpers,
Argive Hera and Athena the Defender.
But they, sitting apart, are pleased just

to look on, while Aphrodite, fond of laughter,

is always bringing aid to the other one and warding off destruction.

And now she has saved him when he foresaw death.

But clearly the victory lies with Menelaus, dear to Ares.

But for our part, let us consider how these matters will be:

will we again stir foul war and dread slaughter,

or should we establish *philotēs* between them?

If, somehow, this should be dear and sweet to all,

let the city of lord Priam live on,

and Menelaus take back Argive Helen."

Insofar as the debate revolves around the possibility of a premature ending to the war, this scene corresponds precisely to the Achaean assembly of Book 2, where a similar provocation by Agamemnon calls into question the future of the war effort.[5] Once again, the politics of the gods shadow the situation of their Achaean counterparts. The two communities seem to be so closely tied together that the gods are compelled to revisit essentially the same problems faced by the Achaeans, albeit from a different perspective.

If they must face the same problems, they must also address them in the same way. For the gods as well as the Achaeans, *epainos* represents the touchstone of an effective collective decision. This emerges clearly from Hera's response to Zeus' proposal:

ὣς ἔφαθ', αἱ δ' ἐπέμυξαν Ἀθηναίη τε καὶ Ἥρη·
πλησίαι αἵ γ' ἥσθην, κακὰ δὲ Τρώεσσι μεδέσθην.
ἤτοι Ἀθηναίη ἀκέων ἦν οὐδέ τι εἶπε
σκυζομένη Διὶ πατρί, χόλος δέ μιν ἄγριος ᾕρει·
Ἥρη δ' οὐκ ἔχαδε στῆθος χόλον, ἀλλὰ προσηύδα·
αἰνότατε Κρονίδη ποῖον τὸν μῦθον ἔειπες·
πῶς ἐθέλεις ἅλιον θεῖναι πόνον ἠδ' ἀτέλεστον,
ἱδρῶ θ' ὃν ἵδρωσα μόγῳ, καμέτην δέ μοι ἵπποι
λαὸν ἀγειρούσῃ, Πριάμῳ κακὰ τοῖό τε παισίν.
ἔρδ'· ἀτὰρ οὔ τοι πάντες ἐπαινέομεν θεοὶ ἄλλοι.
Il. 4.20–29

Thus he spoke, and Athena and Hera muttered at his words.

They sat near to one another and plotted evils for the Trojans.

Athena was silent and said nothing,

indignant at Zeus her father, and a savage anger gripped her.

But Hera's breast could not contain her anger; instead, she said:
"Most dread son of Kronos, what sort of speech have you uttered?
How can you wish to render vain and fruitless my labor
and the sweat I have poured out in toil—my horses have grown weary
as I gather the host to be a curse for Priam and his children.
Do as you like, but we other gods do not all express *epainos*."

Hera and Athena, like the Achaean audience of Agamemnon's speech in Book 2, understand Zeus to be advocating sincerely for a conclusion to the war. Hera expresses their opposition in terms of the withholding of *epainos*. By and large, critics have failed to appreciate the proper force of her remark. Misled, perhaps, by her rhetorical feint—ἔρδ', "go ahead"—they have been quick to assume that there is a real possibility that Zeus could act without divine consensus. One writer offers this representative reading: "Zeus could have his own way on everything; he could even annul something long-fated, even perhaps his own *boulē*. But the repercussions would be so disagreeable that it would not be worth it. . . . 'Go on, do it,' other gods cry when Zeus contemplates going back on something that was settled. . . . 'but we other gods will not all applaud you.' . . . Clearly this threatens something far worse than merely withholding praise."[6] The point being made here is not that the threat to withhold *epainos* is any more consequential than "merely withholding praise" but that this threat is a screen for more substantive consequences.[7] Hera, on this view, insinuates the possibility of subsequent retribution; Zeus' acquiescence is the result of a kind of cost-benefit analysis in which the risk of such retribution outweighs the possible gains. Such a reading, however, ignores the significance imparted to *epainos* by the poem's grammar of reception. As a result, it renders Hera's words overly subtle even as it reduces their practical import. Hera's threat is a real one: Zeus can do as he likes, but without the *epainos* of the group his actions will have no lasting effects. She means to impress upon him the impracticability of such a unilateral decision. The threat of withholding *epainos* is an effective constraint on Zeus' autonomy, and Zeus treats it as such.

The question of whether Zeus sincerely wishes to consider the possibility of a premature ending to the war, or whether, like Agamemnon, he wishes merely to test the resolve of the divine community, has no effect on the dynamics of the scene, nor on the value it sets on consensus. Even if, as the narrator suggests, Zeus makes his proposal merely to goad Hera, nevertheless the rhetoric deployed on both sides clearly articulates the decisive function assigned to *epainos*. And in any case, the subsequent exchange of words exposes real differences of position and preference: when Zeus renounces his proposal, he does so "willingly, but with an unwilling heart" (*Il.* 4.43; this paradoxical statement will eventually need further examination).[8] The differences thus exposed require real negotiation. In fact, the ensuing discussion, in which Zeus accedes to the destruction of Troy, but only in return for assurances that his own wishes will be respected on a future occasion, represents for Egon Flaig the definitive formulation of the "consensus principle" within the *Iliad*'s "political reflections in atheoretical form."[9] Although Flaig does not take note of Hera's reference to *epainos*, his analysis is crucial to an understanding of the term insofar as it elucidates the social transactions on which *epainos* rests. Zeus' negotiations with Hera are aimed at the establishment of a framework that will ensure the full support of all the gods, even if there is no final, positive statement of divine *epainos*.

The scene concludes without any expression of collective sentiment. The community's silence marks a significant discrepancy with the parallel Achaean assembly of Book 2. In both scenes a speaker of questionable sincerity proposes an innovative policy that would entail the abandonment of the war; in both the effect of this proposal is, ultimately, to galvanize support for its contrary, the continuation of the war effort. Among the Achaeans, however, we observe the direct expression of *epainos* for the conservative position, while among the gods we find merely the *withholding* of *epainos* for the innovative one. This discrepancy is undoubtedly due, at least in part, to the persistence of differences among the gods, and even within the mind of Zeus. Zeus may be able to reconcile himself to the destruction of Troy, but he does so with an "unwilling heart"; other pro-Trojan gods are even less able than he to subdue their partisan fervor. Moreover, much of the subsequent narrative actually describes events that can be construed as a temporary suspension of Troy's impending doom. The expression of collective approval for Troy's destruction would seem at odds with all these traces of ambivalence. But there is a further point to be made in connection with the earlier Achaean assembly. Deliberation in human communities tends to highlight the capacity of *epainos* to direct action and to shape the course of subsequent events; it foregrounds consensus as an active force. In the case of divine deliberation, by contrast, what is foregrounded is the consequence of withholding *epainos*, which turns out to be no less effective as a means for directing and shaping events. The disruption or disabling of consensus emerges as an equally meaningful social act, one that, by preventing an innovative course of action, reinforces the status quo.

METAPOETICS

The politics of Olympus thus present the force of consensus in a distinctly different modality from the one privileged in the human sphere. By the same token, discussion among the gods proceeds from a very different perspective on the questions to be decided. For the gods are able to take a long view of events, including future events, and to foresee the consequences of their decisions. Unlike their human counterparts, they have knowledge of what is fated to happen and are therefore able to see beyond the immediate outcome of their choices. Mortal characters must adopt a course of action in ignorance of its ultimate result, on the basis of purely tactical considerations that are often of pressing but short-term importance. Examples include the Achaean decision to construct a defensive wall and the Trojan decision to remain camped on the plain. The gods, however, enjoy a measure of objectivity and distance that allows them to reflect on events in the context of the war as a whole. They are even able to contemplate alternative possibilities and deviations from fate, as they do in Book 4 when considering whether or not to allow the war to be concluded peacefully.

This ability to evaluate developments against the background of a privileged, licensed outcome places the gods in a position analogous to that of the poem's real-world audiences, who are likewise invited at regular intervals to contemplate possible alternatives.[10] What is fated to happen from the gods' point of view is, to one listening to an Iliadic performance, simply what is sanctioned by the traditional and familiar form of the story.[11] Observing events at a comfortable distance and endowed, through knowledge of fate, with a kind of proleptic hindsight, the gods mirror the perspective enjoyed by historical auditors. Among the poem's many internal audiences, theirs is the one that approximates most closely to the experiences of external ones.

Not surprisingly, then, the gods' debates take a distinctly metapoetic turn. That is to say, while human communities measure their choices from the limited perspective of perceived tactical advantage, the gods are consistently compelled to contextualize their deliberations in terms of the merits and faults of making adjustments to the fated course of events—in other words, to the traditional plot of the poem. Admittedly, this is less than fully evident in Book 4. Even though nothing could be more certain than that Troy is fated to perish, Hera's objections focus on her personal investment in the city's destruction rather than the dictates of fate as such. Nevertheless, the pressure to conform to a predetermined arc of development is implicit in her repeated insistence that her efforts be permitted to reach their *telos*, their natural end (*Il.* 4.26, 57): exempting Troy from destruction would unsettle a long-established goal.

Though here implicit, the espousal of fate as a normative force becomes explicit in subsequent iterations of this scene. Twice more do the gods consider granting some reprieve to the Trojan side. Each time the discussion develops according to the same pattern, even employing many of the same verses: Zeus proposes exempting some representative of Troy—first Sarpedon (*Il.* 16.433–38) and then Hector (*Il.* 22.168–76)—from the death apportioned by destiny, to which Hera in the first instance and Athena in the second reply with the now familiar bluff, "go ahead, but we other gods do not all approve" (ἔρδ'· ἀτὰρ οὔ τοι πάντες ἐπαινέομεν θεοὶ ἄλλοι). Significantly, both goddesses cite the constraints of fate as the principal reason why such an expedient would be unacceptable (*Il.* 16.441–42 = 22.179–80). This foregrounding of fate, in relation to the first instance of the scene, coincides with a shift from the general framework of the Troy story and its ultimate endpoint (the destruction of Troy) to the central events of the second half of the *Iliad*. Sarpedon's death will lead directly to Patroklos', and Hector's in turn will point the way to the poem's ultimate conclusion. It is difficult to avoid the impression that the pressure of fate is more keenly felt in these exchanges because they concern a course of action that is not only already under way but that will actually reach fulfillment in the immediate sequel. As a stand-in for poetic tradition, fate can be backgrounded in the debate over Troy's ultimate destiny, since the destruction of the city lies well beyond the limits of Iliadic narrative. It comes to the fore, however, when the narrative structure of the *Iliad* itself is called into question. The insistence on fate, in other words, points to the narrative pressure of the story in progress. It highlights the fact that the gods are discussing matters that are not simply a given of the overall Troy story but in fact constitutive of Iliadic tradition in particular.

The three divine debates over the fate of Troy and its champions form a series with an inherent logic that reflects the structure of the poem as a whole. Distributed across four days of fighting, they track the poem's major divisions and reinforce the roughly tripartite segmentation of the narrative. As each day of fighting is bounded by the *epainos* of Achaeans or Trojans, so each day sees some negotiation of *epainos* among the gods.[12] Moreover, considered as a progression, the three scenes describe a trajectory that parallels the one we have observed among the Achaeans: there is a movement from the disunity evident in the first two iterations to the relative concord achieved in the last, when Zeus meets Athena's objection with a declaration of solidarity and an invitation to manage events as she sees fit (*Il.* 22.183–85). As in the case of the Achaean community, the progression never arrives at its implied endpoint, the establishment of an unambiguous consensus. There is no positive statement of divine *epainos*, only Zeus' conciliatory gesture in response to Athena's threat to withhold it. The ultimate inconclusiveness of this sequence is yet another indication that the fulfillment of the *epainos* motif is to be sought outside the boundaries of the text.

WHOSE *ILIAD*? WHICH *ILIAD*?

Zeus occupies an interesting position in Olympian politics. The progress toward consensus is represented not just in terms of conflict between Zeus and other gods but also in terms of Zeus' own internal conflict. When Hera objects to the idea of sparing Troy, Zeus acquiesces, but not without emphasizing the extent to which he feels torn on the matter: he insists that he concedes "willingly, but with an unwilling heart" (*Il.* 4.43). As Flaig notes, this curiously paradoxical formulation encodes the "affective dissonance" that prevents this scene from producing an unqualified consensus.[13] More than that, however, it suggests that Zeus is not merely at odds with Hera and the other pro-Achaean gods, but at odds as well with himself; he both understands the necessity of Troy's destruction and regrets its demise. This suggestion is confirmed in the discussion of Sarpedon's fate, which Zeus opens by stressing his own "divided heart":

διχθὰ δέ μοι κραδίη μέμονε φρεσὶν ὁρμαίνοντι,
ἤ μιν ζωὸν ἐόντα μάχης ἄπο δακρυοέσσης
θείω ἀναρπάξας Λυκίης ἐν πίονι δήμῳ,
ἦ ἤδη ὑπὸ χερσὶ Μενοιτιάδαο δαμάσσω.
Il. 16.435–38

My heart inclines in two ways as I consider in my mind what I should do—
whether I should snatch him, while he is still alive, from the tearful battle
and set him down in the rich land of Lycia,
or if I should indeed lay him low beneath the hands of Menoitios' son.

The drops of blood Zeus rains down even after the discussion has ended—a highly poeticized sign of his deep regret—show that this is no mere rhetorical ploy designed to win concessions from Hera. It is perhaps a sign of some progress in the last debate, over Hector, that, although Zeus speaks of the grief he feels in his heart (*Il.* 22.169), he makes no mention of an explicit division or conflict. The "affective dissonance" may not have been eliminated entirely, but it seems significantly reduced.

There is a curious convergence between the way Zeus speaks about his own ambivalence and the way the narrator describes the divided opinions of the gods as a group. The "two ways" in which Zeus' heart inclines when he contemplates Sarpedon's death reflect the split between pro-Trojan gods and those who support the Achaeans. Moreover, they prefigure the "two ways" in which the divine community will be disposed when Zeus lifts the ban on direct involvement and invites his peers to join the battle themselves. The gods enter the fray "having a heart [divided] in two ways" (δίχα θυμὸν ἔχοντες, *Il.* 20.32). And when in the next book the theomachy evolves into direct and unmediated combat between pairs of gods, the same divine *thumos* ("heart") is said to be "tossed in two directions" (δίχα δέ σφιν ἐνὶ φρεσὶ θυμὸς ἄητο, *Il.* 21.386). The use of the singular *thumos* in both these cases blurs the line between individual and collective psychology, underscoring the extent to which the gods as a whole collectivize a dynamic that can be comprehended within a single entity—at least in the case of Zeus. The bond between Zeus' "psychology" and group dynamics finds expression in the pleasure he takes when he perceives that his peers' divided *thumos* is compelling them to fight face to face:

ἀμφὶ δὲ σάλπιγξεν μέγας οὐρανός. ἄϊε δὲ Ζεὺς
ἥμενος Οὐλύμπῳ· ἐγέλασσε δέ οἱ φίλον ἦτορ
γηθοσύνῃ, ὅθ᾽ ὁρᾶτο θεοὺς ἔριδι ξυνιόντας.
Il. 21.388–90

The wide heaven resounded around them. And Zeus heard
sitting on Olympus; and his own dear heart laughed
with joy when he saw the gods coming together in strife.

The joy and laughter of Zeus' heart mark his recognition, in an externalized form, of a conflict he had previously experienced within himself. Coming midway between the discussion of Sarpedon's fate and the final divine debate over Hector, in which Zeus is more or less at peace with himself, the theomachy, as an externalization and release of tension, seems to function as a kind of catharsis.

The mirrored divisions that afflict the divine community as a whole and the mind of Zeus in particular stem from divided loyalties and, consequently, conflicting views of the optimal course of events. From the metapoetic standpoint outlined above, they correspond to different visions of the plot of the *Iliad*. For pro-Achaean gods such as Hera, Athena, and Poseidon, the story of Hector's success in battle threatens not only to harm their vested interests but also to subvert, if only temporarily, the generally philhellenic outlines of the Troy story

as a whole. They must therefore be vigilant in ensuring that the impulse to favor the Trojans does not take over the narrative entirely. Those more favorably
inclined toward the Trojans, meanwhile, do not feel threatened by Hector's
temporary ascendancy but find in it, we may suppose, an opportunity to realize
their vision of what the *Iliad* might be, namely, a poem of (circumscribed) victory for the Trojans. This is the implication of Apollo's intervention at the beginning of Book 7, an intervention designed to bring an end to the first day of battle, in which the Achaeans have had the upper hand, and thus lay the groundwork
for the first Trojan triumphs, narrated in Book 8. Apollo does not question the
ultimate fate of Troy, which he accepts as fixed.[14] In spite of his resignation,
however, he acts in order to obtain for his side a kind of attenuated supremacy:
"he was plotting victory for the Trojans" (Τρώεσσι δὲ βούλετο νίκην, *Il.* 7.21).

By translating the verb *boulesthai* with the word "plotting," I mean to highlight the convergence of Apollo's activity with that of Zeus in his capacity as the
designer of the Iliadic plot. The expression *Dios boulē* ("the will of Zeus"), employing a noun, *boulē*, that is cognate with the verb *boulesthai*, is widely used in
archaic Greek poetry as a designation for the plot of a traditional poem.[15] Zeus
is the only other divinity who "plots victory" during the period narrated by the
Iliad, the victory in question belonging to Hector and the Trojans.[16] The phraseology used in Book 7 as an expression of Apollo's intentions elsewhere serves as
a succinct formulation of Zeus' plan to bring honor to Achilles:

Ζεὺς μέν ῥα Τρώεσσι καὶ Ἕκτορι βούλετο νίκην
κυδαίνων Ἀχιλῆα πόδας ταχύν·
Il. 13.347–8[17]

Zeus was plotting victory for the Trojans and for Hector,
out of a desire to glorify swift-footed Achilles.

In taking steps to bring this plan into effect, Apollo momentarily becomes Zeus'
surrogate, stepping into the role of the one who directs the action.

This temporary displacement of Zeus' authority onto the unambiguously
pro-Trojan figure of Apollo may reflect certain aspects of the Iliadic tradition
that have been pushed into the background by our text of the *Iliad*. A manuscript of the ninth or tenth century records an alternative Iliadic proem that,
according to the commentator, was known to the fourth-century (BCE) scholar
Aristoxenos:

Ἀριστόξενος δ' ἐν α´ Πραξιδαμαντείων φησὶν κατά τινας ἔχειν·
ἔσπετε νῦν μοι, Μοῦσαι Ὀλύμπια δώματ' ἔχουσαι,

ὅππως δὴ μῆνίς τε χόλος θ᾽ ἕλε Πηλεῖωνα,

Λητοῦς τ᾽ ἀγλαὸν υἱόν· ὁ γὰρ βασιλῆι χολωθείς . . .

Aristoxenos fr. 91a ed. Wehrli

Aristoxenos, in the first book of his *Praxidamanteia*, says that, according to some, [the *Iliad*] has [this proem]:

> Tell me now, you Muses who dwell on Olympus,
> how wrath and anger took hold of the son of Peleus
> and the bright child of Leto; for he, angered at the king . . .

This introduction to the action of the narrative foregrounds Apollo as the moving force behind the plot and thereby minimizes the importance of Zeus as architect.[18] If, as seems likely, the text from which Aristoxenos' alternative proem derives continued directly with the plague (compare lines 9–10 of our *Iliad*), there would be no mention of the "will of Zeus" at the outset of the poem. This is, so to speak, Apollo's *Iliad*, a version of the Iliadic tradition that is anchored in a particularly direct way to Apollo's point of view, at the expense of Zeus. Such an *Iliad*, framed exclusively by the anger of a pro-Trojan god against the leader of the Greeks, might indeed have tended to cast the story as a tale of Trojan victory.[19]

Our *Iliad*, of course, takes a decidedly more even-handed view, in part by framing the action not, in the first instance, in terms of divine wrath against Agamemnon or the Achaeans but in terms of the more abstract—and more ambiguous—"will of Zeus." The *Iliad* famously begins:

μῆνιν ἄειδε θεὰ Πηληϊάδεω Ἀχιλῆος

οὐλομένην, ἣ μυρί᾽ Ἀχαιοῖς ἄλγε᾽ ἔθηκε,

πολλὰς δ᾽ ἰφθίμους ψυχὰς Ἄϊδι προΐαψεν

ἡρώων, αὐτοὺς δὲ ἑλώρια τεῦχε κύνεσσιν

οἰωνοῖσί τε πᾶσι, Διὸς δ᾽ ἐτελείετο βουλή,

ἐξ οὗ δὴ τὰ πρῶτα διαστήτην ἐρίσαντε

Ἀτρεΐδης τε ἄναξ ἀνδρῶν καὶ δῖος Ἀχιλλεύς.

Il. 1.1–7

Sing, goddess, the baneful wrath of Achilles son of Peleus,
which brought countless woes to the Achaeans,
and cast many valiant souls of heroes down
to Hades, and made their bodies prey for dogs
and all manner of birds, and the will of Zeus was accomplished—
from the time when they were first divided in strife,
the son of Atreus, lord of men, and glorious Achilles.

One of the principal effects of this proem is to produce a certain ambivalence regarding the precise nature of the divine plan that controls the plot. This effect was felt already by ancient critics, who were uncertain as to how to relate the *Dios boulē* hailed in line 5 to the *Cypria*, the first poem of the Epic Cycle, in which the same phrase (Διὸς δ' ἐτελείετο βουλή, *Cypria* fr. 1.7 ed. Bernabé) refers to Zeus' plan to relieve the Earth's distress by destroying the race of heroes.[20] Aristophanes of Byzantium and Aristarchus, two great Alexandrian critics and editors of Homer, evidently made a point of drawing a firm distinction between the *Dios boulē* in the *Cypria* and the *Iliad*'s "will of Zeus," which they understood to refer strictly to Zeus' plan to bring honor to Achilles at Thetis' request.[21] Others, however, recognized in the *Iliad* proem a reference to precisely those extra-Iliadic traditions represented by the *Cypria*.[22] On this view, the *Iliad* represents only one part of a much broader plan that begins long before and concludes after the events related in the poem. Modern scholars have tended to follow Aristarchus, but some have supplemented these short- and long-term versions of Zeus' plan with an intermediate, "medium-term" version: the *Iliad* itself at times suggests that the *Dios boulē*, if it does not cover the whole range of the cosmic plan described in the *Cypria*, at least extends to the final outcome of the Troy story, that is, to the destruction of Troy.[23]

Ancient and modern readers of the *Iliad* have found support for all three of these views, and little means of deciding between them, at least in the case of the proem. On the contrary, the *Iliad*'s opening lines seem deliberately constructed so as to frustrate any precise determination of the scope of Zeus' will. A close examination of the syntax of the proem reveals multiple points of ambiguity that, taken together, make it far from clear whether the *Dios boulē* is independent of Achilles' wrath or, so to speak, subordinate to it, that is, formulated in response to Achilles' quarrel with Agamemnon.[24] The former interpretation is consonant with either the medium- or long-term understanding of the *Dios boulē*, while the latter corresponds to the position of Aristophanes and Aristarchus (that Zeus' will is restricted to the plan to honor Achilles). In short, the opening lines leave open to question the exact relationship between the will of Zeus, as the controlling force of the Iliadic plot, and the broad narrative tradition about the heroes who fought at Troy. The question is important because the *Iliad* can be construed in various ways depending on the answer that is given. The short-term view, correlating the will of Zeus with the consequences of his promise to Thetis, corresponds most closely to Apollo's vision for the poem: the *Iliad* is a narrative of a temporary Trojan victory that stands out against the broader context of the Trojan War tradition. Integrating the *Dios boulē* with this context in the medium term (seeing the destruction of Troy as the endpoint) results in something approximating the perspective of a pro-Achaean god like Poseidon. The *Iliad*, as an expression of the will of Zeus, will then be seen as a story of Achaean success, culminating in the removal of the last obstacle to Troy's destruction. On the longest view, however, the *Iliad* can be understood from an entirely nonpartisan standpoint, as a partial expression of a plan that encompasses the destruction of Achaeans and Trojans alike.[25]

By framing the plot in terms of an ambiguous "will of Zeus," the *Iliad* proem promotes an initially open-ended and impartial understanding of the story, especially by comparison with the variant known to Aristoxenos. But the "will of Zeus" is no mere abstraction, since Zeus himself is a character in the story. Not content to present the *Dios boulē* as a static principle external to the narrative, the narrator depicts it as the product of an ongoing process of negotiation between alternatives. The amphibolies of the proem are thereby carried over into the characterization of Zeus, and the impartiality of the narrative frame is refigured in terms of his internal conflicts.

The first sign of tension between Zeus' conflicting impulses occurs at the very moment that the plan to engineer temporary success for the Trojans is formulated. When Thetis asks Zeus to alter the general course of the war in order to bring honor to her son, Zeus hesitates. Only after an extended silence (ἀκέων δὴν ἦστο ["for a long time did he sit in silence"], *Il.* 1.512), and with evident distress (μέγ' ὀχθήσας ["greatly distressed"], 1.517), does he acquiesce. Clearly, Zeus himself is uncertain as to how to reconcile the short-term plan for Trojan victory with his own longer-term intentions.[26] The same uncertainty resurfaces in the conflicted attitudes he expresses in the subsequent Olympian debates. If, as I have argued, Zeus' unwilling willingness to endorse Troy's destruction and his "divided heart" over Sarpedon correspond to broader divisions in the divine community, that is because they express a tension between alternative perspectives on the Iliadic plot that is represented as much in the opposition of divine factions as in the ambivalence of the proem. The various proposals put forward by Zeus, it should be noted, all favor the Trojan side. They are, therefore, extensions of the policy of Trojan advantage instituted in response to Thetis' request. Zeus' equivocations communicate a fundamental uncertainty over the coordination of this plan for temporary Trojan glory with its larger context.

The debates initiated by Zeus' proposals can, accordingly, be understood as scenes of contest between competing visions for the poem. They enact a struggle, played out both between gods and within the mind of the supreme god, to determine the degree to which the plot will be framed in terms that either reinforce the overall trajectory of the Troy story or stand in contrast to it. The will of Zeus takes shape in these contests, the central question being whether Zeus' *boulē* will remain focused on the pro-Trojan policy implied by his promise to Thetis (and supported by Apollo) or whether it will orient itself around a more long-term set of objectives.

ZEUS' POLITICS OF EXCEPTIONALISM

This is, in essence, a question of how much a theme peculiar to the *Iliad*—Trojan victory—will be permitted to assert itself against the demands of the Troy tradition as a whole. In other words, it is a matter of the normalization of an exception. Moreover, the exception that causes such discord among the gods appears, on closer examination, to be nothing more than a continuation of the exception that sets the whole poem in motion, for the plan to make the Trojans victorious arises only as a consequence of Agamemnon's initial decision to suspend the normal mechanisms of collective decision making. The Olympian debates thus intersect with Achaean politics in at least two essential ways. In the first place, they showcase the dynamics of *epainos*. At the same time, they address themselves to the task of limiting the consequences of the initial state of exception—of ensuring that the irregular situation created by Agamemnon's unilateralism does not overturn the overall tradition but remains limited in scope.

As an extension of Agamemnon's exceptionalism, Zeus' plan to aid the Trojans in fact transfers the disruptive effects of unilateralism from the Achaean community to Olympus. Immediately after Zeus has formulated this plan, Hera complains of his tendency to chart his own course (*Il.* 1.541–42). But the extent to which the new policy requires a suspension of normal procedures analogous to the one imposed by Agamemnon does not emerge clearly until the plan is actually put into effect, in Book 8. As he is about to engineer the Trojan victory envisioned by Apollo, Zeus convenes an assembly in which he directs the gods not to interfere. His speech is remarkable for the way in which it simultaneously invokes and disables the mechanisms of consensus:

κέκλυτέ μευ πάντές τε θεοὶ πᾶσαί τε θέαιναι,
ὄφρ' εἴπω τά με θυμὸς ἐνὶ στήθεσσι κελεύει.
μήτέ τις οὖν θήλεια θεὸς τό γε μήτέ τις ἄρσην
πειράτω διακέρσαι ἐμὸν ἔπος, ἀλλ' ἅμα πάντες
αἰνεῖτ', ὄφρα τάχιστα τελευτήσω τάδε ἔργα.
ὃν δ' ἂν ἐγὼν ἀπάνευθε θεῶν ἐθέλοντα νοήσω

ἐλθόντ᾽ ἢ Τρώεσσιν ἀρηγέμεν ἢ Δαναοῖσι
πληγεὶς οὐ κατὰ κόσμον ἐλεύσεται Οὔλυμπον δέ·
ἤ μιν ἑλὼν ῥίψω ἐς Τάρταρον ἠερόεντα
τῆλε μάλ᾽, ἧχι βάθιστον ὑπὸ χθονός ἐστι βέρεθρον,
ἔνθα σιδήρειαί τε πύλαι καὶ χάλκεος οὐδός,
τόσσον ἔνερθ᾽ Ἀΐδεω ὅσον οὐρανός ἐστ᾽ ἀπὸ γαίης·
γνώσετ᾽ ἔπειθ᾽ ὅσον εἰμὶ θεῶν κάρτιστος ἁπάντων.
Il. 8.5–17

Hear me, all you gods and goddesses,
so that I may speak what the heart in my chest bids me.
Let no female or male divinity
attempt to contravene my utterance, but approve,
all of you, so that I may swiftly bring these matters to completion.
Whomever I perceive, acting on his own volition apart from the other gods,
going and bringing aid to either Trojans or Danaans,
he will return to Olympus stung by inordinate blows.
Or I will take and cast him into gloomy Tartarus,
the farthest reaches, where there is the deepest abyss beneath the earth,
and iron gates and a bronze threshold,
so far beneath Hades as the heavens are above the earth.
Then you will know how far I exceed all the gods in strength.

In demanding that the gods "approve" (αἰνεῖτ᾽) his plan, Zeus seeks something like *epainos* from his peers.[27] Yet the approval he envisions will be extorted, grounded not in the results of collective deliberation but in the assertion of superior force. Zeus exhibits here an authoritarian streak that is of a piece with Hector's forceful silencing of Pouludamas in Book 18 and Agamemnon's threat of violence against Chryses. Although he pays lip service to the will of the group, he is just as willing to disregard it as these other autocrats, at least when it comes to certain short-term goals. The appeal to *ainos* provides thin cover for a policy that requires a temporary suspension of the rules.

Consensus, of course, cannot be imposed by fiat, as the response of the divine community itself indicates. Zeus' injunction meets with silence, a clear formulaic signal, according to the grammar of reception, that the proposed moratorium on divine intervention will be a failed policy (ὣς ἔφαθ᾽, οἱ δ᾽ ἄρα πάντες ἀκὴν ἐγένοντο σιωπῇ ["thus he spoke, and they were all silent"], *Il.* 8.28). In Book 13, in fact, Poseidon begins offering covert aid to the Achaeans, and the narrator indicates that his efforts, which very nearly cause the action to revert to a story of Achaean victory, represent a real threat to Zeus' plan (*Il.* 13.676–78). Poseidon's designs actually take over the plot in the next book, when Hera temporarily nullifies the *Dios boulē* by seducing Zeus and casting him into a deep sleep. On waking, Zeus must restore events to the course dictated by his will; now that the intransigence of the pro-Achaean party has been laid bare, he must rely even more directly on the threat of raw force, which he deploys against both Hera and Poseidon (*Il.* 15.16–33, 162–65). Poseidon relents, but, crucially, he disputes the validity of Zeus' authoritarian politics by reasserting the mechanisms of consensus as the condition for his compliance: if Zeus should allow his Trojan sympathies to overturn entirely the long-term plan for the destruction of Troy, against the will of the pro-Achaean party (identified in full as comprising, in addition to Poseidon, Athena, Hera, Hermes, and Hephaistos), the result will be a permanent, "incurable" rupture in the divine community (*Il.* 15.212–17). Zeus, meanwhile, directs Apollo to lead the Trojans back to a position of dominance, underscoring once more how Zeus' plan temporarily coincides with the Apolline vision for the poem (*Il.* 15.221–35).[28]

But all of this happens later. Although the hollowness of Zeus' approach is evident from the initial silence of his audience, Book 8 nevertheless presents the appearance of a provisionally workable agreement among the gods. The terms of this pact are made explicit in a brief exchange between Athena and Zeus that provides an important guarantee of temporary solidarity. When the gods as a whole have indicated their dissatisfaction by remaining silent, Athena at last replies that her faction will refrain from direct intervention, as Zeus has demanded, but that they will continue to provide counsel (*boulē*) to the Achaeans, "lest they all perish because of your anger" (*Il.* 8.37). This seems to be a significant modification of the spirit, if not the letter, of Zeus' command, yet his response reveals a surprising openness to accommodation:

θάρσει Τριτογένεια φίλον τέκος· οὔ νύ τι θυμῷ
πρόφρονι μυθέομαι, ἐθέλω δέ τοι ἤπιος εἶναι.
Il. 8.39–40

Take courage, dear child, Trito-born: I have not said this
in earnest, but I wish to be in accord with you.[29]

Why this sudden shift in tone? Does Zeus not intend his threat of violence to be taken seriously? Yet the menacing remarks he subsequently directs to Hera and Poseidon confirm that he earnestly means to impose his will by force if necessary. Athena may have a special claim on Zeus' affections, but the discrepancy is nonetheless jarring. It certainly troubled ancient critics, including Aristarchus, who "athetized" (that is, indicated by means of critical signs his doubt about the Homeric authority of the verses as transmitted in the textual tradition) the entire description of the gods' reactions—from the notice about their collective silence through the end of the exchange between Zeus and Athena (*Il.* 8.28–40)—at least in part on the grounds that the lines were copied from other parts of the poem.[30] One of the passages these ancient critics appear to have had in mind is the last in the triple sequence of divine debates, the discussion over the fate of Hector, where, as we will see in a moment, Zeus' accommodating stance toward Athena marks a true moment of reconciliation and resolution. Here, however, the rapprochement has a narrower scope and a more limited (but nevertheless essential) function. The compromise with Athena secures for Zeus' policy a certain restricted effectiveness, even as the silence of the gods as a group indicates its ultimate limitations. That is to say, it permits the plot to advance for the moment in the direction Zeus has dictated—while unrelieved silence would have forestalled any implementation of Zeus' plan.[31]

THE STABILIZING POWER OF CONFLICT AND DISSENT

The story thus progresses, with interruptions, toward the goal that Zeus and Apollo have envisioned: supremacy in battle for Hector and the Trojans. But when the Achaeans have been reduced to utter helplessness, saved from destruction only by the expediency of sending Patroklos into battle, the promise to Thetis is substantially fulfilled. Once the underlying purpose of the plan for Trojan victory has been achieved, the poem arrives at a kind of crisis point, as the narrative changes course and the divine impulse that controls and frames the plot recalibrates itself. This period of adjustment involves a certain amount of ambivalence. As early as Book 15, Zeus reveals that his long-term plan includes Achilles' return to battle as a result of Patroklos' death, his killing of Hector, and ultimately the sack of Troy (*Il.* 15.64–71); but it is not immediately clear how quickly the *Dios boulē* will shift from the pro-Trojan perspective shared by Apollo to a perspective more congenial to the Achaeans' tutelary gods. There are conflicting signals that remind one of the luffing of sails as a ship comes about: Zeus sends Athena to rally the Achaeans in the battle over Patroklos' corpse because, as the narrator tells us, "his mind had turned" (δὴ γὰρ νόος ἐτράπετ' αὐτοῦ, *Il.* 17.546), but only fifty lines later he again "grants victory" to the Trojans and puts the Achaeans to flight (17.596).[32] Similarly, although Zeus has already declared publicly that the death of Patroklos will compel Achilles to return to battle, nevertheless Iris must approach Achilles "in secret from Zeus and the other gods" when she directs him to mount the ramparts (*Il.* 18.168). Iris' furtiveness might possibly have less to do with Zeus than with Thetis, who has just left the scene after instructing her son not to enter battle until she returns with armor—elsewhere, too, the gods seem particularly cautious about coming between Thetis and her son (cf. *Il.* 24.71–76)—but the effect is the same: although the plotline of Trojan victory has clearly reached its conclusion, there are nevertheless traces of a tension concerning the direction the plot should take going forward.

This tension is formally recognized in the great divine assembly that opens Book 20. Like earlier scenes of assembly on Olympus, this one stands in close relation to political developments among the Achaeans. In particular, it echoes important aspects of the climactic Achaean assembly of Book 19. In both cases we are dealing with a maximally inclusive gathering that brings together even those who have not previously participated in deliberation: every river and nymph answers Zeus' summons, as even the steersmen and quartermasters answer Achilles' (*Il.* 20.7–9; cf. 19.42–44). More importantly, however, like its Achaean counterpart, the divine *agorē* does not produce the kind of restoration of solidarity we might expect, given its position in the narrative. On the contrary, it serves only to underscore the existence of fundamental differences among the gods. Zeus invites the Olympians to participate directly in the fight by bringing aid to whichever of the two sides each god favors (ὅπη νόος ἐστὶν ἑκάστου ["as the mind of each inclines"], *Il.* 20.25). There is no formal group response to Zeus' proposal; the gods simply rush to the battlefield "with a divided heart" (δίχα θυμὸν ἔχοντες, *Il.* 20.32). We can compare the way the Achaean assembly of the previous book concludes without any expression of group sentiment, when the troops simply disperse to prepare for battle. Both scenes minimize the suggestion of collective agreement, emphasizing instead the presence of lingering discord.

The subsequent battle represents the fullest expression of this discord. Pitting pro-Trojan and pro-Achaean gods against each other, it gives free reign to their conflicting impulses. It thereby allows their competing visions for the poem's overall tenor to come into direct conflict. The return of Achilles to the battlefield brings this conflict to a crisis point: the short-term plan of Trojan victory has fashioned the *Iliad* as the epic of Hector's supremacy, but Achilles will inevitably displace him in the economy of glory and redirect the story back toward the long-term goal dictated by tradition, namely, the sack of Troy. The confrontation between these two heroes, then, like the clash between the two divine factions, figures a confrontation between two possible framings of the story, one of which would privilege the Trojans and the other the Achaeans.

Zeus' function in this conflict is to mediate between these two alternatives, for, as he recognizes, one frame cannot be allowed simply to replace the other. If the balance of power shifts too precipitously, if Hector's supremacy is undone by absolute triumph for the Achaeans, the result will be just as untraditional as if the Trojans had been allowed to hold onto their victory: Zeus invites the gods to support their respective protégés precisely because he fears that Achilles "might destroy the wall contrary to destiny [ὑπέρμορον]" (*Il.* 20.30). His words recall the "*nostos* contrary to destiny [ὑπέρμορα]" that nearly results from the paradigmatic crisis of Book 2 (*Il.* 2.155).[33] This is not by coincidence: these two possibilities stand in an important relation. They are inverses of each other, representing the limit cases of the two alternative perspectives embodied in the pro-Achaean and pro-Trojan factions. Both positions, if rendered absolute, would lead to an untraditional outcome. The solution to this apparent double bind lies not in the choice of one or the other alternative but in the maintenance of a kind of dialectical opposition between the two. Conflict is the necessary safeguard for the story's traditional outcome because it places an essential check on each of the two partisan tendencies. Zeus, who remains seated on Olympus, "delighting his mind" with the spectacle of the gods' skirmishing (*Il.* 20.23; cf. 21.388–90), is both the facilitator of this conflict and the agent of its eventual sublimation in the *Dios boulē*, which, on the longest possible view, comprises the destruction of all the heroes, Achaeans and Trojans alike.

When Achilles returns to battle, the divine community plays an essential role in keeping the plot of the *Iliad* in line with the broader Troy tradition. Crucially, that role does not depend on the existence of solidarity among them but on the opposite, an irreconcilable conflict of factional interests. In this sense, the theomachy is, to borrow Carl von Clausewitz's famous phrase, a continuation of Olympian politics by other means: it is an intensification of the distinctive modality of Olympian political culture on display in the divine assembly scenes, where it is the withholding of *epainos*, rather than its positive expression, that sustains the plot. Here and elsewhere the divine community exhibits the practical power of dissent as a controlling force. That power is fundamentally conservative, insofar as it acts as a brake on innovative developments, but it does not for that reason obstruct the forward progress of the action. On the contrary, it guarantees the desired result.

CONSOLIDATION OF THE *DIOS BOULĒ*

The last opportunity to observe the positive aspects of dissent among the gods comes with the third, and final, iteration of the divine council scene. When all the surviving Trojans except Hector have fled to the safety of the city and the gods, "some angry, others exulting in victory" (*Il.* 21.519), have returned to Olympus, Zeus proposes one last exemption from the dictates of fate. As the assembled gods watch Hector flee from his pursuer Achilles, Zeus suggests that they consider the possibility of saving him from the death that awaits him. Athena now takes over from Hera as spokesperson for the opposition, although she retains the words Hera had used in insisting that "we other gods do not all approve [*epaineîn*]" (*Il.* 22.179–81 = 16.441–43). The climactic confrontation between the poem's principal heroes thus prompts a final assertion of the capacity of dissent to reinforce the norm.

This exchange is no mere restatement of familiar themes. The substitution of Athena for Hera is only one of several signs that this scene marks an important step forward, toward the resolution of the tensions that have divided the divine community, and Zeus himself, throughout the poem. In the first place, Zeus now seems remarkably willing to accommodate his interlocutor's interests without any residue of ambivalence. Echoing the words he addressed to Athena in Book 8, Zeus declares his readiness to renounce entirely any trace of disagreement with his daughter:

θάρσει Τριτογένεια φίλον τέκος· οὔ νύ τι θυμῷ
πρόφρονι μυθέομαι, ἐθέλω δέ τοι ἤπιος εἶναι·
ἔρξον ὅπῃ δή τοι νόος ἔπλετο, μὴ δ' ἔτ' ἐρώει.
Il. 22.183–85

Take courage, dear child, Trito-born: I have not said this
in earnest, but I wish to be in accord with you.
Do as your mind bids you, and delay no longer.

In Book 8, these conciliatory words concealed the bare-knuckled realities of Zeus' politics of force. Here, however, they mark a genuine accommodation— more, even, since Zeus effectively hands control of the poem over to his daughter, whose own *noos* will now direct the course of events. Does this amount to an abdication of the *Dios boulē*? Hardly, when one considers the particularly close bond that links Zeus to his daughter in the broader epic and mythological traditions. As Sheila Murnaghan has indicated, Athena's position in the divine hierarchy is defined by her role as proponent of Zeus' power; her birth from Zeus' head represents an essential confirmation of his supremacy. She is so closely bound to the workings of Zeus' rule that, in the *Odyssey,* her *noos* doubles for the will of Zeus as the poem's guiding principle.[34] This is not to say that the will of Zeus is wholly irrelevant to the development of that poem; on the contrary, the *Odyssey's* narrator seems at pains to stress the extent to which Zeus' will and Athena's converge.[35] In the *Iliad,* too, Zeus recognizes the "plans of Athena" as an essential component of his own long-term vision for the outcome of the war. When he reveals to Hera the content of his *boulē* in Book 15, Zeus states that after the death of Hector—that is, after the end of our *Iliad*—he will bring it about that the Achaeans "continuously pursue [the Trojans] from the ships until they take steep Ilion through the plans of Athena [Ἀθηναίης διὰ βουλάς]" (*Il.* 15.69–71).[36] This eventual merging of Zeus' will with Athena's "plans" constitutes a return to a normal situation of mutual cooperation, a situation to which the *Iliad,* as in so many other respects, represents an exception. Zeus' endorsement of Athena's *noos* in Book 22 is a precursor to and incremental step toward the restoration of the norm.

If Athena ideally doubles for or reinforces the will of Zeus, then her reconciliation with him points as well to the consolidation of those conflicting impulses that have hitherto seemed to divide Zeus from himself. Gone from the debate over Hector are the earlier intimations of Zeus' internal conflicts, his "unwilling heart" and "divided *thumos.*" To be sure, Zeus expresses regret at Hector's imminent demise (*Il.* 22.168–73), but simple regret is a far cry from the mutually contradictory impulses he gave voice to earlier. "Affective dissonance" is mitigated, if not eliminated entirely. Zeus' lack of ambivalence corresponds to the outcome of the discussion, which effectively puts to rest the tension between the poem's pro-Trojan and pro-Achaean tendencies. By upholding the necessity of Hector's death, the divine community subordinates the story of Hector's success, which represents a brief and localized exception to the broad arc of the Trojan War, to the story of Achilles, and ultimately to the story of Achaean victory. It must be stressed that this decision does not entirely refocus the *Iliad* on Achilles and his compatriots: ending as it does with Hector's funeral and three songs of lament in praise of him, the *Iliad* remains, to some degree, the poem of Hector's glory. But the decision to require his death sets an uncontestable limit on the pro-Trojan policy that has threatened to overturn the fated course of events ever since Zeus reluctantly incorporated it into his own plan with his promise to Thetis in Book 1. Zeus can emerge from the debate without any trace of ambivalence because this final testing of the *Dios boulē* produces an unambiguous vision of the relationship between Hector's story and the wider tradition.

Two important preceding episodes have prepared the way for the emergence of this clarity and the political rapprochement that supports it. Both exploit the encounter between Achilles and a representative of the Trojan side—first Aeneas and then the river god Skamandros—to address some aspect of the tension between Achilles' story and that of the Trojans, whose success Achilles' wrath has temporarily secured. At the same time, they showcase signs of an incipient divine consensus in favor of an accommodation that reconciles the poem's conflicting tendencies. Together, they describe a two-step movement toward resolution in which the Trojans are first granted a version of the redemption for which their proponents hunger, but the priority of Achilles' claim is subsequently reinforced.

The first god to act on Zeus' invitation to take direct action in the war is Apollo, who promptly engineers a duel between Achilles and Aeneas. Aeneas' approach causes some anxiety for Hera, who argues to Athena and Poseidon that they must intervene, either to turn Aeneas back at once or to stand by Achilles, so that he may feel confident of the gods' support (*Il.* 20.119–31). Poseidon, however, advocates provisional noninvolvement—uncharacteristically, for he has previously demonstrated his willingness to take up Hera's call to action (in the *Dios apatē* of Book 14). Now, he declares his readiness to intervene on behalf of Achilles only if the latter's efforts encounter actual obstruction from Apollo or Ares (20.133–43). In the meantime, he is content to await the outcome of the conflict as a spectator, and the other gods, including Apollo and Ares, follow suit. As the two divine factions take their seats on opposite sides of the battlefield, they are said to be "contriving *boulai*" (20.153–54): the narrative thus presents the confrontation between Achilles and a character who, as we will see, qualifies as a double for Hector as a confrontation between competing divine *boulai*.

The confrontation eventually produces a conflict between contradictory poetic and formulaic norms in the subsequent battle narrative. Both Achilles and Aeneas have tradition on their side: poetic destiny requires that each must survive the *Iliad* in order to play the part vouchsafed to him by extra-Iliadic tradition.[37] Their engagement on the battlefield thus gives rise to a kind of impasse, which eventually leads to a breakdown of formulaic conventions. After they have exchanged spear casts, Aeneas prepares to strike Achilles with a large stone he has picked up from the plain. According to the pattern established by similar encounters elsewhere in the poem, such a blow should lead to a decisive victory for Aeneas.[38] But this the *Iliad* obviously cannot allow, even if that means overriding the demands of Aeneas' own traditional glory. Rewriting Iliadic battle conventions, the narrator signals that Achilles' armor would have, in fact, warded off the blow and Achilles would have then dispatched Aeneas with his sword (*Il.* 20.289–90)—if not for the timely intervention of Poseidon, who acts to circumvent the breach of narrative protocols that must inevitably result from the fatal clash of two figures programmed, so to speak, for victory. What is remarkable is that it is Poseidon and not Apollo—Poseidon, who has said that he is prepared to intercede only to support Achilles in the case of interference from the pro-Trojan faction—who now intervenes *on behalf of Aeneas.* The sea god spirits him away to the farthest corner of the battlefield, enjoining him to avoid Achilles at all cost but to fear no other Achaean warrior (20.321–39).

From the start of this episode, Aeneas has been presented as a substitute for Hector, someone who appears on the scene in place of the true object of Achilles' wrath:

αὐτὰρ Ἀχιλλεὺς
Ἕκτορος ἄντα μάλιστα λιλαίετο δῦναι ὅμιλον
Πριαμίδεω· τοῦ γάρ ῥα μάλιστά ἑ θυμὸς ἀνώγει
αἵματος ἆσαι Ἄρηα ταλαύρινον πολεμιστήν.
Αἰνείαν δ᾽ ἰθὺς λαοσσόος ὦρσεν Ἀπόλλων . . .
Il. 20.75–79

But Achilles
was especially eager to enter the fray against Hector
the son of Priam, for his heart bid him to sate Ares,
the fierce warrior, with the blood of this man above all.
But Apollo, who drives the hosts, stirred Aeneas against him . . .

With Poseidon's decision to step in, the forward-looking connections to Achilles' eventual encounter with Hector become even more evident. Before taking action, Poseidon poses the question of Aeneas' fate to his companions, Athena and Hera, as a matter for discussion. His words echo proleptically the speech Zeus makes when suggesting the possibility of saving Hector, from the initial ὦ πόποι ("alas," *Il.* 20.293; cf. 22.168) to the recollection of past sacrifices (20.298–99; cf. 22.170–72). He seems almost to speak for Zeus, to represent his point of view, arguing on the basis not only of destiny but also of Zeus' affection for the line of Dardanos (20.302–8). As in the later debate, Hera demurs from supporting the proposal. She does not veto it, however, but simply leaves it to Poseidon to act as he sees fit. Poseidon is thus put into the unexpected position of being able to fulfill in reality the wish for Trojan deliverance that Zeus three times expresses. With the saving of Aeneas, a staunch member of the pro-Achaean faction crosses party lines to actualize the most fervent desire of Troy's supporters. The scene is a kind of wish fulfillment that finds a place for limited Trojan favoritism even in the context of a general outlook that insists on the priority of Achilles.

At the start of the episode, Hera was concerned that, unless Achilles should "hear from the voice of the gods" that he enjoys divine support, he would experience fear "when some god approaches him in battle" (Il. 20.129–31). Her prescient remark forges a direct link to Achilles' encounter with the river god Skamandros in the next book. Unable to escape from the god's watery toils, Achilles experiences a true crisis of fear. Desperation leads him, as he prays to Zeus, to call into question the most fundamental principles of the Iliad's plot:

Ζεῦ πάτερ ὡς οὔ τίς με θεῶν ἐλεεινὸν ὑπέστη
ἐκ ποταμοῖο σαῶσαι· ἔπειτα δὲ καί τι πάθοιμι.
ἄλλος δ' οὔ τίς μοι τόσον αἴτιος Οὐρανιώνων,
ἀλλὰ φίλη μήτηρ, ἥ με ψεύδεσσιν ἔθελγεν·
ἥ μ' ἔφατο Τρώων ὑπὸ τείχεϊ θωρηκτάων
λαιψηροῖς ὀλέεσθαι Ἀπόλλωνος βελέεσσιν.
ὥς μ' ὄφελ' Ἕκτωρ κτεῖναι ὃς ἐνθάδε γ' ἔτραφ' ἄριστος·
τώ κ' ἀγαθὸς μὲν ἔπεφν', ἀγαθὸν δέ κεν ἐξενάριξε·
νῦν δέ με λευγαλέῳ θανάτῳ εἵμαρτο ἁλῶναι
ἐρχθέντ' ἐν μεγάλῳ ποταμῷ ὡς παῖδα συφορβόν,
ὅν ῥά τ' ἔναυλος ἀποέρσῃ χειμῶνι περῶντα.

Il. 21.273–83

Father Zeus—that none of the gods has undertaken to save wretched me
from the river! Thereafter I would suffer whatever may come.
No other of the Ouranians bears so much responsibility for my plight
as my dear mother, who led me astray with falsehoods:
she said that I would perish beneath the armored Trojans' wall,
by the swift arrows of Apollo.
Would that Hector had killed me, the best of those raised here:
then a noble man would have slain me, and despoiled a noble man.
But now it is my fate to perish by a miserable death,
hemmed in by the great river like a young swineherd
whom a swollen watercourse sweeps away when he crosses it in winter.

Achilles' anguished plea amounts to a repudiation of his own role in the Iliad. Not only does he denounce his mother, who does in fact bear responsibility for the situation, to the extent that her request to Zeus is the mainspring of the epic's action, but he even goes so far as to wish that he might be killed by the very man he is fated to vanquish. It is as if the demonstration of divine favor for Aeneas has, as Hera feared, caused Achilles to doubt the part allotted to him in the story of the *Iliad*—to the point that he is actually willing to resign that part to his archantagonist.

The crisis requires some countervailing indication of divine will that can reassure Achilles—and perhaps, on some level, the audience as well—that his position in the story remains secure. Poseidon and Athena respond immediately to his prayer by appearing before him to provide the in-person encouragement Hera had previously suggested. Speaking for the pair, Poseidon declares their support and dictates to Achilles the part he is to play in the next two books:

Πηλεΐδη μήτ' ἄρ τι λίην τρέε μήτέ τι τάρβει·
τοίω γάρ τοι νῶϊ θεῶν ἐπιταρρόθω εἰμὲν
Ζηνὸς ἐπαινήσαντος ἐγὼ καὶ Παλλὰς Ἀθήνη·
ὡς οὔ τοι ποταμῷ γε δαμήμεναι αἴσιμόν ἐστιν,
ἀλλ' ὅδε μὲν τάχα λωφήσει, σὺ δὲ εἴσεαι αὐτός·
αὐτάρ τοι πυκινῶς ὑποθησόμεθ' αἴ κε πίθηαι·
μὴ πρὶν παύειν χεῖρας ὁμοιΐου πολέμοιο
πρὶν κατὰ Ἰλιόφι κλυτὰ τείχεα λαὸν ἐέλσαι
Τρωϊκόν, ὅς κε φύγῃσι· σὺ δ' Ἕκτορι θυμὸν ἀπούρας
ἂψ ἐπὶ νῆας ἴμεν· δίδομεν δέ τοι εὖχος ἀρέσθαι.
Il. 21.288–97

Son of Peleus, do not be overly anxious and do not fear anything,
for you have two such divine helpers in us—
with the *epainos* of Zeus—myself and Pallas Athena.
It is not fated for you to perish in the river;
he will soon withdraw, and you yourself will know it.
But we will give you sound counsel, if you will heed it:
do not rest your hands from impartial war
until you drive the Trojan host, all who flee, back to the famous walls
of Ilion. But when you have wrested from Hector his life,
go back to the ships: we grant you the winning of glory.

Having previously intervened on behalf of Trojan interests, Poseidon now reaffirms his commitment to Achilles. As in the case of Aeneas, he draws attention to the fact that his actions are in accord with the wishes of Zeus: for the second time we observe the manifestation of an accord that cuts across the gods' fac-tional divisions. That accord can even be characterized as a consensus, since Zeus is said to "express *epainos*" (ἐπαινήσαντος, 21.290).

The formulation is extraordinary: only here in the Homeric corpus does the verb *epaineîn* take as its subject an individual rather than a group. What are we to make of this unique "consensus of one"? Two considerations account for the remarkable phraseology. In the first place, it must be remembered that Zeus is no ordinary individual. As I demonstrated earlier in this chapter, his psychology mirrors the collective sentiments of the gods as a whole. Zeus' personalized expression of *epainos* is therefore not the violation of syntactic and semantic constraints that it might at first appear to be. Insofar as Zeus reflects within him-self the will of the group he represents, his approval can be taken as an indirect indication of an emerging consensus among the gods at large. Moreover, the very obliqueness with which this consensus is signaled becomes intelligible in the context of the general character of Olympian politics. This is the sole in-stance of the *positive* expression of *epainos* among the gods. Yet, as we have seen, the politics of Olympus generally privilege the negative power of the withholding of *epainos*. The gods exert their influence by disrupting or denying consensus. From the point of view of the narrator and his audience, to speak more overtly of a consensus among the gods as a whole would risk misrepresenting the nature of the gods' political practice in the *Iliad*. Projecting that consensus onto Zeus, however, allows the narrative to signal an important moment of collective accord without running into conflict with the general tenor of divine interactions.

Poseidon's message of collective divine support for Achilles provides the nec-essary counterweight for his previous intervention on behalf of Aeneas. By con-firming the place of Achilles in the action underway, *epainos* restores the narrative to a course that might have seemed momentarily undermined by the pro-Trojan gesture of the saving of Aeneas. Taken together, these two scenes perform the important function of regulating the relationship between the pro-Trojan and pro-Achaean points of view that have competed for influence over the Iliadic plot. The Aeneas episode establishes a limited context in which consideration for the Trojans can be acted upon. The encounter with Skamandros subsequently re-affirms the primacy of Achilles within the *Iliad* and thus subordinates all other claims to the primary imperative of his victory over Hector. The two-step narrative sequence reconciles the two competing visions of the *Iliad*'s trajectory by finding a place for both while instituting a clear hierarchy between them. This reconciliation lays the groundwork for the debate over the fate of Hector in Book 22: with a hierarchy in place, Zeus can, if not without regret, nevertheless

without ambivalence accept the death of a beloved Trojan as a necessary consequence of the privilege granted to Achilles.

In this way, these two pivotal scenes provide the framework for the accommodation Zeus is able to arrive at with Athena in the climactic council scene.
They are the crucible through which the poem must pass in order to move from
the "affective dissonance" of the first two iterations of the debate motif (in Books
4 and 16) to the relative harmony and unity of purpose evident in the last. The
crucial step in this process is the establishment of a firm hierarchy of narrative
imperatives that permits the emergence of a *Dios boulē* unencumbered by internal tensions. As a movement from ambivalence and discord to clarity and coherence, this progression follows the fundamental Homeric impulse to reimpose
order in the face of disorder, an impulse that we saw in chapter 4 to be particularly well represented by the paradigmatic narrative of Book 2. At the same
time, the emergence of a clarified divine will coincides with the achievement of
a certain measure of solidarity among the gods, so that the representation of
divine politics can be seen to track the larger-scale pattern of social relationships among the Achaeans, as elucidated in chapter 5: there, too, we see a movement from discord to harmony.

On Olympus as in the Achaean camp, however, that movement never arrives
at its implied endpoint. Among the Achaeans, the realization of a definitive consensus is deferred, displaced onto the flawed *epainos* of the Trojans. Similarly
among the gods, although *epainos* is many times invoked, it is never explicitly
actualized by the group. In fact, the last glimpse the poem offers of the gods in
assembly represents an unmistakable step back from the relative cohesion at-
tained in Book 22. As the gods observe Achilles' mistreatment of Hector's
corpse, a dispute arises, with some gods urging Hermes to "steal" the corpse
from Achilles and others firmly opposing this proposal:

ὣς ὃ μὲν Ἕκτορα δῖον ἀείκιζεν μενεαίνων·
τὸν δ᾽ ἐλεαίρεσκον μάκαρες θεοὶ εἰσορόωντες,
κλέψαι δ᾽ ὀτρύνεσκον ἐΰσκοπον Ἀργειφόντην.
ἔνθ᾽ ἄλλοις μὲν πᾶσιν ἑήνδανεν, οὐδέ ποθ᾽ Ἥρῃ
οὐδὲ Ποσειδάων᾽ οὐδὲ γλαυκώπιδι κούρῃ,
ἀλλ᾽ ἔχον ὥς σφιν πρῶτον ἀπήχθετο Ἴλιος ἱρὴ . . .
Il. 24.22–27

Thus was [Achilles] in his fury abusing glorious Hector,
but the blessed gods felt pity as they looked on him,
and they were bidding the sharp-seeing slayer of Argos to steal the corpse.

This plan pleased all the others, but not Hera

nor Poseidon nor the grey-eyed daughter of Zeus;

they rather maintained the hatred they had from the first for sacred Ilion.

The conflicting preferences of the gods are here expressed by the verb *handanein*, which, as I pointed out in chapter 1, carries distinctly counterconsensual overtones insofar as it signals individualized, as opposed to collective, volition. The absence of cohesive group sentiment is brought home in the subsequent debate, initiated by Apollo after an interval of some twelve days. When the discussion proves inconclusive, Zeus must simply impose a compromise solution (directing Achilles, through Thetis, to accept ransom for the corpse): his decision is executed summarily, without any response formula indicating a collective reaction.[39] This sudden lapse into the politics of individual preference and unilateralism erodes whatever sense of solidarity was established in the debate over Hector. At the same time it returns us to the political climate that dominated at the beginning of the poem, when the divisive preference of Agamemnon, also signaled by the verb *handanein,* unleashed the chain of events that brought us to this point. This is a distinctly closural gesture.[40] Nevertheless, the closure it provides is unsatisfying from the point of view of collective decision making. The *Iliad's* three political communities (Achaean, Trojan, Olympian) seem at various points to be headed for convergence on the ideal represented by *epainos,* yet not one of them arrives there.

All the same, the trajectory of Olympian politics, incomplete though it may be, provides an important indication of where we might look to discover the ultimate resolution of the *epainos* motif. As I have emphasized, the gods, as spectators of events at Troy, are a kind of stand-in for the poem's real-world audience. Their awareness of and reflections on poetic tradition, hypostasized as "fate," point to the existence of a "fourth estate," a fourth community with a stake in the Iliadic narrative: the community of real-world listeners and (later) readers through whose institutions the *Iliad* was transmitted and preserved. Chapter 9 will argue that, by a strategy of displacement analogous to the one that substitutes Trojan *epainos* for the missing Achaean consensus, the *Iliad* projects the ultimate fulfillment of the *epainos* motif onto this fourth community, which bears ultimate responsibility for the Iliadic narrative, just as the gods appear to do within the narrative itself. But first it is necessary to examine the way the poem brings to a close the various thematic arcs I have touched on in this study. Some of the *Iliad's* closural devices are more satisfying than others. These devices are the subject of chapter 8.

PART III

Resolutions

CHAPTER 8

The Return to Normalcy and the Iliad's "Boundless People"

In elucidating the crisis that sets the *Iliad* in motion, I identified several interlocking norms whose violation or suspension defines a state of exception that is more or less coterminous with the *Iliad*'s plot. The most important of these is the norm of collective decision making through *epainos*, but implicated in this are several others, including the compensatory mechanism of *apoina/poinē*, the role of Achilles as exponent of Achaean solidarity, and, at the level of the poem's wording, the formulaic regime by which the facts of Achaean social and political life are expressed. The characteristic Homeric impulse to reimpose regularity on a situation of temporary abnormality demands that the poem's progress toward conclusion be matched by a corresponding progress toward the rehabilitation of these norms. While none of them is fully and completely restored—for reasons that will become clear in the next (and last) chapter—nevertheless, in the poem's final books, each is addressed in a manner that sets it on a more secure and relatively normalized footing.

To anticipate in general terms the argumentation of this chapter: the ransoming of Hector's corpse at the beginning of Book 24 at last reinstitutes a working system of compensation—without, however, restoring the public dimension of that system as it is represented, iconically, on the shield made for Achilles in Book 18. The public dimension of compensation is instead the concern of the funeral games of Book 23, which assign to Achilles a crucial position in the regulation of social relationships. Of particular importance in this connection is the episode of the chariot race, in which the distribution of prizes is bound closely to the poem's final statement of the *epainos* motif. This ultimate instance of *epainos* is faulty from the point of view of the actors involved, but it is constructed in such a way as to restore the rule of *epainos* as both a social and a linguistic norm. Finally, the implications of this reformulation of the rule on the level of the poem's performance and reception are reflected in the *Iliad*'s final scene, the funeral of Hector.

HECTOR'S RANSOM

We saw in the last chapter that the action of Book 24 is framed in terms of a divine community that has regressed to the politics of individual preference, signaled by the verb *handanein*, "please." The resurgence of unilateralism is like the restatement of a musical theme that returns us to the political mood of the poem's beginning. Echoes of Agamemnon's solipsistic commitment to his own preference are to be heard in the objections of Hera, Poseidon, and Athena, and in Zeus' heavy-handed imposition of a solution to the impasse prompted by Achilles' continuing mistreatment of Hector's corpse. Zeus' solution, in turn, calls for the replaying of the event that set the poem in motion—a father's suit to ransom his child—in the hope of resolving harmoniously the dissonance of that opening chord.

Achilles' acceptance of the ransom offered by Priam is the *Iliad*'s ultimate closural gesture.[1] It corrects Agamemnon's willful violation of the established rules of exchange and thus moves us substantially toward the restoration of those essential norms that have been suspended by the state of exception. As Donna Wilson writes, "the successful exchange of *apoina* in Book 24 may be understood to reverse the compounded effects of Chryses' failed offer in Book 1."[2] The most significant of those effects has of course been Achilles' alienation from his community, a circumstance that is elsewhere indexed precisely with reference to the selfsame norms of exchange. In the Embassy, Ajax characterizes Achilles' refusal to accept Agamemnon's gifts and thus to restore the bonds of solidarity as an exception to the general rule epitomized in the fact that "a person accepts *poinē* even from the killer of his dead brother or child; and the killer remains there in the community, having paid much in recompense, while the heart and bold passions of the other, who has received *poinē*, are restrained" (*Il.* 9.632–36). Priam's offer of *apoina*, like the compensation offered by the ambassadors on behalf of Agamemnon, represents another face of the rule put forward by Ajax.

The continuity between Achilles' earlier intransigence and the obstinacy that makes Priam's offer necessary is indirectly suggested by another occur-

rence of the *poinē* motif. As Priam grasps and kisses his hands, Achilles' amaze-
ment is compared to the wonder of those observing an exile who seeks refuge
in a foreign land as a consequence of a murder he has committed in his own
community (*Il.* 24.480–83). This striking "reverse simile"—Achilles is the real
killer, but the simile inverts the relationship between him and Priam with respect to this conspicuous attribute—serves, like similar inversions elsewhere,
to highlight a crucial theme at a climactic moment.[3] In this case, the theme is
that of failed or rejected *poinē:* as Ajax's description of the norm makes clear,
the killer of the simile must seek asylum abroad because the mechanism of
poinē is unavailable or has failed. The relevance of the simile to Priam's situation
lies in the fact that, in a very real sense, it is the failure to accept compensation—or
rather, a sequence of such failures, including, most recently, Achilles' own rejection of the possibility of *apoina* for Hector's corpse (*Il.* 22.345–54)—that now
brings Priam face to face with Achilles. The pivotal role of Patroklos as the middle
term linking Achilles' earlier refusal of compensation from Agamemnon to the
situation that produces Priam's offer of *apoina* is signaled by the same *poinē*
motif: compelled to seek refuge with Peleus after killing a playmate in his native city of Opoeis (*Il.* 23.85–90), Patroklos is likewise brought into connection
with Achilles by the failure or unavailability of *poinē.*

The meeting in Achilles' tent is thus the product, directly or indirectly, of a
number of social dislocations brought about by the foundering of the mechanisms of compensation. By remedying one such dislocation—that is, by securing the return of Hector's corpse for the funerary ritual necessary to accommodate the Trojan community to his loss—the ransom at the same time rehabilitates
the system of compensatory exchange and thus opens the way to a broader restoration of community on both sides. It reinstates a norm that was operative even
for Achilles in the time before the poem's action.[4] More importantly, however,
it triggers for both Achilles and Priam a return to the normal rituals of social
life. Their agreement is punctuated by a sacrificial meal (*Il.* 24.621–27), which
marks the first time Priam has tasted food since the death of Hector (24.641–
42). And while Achilles seems already to have broken his fast—he has evidently
just finished a meal when Priam enters his tent (24.475–76)—nevertheless this
is the first time we observe him participating in the slaughter of animals in connection with rituals of commensality.[5] This return to the ritualized form of the
common meal, which is signaled textually by the restatement of dining formulas that have not been heard since Book 7, is far more significant than the mere
fact of consumption.[6] When urged to participate in a meal in Book 19, Achilles
had divested eating of its social significance by reducing it from a *deipnon,* a

socially meaningful meal, to mere *brōsis*, "food."[7] The meal with Priam, as the concluding act of a social transaction, reinvests the consumption of food with the meaning denied it in the earlier scene; by reinserting Achilles into a working system of social relationships, it provides what was missing in the "reconciliation" with Agamemnon.[8]

Nevertheless, in spite of its obvious social implications, the exchange Achilles transacts with Priam remains remarkably disconnected from collective dynamics. The episode lays considerable stress on the isolation of these two as they negotiate the means to resolve their grief. Priam takes only a single servant with him when he ventures from Troy, and he must leave even that servant outside when he approaches Achilles. Achilles, for his part, is attended by only two servants at the arrival of Priam, who enters unnoticed by all save Achilles. Their meeting is thus presented as an encounter between two individuals cut off from their respective peer groups. Their mutual detachment is not incidental to the way the scene unfolds. Priam's rhetoric relies on an analogy based on decontextualized familial relationships—the analogy between Priam and Achilles' own father. The force of this analogy, the symmetry of its terms, would suffer by the intrusion of collective concerns. If Priam's argument is to have a purchase on Achilles, it is only by virtue of their comparability as individuals and not as members of communities with distinct corporate interests.

Achilles' own rhetoric similarly stresses his autonomy and independence from the collective dynamics that, elsewhere in the poem, have been associated with such agreements. Pressed by Priam to accept the ransom, Achilles replies with an imperious declaration that he is himself minded to release the corpse, at the same time explaining that he recognizes a divine agency behind their meeting:

> μηκέτι νῦν μ' ἐρέθιζε γέρον· νοέω δὲ καὶ αὐτὸς
> Ἕκτορά τοι λῦσαι, Διόθεν δέ μοι ἄγγελος ἦλθε
> μήτηρ, ἥ μ' ἔτεκεν, θυγάτηρ ἁλίοιο γέροντος.
> καὶ δέ σε γιγνώσκω Πρίαμε φρεσίν, οὐδέ με λήθεις,
> ὅττι θεῶν τίς σ' ἦγε θοὰς ἐπὶ νῆας Ἀχαιῶν.
> *Il.* 24.560–64

> Do not now provoke me any more, old man. I am myself minded
> to release Hector to you; and my mother has come to me as a messenger
> from Zeus, she who bore me, the daughter of the old man of the sea.
> And I am well aware, Priam, nor does it escape me,
> that some god has led you here to the swift ships of the Achaeans.

Achilles' emphasis on his own intention, expressed so forcefully here, can be understood as a correction of the behavior of Agamemnon, who had to be compelled to free Chryseis. From another perspective, however, Achilles is asserting a will that is just as free from collective constraint as Agamemnon thought his to be. The only external pressure Achilles recognizes is that of the gods. Of course, there is no opportunity for the Achaeans as a group to express their will regarding the ransoming of Hector's corpse, as they did in the case of Chryseis. But that is just the point. By specifying only his own will and the divine pressure that seems to coincide with it, Achilles' remark emphasizes by omission what is missing from this scene—any involvement of a human community— and the one respect in which this transaction is *not* a correction of Agamemnon's behavior in Book 1. The exchange with Priam may restore the system of *apoina/poinē*, but it has no bearing on the question of collective will.

The arrangement that secures the return of Hector's corpse is a matter of an essentially private agreement between individuals. So too is the twelve-day truce that allows the Trojans to celebrate Hector's funeral. One of the more remarkable features of the ransom episode is the fact that Achilles claims the ability to impose this truce on the Achaeans single-handedly, solely on the basis of his promise to Priam: "It will be as you command," he says to the king, "for I will hold back war for as long as you have indicated" (*Il.* 24.669–70). Once again, the emphasis is on the private transaction of business that could be thought to require collective deliberation and approval. In fact, it is precisely the collective aspect of such a negotiation that comes into view on the other occasion on which arrangements are made for the claiming and burial of corpses, in Book 7. There we see first the Achaeans and then the Trojans discussing in their council and assembly, respectively, the possibility of a temporary truce for the performance of funeral rites (*Il.* 7.323–79).[9] The subsequent request of the Trojan herald Idaios for a formal armistice provides the opportunity for a signal demonstration of Achaean collective sentiment (and of Agamemnon's attitude toward it).[10] This scene clearly looks forward to the meeting of Priam and Achilles in Book 24.[11] Accordingly, it establishes a benchmark against which to measure the divergences of the later episode. By far the most noticeable, and significant, of these is the focus on strictly private relationships, to the exclusion of the collective dynamics the situation seems to call for.[12]

The foregrounding of individual, as opposed to collective, sentiment and the unilateralism of Achilles' promise to impose a truce are of a piece with the dynamics on display in the divine council that opens the book. Although Book 24 clearly resolves certain central themes, nevertheless, with regard to the theme of collective decision making, resolution remains elusive. Absent where we might expect to find it, it must be sought elsewhere. To be sure, it will not be found in the last book of the *Iliad:* there simply are no instances of a decision executed by collective will. There is, however, a profound demonstration of collectivized sentiment in the form of the public celebration of Hector's funeral. The ransom scene may be surprisingly individualistic, but the conclusion of the book puts group dynamics back in the foreground. In this way, the strategy of Book 24 is similar to the overall strategy of the poem: just as the climactic instance of *epainos* is displaced from the Achaeans to the Trojans in Book 18, so too the final expression of communal solidarity is absent from its expected context and resituated among the Trojans. This strategy suggests some broad conclusions about the ultimate community envisioned by the *Iliad;* but before we can begin to elucidate its significance, we must first examine two other, related scenes.

CONFLICT AND COMMUNITY ON THE SHIELD OF ACHILLES

The strangeness of the strictly private nature of Achilles' arrangement with Priam is underscored by means of contrast with earlier scenes: with regard to the negotiation of a truce, by contrast with the agreement made in Book 7, and with regard to the payment of *apoina,* by contrast with the poem's opening scene, in which the acceptance of *apoina* is truly a matter of collective interest. The collective dimension of the *apoina/poinē* system comes across even more clearly in another scene that is crucial for our understanding of the way the poem resolves its central concerns: the dispute over the payment of *poinē* as depicted on the shield made for Achilles in Book 18.

As many have noted, this much-discussed passage bears directly on the situation of Achilles, fitting neatly into the dossier of references to *apoina/poinē* that index his relationships with peers throughout the poem.[13] Here is the text:

λαοὶ δ' εἰν ἀγορῇ ἔσαν ἀθρόοι· ἔνθα δὲ νεῖκος
ὠρώρει, δύο δ' ἄνδρες ἐνείκεον εἵνεκα ποινῆς
ἀνδρὸς ἀποφθιμένου· ὃ μὲν εὔχετο πάντ' ἀποδοῦναι
δήμῳ πιφαύσκων, ὃ δ' ἀναίνετο μηδὲν ἑλέσθαι·
ἄμφω δ' ἱέσθην ἐπὶ ἴστορι πεῖραρ ἑλέσθαι.
λαοὶ δ' ἀμφοτέροισιν ἐπήπυον ἀμφὶς ἀρωγοί·
κήρυκες δ' ἄρα λαὸν ἐρήτυον· οἳ δὲ γέροντες
εἵατ' ἐπὶ ξεστοῖσι λίθοις ἱερῷ ἐνὶ κύκλῳ,
σκῆπτρα δὲ κηρύκων ἐν χέρσ' ἔχον ἠεροφώνων·

τοῖσιν ἔπειτ’ ἤϊσσον, ἀμοιβηδὶς δὲ δίκαζον.

κεῖτο δ’ ἄρ’ ἐν μέσσοισι δύω χρυσοῖο τάλαντα,

τῷ δόμεν ὃς μετὰ τοῖσι δίκην ἰθύντατα εἴποι.

Il. 18.497–508

The people were gathered in the *agorē*. A dispute had arisen
there, and two men were quarreling over the *poinē*
of a man who had died: one claimed the right to pay back all,
pleading before the people, and the other was refusing to take anything;
but both were eager to obtain resolution through a *histōr*.
The people, divided in their sympathies, expressed support for both,
and the heralds restrained them. Meanwhile the elders
sat on polished stones in the sacred circle,
holding in their hands the scepters of the loud-voiced heralds.
To these, then, the litigants rushed, and the elders pronounced judgments one
    after the other.
And in the middle lay two talents of gold,
to give to the one among them who should pronounce the straightest judgment.

In the long history of its interpretation, almost every detail of this description
has been contested.[14] The principal difficulty, which concerns the very nature of
the dispute, centers on the interpretation of lines 499–500. Ought we, following
an opinion recorded in the scholia, to understand these lines as a reference to
an act of payment, alleged by one party (the murderer) to have taken place but
denied by the other?[15] We should then translate, "one was claiming to have paid
all . . . but the other was denying that he received anything," and the issue
would be a simple question of fact: was the *poinē* paid or not? Alternatively, we
may understand the issue as a legal question, that is, as a question of the respective rights of the disputants—the right of the murderer to redeem his own life
by offering compensation, and the right of the victim's family to refuse compensation (and to pursue vengeance instead).[16] In this case, we should translate as I have above, rendering *anainesthai* not as "deny" but as "refuse." I follow the second interpretation because it offers a more convincing explanation of
what is obviously intended to be a matter of complexity: a question of fact would
be easily settled on the testimony of witnesses and anyway would not be likely to
arise in connection with *poinē*, since compensation would, as a rule, be presented publicly precisely in order to establish that the conflict was resolved (as
in the case of Agamemnon's *apoina* in Book 19).[17] Furthermore, in understanding *anainesthai* in the sense of "refuse," I am guided by the semantics and

thematic associations of this key verb as they emerge elsewhere in the poem in connection with Achilles' quarrel with Agamemnon. As Leonard Muellner and others have stressed, one of the arguments in favor of the second interpretation is the degree to which it resonates with the *Iliad*'s central thematic concerns.[18] To my mind, this argument is decisive: if philological and legal considerations cannot conclusively settle the question, we must be guided by the internal evidence of the poem's themes—the same evidence, in fact, that would have shaped ancient understandings of the scene.[19]

The paradigmatic pressure to take *anainesthai* in the sense argued for here stems from the Embassy of Book 9, in which the verb is strategically deployed no fewer than four times in order to characterize Achilles' quarrel with Agamemnon and his rejection of the gifts offered by the ambassadors as a failure of the socially constructive speech designated by the root *an-* (as in *ainesthai* and *ainos*).[20] The power of this episode, with its insistent reuse of the key term *anainesthai*, virtually imposes a congruent interpretation of the scene on Achilles' shield, so that the steadfast refusal of the injured party to accept any amount of compensation parallels Achilles' own refusal. It is no coincidence that Ajax, as one of the ambassadors, appeals to Achilles precisely in terms of the willingness of a murdered man's kinsman to accept *poinē* (*Il.* 9.632–36).

The connection with Book 9 is worth emphasizing because it helps to elucidate the collective dimension of the events depicted on the shield. To designate the disputant's refusal by the verb *anainesthai* is to characterize it as the negation of socially constructive speech, as a denial of an *ainos* that would serve as the basis for a renewed social bond between members of the same community. That such an *ainos* can have broad consequences for the community as a whole is amply demonstrated by the framework of Book 9, in which the struggle to reconcile Achilles and Agamemnon is the linchpin in a wider effort to achieve solidarity in the service of the community's goals, a solidarity that is indexed in terms of the *epainos* motif.[21] That same collective interest is equally evident on the shield, which shows the two disputants pleading not just before a circle of elders but before the assembled community, the *laoi* or *dēmos*.[22] Moreover, *epainos*, as the collective response to a successful resolution of the dispute, can be inferred as the projected outcome of the procedure, even if it is not explicitly specified. The *epainos* of the community is in fact implicit in the relationship between the various groups depicted on the shield.

The *ainos* that would reconcile the two parties to the dispute is presumably to be sought from the elders (*gerontes*), each of whom in turn delivers his judgment on the case. Any of these pronouncements is potentially the *ainos* that will repair the rift created by the murder; for the speaker who attains this mark, who "pronounces the straightest judgment," two measures of gold are set down as a reward.[23] But who is to decide which judgment meets the criterion—who is to judge the judges? A number of proposals have been offered, and all seem at least conceivable.[24] Once again, however, we must be guided by the framework established by the poem itself. If Book 9 points the way, it seems clear that a successful resolution will ideally culminate in communal approval for the result, in an *epainos* that will reconfirm the solidarity of the group. In Book 9, of course, the Achaeans do not achieve this ideal—they must settle for a limited solidarity in the face of Achilles' continued intransigence—but the outlines of the preferred outcome are nevertheless discernible. In any case, even apart from the paradigm of Book 9, the poem's general decision-making apparatus demands that any decision having lasting consequences for the community must ultimately rest on the *epainos* of the group. From this perspective, the most "Iliadic" understanding of the passage would be to assume that the "straightest judgment"— the superlative *ainos*—will be confirmed by the *epainos* of the *dēmos* and that this *epainos* will determine the recipient of the prize.[25]

It is worth noting that, as the final detail in the description of the scene, the awarding of the two talents of gold receives a certain emphasis. This emphasis is entirely appropriate if the award implies the *epainos* motif, a motif that is intricately bound up with the *Iliad*'s teleology. The notice about the prize would then come last not because it is an ancillary, add-on detail but, on the contrary, because it represents the fulfillment of the collective dynamics encapsulated on the shield.

Admittedly, one of the more remarkable features of the scene is the degree to which the roles of the various speakers and observers in determining the result of the process are allowed to remain obscure. It is almost as if there were a positive reluctance to clarify the precise relationship between the crowd, the elders, and the contending parties. Moreover, as Muellner has pointed out, on the basis of the use of *mēden*, "nothing"—the only occurrence of this word, an "epic obscenity," in the Homeric corpus—"we can be certain" that the deceased's relative "will take *absolutely nothing*."[26] That is, in spite of being structured in such a way as to imply the ultimate decision-making power of the community as a whole, the description seems nevertheless to suggest the autonomy (or at least pretended autonomy) of the aggrieved party, who appears determined to decide the issue for himself, regardless of what should transpire among the *gerontes* or *dēmos*.

This divergence of individual will and collective dynamics, however, should not automatically be understood as an indication of the limited capacity of the community to exercise decision-making power. Indeed, it would be rash to infer from this scene any kind of normative vision of a system of justice. The shield description is clearly informed by the thematic structure of the *Iliad*, which, as we have seen time and again, centers not on the norm but on the exception. In the broader context of the poem, the discrepancy between individual and collective and the general reticence of the description as to the actual means of resolving the conflict can be seen as components of a design, shared by the shield and the poem alike, that points to the importance of collective will but defers its ultimate realization.

In fact, the ambiguous relationship between the self-assertion of the deceased's kinsman and the will of the community is homologous to the manner in which the poem as a whole concludes: in spite of an overall emphasis on the importance of the group, the crisis over Hector's corpse—a crisis of determining the appropriate extent of revenge—is resolved by an exchange that is inflected as a purely autonomous act on the part of Achilles.[27] The shield description itself points to this homology by framing the quarrel in terms of the disputants' desire "to obtain a limit" (πεῖραρ ἑλέσθαι, *Il.* 18.501). In one sense, the *peirar*, "limit," is simply the limit on the penalty, that is, a determination as to whether the murderer should be able to pay *poinē* or should be subject to revenge, and also as to the appropriate extent of either *poinē* or revenge.[28] At the same time, the *peirar* is also the "limit" to be set on the dispute itself and on the violence implicated in it: both parties seek an end to their quarrel, but for one that end is to be sought through the continuation, in revenge, of the violence that produced it. So, too, at the end of the *Iliad*, the question is whether the poem's events will be brought to a close through the mechanisms of exchange or whether they will continue as Achilles relentlessly pursues revenge for the death of Patroklos. By explicitly posing the problem of limits, the shield description gestures unmistakably toward the poem's ultimate closural strategy.[29]

The connection thus established can serve as an invitation to reflect on the similarities between both scenes—most notably the willful self-assertion of the protagonists—as well as their differences. The scene on the shield places the search for closure at the center of expanding circles of collective interest, while the reconciliation between Priam and Achilles adopts a much narrower focus, screening out, so to speak, the broader, collective dynamics that carry so much weight in the poem. In this way, the shield highlights, by contrast, what is missing from the poem's conclusion. Yet it is not necessarily more complete for including what the ransom scene lacks; at least, it comes no closer to resolving the discrepancy between individual and collective will. Frozen into a posture of refusal, the murdered man's relative seems permanently to deny the possibility of any acceptable *ainos* from the elders or *epainos* from the people. As a result, an ultimate resolution, in the form of an agreement supported by the community as a whole, remains just as elusive for the figures on the shield as it does for Achilles.

THE CHARIOT RACE AND THE RULE OF *EPAINOS*

If the dispute pictured on the shield evokes by implicit means the collective dimension of compensation that is missing from Achilles' encounter with Priam, a subsequent episode from the funeral games of Book 23 makes it explicit by correlating the distribution of prizes with the *epainos* of the group. The chariot race—the first and by far the most elaborately narrated of the many athletic contests conducted in honor of Patroklos—presents a number of similarities to the shield's depiction of a juridical quarrel. Individual points of connection have often been noted, including the presence of a *histōr*, "judge," in both scenes, comparable roles for the heralds as regulators of disputes, the prominence of the prizes, and other instances of common themes or terminology.[30] We might add as well that the *agōn* of Book 23 is, like the quarrel on the shield, a contest that has arisen in connection with "a man who has died." Of greater significance, however, than these isolated motifs is a broad similarity in terms of the configuration of the actors: both scenes place the competition between contestants at the center of a large group of spectators, who correspond in each case to the community as a whole, and both scenes devote attention to the community's investment in the outcome of the contest. It would be artificial to construct a strict analogy between the two scenes, especially since the chariot race is an extremely complex episode that incorporates a number of embedded conflicts, each presenting certain similarities to the shield's depiction. Nevertheless, those similarities are a sufficient indication that, in spite of its additional complexities, the description of the chariot race is shaped by comparable thematic pressures.

Since both the scene on the shield and the chariot race involve multiple groups of actors, we must first of all establish some points of comparison. The quarrel depicted on the shield involves two related contests: as the disputants vie with one another to generate support for their positions among the elders and the people, the *gerontes* compete to formulate the "straightest" judgment. So, too, the chariot race juxtaposes the contest between the racers themselves with other, related conflicts. First, during the race, we find Idomeneus and Oilean Ajax quarreling over the front-runner (*Il.* 23.450–98); then Antilokhos arguing with Achilles over his decision to award the second prize to Eumēlos (23.540–54); and, finally, we witness a quasi-juridical dispute between Antilokhos and Menelaus over the tactics used by the former in the race (23.566–613).

One might be tempted to correlate the dispute between the murderer and his victim's kinsman directly with the race itself, since these two contests appear to provide the focal points for their respective episodes. On the basis of simple numerical formalism, however, the charioteers (numbering five in total) should properly be compared with the *gerontes* (likewise more than two), leaving the pairings of Idomeneus and Ajax, Antilokhos and Achilles, and Menelaus and Antilokhos as the correlates for the shield's pair of litigants. This configuration produces a particularly clear correspondence in the case of the first dispute to arise in the course of the episode. As the charioteers turn onto the home stretch, Idomeneus declares that he can make out Diomedes in front, and that Eumēlos, who had held the lead going into the turn, must have suffered some reverse. Ajax immediately takes him to task for what he believes is a mistaken observation, to which Idomeneus responds by proposing a wager, with the result to be adjudicated by Agamemnon as *histōr* (*Il.* 23.485–87). Both the wager and the appeal to a *histōr* recall the situation of the dual adversaries on the shield.[31] Meanwhile, it is the outcome of the competition among the charioteers that will ultimately determine the winner of the wager, just as, in the context of the shield, the contest among the *gerontes* ought to dictate the result of the dispute.[32]

In the event, the wager is never formally concluded. Achilles, admonishing the pair for their quarrelsomeness, instructs them simply to wait and see for themselves how the race will conclude (*Il.* 23.490–98). As a result, there is no opportunity to observe the precise mechanism by which the matter would have otherwise played itself out; in particular, there is no opportunity for the community as a whole, the widest circle of spectators, to demonstrate its function in the process. The community comes into view only after the race is concluded, when the distribution of prizes must be determined. As we will see, the assembled Achaeans then seem to play an essential role in ratifying the awards proposed by Achilles. This role corresponds remarkably well to the function imputed to the assembled *laoi* in the description of the shield: there, too, the community appears to bear ultimate responsibility for the awarding of a prize to the one of the *gerontes* who "pronounces the straightest judgment."

Discussions of the part played by the chariot race and the funeral games as a whole in the *Iliad*'s narrative economy often focus on the way the awarding of prizes works to resolve certain central tensions and conflicts. For Wilson, for instance, the funeral games represent the restoration of a "fluid" ranking system bestowing honor and rewards in recognition of demonstrated achievement, a system that had been disabled by Agamemnon in favor of a "fixed" system that guaranteed his preeminence regardless of his personal excellence.[33] When it comes to the chariot race in particular, it is possible to discern in the awarding of prizes a signal improvement over the economics of the confrontation between Agamemnon and Achilles in Book 1. When Agamemnon initially demanded a substitute prize in place of Chryseis, Achilles had pointed out that the lack of an available store of undistributed goods made such a solution impossible:

Ἀτρεΐδη κύδιστε φιλοκτεανώτατε πάντων,
πῶς γάρ τοι δώσουσι γέρας μεγάθυμοι Ἀχαιοί;
οὐδέ τί που ἴδμεν ξυνήϊα κείμενα πολλά·
ἀλλὰ τὰ μὲν πολίων ἐξεπράθομεν, τὰ δέδασται,
λαοὺς δ᾽ οὐκ ἐπέοικε παλίλλογα ταῦτ᾽ ἐπαγείρειν.
ἀλλὰ σὺ μὲν νῦν τῆνδε θεῷ πρόες· αὐτὰρ Ἀχαιοὶ
τριπλῇ τετραπλῇ τ᾽ ἀποτείσομεν, αἴ κέ ποθι Ζεὺς
δῷσι πόλιν Τροίην εὐτείχεον ἐξαλαπάξαι.
Il. 1.122–29

Son of Atreus, most glorious, most acquisitive of all,
how shall the great-hearted Achaeans give you a prize?
Nowhere do we have a store of common goods;
those that we pillaged from the cities have been distributed,
and it is not seemly for the people to collect them back again.
Release now this girl to the god; we Achaeans
will recompense you three- and four-fold, if ever Zeus
grants us to sack the well-walled city of Troy.

Unsatisfied with Achilles' proposal for future compensation, Agamemnon had felt compelled to appropriate Achilles' rightful prize for himself. The situation that arises in the aftermath of the chariot race is altogether similar. When Eumēlos' mishap deprives him of an expected victory, Achilles proposes adjusting the set order of awards so that the mare technically won by Antilokhos with his second-place finish should go to the one whom even Achilles acknowledges as the "best" (ἄριστος, *Il.* 23.536).[34] In other words, Achilles wishes, like Agamemnon earlier, to revoke a prize from its rightful owner and award it instead to one who enjoys a mere claim to excellence, without having demonstrated it.[35] Now, however, Antilokhos is able to propose the solution that the lack of surplus goods earlier made impossible: he suggests that, since Achilles possesses a large store of valuables, he should draw on this reserve in order to provide a supernumerary prize for Eumēlos (23.548–52). Achilles immediately adopts Antilokhos' suggestion, and a crisis that could easily have led to more serious conflict is resolved.[36]

In all these ways, then, the distribution of prizes emerges as a central component of the strategies for achieving resolution that are on display in Book 23. Prizes for athletic competition are, of course, a form of compensatory exchange, so that these strategies can be understood as tying in directly with the *apoina/poinē* motif as it is developed in the poem. The poetic diction of a related tradition provides an interesting point of comparison. In Pindar's epinician poetry, the terms *apoina* and *poinē*, both conveying the general sense of "reward," are frequently used to designate the victory celebration, which is conceptualized as compensation for the tremendous expenditure, physical suffering, and personal risk sustained by the athlete.[37] The relatively greater specialization of Homeric diction, according to which these terms are associated exclusively with ransom and blood-price, respectively, precludes their use in the context of the athletic competitions in Book 23, but Pindar's cognate tradition demonstrates that recompense for athletic victory belongs to the same conceptual sphere as other forms of compensatory exchange.

Pindaric poetry also sheds valuable light on the persistent association we have observed between the themes of compensation, on the one hand, and the socially constructive speech designated by *ainos* and *epainos*, on the other. Pindaric poetry routinely designates the epinician ode itself as the most important form of compensation earned by the victor. Pindar's odes repeatedly correlate the victor's *apoina* or *poinē* with the song of praise performed in his honor, as in *Nemean* 7.14–16:

ἔργοις δὲ καλοῖς ἔσοπτρον ἴσαμεν ἑνὶ σὺν τρόπῳ,
εἰ Μναμοσύνας ἕκατι λιπαράμπυκος
εὕρηται ἄποινα μόχθων κλυταῖς ἐπέων ἀοιδαῖς.

We know of only one way to hold a mirror up to fine deeds:
if, by the grace of Mnemosyne with her splendid headdress,
one finds a recompense for toils in glorious song. (Trans. D. Svarlien)

Since *ainos* and *epainos* (along with the related verbs *aineîn* and *epaineîn*) both function within the conventions of Pindaric diction as designators of epinician poetry, this correlation results in the convergence of compensation and socially dynamic speech (or song), a convergence that finds direct expression in *Olympian* 7 when the speaker declares that he has come

εὐθυμάχαν ὄφρα πελώριον ἄνδρα παρ᾽ Ἀλ-
    φειῷ στεφανωσάμενον
αἰνέσω πυγμᾶς ἄποινα . . .
O. 7.15–16[38]

so that I may praise [*aineîn*] the straight-fighting, towering man who had himself
    crowned on the banks of the Alpheios
as a recompense for his boxing . . . (Trans. D. Svarlien, adapted)

That is to say, Pindaric poetry presents as a unity two motifs that appear closely interrelated but nevertheless distinct in Homeric tradition. Compensation and the social force of (*ep*)*ainos* may reinforce or imply one another in Homer (as in Book 9 or the depiction of the dispute on Achilles' shield), but for Pindar they are simply two different aspects of the epinician moment.[39]

This convergence is made possible by the fact that the language of *ainos* and the language of *apoina/poinē* are really two different ways of speaking about the function of epinician poetry. As Leslie Kurke has demonstrated in her examination of epinician poetics, one of the principal aims of Pindar's odes is to negotiate the anxieties surrounding the reintegration of the victor into his community.[40] The terms *ainos* and *epainos* are eminently appropriate to such a project insofar as they pertain to the kind of efficacious speech that constructs social bonds. *Apoina* and *poinē*—which, as "ransom" and "blood-price," designate the mechanisms by which the disruptive effects of social dislocations (kidnapping, capture, or death) are put to rest—point to the same epinician function of building or restoring solidarity. In Kurke's words, "most significant for our understanding of *apoina* imagery in Pindar is its socially reintegrative function. We must not underestimate the force a term like *apoina* carries with it from its proper context. It must imply to its audience a critical exchange that rescues the community from the threat of internal violence and disintegration."[41] *Apoina* imagery characterizes the ode precisely as an object in an exchange. Since the material of exchange is speech, however, *apoina* and *ainos* converge. In the *Iliad*, meanwhile, *apoina* and *poinē* are always transacted in concrete goods, so they must remain distinct from *ainos*.

They are nevertheless closely connected to the social dimension of speech, for, as much as in the Pindaric system, *apoina/poinē* and *ainos* designate two related aspects of a single social process. Thus, on Achilles' shield, the refusal of *poinē* on the part of the murdered man's kinsman is at the same time a denial of *ainos* (as signaled by the verb *anainesthai*); the same can be said for Achilles' refusal of *apoina* in Book 9 (indicated by the same verb). In the chariot race, where compensatory exchange is such a prominent motif, so too is *ainos;* the two seem to go hand in hand, as reciprocal components of a single social equation. Antilokhos, urging Achilles to draw on his store of valuables, uses the notion of *ainos* to index the solidarity-enhancing result he expects from his proposed solution to the distributive crisis:

ἔστί τοι ἐν κλισίῃ χρυσὸς πολύς, ἔστι δὲ χαλκὸς
καὶ πρόβατ᾽, εἰσὶ δέ τοι δμῳαὶ καὶ μώνυχες ἵπποι·
τῶν οἱ ἔπειτ᾽ ἀνελὼν δόμεναι καὶ μεῖζον ἄεθλον
ἠὲ καὶ αὐτίκα νῦν, ἵνα σ᾽ <u>αἰνήσωσιν</u> Ἀχαιοί.

Il. 23.549–52

You have much gold in your tent, and bronze
and livestock, and you have slave women and solid-hooved horses:
drawing from these give him an even greater prize
than the one you have offered now, so that the Achaeans may <u>praise</u> [*aineîn*] you.

And the episode as a whole concludes with an exchange of a prize for *ainos.* Achilles presents the one remaining prize, which was left unawarded by the adoption of Antilokhos' expedient, to Nestor as a kind of honorary compensation for the athletic competition from which the latter's age bars him (*Il.* 23.620–23). Nestor responds with a lengthy speech that the last line of the episode designates precisely as an *ainos* (23.652).[42]

In spite of this general interest in *ainos*, the collective dimension—*epainos*—finds direct expression only when the distributive system as a whole comes under scrutiny. Achilles' proposal to "correct" the order of awards so that the "best" man, Eumēlos, may take the second prize despite his last-place finish meets at first with the approval of the assembled Achaeans:

ὣς ἔφαθ᾽, οἳ δ᾽ ἄρα πάντες ἐπήνεον ὡς ἐκέλευε.
καί νύ κέ οἱ πόρεν ἵππον, ἐπήνησαν γὰρ Ἀχαιοί,
εἰ μὴ ἄρ᾽ Ἀντίλοχος μεγαθύμου Νέστορος υἱὸς
Πηλεΐδην Ἀχιλῆα δίκῃ ἠμείψατ᾽ ἀναστάς·
ὦ Ἀχιλεῦ μάλα τοι κεχολώσομαι αἴ κε τελέσσῃς
τοῦτο ἔπος· μέλλεις γὰρ ἀφαιρήσεσθαι ἄεθλον . . .

Il. 23.539–44

Thus he spoke, and all were expressing *epainos* for his proposal.

And now he would have given him [Eumēlos] the horse, for the Achaeans
    expressed their *epainos*,

had not Antilokhos, son of great-hearted Nestor,

risen and answered Achilles son of Peleus with a claim for justice:

"Achilles, I shall be especially angry with you if you bring this word

to completion: for you are about to take away my prize . . ."

These lines—particularly the narrator's explanation that "he would have given
Eumēlos the horse, for the Achaeans expressed their *epainos*"—ascribe to the
community the ability to exercise decisive control over the distributive regime in
a way that recalls the implied role of the community in the scene depicted on
Achilles' shield. And yet it quickly emerges that this apparent consensus is flawed,
since one member of the community—one who has a personal stake in the
outcome—objects to the solution endorsed by the group.[43] Antilokhos' assertion
of his own individual will is evidently sufficient to suspend the force of *epainos*.

Interestingly, the suspension seems permanent: even though all the prizes
are eventually awarded in accordance with Antilokhos' counterproposal, there
is no return to a collective mode of ratification or approval. Instead, the narrative is diverted by a new quarrel that arises between Antilokhos and Menelaus
when the latter accuses the former of executing an unfair maneuver during the
race.[44] And even though Menelaus, in conceding the second-place prize to Antilokhos, will eventually lend a kind of support to *ainos* by denying that he is
apēnēs (*Il.* 23.610–11), he nevertheless behaves in a curiously self-assertive way
himself. At first, in an appeal to the juridical structure represented also on the
shield, he invites the Achaean élite to act as judges; but then, with a sudden reversal, he substitutes his own right to adjudicate for this collective procedure,
declaring that he himself will pronounce a "straight" judgment (23.579–80).
Everything then proceeds as if the allocation of the second-place prize were
strictly a matter of a private dispute between Antilokhos and Menelaus. The
overall effect is strikingly similar to the scene on the shield: in spite of a context
that places considerable emphasis on the force of collective will—first in the
ratification of Achilles' proposal and then in Menelaus' appeal to a group framework for conflict resolution—the narrative nevertheless foregrounds the self-
assertion of individuals. Meanwhile, the power exercised by the community,
while made explicit in a way that it is not on the shield, nonetheless remains in
a suspended state, immanent but unrealized.

Even if it remains unrealized, however, the Achaeans' provisional *epainos* is of critical significance at the broadest level of the poem's architecture. This, the last instance of the verb *epaineîn* in the poem, is the keystone in the *Iliad*'s closural strategy so far as the *epainos* motif is concerned. It is no accident that this final opportunity to depict the dynamics of collective decision making supplies the occasion for a rare metanarrative comment that actually formulates the efficiency of *epainos* as a rule of Homeric discourse. The narrator's explanation that "Achilles would have given Eumēlos the horse, for the Achaeans expressed their *epainos* [ἐπήνησαν]" affirms the norm that *epainos* ought to bring into effect the utterance it ratifies. This gloss on the conventions of Homeric narrative is a corrective, at the metanarrative level, to the ambiguity opened up by the state of exception imposed by Agamemnon in Book 1. It is an attempt to restore the transparency of the formulaic system that frames the practice of politics among the Achaeans by stating its rules explicitly. The restoration of the norms of Homeric language also coincides with a return to (or at least movement toward) normalcy in Achaean social life, for Achilles now appears in an approximation of his true identity as the embodiment of sociality, of *philotēs:* the architect of a distributive system that rectifies the inadequacies evident at the poem's beginning, he intervenes actively to settle disputes among his peers. In this way the funeral games, and especially the chariot race, with its final glimpse of the Achaeans engaged as a community in the direction of events through consensus, achieves what has been wanting since the poem's beginning: a restoration of the implied status quo ante, of the norms as they applied before the state of exception that set the poem in motion.

It is essential to note, however, that this restoration is fully realized only at the metanarrative level. In the world of the poem's dramatic action, *epainos* never regains its proper efficiency; the ability of consensus to shape social and political realities is held in check by the dissent of individuals, as in the shield's depictions. It is only in the frame that surrounds these representations, in the code of Homeric discourse as formulated by the narrator for the benefit of the audience, that we observe the reaffirmation of the rule. If the poem seems to follow a trajectory leading from the violation of the norm to its eventual restoration, that trajectory reaches its fulfillment only in the interaction between the Homeric performer and his audience—that is, at the level of the performance and its reception. Although there is a kind of attenuated resolution of certain themes (Achilles' renewed participation in social life, his acceptance of Priam's ransom), true resolution of the consensus theme occurs not in the world of the poem but in the real-life world of the performer and his audience.

There is a striking resemblance here to the picture drawn by Johannes Haubold in his study of the relationship between the communities represented within the Homeric poems and the historical *polis* communities for which Homeric poetry was performed. For Haubold, the "people" (*laoi*) depicted in the *Iliad* and *Odyssey* represent pre- or protopolitical communities that can be thought of as the ancestors of the historical *poleis*, which, in their festivals and collective rituals, provided a context for the performance of Homeric poetry. The Homeric *laoi* exhibit many features characteristic of their eventual heirs, but they are nevertheless afflicted with inadequate social and political structures that, within the poems themselves, can never be corrected.[45] These flawed communities, however, provide the benchmark against which to measure the success of their descendants, whose civic rituals and institutions bring fulfillment to a potential that "can only ever be hinted at, never *narrated*" in the Homeric epics.[46]

Crucial to this manner of interpretation—which is fundamentally in harmony with my own—is the notion that the *Iliad* (as well as the *Odyssey*) points beyond itself to an implied context of reception in the present time of performance, from which vantage point the problems that afflict the represented communities can be perceived and contrasted with the resolutions achieved in the audience's here and now. Nowhere is this gesture more plainly evident than in the *Iliad*'s last instance of the *epainos* motif, where the narrator speaks directly to the audience in order to confirm the validity of a convention that nevertheless remains in abeyance within the narrative itself. But this is far from the only manifestation of a tendency to look beyond the limits of the *Iliad*. Particularly in the scenes I review in this chapter—scenes that fulfill important functions in the poem's closural strategies—we observe again and again embedded audiences that can be understood as figuring the ultimate audience of the poem. The Achaean *laoi* assembled at the funeral games are a case in point: their imperfect *epainos* not only provides an opportunity for the narrator to address his auditors directly; it also provides the key term that links the embedded audience to the real-world audience, as prototype to perfected version. Likewise, the scene depicted on Achilles' shield, with its multiple groups of auditors poised to interpret events, presents a picture of expanding levels of interpretation that culminates, implicitly, with the *Iliad*'s historical audiences.

Here is how Gregory Nagy describes these ever-expanding circles of evaluation: "The logic of the litigation scene spills over into the logic of a surrounding circle of supposedly impartial elder adjudicators who are supposed to define the rights and wrongs of the case. Next, the logic of this inner circle of elders spills over into the logic of an outer circle of people who surround the elders, the people who will define who defines most justly. Next, it spills over into the logic of the outermost circle, people who are about to hear the *Iliad*. . . . Ultimately, these people are even ourselves." [47] As in the chariot race, the *laoi* who assemble to observe the contest are a stand-in for the poem's implied audience. As I argued above, the reaction expected from them is an *epainos* that will ratify one of the elders' judgments as the "most straight"; insofar as it is perpetually deferred, this reaction parallels the incomplete, unrealized consensus of the Achaeans in the chariot race. In both cases, the embedded audiences figure the audience (or audiences) envisioned by the *Iliad*. Their incipient or imperfect responses project onto this external audience the fulfillment of the *epainos* that remains only partial and qualified within the poem.

What does it mean to speak of the fulfillment of *epainos* at the level of this "outermost circle"? In what sense can a real-world audience be conceived of as participating in the political dynamics that mold the *Iliad*'s trajectory? It is one thing to speak of the reaffirmation of the norms of a narrative code, quite another to suppose that such metanarrative activity is somehow comparable to the kinds of decision-making processes depicted within the *Iliad*. In the concluding chapter I argue that audiences engaged in the evaluation of Iliadic narrative were (and are) participants in a long-term decision-making process that has shaped the *Iliad* as we know it. The clearest figure for this process within the poem is in fact the litigation scene on Achilles' shield, where the embedded audience is confronted with a series of performances—the judgments of the elders—each of which represents a distinct view of the Iliadic quarrel that has set the process in motion. The audience must decide which of these performances constitutes the most just portrayal, and their decision will determine the outcome of the case. In the same way, the *Iliad*'s implied audience is called upon to evaluate performances of Homeric poetry, and their judgment is imagined as the ultimate arbiter of what counts as a legitimate performance of the *Iliad*.

The manner in which the reception of Iliadic poetry becomes constitutive of the Iliadic tradition is explored in the next chapter. For now, I wish to conclude this discussion of the *Iliad*'s closural strategies by focusing on one last instance of an embedded audience—in fact, the last embedded audience to be found in the poem. In line with what I have suggested here about the teleology of the poem's thematic development, this final depiction of an internal audience focuses precisely on the response to a poetic performance. The poem thus concludes its sustained examination of collective dynamics with a shift from politics to aesthetics, from political decision making to the reception of poetry. Curiously, this shift happens not among the Achaeans but among the Trojans.

THE FUNERAL OF HECTOR: LAMENTATION AND COMMUNITY

The last two books of the *Iliad* present a more or less continuous narrative of death ritual. The ceremonies for Patroklos lead smoothly into the funeral of Hector, with the intervening scene—Priam's mission to ransom Hector's corpse—actually initiating the burial rites: the washing of the corpse by Achilles' servants is the first in the series of prescribed ritual actions that culminates in the erection of the burial mound.[48] From a certain point of view, in fact, the burial of Hector represents the only way of successfully concluding Patroklos' death ritual. Apollo remarks early in Book 24 that, while humans are ordinarily able to "let go" of even a brother or a son after they have properly mourned him, Achilles' continuing mistreatment of Hector's corpse is a sign of his inability to bring the period of mourning to a close (*Il.* 24.46–52). The funeral rites performed for Hector at the end of the book are therefore not simply the sequel to the games of Book 23 but their necessary conclusion.

The centerpiece of Hector's funeral is the series of three laments sung by female members of his household, Andromache, Hecabe, and Helen.[49] Their performances bring to the fore a mode of collective action and response that, although it has appeared in previous scenes, now gains importance as the means by which the Trojans demonstrate their membership in the community. If Book 23 establishes the solidarity of the Achaeans through their collective spectatorship at the games and their collective response to the awarding of prizes, Book 24 does the same for the Trojans by focusing on their responses, as a group, to the performances of the mourners.

A readily discernible isomorphism links these responses to the more properly political behaviors that have occupied my attention elsewhere in this study. The relation between performer and group unfolds according to the same dynamics that characterize deliberative assemblies: in both cases, a principal speaker (or singer) delivers an utterance, which is then affirmed by a demonstration of collective sentiment on the part of the audience.[50] Syntax underscores the affinity between these two modes of collective behavior: like the elements of the *Iliad*'s grammar of reception, group reactions to the performance of a mourner are typically expressed by means of a formula that employs the preverb *epi-* to indicate the relation between utterance and response. With a line like ὣς ἔφατ᾽ Ἀτρεΐδης, ἐπὶ δ᾽ ᾔνεον ἄλλοι Ἀχαιοί

Il. 3.461

Thus spoke the son of Atreus, and the other Achaeans were expressing *epainos*

we can compare the recurring formula

ὣς ἔφατο κλαίουσ᾽, ἐπὶ δὲ στενάχοντο γυναῖκες.

Il. 19.301, 22.515, 24.746 (cf. 24.722)

Thus she spoke, lamenting, and the women groaned in response.

Such correspondences are not insignificant. They are evidence of a shared dynamic that explains the ease with which the narrative is able to shift its focus from collective deliberation to collective mourning.

The transition begins as early as Book 19, with the laments performed by Briseis and Achilles over the corpse of Patroklos. As I pointed out in chapter 5, Book 19 is where we would expect to find a climactic *epainos* formalizing the restoration of Achaean solidarity. This *epainos*, however, has been usurped by the Trojans in Book 18; meanwhile, the motif of collective decision making fades from view among the Achaeans until the funeral games of Book 23. In its place we find a new emphasis on the group dynamics of funerary ritual that continues with the laments of Priam and Andromache for Hector in Book 22 (416–29, 477–515) and culminates in the sequence of three laments that conclude the poem.[51] Within this series we can observe a progression from private to public contexts of mourning. The laments of Book 19 occur in the domestic setting of Achilles' tent, but in Book 22 Priam and Andromache (as well as Hecabe) express their grief among the Trojans assembled on the city wall. The final sequence of laments recapitulates this move from private to public: Hector's body is laid out in the domestic space of the palace (*Il.* 24.719–20), and as Andromache initiates the lamentation, she is clearly performing before a group of women associated with the household; but Helen's lament, the last of the series, evokes a response from the entire *dēmos*, the civic body of Troy (24.776). The inconsistency of situating such a response in a domestic setting should be interpreted not as a flaw in the composition but as a sign of the importance the narrative attaches to the shift from private to public, which overrides the demands of mere verisimilitude. This shift, it must be underscored, coincides with the shift from an Achaean to a Trojan milieu. As in the case of the *epainos* motif, a trajectory that has its beginning in the Achaean community reaches its culmination at Troy.[52]

This trajectory becomes particularly evident if we examine the actual responses each lament receives, paying attention to the particular segment of the community involved in each instance. As in the case of deliberative proposals, the reactions to the performances of mourners provide a fairly precise index of the scope of the participating group. In deliberative contexts, response formulas specify, for example, whether it is the Achaeans as a whole or just the *basilēes* whose will is being expressed, while the use of discrete formulas underscores the distinction between different political communities (Achaeans versus Trojans). The language of deliberative response thus traces the articulation of the poem's various groups and subgroups. The same can be said of responses to displays of grief. The language used to describe them specifies precisely which segment of the community is being called upon to support the performance of the mourner and thereby sketches an outline of the internal organization of the social body.

The responses to the first laments in the series—those performed by Briseis and Achilles in Book 19—suggest a straightforward division of the social group along gendered lines, according to whether the performer is male or female:

(Briseis)
ὡς ἔφατο κλαίουσ', ἐπὶ δὲ στενάχοντο γυναῖκες
Il. 19.301

Thus she spoke, lamenting, and the women groaned in response

(Achilles)
ὡς ἔφατο κλαίων, ἐπὶ δὲ στενάχοντο γέροντες
Il. 19.338

Thus he spoke, lamenting, and the elders groaned in response.

In both cases, the laments are performed before a select group of intimates: either the women of Achilles' household or the small group of Achaean leaders Achilles has permitted to remain with him. In Book 22, with the laments performed for Hector on the city walls, we find a similarly gendered distribution of performers and audiences:[53]

(Priam)
ὡς ἔφατο κλαίων, ἐπὶ δὲ στενάχοντο πολῖται
Il. 22.429

Thus he spoke, lamenting, and the townsmen groaned in response

(Andromache)

ὡς ἔφατο κλαίουσ', ἐπὶ δὲ στενάχοντο γυναῖκες

Il. 22.515

Thus she spoke, lamenting, and the women groaned in response.

Now, however, there is a specifically *civic* inflection to at least one of the responses (the reaction to Priam's lament), and in both cases the audiences are much broader than a small circle of intimates. The expansion of the boundaries of the attending group to include the civic community at large coincides with the shift from a domestic to a public setting. What is largely a private, exclusive function among the Achaeans takes on a more inclusive aspect among the Trojans.[54] Notwithstanding the deficiencies of their political life, when it comes to grief and mourning, the Trojans exhibit a far more collective experience of performance than their Achaean counterparts. In this respect, they realize more fully the inherent potential of lament as a meaningful politico-poetic act, a performance that not only gives expression to personal feelings of loss, but that also—perhaps even more so—gives expression to the solidarity of the group in the face of loss.[55]

The collective dimension of Trojan mourning is most fully realized during Hector's funeral, in the course of which the series of audience reactions contributes to a progressively more articulated sense of social structure. The return of Priam prompts an initial outpouring of grief at the city gates, as the Trojan people assemble to meet Hector's body. The gestures of sorrow performed by Andromache and Hecabe elicit a group response, but the group in this case is designated simply as a *homilos,* "throng," a word that suggests an undifferentiated mass of people lacking a cohesive collective identity (κλαίων δ' ἀμφίσταθ' ὅμιλος ["weeping, the throng surrounded them"], Il. 24.712).[56] The lamentation sequence that subsequently takes place within the palace gradually gives shape to this chaotic assemblage.

The sequence begins with the isolation of a gendered subgroup familiar from previous examples, continues with a response that curiously avoids, even undermines, the establishment of such categories, and concludes by affirming the involvement of the civic community as an undivided whole:

(Andromache)

ὡς ἔφατο κλαίουσ', ἐπὶ δὲ στενάχοντο γυναῖκες

Il. 24.746

Thus she spoke, lamenting, and the women groaned in response

(Hecabe)

ὣς ἔφατο κλαίουσα, γόον δ' ἀλίαστον ὄρινε

Il. 24.760

Thus she spoke, lamenting, and she stirred up relentless wailing

(Helen)

ὣς ἔφατο κλαίουσ', ἐπὶ δ' ἔστενε δῆμος ἀπείρων

Il. 24.776

Thus she spoke, lamenting, and the boundless *dēmos* groaned in response.

The middle term in this sequence deserves particular attention. It departs from the established pattern of such response formulas by avoiding any specification of the group to which it refers. It is exceptional in this regard; and, as an exception to a system of formulas that give expression to fundamental mechanisms of social life, it bears a certain resemblance to the anomalous response that signals the state of exception in Book 1. In both cases we are confronted by an avoidance of those familiar patterns of language that might serve to clarify the precise meaning or extent of the phenomenon in question. The way in which the response to Hecabe's lament is described obscures rather than elucidates the nature of the group involved. Moreover, attending to the semantic overtones of the verb *orinein,* which elsewhere signifies the "atomizing" effect of socially deleterious speech, we can detect in this response an indication that the social structure of the Trojan community is being somehow dissolved.[57] If so, however, it is only as an intermediate step on the way from a segmented, essentially private view of Trojan society (evident in the response to Andromache's lament) to the constitution of the body politic as a cohesive unity. The "atomizing" of the mourners is the necessary precursor to the emergence of the *dēmos apeirōn,* the "people without limit," out of the distinct, segregated subgroups that have characterized collective mourning up to this point. The movement from the dissolution of social structure to the restoration of the community at a new level of organization is not only a common feature of death ritual as described by anthropologists and sociologists;[58] it is also a pattern familiar from the *Iliad,* having been established by the paradigmatic instance of *epainos* in Book 2 (discussed in chapter 4). Both here and in Book 2 we observe the reestablishment of solidarity at the broadest level after a period of social disorder.

The fundamental similarity of these two examples provides yet another indication of the extent to which poetic performance converges with—and even replaces—decision making as a context for the display of group identity and collective sentiment in the later books of the *Iliad*. Of course, an audience's response to the performance of lament is not in any sense deliberative; there is no question to be decided upon. Nevertheless, as in the case of deliberative proposals, responses are indicative of the degree of social support any given performance receives. (In this regard they are a manifestation of the political dimension of lament as a performance that expresses and consolidates social cohesion.) And the possibility of identifying different responses conveying different degrees of support suggests that, even in the case of lament poetry, audience response can be evaluative. The series of laments in Book 24 results in a hierarchy of responses organized according to the scope of social integration evidenced by each. Although this is not an agonistic context, there is an obvious similarity to the situation presented on Achilles' shield: multiple performers present their views sequentially on the crisis that has befallen the community (a crisis centering once again on "a man who has died"). And while the audience is not called upon to judge which performance is truest or best, their responses are scaled in such a way as to indicate which is widest in appeal, which is able to muster the resources of the community on the broadest possible level.

As on the shield, the widest circle of people involved in the process of performance and evaluation is the *dēmos*. By contrast with the shield, however, where the *dēmos* and the scene as a whole are strictly bounded by the limits of the image and ultimately of the shield itself, the *dēmos* that participates in Hector's funeral is explicitly said to be *apeirōn*, "without limit."[59] What significance ought we to assign to this epithet? Narrowly understood, it stresses the contrast between the restricted response to Andromache's lament and the universal appeal of Helen's, whose audience is "without limit" in the sense that it includes every member of the Trojan community. But a broader understanding is possible, an understanding that takes into account the Iliadic technique of using embedded audiences to figure the poem's implied audience. On this view, the audience of Helen's lament is "without limit" precisely because it looks beyond the confines of the *Iliad* to the real-world audiences the poem envisions for itself. The boundless *dēmos* spills over into the present of the poem's performance; included in it is, potentially, every hearer or reader of the *Iliad*. Helen is eminently qualified to be the one to address this ever-expanding audience, for, of all the characters represented in the poem, she is uniquely aware of the epic tradition that envelops her, and uniquely able to appropriate the functions of the epic poet.[60]

Even if Helen is particularly well suited to command such an expanded audience, why should that audience be anchored in the Trojan community? Why should the Trojans, and not, as we might expect, the Achaeans, provide the embedded audience that seems to figure most explicitly the activity of the poem's real-world appreciators? The answer may be as simple as the fact that the Trojans *are not* Achaeans. Building on Haubold's insight regarding the relation between the Achaeans and the *polis* communities of which they are the notional ancestors, and to which the poem's real-world audiences belong, we can discern an underlying rationale for the pattern of displacement that shifts climactic instances of collective action from the Achaeans to the Trojans. Within the *Iliad*, the mechanisms of community among the Achaeans must always remain flawed, incomplete, and imperfect, since, from the standpoint of their notional descendants, it is only in the later world of the *poleis* that their potential is fulfilled.[61] This is the reason why, as we saw in chapter 6, the climactic *epainos* that seals Troy's fate is displaced to Hector's camp. It is likewise the reason why the motif of poetic response, which begins among the Achaeans, culminates with Helen's performance before a Trojan audience. The poem must include some indication of the perfected experience it projects onto its implied audience, but it cannot situate it among those who must remain imperfect. As a result, we encounter a dislocation of crucial motifs from the Achaean ships to Troy, a dislocation that can be interpreted as a sign of the poem's reach into the present of performance.[62]

The universal response of the boundless *dēmos* provides an effective and fitting conclusion to the *Iliad*'s collective dynamics. Although it is not in the narrow sense political (that is, deliberative), it brings to fulfillment in the sphere of poetic performance and reception the poem's drive to place the solidarity of the community on the broadest possible foundation, by establishing a community that extends even beyond the limits of the poem's represented world. This shift from politics to poetry is, along with the metanarrative character of the gods' debates about the plot of the poem (as discussed in chapter 7), the clearest indication within the text that the *Iliad*'s sustained interest in collective sentiment, political and otherwise, ultimately aims at the Iliadic tradition as such. The next chapter will review other indications, outside the text of the *Iliad*, that the poem's treatment of collective decision making can and should be understood as a means of reflecting on the forces that shape a poetic tradition of Panhellenic status. The claim to Panhellenic authority is far from incidental to these reflections. On the contrary, it is implicitly asserted by the universalism of the poem's final image of an audience unlimited in scope.[63]

CHAPTER 9

The Politics of Reception

Collective Response and Iliadic Audiences within and beyond the Text

Previous chapters have advanced the claim that the *Iliad*'s depictions of collective decision making point, implicitly but unmistakably, beyond the poem to its real-world audiences. In the transference of *epainos* from the Achaeans to the Trojans, in the metapoetic character of the debates on Olympus, and especially in the image of the "boundless people" whose collective response to a poetic performance concludes the poem, we catch glimpses of the "fourth estate" that lies just beyond the poem's horizon: the historical communities whose festivals provided the context for rhapsodic performances and who constituted the poem's true stakeholders. The very possibility of tracing such gestures within the text implies "an organic link between reception and performance," which is to say, a poetic tradition that remained sensitive, in the course of its evolution, to the process of reception, and that was accordingly able to incorporate reflections on that very process.[1] But important questions remain. Is there evidence external to the poem that historical audiences recognized some semblance of their own experience in the *Iliad*'s representation of political dynamics? And, more importantly, a question that is prior even to the search for such evidence: what, in general terms, was the nature of this experience, such that it could find meaningful expression in the Iliadic image of collective decision making? The concluding chapter of this study begins with an exploration of this second question, as a way of setting the stage for a broader consideration of the relationship between the *Iliad* and the history of its reception.

PASSIVE TRADITION BEARERS AND THE SHAPING
OF A PANHELLENIC TRADITION

It has become an established tenet of Homeric criticism that the *Iliad* and *Odyssey* are to be understood as Panhellenic in scope—that is, as appealing, notionally at least, to all Greeks, as opposed to a variety of other texts and traditions that betray a more local, or "epichoric," orientation.[2] The rubric of Panhellenism thus becomes a useful way of distinguishing the Homeric epics, in terms of content, form, diffusion, and institutionalization, from lyric and even other epic traditions that express a more restricted set of concerns, often because of ties to local cults.[3] There is a tendency to speak of the Panhellenic quality of Homeric poetry as though it were something absolute, an unqualified universalism that sets the poems on the far side of an impermeable boundary. As Gregory Nagy has stressed, however, Panhellenism is not an absolute but a relative phenomenon, a tendency and an ideology rather than an uncontested reality.[4] It is not, for example, that the *Iliad* is Panhellenic while the *Aithiopis* (one of the poems of the Epic Cycle) is not but that the *Iliad* is *more* Panhellenic, which is to say that it reflects a tradition that has developed in the direction of greater ecumenicalism rather than greater local specificity.[5]

As this formulation implies, to relativize the notion of Panhellenism is to recognize it as the product of a developmental process that privileges certain elements of a tradition over others. This is not a matter of the wholesale or instantaneous adoption of a universalizing orientation at the expense of a local one but of an evolving interaction between the two. Like the divinities of Greek cult, whose identities were implicated in a constant negotiation of tensions between local and supralocal perspectives, Greek poetic traditions—the Homeric tradition included—provided a matrix for the interplay of these same points of view.[6] A story told by Herodotus about the tyrant Kleisthenes of Sikyon illustrates the way in which epic poetry could be invested with local significance, notwithstanding its relatively Panhellenic orientation: at war with Argos, Kleisthenes reportedly banned rhapsodes from performing in his city, on the grounds that the "Homeric" verses they performed praised the "Argives" (5.67).[7]

Herodotus' anecdote draws attention to another crucial aspect of the tension between epichoric and Panhellenic perspectives. Far from being a solely abstract phenomenon, in the performance culture of archaic and classical Greece, this tension was always experienced and expressed concretely, in the framing, execution, and reception of particular performative events. A variety of factors might influence the relative orientation, Panhellenic or otherwise, of a given event, including the institutional or ritual context (rhapsodic contests at the Great Panathenaia, for example, would have a more Panhellenic cast than similar contests at the Brauronia, a local festival in the Attic town of Brauron); the status of the performer (a member of the rhapsodic guild known as the *Homēridai* would have a far greater claim to authority than an amateur performer); and, finally, the disposition of the audience, who would bring to each performance the sum total of their experience of epic narratives, both local and Panhellenic, as well as a wealth of related information deriving from folktales, iconography, and so on.[8] Kleisthenes of Sikyon himself exemplifies the extent to which the attitudes of audience members—in this case, a particularly authoritative audience member— might affect the way the meaning of a performance was framed.

Kleisthenes' intervention as related by Herodotus could be considered an exceptionally strong case of what folklorists describe as the influence of "passive tradition bearers." This term, introduced by Swedish folklorist Carl von Sydow, refers to those members of a community who, although they may not be competent themselves to perform and transmit to others a given element of tradition (or authorized to do so), are nevertheless knowledgeable about it to a greater or lesser degree, and are therefore able to judge and evaluate the activities of "active tradition bearers," whose competence extends to performance.[9] Passive tradition bearers exert a powerful control over tradition, a control that can be observed both synchronically and diachronically.

Synchronically, at the level of the individual performance, passive tradition bearers "act, to some extent, as a check on tradition. If some deviation should be made, they can easily correct it, and they do so, which is of great importance for the unchanging survival of the tradition."[10] Knowledgeable audience members can, by their comments or other forms of approval or disapproval, signal and set right the perceived deficiencies in an expert's performance. The diachronic impact of such passive tradition bearers is a consequence of von Sydow's important observation that "the border-line between active and passive bearers of tradition is, of course, far from being fixed; it is ever fluctuating."[11] Just as an active bearer might become passive for a variety of reasons, including the decline of interest among other passive bearers, so too passive tradition bearers can and do become active, as indeed is always the case when it comes to the maturation of any given active bearer. Today's audience members are tomorrow's performers. For this reason, passive tradition bearers function as a kind of filter or bottleneck that largely determines what traditions will be continued among the next generation of active bearers.[12] Roman Jakobson and Petr Bogatyrev, in their influential discussion of "preventive censure," make a similar point: "Let us suppose that a member of a community has composed something. Should this oral work . . . be unacceptable to the community for one reason or another, should the remaining members of the community not adopt it, then it is condemned to failure."[13]

Kleisthenes' extraordinary measure against the rhapsodes, although it takes a peculiarly interventionist form, is nevertheless emblematic of the "passive" control that audiences exert over performance traditions. Considered as a kind of speech act, a performance is an utterance that requires the assent and approval of the group in attendance in order to be efficacious, or, in Austin's terms, "felicitous."[14] The efficaciousness of a performance can be measured in terms of its perceived legitimacy and its ability to promote the continuation of the tradition. Some traditions make explicit the essential relation between passive tradition bearers and the efficaciousness of performance by formalizing the expression of collective approval. Among the Kuba of central Africa, for instance, the presentation of testimony at chiefs' councils incorporated elaborate formulas whereby the assembled dignitaries expressed their assent to the chief's pronouncements.[15] In other traditions, a prescribed pattern of exchange between the principal performer and a respondent figures concretely the audience's support for the performance in progress.[16] And there are less formal means by which traditions may acknowledge the importance of the community's standards for effective performance.[17]

The Kuba chief's council bears an obvious resemblance to a situation of collective decision making. In fact, insofar as the chief's testimony deals with questions of direct political significance to the community, the communal ratification of the tradition performed by the chief *is* a situation of collective decision making. At the same time, the ritualized expression of group approval among the Kuba simply externalizes what is inherently true of any oral performance tradition, namely, that every performance is a negotiation, between performer and audience and between audience members, over the legitimacy of the tradition's current realization. From this point of view, any performance can be thought of as a collective decision, insofar as its success—its ability to embody the tradition and so to shape future performances—requires the approval of the audience. A performance is successful, efficacious, by virtue of the consensus of those in attendance in favor of its legitimacy. Moreover, the tradition, viewed diachronically, can be understood as an extended process of collective decision making, whereby a succession of audiences regulates the content of the tradition, endorsing some multiforms and rejecting others. The state of the tradition at any given time will reflect the converging (and sometimes competing) preferences of many previous performative communities. In a meaningful sense, it can be considered the product of an intergenerational and often geographically diverse consensus.

The relevance of such a notion of consensus is a direct consequence of the observable influence of passive tradition bearers on the shaping of oral traditions worldwide. This notion is furthermore the key to understanding why scenes of collective decision making should be the locus for metapoetic reflection within the *Iliad*. There is a fundamental formal parallel between the shaping of a poetic tradition by its community (or communities) of reception and the determination of group action or policy by consensus—a parallel to which the *Iliad* can be observed to respond.

I have said that Herodotus' anecdote about Kleisthenes is emblematic of the influence that audiences may exercise over poetic traditions, but a few qualifications are in order. In the first place, it is not at all obvious that Kleisthenes represents the collective sentiment of his community. In fact, when viewed against the background of Herodotus' broader interest in the autocratic behavior of tyrants, his story appears to suggest that Kleisthenes' intervention is the consequence of an idiosyncratic point of view imposed upon, rather than arising from, the rhapsodes' audience. In unilaterally expelling the bearers of "Homeric verses" from his city, Kleisthenes seems almost to be modeling his actions on the most visible exemplum of autocratic behavior offered by the Homeric tradition: Agamemnon. Furthermore, his intervention is motivated not by any concerns over the accuracy or legitimacy of the tradition as such but only over its framing. From his point of view, the legitimately traditional content of these "Homeric verses" is contextually unacceptable in terms of the relatively epichoric lens through which he views the performance. All the same, Herodotus' anecdote demonstrates an important point: the continuity of a tradition depends not just on the availability of active bearers of the tradition but as much or more on its favorable reception among passive bearers.

In the context of an ancient poetic ecology in which traditions of a relatively more Panhellenic and a relatively more local orientation circulated side by side, the question of framing would have been just as important to audiences in general as it was, apparently, to Kleisthenes. The "framing" of a performance necessarily involves the complex interaction of a variety of factors. Nevertheless we can say that an event will be framed in a relatively Panhellenic way when the audience is implicitly or explicitly called upon to view the performance from a translocal perspective. The perspective the audience is invited to adopt makes no small difference to the nature of the constraint represented by their approval as passive tradition bearers. In the case of a locally oriented event, the performance will be constrained by epichoric traditions, to the extent that these are known to performer and audience: a legitimate performance will have to conform to these traditions. In the case of a performance that is framed in a more ecumenical way (at which the audience is invited to suspend, to a certain extent, its local prejudices), the performance may be liberated to a greater or lesser degree from the requirements of local tradition—but it is nevertheless constrained by the knowledge, on the part of both performer and audience, of what Jim Marks has recently called the "synthetic narrative" of the Panhellenic "borderless text," that is, the emerging body of Panhellenic narratives about Troy.[18]

Both Panhellenizing and locally oriented performances, then, are subject to traditional constraints, but there is an important difference in the nature of these constraints, insofar as the Panhellenizing performance is simultaneously characterized by a relative autonomy from epichoric standards.[19] From the point of view of local tradition, this autonomy is liable to be perceived as an innovative departure from the locally guaranteed version of events. We may take as an example the death, as reported by the *Iliad*, of the Boeotian hero Askalaphos (*Il.* 13.518–20). Richard Janko stresses the deviation of this Homeric account from earlier traditions, recoverable from Dictys of Crete, that assigned to Askalaphos a significant role later in the Trojan War.[20] These traditions were most likely tied to and maintained by the hero's Boeotian cult.[21] Even in Boeotia, they might have been known only to a minority of those attending a performance of the *Iliad;* but those who did bring to such a performance knowledge of the local hero's extra-Iliadic adventures would naturally have been inclined to regard the Homeric version as an innovative divergence from the "facts" as established by cult. Such a perception, of course, would say nothing about the actual chronological priority of one or the other tradition.

These considerations imply a subtle differentiation between two ways in which the collective constraint exercised by passive tradition bearers might—notionally speaking—operate. In the context of a locally oriented performance, before an audience sensitive to the demands of epichoric tradition, collective endorsement or acceptance of a performance will be fundamentally conservative: a confirmation of local norms. The more Panhellenic the frame applied by the audience, however, the greater is the room for the suspension of these norms in favor of the divergent constraints of Panhellenic tradition. In this case, collective approval is liable to be felt as at least partly innovative, insofar as it endorses a narrative that conflicts in certain particulars with local "truths."[22] Of course, the influence brought to bear by passive tradition bearers is always in a sense conservative, since it is premised on the norms established by the tradition. But the poetic culture of archaic and classical Greece, with its combination of centripetal and centrifugal forces, provided an environment in which this essentially conservative force could be played out at different levels, involving communities of reception constituted at different scales. In this way, the consensus that shaped a Panhellenic tradition like the one that produced the *Iliad* could be understood as simultaneously conservative and innovative: conservative so far as the Panhellenic "synthetic narrative" was concerned, and innovative from the point of view of local traditions.

ILIADIC TRADITION AND THE POETICS OF CONSENT

These reflections on the nature of the constraint exercised by passive tradition bearers help to give a cohesive and intelligible shape to the *Iliad*'s portrayal of collective decision making. As difficult as it may be to map the poem's vision of consensus as a political ideal onto recoverable sociopolitical systems of the archaic period, that vision nevertheless corresponds remarkably well to the dynamics of poetic tradition as outlined above.[23] This is especially true when it comes to the peculiar tension between innovation and conservatism that has emerged from the examination of the *epainos* motif in earlier chapters.

As we have seen, *epainos* is primarily—but not exclusively—a conservative phenomenon. In the large majority of instances, whether it is expressed positively or negatively (by the withholding of it), *epainos* represents a social force that merely confirms the status quo. In fact, there are only three occasions on which the expression of *epainos* endorses an innovative proposal, one that does more than simply call for the continuation of an established course of collective action. These are: the Achaeans' approval for Agamemnon's verdict on the outcome of the duel between Menelaus and Paris at the end of Book 3 (*Il.* 3.461), the approval of the Achaean *basilēes* for Nestor's proposal to build a pyre for the fallen warriors and a fortifying wall for the camp (*Il.* 7.344), and the exceptional *epainos* of the Trojans for Hector's proposal to stay camped on the plain (*Il.* 18.312). The first of these decisions constitutes a threat to the traditional outcome of the Troy story and is ultimately neutralized by the divine apparatus; the last reinforces the traditional outcome, but with catastrophic results for the Trojan community. On the whole, then, the rarity of innovation and the predominantly negative consequences when it does occur tend to confirm the view that *epainos* is a fundamentally conservative force, just as the tradition-based constraint exercised by passive tradition bearers is fundamentally conservative.

At the same time, however, the *Iliad* does indicate that *epainos* can accommodate innovation, provided, as in the case of the traditional dynamics outlined above, that it is executed or framed at the appropriate scale. A first intimation of this all-important matter of scale occurs already in the first instance of collective support for an innovative proposal, the Achaean *epainos* that concludes Book 3. Part of the irregularity of this situation—apart from the nature of the proposal itself, which threatens to end the war prematurely—is the fact that a proposal calling for action on both sides receives the support of only one, while the attitude of the other side is left in question.[24] The overall effect of the discrepancy between the scope of the proposition and the scope of the response is to draw attention precisely to the problem of scale, to the question of how ecumenical in appeal an innovative proposal must be if it is to achieve results.

A more complex relation between innovation and scale emerges from consideration of Nestor's proposal in Book 7 and its aftermath. The proposal to construct fortifications around the Achaean camp is unquestionably innovative—Nestor's *mētis*, "contrivance," for the defense of the ships is an extraordinary measure, made necessary only by Achilles' withdrawal from the battlefield—but it is easily approved and executed, with consequences that appear to last for the rest of the poem.[25] However, an important limitation is set on the consequences of this proposal outside the poem, a limitation that, as we will see, is closely tied to the question of how the building of the wall will be framed in relation to events of more local importance. The issue of scale does not in this case arise in connection with the proposal's immediate audience, namely, the Achaean *basilēes*. While it is always possible to consider the Achaeans as a Panhellenic community, and so as figuring in themselves the operation of social forces with a relatively broad compass, there is nothing in the description of Nestor's audience to suggest an ecumenicalism comparable to the one evoked as a possibility in Book 3. Instead, it is in the reaction of a more distant audience— the gods on Olympus—that the questions of framing and scale are explicitly brought to the fore.[26]

The objections of Poseidon are the vehicle by which these concerns are introduced. As the gods, seated around Zeus, look on, Poseidon voices his anxiety that the *kleos*, "glory," of the Achaean wall will obscure the glory of the wall of Troy, which he and Apollo constructed:

Ζεῦ πάτερ, ἤ ῥά τίς ἐστι βροτῶν ἐπ' ἀπείρονα γαῖαν
ὅς τις ἔτ' ἀθανάτοισι νόον καὶ μῆτιν ἐνίψει;
οὐχ ὁράᾳς ὅτι δ' αὖτε κάρη κομόωντες Ἀχαιοὶ
τεῖχος ἐτειχίσσαντο νεῶν ὕπερ, ἀμφὶ δὲ τάφρον
ἤλασαν, οὐδὲ θεοῖσι δόσαν κλειτὰς ἑκατόμβας;
τοῦ δ' ἤτοι κλέος ἔσται ὅσον τ' ἐπικίδναται ἠώς·
τοῦ δ' ἐπιλήσονται τὸ ἐγὼ καὶ Φοῖβος Ἀπόλλων
ἥρῳ Λαομέδοντι πολίσσαμεν ἀθλήσαντε.

Il. 7.446–53

Father Zeus, who is there among mortals on the boundless earth
who will still communicate his mind and his designs to the immortals?
Do you not see that the long-haired Achaeans have now
built a wall about their ships, and around it they have driven
a trench, but they did not give splendid hecatombs to the gods?
Its *kleos* will surely spread as far as the dawn's light,
but that wall will be forgotten, which I and Phoibos Apollo
toiled to build for the hero Laomedon.

Kleos, of course, is shorthand for the "fame" that is promoted by and embodied in poetic tradition, especially epic tradition.[27] In this case, we are dealing with two competing *klea* that each correspond to the story of an important act of foundation, or *ktisis*—the foundation of the *polis* of Troy, on the one hand, and of the quasi-*polis* of the fortified Achaean camp, on the other.[28] Such acts of foundation are in fact attested as subjects of an important class of archaic epic and elegiac traditions known collectively as "*ktisis* poetry."[29] From our point of view, one of the most important features of *ktisis* poetry is that, as the expression of the bond between a particular community and its place of settlement, it is "fundamentally local rather than Panhellenic in orientation."[30] Poseidon, in effect, acts as the spokesman for local traditions, and for the local tradition of Troy in particular, expressing the concern that the poetic fame of this new foundation will obliterate the preexisting fame of the earlier foundation of Troy.[31]

Poseidon frames the poetic tradition of the Achaean wall—which can arguably be equated with the poetic tradition of the *Iliad* itself—in terms of local significance, as one among many *ktisis* traditions.[32] As such, he views it as a direct competitor for the local tradition of Troy's foundation. Zeus, however, quickly reassures him, reframing the significance of the wall in such a way as to minimize its effect on the *kleos* Poseidon derives from local traditions:

ὦ πόποι ἐννοσίγαι᾽ εὐρυσθενές, οἶον ἔειπες.
ἄλλός κέν τις τοῦτο θεῶν δείσειε νόημα,
ὃς σέο πολλὸν ἀφαυρότερος χεῖράς τε μένος τε·
σὸν δ᾽ ἤτοι κλέος ἔσται ὅσον τ᾽ ἐπικίδναται ἠώς.
ἄγρει μὰν ὅτ᾽ ἂν αὖτε κάρη κομόωντες Ἀχαιοὶ
οἴχωνται σὺν νηυσὶ φίλην ἐς πατρίδα γαῖαν
τεῖχος ἀναρρήξας τὸ μὲν εἰς ἅλα πᾶν καταχεῦαι,
αὖτις δ᾽ ἠϊόνα μεγάλην ψαμάθοισι καλύψαι,
ὥς κέν τοι μέγα τεῖχος ἀμαλδύνηται Ἀχαιῶν.
Il. 7.455–63

Ah, mighty earth-shaker, what have you said!
Some other of the gods might fear this contrivance,
one who is far weaker than you in strength of arm and might,
but your *kleos* will surely spread as far as the dawn's light.
Come now: when the long-haired Achaeans
depart with their ships for their dear fatherland,
break apart the wall and sweep it all into the sea,
and cover over the wide seashore with sands,
so that the great wall of the Achaeans is destroyed.

Zeus' concession to Poseidon would seem at first glance to be a severe limitation on the *kleos* associated with the wall—the *kleos* associated with the *Iliad*
itself. Crucially, however, this limitation is at the same time what liberates the
wall from a *merely* local significance. By obliterating the basis for its local prestige, the destruction of the wall opens up the possibility of a significance that
transcends the epichoric level and rises to truly Panhellenic proportions. Relevant here are Nagy's comments on a similar act of obliteration, the destruction
by Thespiai, probably in the period between 700 and 650, of Askra, the Boeotian village identified in the *Works and Days* as the birthplace of Hesiod (639–
40). Writing of the "transcendence" that elevates Hesiodic poetry above local
traditions to a Panhellenic level, Nagy explains: "This transcendence is of course
facilitated by the historical fact that the figure of Hesiod has no native city to
claim him, since Askra was destroyed by Thespiai. Because Askra is no more,
its traditions need not infringe on those of other cities. By allowing Hesiod to
speak as a native of Askra, the pan-Hellenic tradition is in effect making him a
native of all Greek cities . . ."[33] The difference between these Homeric and Hesiodic strategies for advancing Panhellenic claims is that the latter appropriates a

historical act of destruction, while the former fabricates an imagined one. The fabrication amounts to a kind of anti-*ktisis*, a poetic obliteration that establishes the Panhellenic validity of the Iliadic account of the wall by (literally) undermining the foundations of that account in a putative local tradition.[34] The *Iliad*, in other words, summons the local mode of *ktisis* poetry as a foil for its own Panhellenic narrative. Zeus drives home the point by denying the *Iliad* any basis in this epichoric register.

Thus, the innovation inaugurated by the Achaean *epainos* of Book 7 is ultimately accommodated or normalized—brought into harmony with a broader ecology of poetic traditions real or imagined—by an act of forcible reframing that situates the significance of the wall on an exclusively Panhellenic level. It should be noted that this reframing coincides with the restoration of a state of divine solidarity that appears to have existed before the arrival of the Achaeans at Troy but to have been suspended during the period of the war. Apollo and Poseidon—divinities whose partisan fervor very nearly brings them to blows in the theomachy of Book 21 (*Il.* 21.435–69)—cooperated in the construction of the walls of Troy, and they will cooperate again in the destruction of their Achaean counterpart.[35] The Panhellenizing act of obliteration by which the innovative proposal is integrated into a broader context therefore corresponds to the emergence of collective solidarity on a level beyond the merely human consensus that brings the wall into being. In this way, the poem's treatment of the wall models a complex set of interactions between the operation of communal judgments at various scales, the accommodation of innovation within a system that generally favors the status quo, and the tension between epichoric and Panhellenic frames. Moreover, the emphasis on *kleos* gives the entire episode a distinctly metapoetic cast. Overall, it offers an outstanding example of the way in which the thematics of collective decision making figure the operation of poetic tradition.

EPAINOS IN PERFORMANCE

If the *epainos* motif embeds within the text a figure for the dynamics that shaped the Iliadic tradition, it may also have enacted that force performatively, at least at certain stages in the development of the poem. At issue is the relation between the distribution of the *epainos* motif and possible performative divisions within the text of the *Iliad*. Numerous attempts have been made to discern within the poem meaningful points of articulation corresponding to the pauses that would be necessary in the performance of such a monumental composition. Discussions of the problem remain controversial at every level, whether it is a matter of the divisions between individual books (or "rhapso-dies") or of larger-scale compositional patterns.[36] Nevertheless, among those researchers who accept the premise of a correlation between performative and compositional units (as do I), it has become increasingly common to posit an organization of the poem in three "movements" (in Oliver Taplin's terminol-ogy), which correspond roughly to the periods before, during, and after the day of Hector's great triumph over the Achaeans. It is as yet impossible to speak of a consensus: scholars have fixed the boundaries between these movements at various points, and there is no shortage of competing schemes.[37] Many of the discrepancies between these schemes, however, may be accounted for on the reasonable hypothesis that the *Iliad* includes multiple sets of compositional and performative boundaries, corresponding to multiple stages in the development and fixation of the text.[38] The three "movements" discerned by Taplin and others would then represent only a particular stage in the poem's performance history. What is important for my purposes is that there is good evidence for such a tri-partite framework, and, furthermore, that the outlines of this framework coin-cide in important ways with the distribution of the *epainos* motif.

Among those who advocate for a three-part compositional and performative structure, the most widely shared view, representing a plurality, if not a major-ity, of voices, fixes the poem's first internal segment boundary at the end of Book 9, and the second at either the mid- or endpoint of Book 18.[39] The relation between the resulting three-part structure and the distribution of the *epainos* motif can be observed most clearly in connection with the sequence of Olym-pian debates. Regardless of precisely where one fixes the boundaries, in fact, each of the poem's three movements includes one of the three scenes in which the gods deliberate about a possible alteration of poetic destiny in terms of the con-straints imposed by collective will. As I have argued, these scenes highlight the relationship between *epainos* and the shaping of the plot; their arrangement in a manner that closely tracks the poem's overall architecture serves to under-score this relationship.

More interesting patterns emerge from consideration of the arrangement of scenes within narrative segments. If we adopt the most widespread view of segment divisions (with boundaries at the end of Book 9 and at or near the end of Book 18), we find that each segment concludes with a climactic expression of collective sentiment: the *epainos* of the Achaean *basilēes* for Diomedes' proposal (*Il.* 9.710), the Trojan *epainos* for Hector (*Il.* 18.312), and the response of the *dēmos apeirōn*, the "boundless people," to Helen's lament (*Il.* 24.776). In other words, these potential performative units are punctuated by scenes that figure the control exercised by collective will over the validity of traditional performances. Moreover, with the Trojan consensus of Book 18 excepted, both the remaining instances of innovative *epainos* (*Il.* 3.461 and 7.344) are embedded within the first movement, preceded by the paradigmatically conservative response that prevents the Achaeans from fleeing in Book 2 and followed by the similarly conservative decision that brings the movement to an end in Book 9. The innovative potential of *epainos* is literally contained by assertions of its fundamentally conservative force. As a performative unit, then, this movement enacts the power of collective will to accommodate innovation in the service of a fundamentally conservative goal. Similarly, by concluding a major performative segment with an embedded expression of *epainos*, a performer could give concrete expression to the power his audience exercised over the shape of the tradition. The question of performative divisions in the *Iliad* must remain a matter for speculation. Such speculation, however, provides a tantalizing indication of how the relation between the *epainos* motif and the dynamics of epic tradition might have been given concrete expression in performance.[40]

EPAINOS BEYOND THE *ILIAD*

Looking now beyond the text of the *Iliad*, it is possible to discover indications that the metapoetic significance of the *epainos* motif was not merely an implicit or potential aspect of the Iliadic tradition, awaiting realization in some hypothetical context of performance, but an acknowledged part of the way that at least some tradition bearers and readers conceptualized the process of reception.

A first such indication can be traced in the language used by professional performers of Homeric poetry—that is, rhapsodes—to describe the very activity of performance. We possess a unique document of the rhapsodes' professional vocabulary in Plato's *Ion*, a dialogue that presents a conversation between Socrates and an eponymous rhapsode from Ephesos.[41] Although Plato undoubtedly manipulates his portrayal of Ion in the service of his own philosophical agenda, he nevertheless makes use of "a variety of authentic expressions and turns of phrase that echo the talk of real rhapsodes as they once upon a time practiced their art."[42] Among these is the idiosyncratic usage of the verb *epainein* with the meaning "recite, declaim publicly" (LSJ s.v. iv), as at *Ion* 541e1–2: ἀλλὰ γὰρ σύ, ὦ Ἴων, εἰ μὲν ἀληθῆ λέγεις ὡς τέχνῃ καὶ ἐπιστήμῃ οἷός τε εἶ Ὅμηρον ἐπαινεῖν, ἀδικεῖς ("But, Ion, if you are right in saying that you are able to <u>recite</u> Homer by virtue of a systematic art and knowledge, you are cheating me . . .").[43]

The rhapsodes' metadiscourse about the practice of their art must be connected with the traditional phraseology that comprises the substance of that art. Far more than simply configuring the quotation of Homeric verses as a kind of "praise" accruing to the legendary poet (as a strictly "classical" understanding of the semantics of *epainein* might suggest), this rhapsodic way of speaking constructs an essential bridge between the dynamics of reception, as encoded in the Homeric use of the term, and performance. The periphrasis in fact collapses the two together, equating the public recitation of Homeric verses with an act of endorsement that sustains and shapes the Homeric tradition in the here and now.[44] The mentality underlying this turn of phrase emanates from the point of view of the tradition bearer who perceives his position as the mediator between past and future versions of the tradition: the rhapsode's performance effectively ratifies the Homeric text, approves the utterance of previous performers for continuation into the future. In this way, the rhapsode becomes a kind of spokesman for the community, an embodiment of collective approval, and his actualization of the tradition becomes the *epainos* that determines the shape of the tradition going forward.

Here, as elsewhere, Plato demonstrates a remarkable sensitivity to the linguistic habits of skilled professionals. More revealing still is the way that Plato's Socrates speaks about the shaping of Homeric tradition when he begins to articulate his poetic program for the ideal city in *Republic* 2. As he makes a set of increasingly specific suggestions about the kinds of *muthoi* that are to be employed in the early education of the city's guardians, Socrates uses a variety of verbs to capture the notion of "inclusion" or "exclusion," including *enkrinein* (377c1, 2), *apokrinein* (377c2), *ekballein* (377c5), *paradekhesthai* (378d5), and *apodekhesthai* (379c9). But when he comes to speak about specific changes that must be made to the *Iliad* in order to make it serviceable to the state, he adopts a distinctly rhapsodic—and, more importantly, Iliadic—way of speaking:

τὴν δὲ τῶν ὅρκων καὶ σπονδῶν σύγχυσιν, ἣν ὁ Πάνδαρος συνέχεεν, ἐάν τις φῇ δι᾽
Ἀθηνᾶς τε καὶ Διὸς γεγονέναι, <u>οὐκ ἐπαινεσόμεθα</u> . . .

Rep. 379e2–4

But the violation of the treaty oaths and libations, which Pandaros confounded, if anyone should say that this came about through Athena and Zeus, <u>we will not approve</u> [*epainein*] . . .

A few pages later, when he next comes to speak about a specific adjustment to the content of the *Iliad*, Socrates again makes use of the same locution:

πολλὰ ἄρα Ὁμήρου ἐπαινοῦντες, ἀλλὰ τοῦτο <u>οὐκ ἐπαινεσόμεθα</u>, τὴν τοῦ ἐνυπνίου πομπὴν ὑπὸ Διὸς τῷ Ἀγαμέμνονι·

Rep. 383a7–8

So, though we approve much in Homer, this <u>we will not approve</u> [*epaineîn*]: Zeus' sending of the dream to Agamemnon.

The use of the verb *epaineîn* to refer to the approval (or, in negation, the disapproval) for a certain way of telling the *Iliad*'s story doubtless owes something to the rhapsodes' term for public performance: at issue here are precisely those verses that will be licensed, so to speak, for public use. Socrates' language, however, is more than just an appropriation of rhapsodic terminology—it is a direct allusion to the metapoetic value of the *epainos* motif as it is deployed in the *Iliad*.

Socrates' first example of a passage that must be excised from his "approved" version of the *Iliad*—the collapse of the truce in Book 4 through the agency of Zeus and Athena—speaks volumes. The mention of the involvement of the gods would be enough to remind any reader of the divine council that precedes and prompts Pandaros' treacherous bowshot. In fact, Socrates' argument bears more on this council scene than on Pandaros' actions, since his point is that poetry, to be pedagogically useful, must not ascribe to the gods responsibility for evils. The divine council of Book 4, of course, is the first occasion on which we observe the gods debating the contours of the Iliadic plot, and they do so in language that Plato deliberately evokes: Socrates' negation of *epainos* (οὐκ ἐπαινε-σόμεθα) alludes to the nearly identical rhetoric of Hera (οὔ τοι πάντες ἐπαινέομεν ["we do not all express *epainos*"], *Il.* 4.29).[45] Thus, at the very moment that he first offers concrete suggestions for the reshaping of the Iliadic tradition, Socrates conjures the first episode to raise the same possibility within the poem—suggesting, furthermore, that the *Iliad*'s own reflections on this subject ought to be expunged in favor of the philosopher's superior understanding.

The significance of this gesture should not be underestimated. In Socrates' playful manipulation of Iliadic themes, we find positive proof that at least one ancient reader—a reader no less authoritative than Plato himself—recognized the Iliadic treatment of the *epainos* motif as a way of reflecting on the decisive power of reception to shape the contours of tradition, and a statement of the ulti-mate dependence of tradition on the collective values of the community to which it belongs. Plato, in other words, read the *Iliad* as I do; and he evidently expected his reader to do so as well.[46]

A much later (Hadrianic) source provides evidence that Plato's reading, far from being idiosyncratic, in fact resonated with the way that others understood the *Iliad*'s treatment of collective decision making in the fourth century BCE. The document in question is the so-called *Certamen* or *Contest of Homer and Hesiod*, which recounts a poetic *agōn* between the two great poets, prefaced by remarks on their origins and concluded by a brief account of their subsequent travels and their respective deaths.[47] The text as we have it has a complicated history. Although a reference to Hadrian places it squarely in the second century CE, Nietzsche suggested as early as 1870 that much of our text derives from a fourth-century work, the *Mouseion* of Alcidamas, who competed with Plato and Isocrates as an educator in Athens.[48] With the discovery of two papyrus fragments, Nietzsche's hypothesis gained widespread acceptance.[49] Today, scholarly consensus holds that the bulk of the narrative goes back to Alcidamas, who may himself have been drawing on even earlier traditions.[50] It seems likely to me that some form of the contest myth predated Alcidamas, but, from my point of view, the important thing is that the story of a competition between Homer and Hesiod—a story in which Hesiod's triumph was attributed to the verdict of the presiding judge—can be more or less securely traced to Alcidamas, in substantially the same form in which we know it.[51]

As Barbara Graziosi has shown, ancient biographical narratives about the poet Homer "represent a rich and nuanced body of evidence for the early reception of epic"—and the *Contest* is no exception.[52] It is not difficult to detect in this story some form of critical reflection on the two most prestigious representatives of archaic Greek epic. In the view of Gregory Nagy, the issue at stake is the degree of Panhellenic appeal enjoyed by the two traditions: "the myth of [Hesiod's] victory compensates for the fact that the poetry of Hesiod is relatively less Panhellenic than that of Homer."[53] Without a doubt the text establishes a contrast between the two poets in terms of the breadth of their appeal. Competing in Chalkis at the funeral games of the Euboean king Amphidamas, Homer is repeatedly acclaimed the winner by the assembled Hellenes (οἱ Ἕλληνες, 176, 205 ed. Allen)—the term underscores that Homer is the favorite of a composite audience representing all Greeks, not merely the local Euboean community—while Hesiod owes his victory to the idiosyncratic preference of the local king, Panēdēs.[54] And even if we should hesitate to see in this detail a relative denigration of Hesiod's Panhellenic status, we can nevertheless agree with James Porter that the *Contest* narrative offers "a reflection on the relative value of the two poets."[55]

What is remarkable—and of cardinal interest for the present discussion—is that this value is expressed precisely in terms of the Iliadic representation of *epainos*. More than that: the decisive scene of Panēdēs' judgment is constructed in a manner that recalls more or less directly the opening assembly of the *Iliad*. Following a command performance, the assembled Hellenes express their approval for Homer (the verb is *epainein*) and bid Panēdēs to declare him the victor, but the king, playing the role of Agamemnon, defies collective will in favor of his own inclination:

θαυμάσαντες δὲ καὶ ἐν τούτῳ τὸν Ὅμηρον <u>οἱ Ἕλληνες ἐπήνουν</u>, ὡς παρὰ τὸ προσῆκον γεγονότων τῶν ἐπῶν, καὶ ἐκέλευον διδόναι τὴν νίκην. ὁ δὲ βασιλεὺς τὸν Ἡσίοδον ἐστεφάνωσεν εἰπὼν δίκαιον εἶναι τὸν ἐπὶ γεωργίαν καὶ εἰρήνην προκαλούμενον νικᾶν, οὐ τὸν πολέμους καὶ σφαγὰς διεξιόντα. τῆς μὲν οὖν νίκης οὕτω φασὶ τυχεῖν τὸν Ἡσίοδον . . .

Cert. 205–11 (ed. Allen)

Wondering once again at Homer, <u>the Hellenes approved him</u>, on the grounds that his verses surpassed what the occasion required, and they urged [the king] to award him the victory. But the king crowned Hesiod [as the victor], saying that it was just for the one encouraging agriculture and peace to be victorious, not the one recounting battles and slaughter. And so they say Hesiod won the victory . . .

Ernst Vogt found in the judgment of Panēdēs—which in fact became a proverbial label for a bad decision—a "flagrant injustice."[56] Others have taken issue with his view, seeing no explicit indication in the text of an adverse assessment of the king.[57] The indications are there, however—in the narrative's intertextual underpinnings. By setting himself in opposition to collective will, Panēdēs aligns himself with the counterconsensual behavior of Agamemnon, which, as we have seen, is not merely a premier example of injustice but also a violation of social norms. The king's affinity with Agamemnon is signaled also by the odd name that the text bestows on him: Panēdēs, the one to whom "all is pleasing" (*pan*, "all," + *hēdus*, "sweet, pleasing").[58] This compound exploits the same lexical cue that sets Agamemnon apart from the community: recall that Agamemnon's singular preference is designated in Book 1 and elsewhere by the verb *handanein*, "to please," cognate with the second element of the Euboean king's name. In other words, Panēdēs' divergence from the sentiment of the assembled Hellenes is constructed in terms that are carefully taken over from the *Iliad*'s portrayal of consensus and its discontents.

There is, however, an alternative background and an alternative model of kingship against which Panēdēs' judgment might be viewed. If the Homeric intertext figures him as a definitively unjust king, the Hesiodic one, which is arguably no less important, rehabilitates him. By siding with Hesiod and promoting the latter's vision of peaceful agricultural prosperity, Panēdēs shows himself to be at odds with the unjust kings of the *Works and Days,* whose crooked judgments in favor of Hesiod's delinquent brother Perses threaten to undermine that prosperity. The *Contest* thus charts a course between two paradigms of unjust kingship, one Homeric and the other Hesiodic. Panēdēs' task, in one sense, is to choose which kind of unjust king he would rather be. The passages on which he bases his decision—the king asks each of the poets to recite the best lines of their respective oeuvres—have puzzled some scholars, on the grounds that they seem not to be the most representative.[59] But in fact they serve as perfect illustrations of the values implied by Panēdēs' alternatives. Hesiod offers a version of *Works and Days* 382–91, a bit of agricultural advice to Perses aimed at procuring the kind of security that would eliminate the need for recourse to corrupt kings. Homer, on the other hand, recites a composite of *Iliad* 13.126–33 and 339–44, lines that, uncharacteristically for that poem, stress the concerted action of large masses of anonymous fighters. Homer, that is, presents one of the *Iliad*'s most concise and powerful expressions of solidarity. It is precisely this solidarity that Panēdēs rejects when he rejects Homer—simultaneously, as it happens, embracing the Homeric model of (unjust) kingship.

The *Contest of Homer and Hesiod* offers a unique window onto the ongoing reception of these two Panhellenic poetic traditions in the fourth century (and possibly even earlier). What is, for my purposes, most fascinating about this text is the framework it adopts for figuring the process of reception. Like Plato's Socrates, the *Contest* narrative takes over one of the *Iliad*'s most iconic scenes of collective decision making and appropriates the *epainos* motif in order to stage its own reflections on poetic tradition. These acts of appropriation are faithful extensions of Iliadic themes, as well as evidence for the degree to which the poem's treatment of *epainos* could be recognized as a way of attending to traditional dynamics even by classical audiences and readers. While Plato exploits the motif in order to highlight the role of collective values in shaping the community's poetic inheritance, the *Contest* uses it as shorthand for the Panhellenization of traditions. Crucially, in this text the Panhellenic reception of Homer (and Hesiod) is figured in terms of a unique political situation: a "state of exception." The Panhellenic consensus over the value of a Homer or a Hesiod involves compromises, as the tensions between local and universalizing perspectives (corresponding to those of Panēdēs and the Hellenes, respectively) play themselves out. For this reason, a Panhellenic tradition will perhaps always be in some sense exceptional, involving a suspension of one or another set of norms.

BEYOND "TRADITION" AND "INNOVATION"

The *Iliad*, as we have seen, presents itself as just such an exception. The entire plot arises from the state of exception initiated by Agamemnon in Book 1 and develops as a response to the suspension of norms on a variety of levels. The most concrete sign of the poem's exceptional status is the Achaean wall, which, in the words of James Porter, stands in a relationship of "functional identity . . . with the plot of the *Iliad*."[60] Constructed solely to meet the emergency of Achilles' absence from the fighting, the importance of the wall to the Trojan story begins and ends with the *Iliad*. Meanwhile, as a focal point for tensions within the divine community, the wall delineates a period in which a normally cooperative environment among the gods is temporarily supplanted by one of intense antagonism. In other words, the wall constitutes a material signifier of the poem's singular status.

This singularity has always resonated with readers. Although the loss of much early Greek poetry makes it difficult to measure the poem directly against its context, critical assessments have often focused on the ways in which it can be presumed to have stood apart from its background, for instance, in terms of its monumental scope or its relation to the Epic Cycle.[61] For many writers, it is precisely in such arguments about the distinctive qualities of the *Iliad* (and the *Odyssey*) that one can trace the originality of the poet or poets to whom the poems are credited or otherwise glimpse the moment at which a decisive break with tradition produced the Homeric epics. The *Iliad*'s distinctiveness, however it is imagined or reconstructed, thus becomes the means of charting the line between tradition and innovation.[62] This is in spite of the inherent difficulties involved in measuring the traditionality of the poem in the nearly complete absence of appropriate benchmarks.[63] But as I have suggested—partly with reference to the wall itself—there is another way to assess the evident uniqueness of the *Iliad*, both as a matter of the text's objective characteristics and as a matter of its rhetoric of self-presentation. The *Iliad*'s exceptionalism can be understood as the result of its position in the ecology of traditions, that is, as an expression of a Panhellenizing tendency that must inevitably seek a measure of differentiation from more localized traditions.

From this perspective, the issue of the *Iliad*'s singularity is entirely distinct from the question of the "originality" of the poet—or poets, or tradition—that produced it. Indeed, it supersedes the problematic opposition between "tradition" and "innovation" altogether. Those qualities that make the *Iliad* exceptional may well be "innovative" from one point of view—the point of view of a competing or epichoric tradition. But that is not to say that they are not themselves rooted in a tradition of their own. The ambiguity of these categories is the key to the poem's seemingly contradictory ability to sustain both conservative and innovative impulses simultaneously.

The most surprising thing about the *Iliad*'s poetics of consent is the way that it anchors a narrative defined, for the most part, by the violation of norms to a system of values that centers on the collective approval of the community. This is not the kind of strategy one would expect to find in the work of a poet or group of poets conscious of their originality with respect to traditional norms, nor in a text that arises from a definitive break with tradition. To be sure, the state of exception depicted by the poem might be thought to suggest such a break, as though, by spotlighting the suspension of norms, the poem were drawing attention to its own deviation from traditional precedent. Porter in fact raises the possibility of such a reading in his discussion of the Achaean wall.[64] But here I return to the point I made above in connection with Poseidon's objection to the wall and Zeus' reply: the debate over the wall, the most concrete sign of the *Iliad*'s exceptionalism, predicates the prestige of the Iliadic tradition on the normalization of the exception—the destruction of the wall—and the reconsolidation of collective support for this outcome. The poem may, within certain carefully delineated boundaries, give free reign to unprecedented developments, but ultimately the normative force of collective sentiment works to reassert the standards agreed upon by the community.[65]

The *Iliad* stops short of dramatizing the complete restoration of collective frameworks. As I stressed in earlier chapters, the consensus at which much of the poem seems to aim is only ever implied, never fully achieved. But the absence of a functional consensus from the text cannot be a reason for dismissing its central importance to the poem's rhetoric of self-presentation. On the contrary: the difficulties that beset communities within the text are only so many signs of an awareness, embedded within the tradition, of the need to look beyond the text, to the here and now of performance, for the source of the collective norms governing the tradition. The *Iliad*'s several struggling social groups present imperfect images of a power collectively to determine social realities that is finally realized only in the world of performance, in the community that emerges across time and space in the sequence of Iliadic audiences.[66] This diachronic and translocal community, engaged in a long-term process of collective decision making that shapes and determines the tradition, obviously transcends any single occasion for performance. For this reason, the poem's interest in collective dynamics culminates in a "boundless people" that extends notionally beyond the text, escaping the spatial and temporal bounds of the Troy story.

The real-world audiences comprising this "boundless people" at the broadest level would always be called upon to evaluate Iliadic performances against their own experiences, and so to make a variety of judgments regarding what was traditional and what was innovative from their several points of view. These judgments must have been extraordinarily diverse, both across different audiences and among members of the same audience. As Ruth Scodel has argued in detail, the *Iliad*'s "rhetoric of inclusion"—the variety of techniques and incidents that seemingly presuppose the audience's familiarity with the story—cannot be taken as an indication that any given motif is indeed traditional from the audience's perspective, or even that it is traditional in the objective sense.[67] By the same token, the poem's numerous indications that its content is somehow singular or exceptional cannot be taken as a sign of innovation, objective or otherwise. Like Scodel's "rhetoric of inclusion," this "rhetoric of exceptionalism" is an expression of the tradition's drive to establish a community of stakeholders to whom the poem and its tradition will belong, and whose normative expectations for how the story should be told will realize the poem's implicit demand for the restoration of norms.

The solution to the *Iliad*'s crisis of exception emerges in the here and now of performance, as audiences engage in the construction of an evolving consensus that affirms the norms of an exceptional tradition. That consensus is still evolving today as we, the modern successors to so many generations of audiences and readers, continue to debate the meaning of this remarkable poem. Its capacity to reveal meaning, of course, vastly exceeds its reflexive commentary on the nature of poetic and political collectivities. The poetics of consent is only one strand in an extraordinarily rich and textured fabric. We can be guided, however, in our pursuit of meaning by the *Iliad*'s own modeling of interpretive communities: we can recognize that an ultimate consensus, an ultimate determination of the poetry's significance, will always remain elusive, always just beyond reach. The constitution of an interpretive consensus is an open-ended, continuously unfolding process. This is what ensures that the experience of poetry—even poetry that sets solidarity and cohesion as its highest values—can never be reduced to a totalitarian prescriptiveness, a tyranny of the collective. The search for consensus is an invitation to the continuation of discussion and debate.

Epainos *and the* Odyssey

George Bolling stipulated that "a Homeric grammar should be written in three parts: a description of the *Iliad,* a description of the *Odyssey,* a comparison of these descriptions."[1] This principle certainly holds true for what I have called the "grammar of reception," with respect to which we find significant differences between the two Homeric poems. The narrow limits of a short afterword do not permit me to provide a complete description of the *Odyssey's* grammar, nor a complete comparison with that of the *Iliad.* But a brief indication of the most salient features of collective response in the *Odyssey* will provide a useful starting point for analysis of that poem's treatment of the relation between political and poetic dynamics. We will find that, as in so many other respects, the *Iliad* and the *Odyssey* develop visions that are neither divergent nor identical but complementary. In particular, in reflecting on the relation between poetic tradition and the community to which it belongs, the *Odyssey* tends to focus more on active than on passive tradition bearers—on performers rather than audiences.

As I noted in chapter 1, the only two response formulas shared by the *Iliad* and the *Odyssey* are (in terms of the *Iliad's* system) the definitively inefficient and the definitively efficient responses—silence and *epainos.*[2] This fact is, in itself, indicative of certain norms established by the epic tradition at the broadest level, above all the principle that decisions should ordinarily be made by *epainos.* Each poem makes use of a set of additional formulas in accordance with its own particular thematic concerns. So, for instance, the *Odyssey* introduces formulas that highlight public wonder at Telemachus' newly assertive pronouncements, and also the disheartening effect that Odysseus' commands not infrequently have on his companions.[3] Perhaps the most significant Odyssean addition to the basic system, however, is a formula that frequently and almost exclusively characterizes the deliberations of the Suitors, exemplified by the line ὣς ἔφατ' Ἀντίνοος, τοῖσιν δ' ἐπιήνδανε μῦθος ("thus spoke Antinoos, and his *muthos* pleased them," *Od.* 18.50).[4] The use of a form of *handanein*, which we have seen to be the *vox propria* for divisive, individualized preference, seems deliberately designed to mark the Suitors as a deficient community, even an anticommunity, organized not around collective interests but around the coordination of selfish ones.[5]

And yet the Suitors are, on rare occasions, capable of *epainos*. When Telemachus expressly calls on Antinoos and Eurumakhos to express approval for his injunction not to interfere in the boxing match between Iros and the disguised Odysseus (ἐπὶ δ' αἰνεῖτον βασιλῆες ["you two kings approve"], *Od.* 18.64), they and the rest of the Suitors oblige (ὣς ἔφαθ', οἱ δ' ἄρα πάντες ἐπήνεον ["thus he spoke, and they all expressed *epainos*"], 18.66).[6] And on one significant occasion they come to a true consensus without being compelled to do so: when Antinoos proposes the plot to kill Telemachus in an ambush, the group readily responds with *epainos* (*Od.* 4.673). The formulation of this plot occupies a crucial position in the poem's narrative economy, bringing as it does the Telemachy (the first four books of the poem; with Book 5 the focus shifts to Odysseus) to a close. It also creates considerable suspense, as the audience awaits fulfillment of what should be, according to the rules of the formulaic grammar, an effective proposal, that is, one that achieves its purpose. Narratologically, then, this moment of *epainos* is analogous to the Achaean *epainos* that concludes *Iliad* Book 3: in both cases an apparently efficient response to a proposal that would lead to an unacceptable outcome (in terms of the traditional plot) creates a cliffhanger effect. And in both cases divine intervention is necessary to ensure that aberrant *epainos* does not derail the plot.[7]

One of the more striking features of the *Odyssey*'s grammar of reception is the manner in which it is applied to certain of Odysseus' nondeliberative utterances, specifically, to his narrative of his adventures before an audience of Phaeacians (the so-called *Apologoi*). Not that it is unusual or unexpected to find response formulas used in nondeliberative contexts. As we saw in chapter 1, some of the *Iliad*'s response formulas have wider applications; and the *Odyssey*, though relatively poorer in deliberative scenes, is richer in terms of those that depict narration (or poetic performance) as an independent activity.[8] And yet, if it is true that, in Iliadic contexts, *epainos* reflects in some way the collective support of the community for its poetic traditions, then it cannot but strike us as odd that Odysseus himself—a quasi-poet in his own right, as is often stressed—receives for his performance in the *Apologoi* not *epainos* but its opposite. Both when he pauses and when he finally concludes his narrative, Odysseus meets with the stunned silence of his audience:

ὣς ἔφαθ᾽, οἱ δ᾽ ἄρα πάντες ἀκὴν ἐγένοντο σιωπῇ,
κηληθμῷ δ᾽ ἔσχοντο κατὰ μέγαρα σκιόεντα.
Od. 11.333–34 = 13.1–2

Thus he spoke, and they were all silent,
held still by enchantment throughout the shadowed halls.

Granted, the "silence" formula is among the most versatile of response formulas.[9] Nevertheless, if patterns of collective response are to have any meaningful correlation with poetic dynamics, is it not problematic to find the audience to Odysseus's most poetic performance reacting in an apparently "inefficient" manner? The problem seems especially acute if we recall that, as we saw in chapter 9, texts other than the Homeric poems, apparently reflecting the usage of the rhapsodes themselves, readily apply the language of *epainos* to the reception of Homeric poetry.

The difficulty recedes if we consider more carefully what "efficiency" and "inefficiency" should mean in this context. Transferring these concepts from the realm of deliberation to that of poetic tradition, we must think what it means for a performance—not a proposal—to be efficacious. In an environment governed by oral tradition, an efficacious performance is above all one that is taken up as a model by subsequent performers. Like an efficacious proposal for collective action, such a performance has a lasting effect on the community, providing as it does the basis for later reperformances. This is evidently the import of the rhapsodes' use of *epaineîn*: by "approving" Homer through the quotation of Homeric verses, a rhapsode affirms the relationship of his performance to the ultimate (notional) model, the performance of Homer himself. From this point of view, it becomes clear why the Phaeacians cannot express *epainos* for Odysseus' performance. Who in their community would ever be able to reperform the *Apologoi*? Odysseus' incomparable narrative abilities and his singularly authoritative knowledge of events—to say nothing of the first-person form in which his story is cast—make his narrative unrepeatable by anyone in the world he inhabits.[10] Odysseus' tale is one that can never be taken up directly by the community. It requires a uniquely powerful and authoritative force—the Muse, by way of the figure of Homer and the Homeric tradition—to transform his tale into a form that is capable of being sustained and transmitted by others. That form is the *Odyssey*.

As a performer, then, Odysseus is cut off from every community, in the sense that his performance is disconnected from the social networks that ordinarily sustain poetic tradition. The operation of such networks is a major preoccupation of the *Odyssey*, which exploits the opposition between the two singers Phēmios and Dēmodokos precisely in order to explore contrasting relationships between poet and community. Dēmodokos' very name signifies the close connection he enjoys with his community of listeners: he is the one who is "accepted [-*dokos*] by the people [*dēmos*]," an interpretation that is reinforced by the narrative itself, which assigns to him the epithet λαοῖσι τετιμένον, "honored by the people" (*Od.* 8.472).[11] The precise nature of the "acceptance" at issue is suggested by the verbal component of Dēmodokos' name. The -*dokos* element is cognate with the verb *dekhesthai*, "receive, accept," which refers in the *Odyssey* to, among other things, the acceptance—that is, the putting into effect—of a speech act, as in Antinoos' reluctant acknowledgment of the necessity of abiding by Telemachus' stern command:

καὶ χαλεπόν περ ἐόντα δεχώμεθα μῦθον, Ἀχαιοί,
Τηλεμάχου· μάλα δ᾽ ἥμιν ἀπειλήσας ἀγορεύει.
Od. 20.271–72

Let us accept the *muthos* of Telemachus, Achaeans,
though it be harsh; he speaks with special threats for us.[12]

If Dēmodokos is "accepted" by the community, it is not so much for who he is as for what he says (or rather, sings). The honor in which he is held is a direct consequence of the honor bestowed on his songs, which are, by implication, taken up, received, "accepted" by the Phaeacian community.[13] While Odysseus' tale is an isolated singularity that can only stun his listeners into silence, Dēmodokos' songs are, it is suggested, fully integrated into the life of the group.

The figure of Dēmodokos, then, may be taken as iconic of an ideal situation in which songs and singing are embedded in and sustained by the social life of the community. His opposite in this regard is the singer attached to the house of Odysseus on Ithaca, Phēmios. That is not to say, of course, that Phēmios' songs are not appreciated by his audience. The Suitors evidently enjoy his singing enough to compel his presence at their feasts (*Od.* 22.350–53). But there are signs of a certain disconnect between Phēmios and the community to which he belongs, or at least of some disruption of the network that would ordinarily support his role as tradition bearer (not the least being the very fact that he must be compelled to sing for the Suitors). When we first see him perform, not all his hearers are pleased: Penelope asks him to stop singing the *nostos*, "homecoming," of the Achaeans—a song that pains her—and perform instead some other selection from his stock of songs (*Od*. 1.328–44). Telemachus excuses his performance by citing the predilection of audiences for the "newest" song (*Od*. 1.351–52), an argument that not only opens up a potential gap between the preferences of Phēmios and those of his audience but also seems, curiously, to distinguish the song performed for the Suitors from a genuinely traditional repertoire.[14] (A traditional song, one circulated and transmitted within the community, would presumably not seem "new" at all.)

The most striking, and telling, indication of a gap between Phēmios and his community is his own self-characterization when he pleads with Odysseus for his life:

αὐτοδίδακτος δ᾽ εἰμί, θεὸς δέ μοι ἐν φρεσὶν οἴμας
παντοίας ἐνέφυσεν·
Od. 22.347–48

I am self-taught, and a god has imbued my mind with songs
of all kinds.

Phēmios' claim to be *autodidaktos*, "self-taught," has been much discussed, mostly in the context of attempts to reconcile this apparent assertion of creative autonomy with the simultaneous avowal of divine inspiration.[15] But this (probably false) dichotomy distracts us from what is really at stake in the remark, the key to which must be sought in its utility as an argument for why the singer should be spared. Phēmios is contending that he ought not to be associated with the Suitors; that, in spite of the fact that he regularly sings for them, he ought not to be considered a part of their community. In claiming to be *autodidaktos*, he is claiming that his activities as poet—the songs he sings—do not in any way derive from the company he keeps. Both assertions—that he is "self-taught" and that he is divinely inspired—are ways of representing his songs as socially disembedded and therefore untainted by the Suitors. While Dēmodokos is implicitly positioned as the mouthpiece of Phaeacian values and traditions, Phēmios stresses that he does not speak for the Suitors, or the Suitors for him.[16]

Phēmios' disengagement from the community that surrounds him resonates with a number of other figures in the poem. The most memorable, certainly, is the Cyclops Polyphēmos, whose name not only recalls that of the Ithacan bard but even seems to substitute for it when Odysseus refers to the singer by the striking periphrasis *poluphēmos aoidos*, "singer of many songs" (*Od.* 22.376). Like Phēmios, Polyphēmos is cut off from his social group (*Od.* 9.187–89), even by the standards of the Cyclopes, who are an antisocial lot (cf. *Od.* 9.112–15). More obviously analogous to Ithaca's isolated singer, however, is the poet whom Agamemnon leaves behind to watch over his household in his absence; this man is forcibly detached from the community at Argos and marooned on a desert island by Aigisthos, who must get him out of the way before he can seduce Clytemnestra (*Od.* 3.267–71). Notably, the loss of the singer leads ultimately to the destruction of the household, for it was, it seems, largely his influence that maintained the queen's loyalty. The implication is that social order is directly or indirectly supported by the active circulation of poetic traditions within the community.[17] The disengagement of the singer, whether forcible or not, is a sign of social dysfunction, in Argos as on Ithaca.

The destructive consequences of the disconnect between performer and group bring me back to Odysseus, who, as I have said, is undeniably a stand-in for the singer of tales. He can even be understood on returning to Ithaca as a kind of replacement for Phēmios. Numerous elements in the scene of the archery contest suggest that Odysseus' performance with the bow substitutes for the entertainment provided by Phēmios in Book 1. First, Telemachus' exchange with Penelope concerning the stranger's right to handle the bow replays their earlier exchange over Phēmios' right to sing as he pleases: in both cases, Telemachus concludes the discussion by claiming ultimate authority over affairs in the house.[18] Then, the narrator compares the bow to a lyre (or, rather, a *phorminx: Od.* 21.406–9), a metaphor that Odysseus himself exploits with his ominous remark, "Now it is time for the Achaeans to have their supper while it is light, and then to make merry in another fashion, with song and dance and with the lyre [μολπῇ καὶ φόρμιγγι]—for these are the adornments of a feast" (*Od.* 21.428–30). These words pointedly recall the way in which the narrator introduces Phēmios' singing in Book 1.[19] If Penelope was displeased by that song, the Suitors will be even more so by the entertainment that their strange new singer provides. I have already indicated that, as a performer of narrative, Odysseus is cut off, disconnected from his audiences. That disconnect takes on a lethally concrete form at the end of the *Odyssey:* never was there a more alienated performance than the one Odysseus enacts with his "lyre" for the Suitors.

The Suitors are not the only ones who suffer, however, as a result of Odysseus' inability to connect with those around him. Odysseus, to put it mildly, has a leadership problem, and the Companions, too, must bear the consequences.[20] The detour we have taken through the *Odyssey*'s depictions of poetic performance and performers permits us to set the difficulties Odysseus faces in his interactions with the Companions in a larger context, one that encompasses performative dynamics more generally.

The clearest indication of Odysseus' disconnect as a narrator is, as I have indicated, the "inefficient" response he receives among the Phaeacians. An analogous disconnect as a leader manifests itself in the context of his deliberations with the Companions, where again the grammar of reception is put to effective use as a vehicle for certain crucial themes. From the point of view of this grammar, we can observe several striking irregularities that seem to emphasize the extent to which Odysseus is marginalized within or excluded from the decision-making group. Twice, for instance, we find a reversal of the ordinary dynamics of collective decision making, according to which a single individual makes a proposal to the group, who then reject or accept it: on two occasions the Companions make a collective proposal to Odysseus, who once ignores their suggestion (to his regret: *Od.* 9.224–29) and once acquiesces (*Od.* 10.469–75). And arguably their two most fateful decisions (to open Aiolos' sack of winds and to sacrifice the cattle of Helios) are made in the absence of Odysseus, as though to underscore his detachment from the group and its dire consequences.[21] The single most remarkable violation of decision-making norms, however, is reserved for the dramatic climax in Odysseus' account of his fraught relationship with the Companions. As they near Thrinakiē, the island on which Helios keeps his cattle, Odysseus pleads with his shipmates to sail on. Their hearts "break" (τοῖσιν δὲ κατεκλάσθη φίλον ἦτορ ["their dear hearts broke"], *Od.* 12.277); Eurulokhos replies with a speech urging that they put in for the night, and it is this ruinous proposal that carries the day:

ὣς ἔφατ᾽ Εὐρύλοχος, ἐπὶ δ᾽ ἥνεον ἄλλοι ἑταῖροι.
καὶ τότε δὴ γίνωσκον, ὃ δὴ κακὰ μήδετο δαίμων,
καί μιν φωνήσας ἔπεα πτερόεντα προσηύδων·
ʿΕὐρύλοχ᾽, ἦ μάλα δή με βιάζετε μοῦνον ἐόντα. . . .ʾ
Od. 12.294–97

Thus spoke Eurulokhos, and the other companions expressed *epainos*.
And then indeed I recognized that a *daimōn* was plotting evil.
Speaking, I addressed winged words to him:
"Eurulokhos, truly by force do you compel me, who stand alone . . ."

The Companions' decision recalls the exceptional *epainos* of the Trojans in *Iliad* 18: in both cases an ill-founded consensus is attributed to the malign influence of a divinity. And this *epainos* is no less exceptional—indeed, it is perhaps even more so, insofar as it violates one of the fundamental principles of consensus-based decision making, namely, that a single objection (to say nothing of one posed by the group's most authoritative member) should be enough to forestall the outcome. In the *Iliad*, Antilokhos (hardly a hero of the same rank as Odysseus) is able to prevent *epainos* from taking effect.[22] Here, not even the leader's own claim of being subjected to *biē*—"force" or "compulsion"—carries enough weight to obstruct a questionable consensus.[23] There could be no clearer expression of Odysseus' deep and abiding estrangement from the life of the community.

Odysseus' estrangement as a leader is of a piece with his estrangement as a performer: in both cases the difficulty he faces is an inability to convey his words in a way that would make them effective in the community at large, that is to say, efficacious in shaping the words and actions of others.[24] Like his performance among the Phaeacians, his proposals to the Companions seem strangely inefficient. Perhaps there is a sense in which these proposals, like his performance, are too idiosyncratic, too deeply rooted in his own unmatchable mastery of the situation, to be taken up by others: Odysseus likes to play his cards close to the vest and frequently conceals the motives for the plans he pursues.[25] This, I submit, is one reason, perhaps the ultimate reason, why all those around him—all those in the broader community, that is, excluding the members of his own household—seem doomed to perish. Odysseus may be uniquely wise, the bearer of poetic and political wisdom with the potential to sustain social order (as we see in the *Iliad*), but that wisdom does little good if it cannot be effectively transmitted to and circulated among others. The *Odyssey* permits Odysseus to be the inimitable singer of his own *kleos*, but at considerable cost to those would-be members of his community of reception.[26] Such a community is realizable only in the world outside the poem, the world in which it is Homer's *Odyssey*—not Odysseus'—that calls for our acceptance and approval.

Notes

1. As a useful working definition of a "collective decision," I adopt the formulation of Tideman 2006: 6: "A process that identifies a pattern of future coordinated actions as the intended actions of the members of a collectivity, and creates corresponding intentions in enough members of the collectivity that in the ordinary course of events the pattern is realized." We will see that the *Iliad* generally regards the support of *all* the members of the collectivity as necessary for the realization of collective action.

2. Walsh 2005: 14. Walsh (18n56) notes two other instances of "folk definition" embedded within characters' speech in the *Iliad*.

3. I adopt the term "interpretive community" from Fish 1980, who uses it to indicate the way in which interpretive norms—the limits of what may constitute a "correct" interpretation—are established by the consensus of a particular community of readers. Although the issues Fish confronts are distinct from those at stake here, his emphasis on the collective determination of interpretive values is eminently relevant. In the context of my arguments, interpretation should be understood as being coextensive with reception.

4. "Le mot ἐπαινεῖν . . . précise souvent chez Homère une idée d'efficacité quasi juridique" (Gernet 1948: 186; reprinted in Gernet 1955, quotation on p. 16).

5. See Haubold 2000, esp. pp. 32–35; Barker 2009, ch. 1, on the "institutionalization" of dissent in the *Iliad*. For speakers' appeals to *themis*, see *Il.* 2.73 (Agamemnon) and 9.33 (Diomedes), with the remarks of Barker 2009: 62–63; cf. Agamemnon's "procedural" remark at *Il.* 19.79–80.

6. Here and elsewhere I make a rough equivalence between "politics" and "collective decision making." "Politics" and "political" are to be understood in such formulations as shorthand for the arena in which matters of significance to the social group as a whole are contested. Like Hammer, who defines "politics" as "a realm in which people think about themselves, and constitute themselves, as communities" (Hammer 2002: 32), I wish to keep "politics" distinct from the institutions of the *polis*. The degree to which these institutions can be traced in the Homeric poems remains a matter of controversy in Homeric studies, although scholars today do generally accept that the *polis* has left a significant imprint on the poems: see, e.g., Scully 1990, Seaford 1994, and the references cited by Hammer 2002: 205n50.

7. Finley 1977: 80–81. Cf. Raaflaub and Wallace 2007: 28, "there is . . . no formal obligation to respect the people's opinion"; Catanzaro 2008: 273, "la componente dei molti riunita in assemblea ha scarsa, se non scarsissima, autorità in materia decisionale e si limita, spesso, ad approvare o a contestare le scelte dei capi"; Barker 2009: 35n20, "the group do not even possess the power of ratifying policy." For a survey of some alternative views, see Ruzé 1997: 14–15.

8. Cartledge 2009: 33. For Węcowski 2011: 77–78, by contrast, it is precisely in this episode that the poem reveals an awareness of collective modes of decision making.

9. Hammer 2002: 146–47. Hammer nevertheless upholds the common position that "the leaders appear free to follow or ignore whatever might be the expressed sentiment" of the people (145). A similar ambivalence characterizes the remarks of van Wees 1992: 32–33, who contends that, while "the people . . . have no vote or any say in the matter," nevertheless, "decisions taken by the princes are supposed to express the will of the people." Weber's description of "plebiscitary democracy" can be found at Weber 1978: 266–71.

10. Cf. Green 2010: 145 on Weber's model: "A plebiscitary leader pursues a substantive agenda that is his or her own, not that of the People, and thus possesses an extraordinary degree of independent decision-making authority."

11. Allan and Cairns 2011 (quotation from p. 117; see p. 115 for the de iure / de facto distinction).

12. Flaig 1994; quotation from p. 31 ("Der Dichter leistet politische Reflexion in atheoretischer Form"). Others have discussed Homeric deliberation in terms of "consensus," although Flaig's discussion remains the most rigorous: see, e.g., Patzek 1992: 131–32 and Farenga 2006: 109–73. Both of these writers voice reservations about the extent to which the consensus they observe genuinely expresses collective sentiment (cf. Farenga 2006: 135). See also Cantarella 1979: 104–29 on the relationship between consensus and power in the constitution of authority.

13. For a more complete overview of the sociological and political conditions necessary for the operation of consensus as a decision-making principle, see Flaig 1994: 15–17 (recapitulating the discussion of Flaig 1993: 140–41). My quotations refer to these pages.

14. Cf. Sartori 1975: 144–45 on the "principle, or mechanism, of *deferred reciprocal compensation*" (emphasis original).

15. On decision making by majority rule, and the absence of such a concept in the *Iliad*, see Ruzé 1984 (esp. p. 248); on the concept of majority rule in Greek thought more generally, see Loraux 1990.

16. Sartori 1975: 142–43. The conditions of possibility for such a comparison pose a philosophical problem in their own right (for instance in the context of the "problem of other minds"), but they may be taken for granted in the context of the pragmatic perspective adopted here: cf. Flaig 1993: 140. In applying this model to the *Iliad*, I assume that the poem recognizes rational criteria for deliberation; see on this point Schofield 1999: 3–30, who convincingly refutes Finley's assertion that rational, principled debate has no place in the world of the heroes (cf. Finley 1977: 114).

17. Flaig 1994: 21n32 suggests that there is no indication in the text of the means by which the gods would express their approval, were they to be presented with an accept-

able proposal. In fact, Hera points fairly precisely to such a mechanism, by negating it: we can infer from her words that, if consensus were achieved, the gods' expression of approval would be indicated by some version of the *epaineîn* formula discussed in chapter 1.

18. For more on the metanarrative perspective of the Olympians, see chapter 7.

19. For discussion of three historical consensus-based decisions in three distinct societies, see Boehm 1996. For a description of the consensus-based society of Samoa, mediated by the views of native informants, see Huffer and So'o 2003, who give a good sketch of the actual process of making decisions by consensus on p. 295. On the decision-making procedures of committees, see Sartori 1975, esp. pp. 143–47.

20. Cf. Bailey 1965: 8–9 (on the politics of village life in India): "some of the apparent anxiety to damp down dispute . . . springs from the fact that everyone knows that if the decision is not the result of an agreed compromise, then it cannot be implemented. . . . conflicts will tend to be resolved by compromise if the majority know that the minority must be carried with them on pain of taking no action at all." (On the inadequacy of "compromise" as a descriptor of the solution reached by consensus, see Sartori 1975: 144–45; Flaig 1993: 140, 1994: 15.)

21. For a thorough discussion of "consent" and "consensus" in this sense, see Partridge 1971.

22. See Murphy 1990 and Huffer and So'o 2003: 286.

23. The difference between consensus and unanimity in this regard can be observed clearly in the case of one-off decisions by majority rule (e.g., popular referenda): unanimity is, at least in principle, possible in such cases, but consensus (in the sense developed here) is not, since the decision is not part of an ongoing decisional context that would permit the operation of the "principle of deferred compensation."

24. Barker 2009: 31–88.

25. Cf. ibid., 5: "representations of debate may be best understood in terms of institutional dissent, by virtue of which authority is challenged and alternative views are not only tolerated, but also somehow incorporated, managed and utilized . . ."

26. I refer here to Barker's (2009: 18n62) criticism of Loraux 2002. In general, I find myself in near total agreement with Barker. The most significant point at which I diverge concerns my reading of the initial assembly of Book 1 (which, in fact, Barker does not recognize as an assembly), set forth in chapter 3. I read this scene as an exception to a set of norms established by the Iliadic tradition and the tradition of archaic epic at large; my arguments presuppose familiarity with these norms on the part of the audience, in accordance with my understanding of Homeric poetry as a traditional medium. Barker, on the other hand, argues that the *Iliad* presents the gatherings of Book 1 not as exceptions to an established practice but as institutional firsts (see esp. Barker 2009: 52n38, which tempers the arguments of Barker 2004).

27. Flaig 1994: 30.

28. Flaig 1993: 142–43. On the procedures of the Roman senate, which regularly reached a decision without recourse to strict majority rule, see Flaig 1994: 14n3; for a discussion of consensus in the political culture of the Roman Republic more broadly, Flaig 1995. It is significant in this regard that those ancient writers who did, exceptionally,

stress the importance of councils in the Homeric poems—Philodemus in his *On the Good King According to Homer* and Dio of Prusa in the 56th *Oration*—"wrote with their attention on the Roman world and the position of the senate" (Murray 1965: 176).

29. On the opposition between majority rule and consensus as, respectively, zero- and positive-sum methods of decision making, see Sartori 1975. For a more positive view of the role of consensus in the political life of early Greek communities, see Hölkeskamp 2000 (esp. pp. 35–40), who contends that both the *Iliad* and early inscribed laws project consensus as a value.

30. The civic ideal of *homonoia*, valued particularly highly in Spartan political discourse, is not a good match: as Cartledge 2009: 24 stresses, *homonoia* is "not merely consensus or passive acquiescence in the will or power of the majority, but literally and full-bloodedly 'same-mindedness,' absolute and total unanimity." On *homonoia*, see also Bonazzi 2006.

31. Flaig 1994: 30–31.

32. Loraux 2002: 30.

33. Raaflaub and Wallace 2007: 24; cf. Raaflaub 1997: 626–28 and 1998: 169, suggesting that "the burden of proof" has shifted "to the side of those who continue to deny the substantial historicity of Homeric society or the 'Homeric world.'" Raaflaub dates this "Homeric society" somewhat later than Finley, assigning it to the late ninth or eighth century (1997: 628; a slightly later date seems to be allowed by Raaflaub and Wallace 2007: 24).

34. See, e.g., Carlier 1984: 210–14, Donlan 1997, Morris 1986, van Wees 1992. A concise review of various historicizing approaches can be found in Węcowski 2011.

35. Cf. Hammer 2002: 33 on the "historical context for the activity of politics that we see in the *Iliad*."

36. Snodgrass 1974 (reprinted as ch. 10 in Snodgrass 2006). For a response to Snodgrass, see Morris 1986: 105–15. It should be noted that Snodgrass allows for the possibility of differences between the *Iliad* and the *Odyssey*: even considered separately, each poem presents an amalgamation of social and material details.

37. Cf. Ulf 2002 and 2011: 12, 18.

38. A point of view eloquently and succinctly expressed by Allan 2006: 9n40: "Homeric society itself is a fiction . . . not only in the obvious sense of 'existing within a work of literature,' but also in the stronger sense that it does not track a particular historical society. Like the epic *Kunstsprache*, Homeric society has developed to suit the purposes of generations of bards." Cf. Cartledge 1996: 687–88. For concise inventories of comparable views (and counterviews), see Raaflaub 1998: 190n25, Hammer 2002: 205n49.

39. So, e.g., Raaflaub and Wallace 2007: 24.

40. Snodgrass 2006: 173.

41. See, e.g., Taplin 1992: 33–35, Seaford 1994: 144–54, Cook 1995: 3–5, 168–70, West 1995, Jensen 1999 and 2011. Arguments for a later date have long been put forward (e.g., by Sealey 1957, Kullmann 1960: 381, Burkert 1976), but have noticeably gained momentum in recent years. For a useful survey of references, see Cook 2004: 50n52.

42. So Whitmarsh 2004: 40.

43. Nagy first outlined his "evolutionary model" in Nagy 1981; see also the detailed discussion in Nagy 1996b, chs. 5–7. For the role of reception in the shaping of the texts, see Nagy 2009a: 283, 2012: 37–38.

44. Cf. the judicious comments of Burgess 2001: 52: "The evidence supports the argument for a long Homeric compositional tradition leading to fixation of texts only in the sixth century. A Homeric performing tradition that remained continuously fluid, yet became increasingly stabilized, would explain the presence of elements from different time periods, including the Archaic Age"; Osborne 2004: 206: "Any reading of the *Iliad* or *Odyssey* needs to be informed by an appreciation that the epic tradition had been formed and shaped through successive very different social arrangements and material cultures."

45. I am not suggesting that Odysseus' boar's-tusk helmet (*Il.* 10.261–65)—to take one of the most famous Homeric anachronisms as example—necessarily implies a Bronze Age version of either the *Doloneia* or the *Iliad*. My point is that we must think in terms of traditional narratives and not simply in terms of traditional diction as an abstract system acquired and transmitted independently of its narrative settings. Singers do not learn and transmit the language of epic songs as a disembedded system—they learn *songs*. (On the acquisition of the art of epic singing, see Lord 2000: 13–29.) Still, it is worth recalling Palmer's observation that, given the negative semantics of the name *Akhilleus* in the absence of a supporting heroic narrative, the appearance of this name on Linear B tablets suggests the existence of an *Akhilleid* as early as the thirteenth century BCE (Palmer 1979).

46. Various dictation theories have been proposed. The most prominent are represented by Jensen 1980 and 2011, West 1990, Powell 1991, and Janko 1994: 37–38.

47. Forceful arguments, however, are still being made in favor of a relatively early date for the fixation of the texts. I note in particular Frame 2009, who situates the creation of the *Iliad* and *Odyssey* in the late eighth century, in the context of the Panionia (see esp. pp. 551–620).

48. On the need to situate Homeric poetics in a diachronic perspective, see González 2013. The tension between synchronic and diachronic perspectives is a theme that runs throughout the work of Gregory Nagy; see, e.g., Nagy 1976a. Following Nagy 1990b: 4, I equate the term "synchronic" with "the workings of a system as it exists at a given time and place," and "diachronic" with "the transformations of this system through time."

49. Hölkeskamp 2009 offers an outstanding example of the results that can be achieved by this method. See also Wilson 2002: 143–44.

50. For instance, the poem's representation of Agamemnon's autocratic and counter-consensual exercise of power is potentially relevant to the way tyranny is configured in the discourse of the early *poleis*. Read against the dynamics I trace in chapters 3 and 5, Alcaeus' lines on the role of *epainos* in establishing the tyrannical power of Pittakos are especially provocative (fr. 348 ed. Lobel-Page). In chapter 9, I note other examples of resonance with historical and literary autocrats. Haubold 2000 (esp. ch. 3) provides an illuminating discussion of the relationship between the Iliadic narrative and the self-awareness of historical Greek communities.

51. The Panathenaia features prominently in Nagy's "evolutionary model." Frame 2009: 515–647 has made a case for the Panionia as the context for the creation of the Homeric poems. Whitman 1958: 76, 81 names both of these festivals as well as the Delia as likely contexts for performance of the *Iliad;* for more on the Delia, see Nagy 2010b: 12–20.

52. Cf., e.g., van Wees 2002: 115 (the Achaean host as a reflection of Panhellenic festivals), Wickersham and Pozzi 1991: 5 (similarly for the funeral of Patroklos), Haubold 2000: 188–95 (on the resonance of Homeric poetry with the Panathenaia).

53. Nagy 1999: 7.

54. For the pervasiveness of the zero-sum mentality in Greek society, cf. Griffith 1990: 188 (with references). Graziosi 2001 gives a fascinating account of the way in which Homeric tradition, as exemplified by the *Certamen* (which she tentatively derives from rhapsodic traditions), can picture itself as engaged in a positive-sum contest.

55. In this regard the presentation of Homeric poetry at a religious festival is a preeminent example of a "ceremony," in the sense developed by Redfield 1994: 163: "Any given ceremony . . . will be efficacious largely to the degree that it is perceived to be a repetition of earlier ceremonies. . . . Ceremony thus implies both the diachronic continuity of the community and its synchronic cohesion." Redfield goes on to note that the cohesion established by such ceremonies is "consensual" and furthermore that "the analogies between ceremony and performed art are obvious" (164).

56. These limitations are stressed by Cassio 2009: 109.

57. The link between the dynamic process of "evolution" and textual fixity may seem paradoxical, but it is based in the realities of oral tradition: in a predominantly oral culture, institutions are more likely than texts to be considered authoritative. We should therefore look for an institutional context (such as the Panathenaic festival) as the catalyst for textual fixity.

58. Georg Danek (2010: 40) takes up the view of the Homerist and Slavist Zlatan Čolaković, who maintained, on the basis of comparison with Avdo Međedović, Parry's famous "Yugoslav Homer" (the words of Albert Lord, as quoted by Mitchell and Nagy in Lord 2000: xii), that Homer himself was a "post-traditional singer" (Čolaković 2004, 2007). I offer a refutation of this problematic notion of "post-traditionality" in Elmer 2010.

59. Ford 1992: 1–12, Taplin 1992: 4.

60. Austin himself excluded poetry from the category of speech act (cf. J. L. Austin 1975: 9), but Johnson (1980: 52–66) has offered a forceful critique of this exclusion. Fish 1980: 231–44 makes a strikingly similar argument regarding Searle's version of speech act theory.

61. On the importance of "uptake" to the speech act as a whole, see J. L. Austin 1975: 116–17, 139. Cf. Ohmann 1972: 129 on the "social" aspect of Austin's "felicity" and the formulation of Fish 1980: 222–23: "illocutionary force . . . refers to the way an utterance is taken . . . by someone who knows the constituting procedures and their value." There is an unfortunate tendency among some writers to equate the speech act with the performative utterance, a reduction that deprives the concept of "speech act" of much of its significance.

62. Parry's writings, in which he frequently stresses the need for the interpretation of Homeric poetry to avoid criteria originating in written literature, are collected in M. Parry 1971. Lord's most influential book is *The Singer of Tales*, first published in 1960 (2nd ed. 2000). For my present purposes, the most important aspect of Lord's work is his analysis of the relationship between formula and theme.

63. Machacek 1994 is representative of the best work in response to Parry: the author shows that, while formulaic constraints may appear to be ironclad at the level of the single verse, flexibility emerges in the development of ideas across sequences of verses. A number of studies have shown that, in spite of Parry's claim that the "fixed" or "ornamental" epithet is always used indifferently to its context (cf. M. Parry 1971: 141), such epithets can in fact show some context sensitivity: see, e.g., N. Austin 1975, Sacks 1987, Lowenstam 1993, Martin 1993, Beck 1999. Shive 1987 is often cited as a refutation of Parry's basic principles of "economy" and "extension," but his work is flawed: see Nagy 1988. For a more nuanced examination of "breaches" of economy and extension, see Friedrich 2007.

64. On traditional theme as the equivalent, on the level of content, to traditional formula, on the level of wording, see Lord 2000, ch. 3. Note that Lord uses "theme" to mean a traditional *sequence* of ideas or motifs: e.g., the "council" theme includes as constituent motifs the summoning of advisors, a request for advice, the delivery of good or bad advice by the counselors, etc. Following Nagy 1990b: 4n15, I will use the term "theme" to indicate "a traditional unit of composition on the level of meaning," i.e., as any unit of traditional content, however restricted in scope, that has some correlate in the traditional diction of Homeric poetry.

65. Nagy 1999: 4.

66. A crucial example, the substitution of the quasi-*hapax* ἐπευφήμησαν for a more "normal" verb of response at *Il.* 1.22, provides the starting point for the discussion in chapter 3.

67. See, e.g., Segal 1994: 113–83 and Olson 1995.

CHAPTER 1: THE GRAMMAR OF RECEPTION

1. See LSJ s.vv. ἐπαινέω 2, ἔπαινος 1 and 2.

2. Snell 1953: 1.

3. Some continuities between Homeric, archaic, and later usage are traced in chapter 2.

4. The first volume of the *Lexikon*, which was published in separate fascicles under the supervision of various editors, appeared in 1955, the last in 2010. Snell and his coeditors U. Fleischer and H. J. Mette outlined their lexicographical principles on pp. i–vi of the inaugural volume; for *Wortfeldforschung*, see p. ii.

5. *LfgrE*, s.v. αἰνέω, ἐπαινέω 1: "ja sagen, zustimmen." The bulk of the Homeric examples are listed under this definition. Note that, contrary to Allen's practice in his OCT edition (which is otherwise the basis for the *Lexikon's* citations), H. J. Mette, the author of the article, treats the preverb as an adverbial preposition, printing *Il.* 7.344, for instance, as ὣς ἔφαθ᾽, οἱ δ᾽ ἄρα πάντες ἐπ᾽ ἤνησαν [instead of ἐπήνησαν] βασιλῆες. Only in cases with a direct object does he treat the word as a true compound, which he nevertheless

treats together with the simplex form under the definition "zu jemandem (etwas) ja sagen, ihn (es) anerkennen" (s.v. 2). Regardless of whether ἐπί is treated as a preverb or preposition, it has a decisive impact on the meaning of the expression, which must therefore be treated as an independent lexeme.

6. The single exception (Ζῆνος ἐπαινήσαντος, *Il.* 21.290), in which the deliberative and collective dimensions are still implicit, is discussed in chapter 7.

7. Cunliffe and Ebeling each devote a separate entry to ἐπαινέω, glossing it as "to express approval *to*, to agree or concur *with* . . . to express approval *of* . . . ; to approve, assent, concur" (Cunliffe 1924 s.v.); "comprobo, assensu meo excipio . . . ; assentior" (Ebeling 1885 s.v.). Ancient commentators assigned to *epainein* the basic notion of "approval": cf. the D scholia at *Il.* 3.461 and 4.380 (συγκατετίθεντο) and Eustathius 1.768.16 (ed. van der Valk): τὸ δὲ ἐπήνεον ἀντὶ τοῦ συνήνουν, συγκατετίθεντο.

8. Martin 1989.

9. J. L. Austin 1975. Austin emphasizes the distinction between the performative and the speech act when he speaks of "the doctrine of locutionary and illocutionary acts in the total speech act," asserting that "the total speech act in the total speech situation is the *only actual* phenomenon which, in the last resort, we are engaged in elucidating" (148; emphasis original). Although Austin does not, to my knowledge, make use of the term "felicity conditions," this has become the standard way scholars refer to the conditions outlined in Austin's lectures for the "felicitous" or "happy" accomplishment of a speech act.

10. J. L. Austin 1975: 116–17; see also p. 139.

11. The verb is always used absolutely in the *Odyssey*. In the *Homeric Hymn to Hermes*, the verb is construed with both an accusative and a dative (μῦθον ἐπαίνει πρεσβυτέροισι, 457). Note that the object is, once again, a *muthos*.

12. Cf. *Il.* 9.710–11, where the proposal *is* designated as a *muthos*.

13. Parry's formulation of the principle of "thrift" (later writers prefer the term "economy") can be found at M. Parry 1971: 276.

14. Edwards 1969 and Riggsby 1992 both note apparent violations of economy but support the validity of the concept. For the usefulness of Parry's notion of economy in the analysis of formulaic phraseology (with specific reference to the first of the five formulas I discuss below), see J. Foley 1995: 25. At p. 12, Foley emphasizes that the meaning of Homeric formulas exceeds the mere lexical values of words: this insight is crucial to the method I pursue in the following pages.

15. See chapter 6.

16. Lowenstam 1981: 17–22 discusses the "constraints" or "restrictions" of formulaic diction that allow us to infer from the deployment of a given formula the presence of themes, motifs, or contexts with which that formula is traditionally associated.

17. Cf. Nagy 1974: 85–89 on the metrical constraints governing speech frame formulas. Beck 2005 provides a detailed analysis of framing conventions in a variety of contexts (see chapter 5 for deliberative settings in particular); her appendix IV surveys all Homeric speech frame formulas.

18. All but (arguably) three Iliadic instances of deliberative reception (*Il.* 2.142, 3.111, and 9.173) are described using some variation either on an expression belonging to this

system or on the familiar κλύον ἠδ' ἐπίθοντο formula. The special circumstances motivating the exceptional phraseology of *Il.* 9.173 are discussed more fully in chapter 5. Agamemnon's proposal at *Il.* 2.110–41 is likewise exceptional. In fact, he does not intend his proposal to be efficacious, and the response in question is explicitly identified as the result of insufficient knowledge about the context of this proposal: ὣς φάτο, τοῖσι δὲ θυμὸν ἐνὶ στήθεσσιν ὄρινε / πᾶσι μετὰ πληθύν, ὅσοι οὐ βουλῆς ἐπάκουσαν ("thus he spoke, and he stirred the *thumos* in the chests / of all those in the rank and file, as many as had not heard his speech in the council," *Il.* 2.142–43). See chapter 4 for the implications of the fact that line 142 is a variation on a formula customarily used to describe the reaction of an *individual;* I draw attention also to the fact that this response is explicitly limited to certain members of the group, i.e., it is not properly collective. *Il.* 3.111 (οἳ δ' ἐχάρησαν Ἀχαιοί τε Τρῶές τε ["the Achaeans and the Trojans felt joy"]) is a complex case. Note that this line represents the response to Menelaus' reformulation of a proposal that has already been made by Hector, and that has already been received with one of the terms of our system (*Il.* 3.95). In any case, this passage must be read in connection with *Il.* 19.74–75, where we find a description of a group response to a public pronouncement of Achilles: ὣς ἔφαθ', οἱ δ' ἐχάρησαν ἐϋκνήμιδες Ἀχαιοί / μῆνιν ἀπειπόντος μεγαθύμου Πηλεΐωνος ("thus he spoke, and the well-greaved Achaeans felt joy, / since the great-hearted son of Peleus was forswearing his *mēnis*"). (See chapter 5 for discussion of these lines, and of the fact that in Book 3 we are dealing with the unique problem of "cross-cultural" reception.) This reaction does indeed occur in the most marked assembly in the poem (Achilles summons *all* the Achaeans, even those who did not, it seems, ordinarily participate in assemblies: *Il.* 19.42–45); the emphasis is due to the fact that Achilles' pronouncement is a singularly important juridical act, the forswearing of his *mēnis*. Nevertheless, this pronouncement is not a proposal submitted to the group for approval; it concerns rather Achilles' personalized relationship with Agamemnon (I refrain from calling this relationship "private," because it undoubtedly has implications for the community). The juridical nature of Achilles' illocution is the technical reason why it must be made in public. Note that all these apparent exceptions involve descriptions of an audience's *attitude* toward a pronouncement, not of their *expression* of that attitude.

19. As I point out below, the identical formula occurs on a number of other occasions in contexts other than collective decision making (see, e.g., *Il.* 7.92, 9.430, 10.313, 23.676).

20. The key verb *epainein* occurs as well in the following lines: *Il.* 2.335, 4.29, 4.380, 16.443, 18.312, 21.290, 22.181, 23.540. Though not all of these occurrences are formulaic, they all rely for their meaning on the function of the *epainein* response in the grammar of reception outlined here. See the index for references to discussions of each of these passages.

21. The *epainein* formula occurs in the *Odyssey* with slight variations arising from the context. Examples: *Od.* 16.393 (ὣς ἔφαθ', οἱ δ' ἄρα πάντες ἀκὴν ἐγένοντο σιωπῇ ["thus he spoke, and they were all silent"]), 7.226 (ὣς ἔφαθ', οἱ δ' ἄρα πάντες ἐπήνεον ἠδ' ἐκέλευον ["thus he spoke, and they all expressed *epainos* and bade (Alkinoos to arrange for Odysseus' homecoming)"]), 12.294 (ὣς ἔφατ' Εὐρύλοχος, ἐπὶ δ' ᾕνεον ἄλλοι ἑταῖροι ["thus spoke Eurulokhos, and the other companions expressed *epainos*"]).

22. The formula in question is exemplified by *Od.* 18.50, ὣς ἔφατ' Ἀντίνοος, τοῖσιν δ' ἐπιήνδανε μῦθος ("thus spoke Antinoos, and his *muthos* pleased them"; cf. 13.16, 16.406,

18.290, 18.422, 20.247, 21.143, 21.269). The semantics of *handanein*, discussed more fully below, signal that the Suitors' community is shaped not by a truly collective will or consensus but merely by the coordination of individual interests. Other formulas that might be included in an Odyssean grammar of reception include ὡς ἔφαθ', οἱ δ' ἄρα πάντες ὀδὰξ ἐν χείλεσι φύντες / Τηλέμαχον θαύμαζον ("thus he spoke, and they all, biting their lips, / wondered at Telemachus"), which three times (*Od.* 1.381–82, 18.410–11, 20.268–69) describes the reaction of the Suitors to a *muthos* by Telemachus, though not in explicitly deliberative contexts; and ὡς ἐφάμην, τοῖσιν δὲ κατεκλάσθη φίλον ἦτορ ("thus I spoke, and their dear hearts broke"), which occurs in a variety of contexts but can also indicate the reaction of the Companions to Odysseus' instructions (cf. esp. *Od.* 12.277). See the afterword for more on the specifically Odyssean treatment of the themes analyzed in this study.

23. For discussions of this formula and its discursive significance, see esp. J. Foley 1995, Person 1995, A. Porter 2011. All three authors include in their analyses occurrences of the formula outside the deliberative context, but their discussions nevertheless reinforce the conclusions presented here. Beck 2005: 44 notes that the formula "appears almost exclusively in the middle of group conversations" (where the category "conversation" includes deliberation). This is what we should expect if, as I claim, silence is the functional equivalent of the rejection of a proposal: the conversation must then continue until an executable policy emerges. See also Montiglio 2000: 63–66, Kelly 2007: 85–86.

24. Thus J. Foley 1995: 14: "the radical, unexpected action [proposed by the speaker] never materializes without an immediate or an eventual qualification, that is, without a substantial attendant drawback that may be crippling to or dismissive of the proposal but at the very minimum constitutes a change of narrative direction from that suggested by the initial speaker." A. Porter 2011, emphasizing the metonymic relationship between the "silence" formula and the acceptance of a *subsequent* proposal, presents a complementary perspective: for him, too, silence implies the rejection or modification of the preceding speech.

25. Heiden 1991: 10.

26. Cf. *Il.* 8.39–40: θάρσει Τριτογένεια φίλον τέκος· οὔ νύ τι θυμῷ / πρόφρονι μυθέομαι, ἐθέλω δέ τοι ἤπιος εἶναι ("Take courage, dear child, Trito-born: I have not said this / in earnest, but I wish to be in accord with you"). These verses are repeated in the debate over Hector's fate in Book 22 (*Il.* 22.183–84). Comparison with that scene, in which Athena actually forces Zeus to withdraw his proposal, suggests that here, too, her position should be understood as a rejection of Zeus' position rather than as qualified approval for it. To judge by the scholia (cf. the A scholia at *Il.* 8.28, 8.39–40, 22.183–84), certain ancient critics saw the connection with Book 22 as evidence that these and other lines (including the "silence" formula) had been imported into Book 8 from other parts of the poem. Perhaps these critics were also troubled by the appearance of the "silence" motif in a context where the proposal is apparently accepted.

27. J. Foley 1995: 16–17 comments on the Homeric technique of delaying fulfillment of the norms of traditional phraseology.

28. A similar argument might be made about the occurrence of the "silence" formula at *Il.* 3.95, where it marks the response to Hector's proposal to settle the war by

means of a duel. Although the armies enact this proposition, insofar as they stage the duel, they will of course fail to settle the war thereby. The silent response of Hector's audience is an implicit sign that his proposal will not achieve its intended result. (At the same time, this silence resonates, so to speak, with the motif of the battlefield challenge, on which, see below.) On the way this scene explores the limits of community by constructing a temporary Greco-Trojan collectivity, see Elmer 2012.

29. Cf. *Il.* 7.92. The formula can also refer to the response to a challenge in an athletic contest (*Il.* 23.676, *Od.* 8.234) and, in the *Odyssey*, the response to a storyteller (*Od.* 11.333, 13.1). J. Foley 1995: 22 finds these last two examples to be exceptional; I offer a different explanation in the afterword.

30. Even though it is offered in a *boulē* (*Il.* 10.195), Nestor's proposition that one of the Greeks should undertake a night mission ought to be seen as a challenge rather than a deliberative proposal: no course of action to be taken by the group as a whole is at issue. (Moreover, the *kleos* motif makes a thematic link between Nestor's speech and Hector's challenge in Book 7; cf. *Il.* 10.212 with 7.91.) For this reason, Nestor's proposal is not voided even though it is at first received with silence (*Il.* 10.218). The same could be said about the Trojans' response to an identical proposal made by Hector (*Il.* 10.313).

31. See Lowenstam 1981: 21 on the way that the formula χειρὶ παχείῃ ("with a stout hand") is "unmarked among men, but marked among women."

32. Gernet 1948 argues for the convergence of the procedures of the athletic *agōn* with those of the assembly. In fact, when the *agōn* requires a collective decision to be made, the response of the group is designated by the properly (and exclusively) deliberative verb *epainein*. Conversely, the fact that *epiakhein* does not imply decision-making force in the funeral games suggests that, even in assemblies, the verb does not denote a fully efficient response.

33. Considered in more detail in chapter 5.

34. In Book 7, e.g., the Achaeans shout in response to Diomedes' short speech (*Il.* 7.403), but Agamemnon's language—specifically, his use of the verb *handanein*—makes it clear that he regards his own will as decisive. (More on this scene in chapter 5.)

35. The formulaic phrase Ἀργεῖοι δὲ μέγ᾽ ἴαχον occurs in this metrical position only on these two occasions. (It occurs in line-initial position at *Il.* 4.506 and 17.317.) I devote more attention to Agamemnon's dysfunctional leadership, as evidenced especially by the development of the *epainos* motif, in chapter 5. With respect to the passage discussed here, it might be noted that Agamemnon begins his remarks as an address to Nestor (and not to the assembled Achaeans), although he concludes with directives for the community as a whole.

36. See, e.g., *Il.* 18.576 (πὰρ ποταμὸν κελάδοντα ["beside a noisy river"]) and 21.16 (ῥόος κελάδων ["noisy stream"]), and note that the participle may even be used as the proper name of a river (7.133). For the form, see LSJ s.v. κελάδω.

37. Cf. Mackie 1996: 23: "The formulas used to construct Homeric assembly scenes are strangely lacking from the *Iliad*'s accounts of Trojan assemblies." At pp. 92–93, Mackie contrasts the verbs *epikeladein* and *epainein* as distinctive indicators of approval among the Trojans and Achaeans, respectively.

38. The *Odyssey* does not observe this rule that the imperfect tense indicates an "incomplete" expression of *epainos*. In fact, *epainein* always occurs in the imperfect tense in the *Odyssey*, but it designates an efficient response nevertheless: see *Od.* 4.673, 7.226, 8.398, 12.294, 12.352, 13.47, 18.66. We observe here another difference between the poetic grammars of the *Iliad* and *Odyssey*.

39. See Barker 2009: 29–88.

40. On this passage, see Frame 2009: 175–82, who stresses that the like-mindedness of Nestor and Odysseus during the war contrasts with their parting of ways later in this same episode (*Od.* 3.159–66).

41. The connection to Iliadic themes is arguably even clearer in the case of the alternative proem attested by Aristoxenos (fr. 91a ed. Wehrli), in which the *mēnis* and *kholos* that set the poem in motion belong both to Achilles and Apollo.

42. I return to the notion of *kosmos* in chapters 2 and 4. The catastrophic assembly that is summoned "contrary to *kosmos*" in Nestor's narrative can be compared directly with the assembly that opens *Iliad* 2, where Thersites' propensity to speak οὐ κατὰ κόσμον ("without order," *Il.* 2.214) is precisely the disorderly force that must be overcome before Odysseus can restore consensus (see chapter 4).

43. We can detect in this usage a connection between the *Iliad*'s language of collective decision making and later ways of speaking about the legally sanctioned procedures of political life. *Handanein* is epigraphically attested in Crete, Phokis, and Lokris as the *vox propria* for decisions enacted by the community: see, e.g., *SEG* 27.620 (Dreros); *IC* IV.78 (Gortyn); *SEG* 35.991 (Lyttos); *FD* III 4.369 = *CID* 1.8 (Delphi); *IG* IX 1² 3.718, 38 (Lokris). In Crete, the traditional formula appears to have been ἔϝαδε πόλι (Ruzé 1984: 302), with the collective noun *polis* implying that the preference subsumes the entire community. In Iliadic usage, by contrast, *handanein* takes only a singular or plural complement. That is, it signals the preference of either one or many *individuals*, viewed independently from their collective identity. See also Gallavotti 1977: 132, who connects the Homeric usage with the Cretan inscriptions, and notes as well Hipponax fr. 132 ed. West (ἄδηκε βουλή).

44. Within the *Iliad* these themes are of course revisited many times. I draw attention to one notable instance in the description of Achilles' shield. The image of the "City at War" depicts an army paralyzed by divided opinion over which strategy to pursue; their dilemma is expressed by means of the same *handanein* formula as in Nestor's tale (δίχα δέ σφισιν ἥνδανε βουλή, *Il.* 18.510). As noted by Edwards 1991: 218, the "two *stratoi*" on the shield may well be simply two "regiments" of a single army shown, in accordance with second-millennium iconographic conventions, as encircling a city viewed in cross-section. If so, this image of a divided community has obvious relevance to the situation of the Achaeans. For the similar way in which the "City at Peace" figures dynamics among the Achaeans, see my comments in chapters 5 and 8.

45. See Blanc 1985, esp. p. 257 and pp. 259–63.

46. Phoenix constructs a direct link between his notion of *litē*, "entreaty," and the relationship of *philia*: see *Il.* 9.520–22. I have taken these two examples from Blanc 1985,

who offers as well a number of other illustrations of the connection between *anainomai* and *apēnēs*.

47. Cf. *Il.* 11.647, 23.204 (the refusal of a proffered seat); *Od.* 4.651, 18.287 (the refusal of gifts).

48. Nagy 1999: 74–78 (quotation on p. 78). Note Achilles' earlier use of the *loigon amunai* formula at 1.67, when he summons an assembly to address the crisis of the plague.

CHAPTER 2: CONSENSUS AND *KOSMOS*

1. Milman Parry's studies of Homeric formulas led him, famously, to deny that fixed formulaic epithets could bear any context-specific significance in the minds of either poet or audience, so that, e.g., the meaning of the formula πολύτλας δῖος Ὀδυσσεύς ("much-enduring, glorious Odysseus") would be reduced to the "essential idea" "Odysseus." A sizeable portion of the responses to Parry have concerned themselves with refuting this thesis. A number of studies have shown that formulaic epithets (and by extension formulaic language more generally) can indeed convey denotative and connotative meanings that resonate with particular contexts. See above, introduction, n. 63.

2. For *ainos* in the sense of "praise," cf. *Il.* 23.795, *Od.* 21.110; for *ainein*, *Il.* 10.249, 24.30. (The line between "praise" and "approve" is not always clear: cf. *Il.* 23.552.)

3. "Praise" features prominently in all the entries in LSJ for *ainos* and related terms.

4. Cf. L. Edmunds 1985: 105.

5. Gernet 1948: 186.

6. Dumézil 1943 and 1969: 103–24, the latter being a compressed, definitive reformulation of the former. For the complementarity of praise and blame, see Nagy 1976b and 1999 passim. For an illustration of this complementarity in a non-Indo-European society, cf. Opland 1980: 299 on the Zulu/Xhosa *imbongi*: "Praise and censure are twin aspects of his truthtelling."

7. For Servius' "election," see Dumézil 1943: 137–46, noting that Livy and Dionysius place Servius' public confirmation as king at opposite ends of his career; also Dumézil 1969: 109–10.

8. Including, above all, social order among humans: see Doniger O'Flaherty 1976: 329–30 on Pṛthu's restoration of class division after Vena's mingling of the castes, and Dumézil 1969: 120–21 on Pṛthu's connection strictly to the human sphere in the oldest layer of the tradition.

9. Dumézil 1943: 56: "autant et plus que noblesse, louange oblige."

10. *Taittirīya Brāhmaṇa* 2.7.5; cf. Dumézil 1943: 73–75, 1969: 105. The adjective *nārāśaṃsī* is a derivative of *narāśaṃsaḥ*, an epithet of Agni, who is called "praise of men" by virtue of his function as conveyor of praise between men and gods. This epithet is the exact cognate of Mycenaean Greek *Kessandros*, a forerunner of later Greek *Kassandros*, *Kassandrā*: Watkins 2000: 40 (s.v. *kens*-); cf. R. Schmitt 1967: 98–101. For more on Mycenaean onomastics, see below.

11. *The American Heritage Dictionary of Indo-European Roots* (Watkins 2000), s.v. Cf. Benveniste 1969: 2.144, who summarizes the views of the lexica with the gloss "proclamer

solennellement." For ease of presentation, I ignore here the difference between velar and palatovelar consonants, which has no bearing on my arguments. It should be noted, however, that the initial consonant of the root is reconstructed as a palatovelar, which is commonly distinguished from velar *k* by the addition of a diacritic.

12. Dumézil 1969: 103; cf. the provisional and avowedly reductive definition at Dumézil 1943: 25: "situer (un être, un acte, une opinion . . .) à sa juste place hiérarchique par une appreciation solennelle."

13. Note his regular use of the gloss "la louange efficace," as, e.g., at Dumézil 1943: 86, 108, and 1969: 122.

14. Benveniste 1969: 2.143; cf. his definition of Old Persian *θanh-/θah-*, another reflex of **kens-*: " 'affirmer avec autorité come étant la vérité; dire ce qui est conforme à la nature des choses; énoncer la norme de conduite.' Celui qui 'parle' ainsi est en position souveraine; *en déclarant ce qui est, il le fixe;* il énonce solennellement ce qui s'impose, la vérité du fait ou du devoir" (147; emphasis mine). His critique of Dumézil can be found on p. 145.

15. García-Ramón (1992a: 45, 1992b: 248, 1993: 115) adopts Dumézil's minimal definition "déclaration qualifiante," where "qualifiante" signals, among other things, the creation of norms and obligations.

16. See García-Ramón 1992b.

17. Froehde 1877.

18. Chantraine 2009, s.v. *kosmos*, with references to earlier literature. Dumézil himself did not acknowledge the connection between **kens-* and *kosmos* in his 1943 book (cf. p. 133: "un des vieux mots politico-religieux communs à l'indo-iranien et au latin, et, reserve faite du tokharien, à eux seuls") but declared himself in support of the derivation at a scholarly meeting in 1945, citing "considérations sociologiques" (as reported in the *Bulletin de la Société de Linguistique de Paris* 42 [1942–1945], p. xvi).

19. For a discussion of the way that *kosmos* "belongs equally to words and the world," see Elmer 2010: 290–97 (quotation from 296). That essay focuses on a synchronic analysis of the meaning of *kosmos* within rhapsodic discourse and therefore does not take into account the implications of the derivation from **kens-*. To the bibliography cited there should be added Haebler 1967 (critiqued by García-Ramón 1992a: 42). It is tempting to discern some notion of authoritative speech in the use of the term *kosmoi* to designate the chief magistrates of certain Cretan cities (cf., e.g., Ephoros *FGrH* 70 F 149.22, Arist. *Pol.* 1272b1–23, *SEG* 27.631).

20. *Kosmeîn: Il.* 2.704, 2.727; *diakosmeîn: Il.* 2.476, 3.1.

21. See Benveniste 1969: 2.145 on the way that Dumézil "sociologizes" his linguistic reconstructions. For Dumézil's own view of the relation between linguistics and sociology, see Dumézil 1943: 20–21, 25–27.

22. Dumézil 1943: 26–27.

23. Opland 1980 (quotation from p. 301).

24. Caton 1990: 28 (exchange), 55 (praise and blame).

25. Mauss 1990; for the term "potlatch," see pp. 6–7, and for the notion of the "total social fact," pp. 38 and 78. Dumézil refers to Mauss' original publication in the *Année sociologique* (1925) at 1943: 56. The notion of potlatch ordinarily foregrounds the competi-

tive destruction of wealth, what Mauss refers to as the "agonistic" quality of exchange (Mauss 1990: 6); Benveniste 1969: 1.76 emphasizes that, in Indo-European societies, the agonistic quality of potlatch is typically consigned to the background. An obvious exception, of course, is the "lavish expenditure of wealth" in the agonistic context of Panhellenic athletic festivals: see the discussion of Kurke's work on Pindar, below. Mauss himself detected traces of potlatch in the *Iliad*, although he felt that Greeks of the Geometric period no longer fully understood the custom: see Mauss 1921 and Calder 1984. For more on potlatch in the *Iliad*, see Bader 1978: 197–99, Donlan 1989: 2, Scodel 2008: 43 (potlatch is "not a Homeric practice," but "heroes sometimes engage in what could be called a 'potlatch strategy'").

26. Watkins 1995: 68–84. Nagy 1990a: 187–90 emphasizes the importance of the relation between patron and community and goes on to discuss specifically Greek developments in the treatment of the inherited notion of the poet's *misthos*, "wages."

27. On the relation between *nārāśaṃsī* and *dānastuti*, see Bloomfield 1897: 688–90; Dumézil 1943: 70–72, 79, and 1969: 104. Noting the existence of cognate poetic forms in other IE traditions, Watkins writes (1995: 73): "Perhaps the single most telling indication of the common Indo-European origin of the reciprocal poet-patron relation . . . is the existence of a special literary genre in Vedic, Greek, Celtic, and Germanic, which we can call by its Sanskrit name *dānastuti*."

28. On the etymology of medieval Irish *dúan*, see Watkins 1976; for discussion of IE **dap-*, see Benveniste 1969: 1.74–77.

29. Ibid., 1.76.

30. On *ainos* and *epainos* as conventional self-designations for Pindar's medium of praise poetry, see Nagy 1990b: 147.

31. Kurke 1991. Nagy 1990b: 136–45 offers another view of the Pindaric notion of compensation, focusing more on the ritual dimension of Greek athletics and epinician. Nagy stresses that, as the performance of the victory ode is compensation for the athlete's ordeal, that ordeal is in turn compensation for the primordial death of the hero in whose honor the competition is held. This cultic dimension is essential: as Mauss emphasized, the "total social fact" of potlatch encompasses both horizontal social relationships and vertical relationships with cosmic entities (ancestors and gods); cf. Kurke 1991: 96, 114–16.

32. Kurke 1991: 99.

33. Ibid., 102–6 and passim. On the ode as the means by which the victor is reincorporated into the community, see also Crotty 1982: 104–38 (esp. 121 on the ode as an "act of inclusion").

34. For the collective identity embodied in the epinician chorus, cf. Nagy 1990b: 142: "the chorus represents, reenacts, the community of the polis. In the case of an epinician performance, the ritual experience of a single person's athletic victory is being communalized through the chorus."

35. I discuss the Pindaric resonances and the overall significance of this passage in greater detail in chapter 8. Nagy 1999: 235–38 also detects connections to epinician poetics in the *ainos* related by Odysseus to Eumaios in *Od.* 14.462–506 (designated as an *ainos* at 14.508).

36. On potlatch in the *Iliad*, see Bader 1980: 74–79.

37. Two other passages exhibit a connection between *ainos* and the circulation of goods. In the first, *Od.* 14.508–22, Eumaios offers the disguised Odysseus a cloak in recognition of the underlying meaning of his *ainos* (see below for *ainos* in the sense of "coded narrative"). The second occurs at the end of the chariot race: when Achilles awards to Nestor the surplus prize that remains after the adjustment recommended by Antilokhos, the elder Neleid responds with a speech designated by the narrator as an *ainos* (*Il.* 23.652). This speech does not have any explicit praise function (unless it be praise of Nestor's own erstwhile athletic prowess), but it does claim an important position in the cycle of compensation, which may be enough to qualify it as *ainos*. (Frame 2009: 158n52 suggests that Nestor's speech is an *ainos* because it communicates a coded message; see below for more on *ainos* in this sense.) Nestor concludes his speech with a prayer that the gods reward Achilles for his generosity. He thereby adds a vertical dimension to the horizontal sphere of exchange, invoking the cosmic implications of this "total social fact" (see above, chapter 2, n. 31).

38. Arguably the best illustration in alphabetic Greek of the link between **kens-* and social order is the Spartan use of the term *kosmos* to designate the social and political system as a whole (and the order it fosters): cf. Herodotus 1.65.4, with Nagy 1985: 32.

39. García-Ramón 1992a, 1992b, 1993.

40. García-Ramón 1992b (with complete argumentation, including criticism of alternative interpretations), 1992a: 40. García-Ramón (1992b: 250–51) notes also *ka-e-sa-me-no /Kaʰēsamenos/* and the "Kurzform" *ka-e-se-u /Kaʰēseus/*.

41. κέκασμαι < IE **(s)kend-* (where the *k* is again the palatovelar). According to García-Ramón, the names deriving from **kens-* are absorbed into these names deriving from a different root (or replaced by names with parallel semantics).

42. In support of this interpretation, García-Ramón 1992b notes that the name of Cassandra is given as Κεσ(σ)άνδρα in a number of archaic vase-inscriptions. See Davreux 1942, nos. 48, 49, and 116.

43. García-Ramón 1992b: 249; cf. 254–55 and 1992a: 40–41.

44. Jaeger 1945: 433n41.

45. So the entry in Chantraine 2009: "αἶνος, m., se dit d'abord de paroles, de récits chargés de sens . . ."

46. Richardson 1993: 240; Bader 1989: 160n138; Verdenius 1962: 389.

47. L. Edmunds 1985: 105.

48. Nagy 1990b: 31; cf. 148.

49. Blanc 1995: 191, 194; cf. Blanc 1985: 259n21.

50. See above, chapter 1. The examples are taken from Blanc 1995: 193. A more complete dossier of parallel passages is assembled at Blanc 1985: 262–63.

51. Ancient grammarians seem already to have proposed an etymological connection between *apēnēs* and the *ainos* family (specifically, *aineîn*): see *Etymologicum Gudianum* s.v. *apēnēs* (and cf. Blanc 1985: 260–61). Eustathius (1.768.21–769.1 ed. van der Valk) correlates *apēnēs* with the notion of refusal, which he designates in terms of *epainos*: ὁ δέ γε προειρημένος ἀπηνὴς λέγοιτο ἂν καὶ ἀπηλεγής, ὃς ἀπηλεγέως ἀποείποι ἂν, ὡς μὴ ἐπαινῶν δηλαδή, τουτέστι συγκατατιθέμενος.

52. The long vowel of *apēnēs* would be the result of an analogical application of Wackernagel's Law, which refers to the lengthening of an initial vowel in the second member of a compound (cf. Blanc 1995: 193–94).

53. Fick 1877: 242.

54. Blanc 1995; see pp. 185 and 192 for the previous attempts of Bechtel and Brugmann to support Fick's hypothesis.

55. Blanc 1995: 199; see also Chantraine 2009, *Supplement* s.v. αἶνος. On the semantic alternation GIVE/TAKE in the sphere of exchange, see the definitive formulation of Benveniste 1966: 316–17.

56. In part because it is founded on the concordance of only two branches of Indo-European (for the methodological principle that a secure etymology should rest on the evidence of three or more languages or language families, see Meillet 1967: 54) but also, as Jeremy Rau points out to me, because the evidence permits only a root equation, without morphological overlap.

57. Blanc 1995: 212–22 surveys the attested semantics of *ainos* and its verbal derivatives, offering an explanation in each case based on the meaning of his reconstructed root *h_2en- "accept, approve, consent." My comments here are intended to provide a broader perspective on select uses of *ainos*.

58. Cf. Blanc 1995: 218. As Blanc notes, some recollection of this deliberative use of *ainos* appears to be preserved among the Byzantine lexicographers: cf. *Etymologicum Magnum* 36.16–18: αἶνος· γνώμη, παροιμία, παράδειγμα· ἔπαινος. καὶ ἡ χειροτονία καὶ ψήφισμα. See also L. Edmunds 1985: 105.

59. Other examples of *ainos* in this sense: Archil. 174.1, 185.1 ed. West; Call. fr. 194.6 ed. Pfeiffer; Theoc. 14.43.

60. Nagy 1990b: 148.

61. A polite formula: Jacoby 1931: 126n1. Cf. West 1978: 206: "Perhaps it is not so much being polite as pressing the kings to agree."

62. It is significant that Antilokhos designates his audience both as knowledgeable and as socially proximate (*philoi*): these are two of the three "qualifications" for the ideal audience of *ainos* identified by Nagy 1990b: 148. (The third, not represented here, is the ethical standard implied by terms such as *agathos*, "noble"). For a cognate system of requirements in Avestan, see Schwartz 2003.

CHAPTER 3: ACHILLES AND THE CRISIS OF THE EXCEPTION

1. Lesky 1961: 16–17.

2. Cf. Catanzaro 2008: 277. For Wilson 2002: 42, formal similarities are enough to qualify the scene as an assembly; Ruzé 1997: 103 also counts it as such. Barker 2009: 34, employing the term *agorē* as a strict criterion—overly restrictive, in my view, since it excludes the divine assembly of Book 4, introduced by the verb ἠγορόωντο ("they were holding an assembly," *Il.* 4.1)—does not count Chryses' plea as an assembly scene, although he notes the significance of the ambiguity at 41n5; cf. his comment on p. 52: "presumably some kind of assembly must be taking place."

3. Grote 1869: 66–69; cf. the remarks of Ruzé 1997: 13. This view of Homeric politics is frequently expressed by writers who take the Homeric texts as a starting point for discussions of later political developments, e.g., Raaflaub and Wallace 2007: 28 (there is "no formal obligation to respect the people's opinion" in Homer).

4. Finley 1977: 80–81. *Pace* Finley, shouting always indicates a positive (though not necessarily efficacious) response in the *Iliad*.

5. E.g. Cantarella 1979: 104–23, Hölkeskamp 2000: 25–26. Taplin 1992 cautions against overrating "the hierarchical standing of Agamemnon" (63) and argues more generally that Agamemnon's prerogatives remain to a certain degree ambiguous (48–49). Ruzé 1997: 14–15 identifies a number of Homeric scholars who have argued for a version of popular sovereignty in the poems, beginning with F. Moreau and A. Fanta in the nineteenth century.

6. Carlier 2006: 106; cf. Carlier 1984: 185–87 and 1999: 278–83.

7. King 1987: 492. For a critique of attempts to discern sovereign kingship in the Homeric poems, see Thalmann 1998: 246–48.

8. Cf. Finley 1977: 82: "Viewed from a narrow conception of formal rights, the king had the power to decide, alone and without consulting anyone."

9. Allan and Cairns 2011, esp. p. 115.

10. Wilson 2002: 8.

11. Said 1975. "Intention" here must be understood not in the conventional way, as the direction imposed by an individual authorial consciousness, but as the continuity of meaning production implied by a particular beginning, "the created *inclusiveness* within which the work develops" (12; emphasis original).

12. See my comments in chapter 1.

13. Although Barker 2009 reads the poem in terms of the institutionalization of new political practices, he acknowledges the difficulty posed by the audience's awareness of tradition at 52n38. There he contrasts his arguments with his earlier work (Barker 2004), in which he advocated for the more radically "foundationalist" position that the *Iliad* presents the assembly convened by Achilles as a true first. While I am substantially in agreement with Barker 2009, I believe my perspective to be truer to the experience of ancient audiences, who would be inclined to judge the poem's political narrative against traditional norms.

14. The state of exception has come to greater prominence in the political philosophy of recent decades, largely through renewed attention to the work of Weimar (and later Nazi) jurist Carl Schmitt, whose *Political Theology*, a treatise on the connection between sovereignty and the state of exception, begins with the dictum, "Sovereign is he who decides on the exception" (C. Schmitt 2005: 5). For my purposes, the most important of the commentators on Schmitt is Giorgio Agamben, who has explored Schmitt's ideas in two works (Agamben 1998, 2005). For the appeal to *themis* by Homeric characters as the assertion of a contested principle, see Barker 2009: 62–63.

15. See the note of G. Schwab at C. Schmitt 2005: 5n1.

16. Russo 1978: 47–49. For the relative fixity of the end of the verse, a feature of Indo-European metrics that J. Foley 1990: 82 terms "right-justification" and identifies in South Slavic oral epic as well, see Nagy 1974: 30–31. Nicolai 1983 nicely complements Russo's essay: he describes the *Iliad*'s essential plotting device as the deviation from an

expected or reasonable course of events caused by the faulty decision making of a prominent individual. Significantly, for Nicolai, the implicit message of this plot structure is that collective will ought to be invested with the power to correct the errors of individuals by controlling and directing policy for the group.

17. Agamben 2005: 36–37. Cf. also Agamben 1998: 20: "Just as in an occurrence of actual speech, a word acquires its ability to denote a segment of reality only insofar as it is also meaningful in its own not-denoting (that is, as *langue* as opposed to *parole*, as a term in its mere lexical consistency, independent of its concrete use in discourse), so the rule can refer to the individual case only because it is in force, in the sovereign exception, as pure potentiality in the suspension of every actual reference."

18. Agamben 2005: 23 and passim.

19. Cf. ibid., 36: "the state of exception separates the norm from its application in order to make its application possible. It introduces a zone of anomie into the law in order to make the effective regulation [*normazione*] of the real possible" (translator's parenthesis). See also ibid., 60.

20. Brenkman 2007: 59–61. See Schmitt 2005: 5.

21. Ibid., 61: "Whatever agency makes the declaration . . . lays itself open to challenge, limitation, even crisis. The very conditions of the legitimacy of its own rule shift. . . . [the] *appeal to necessity* opens the way for the public, the press, the legislature, and the courts to assume responsibility for scrutinizing and questioning the leader's decision and exercise a judgment of *their own*" (emphasis original).

22. It must be stressed that Agamemnon is not a sovereign deciding on the exception in the constitutional sense. Nevertheless, he attempts to use his authority to overturn certain principles of deliberative procedure; the consequences of this attempt determine the limits of his authority.

23. Sinos 1980: 34.

24. On the relationship between Achilles' *mēnis* and his overall commitment to *philotēs*, see Muellner 1996: 133–75.

25. If Agamemnon had accepted Chryses' *apoina*, he would not be without a *geras*, since he would have the ransom in place of the girl.

26. Cf. Taplin 1992: 52: "a significant element in the perennial power of Homer is the challenges of evaluation which he sets his audience. That is why the poem begins with two scenes which provocatively demand ethical opinion without explicitly supplying it: Agamemnon's treatment of Chryses, and his great dispute with Achilleus."

27. Cf. White 1984: 33, Taplin 1992: 62.

28. *Il.* 1.366–69. According to the *Cypria* (as reported by Eustathius 1.184.30 ed. van der Valk) and the bT scholia at *Il.* 1.366, Chryseis had gone to Thēbē to perform a sacrifice to Artemis. Two alternative versions can be found in Eustathius and the scholia: that Chryseis was in fact a citizen (*polītis*) of Thēbē and that she had fled to Thēbē with other residents of Chrysē because Thēbē was better fortified. (All these testimonia are usefully collected by Bernabé 1996 as *Cypria* fr. 28.)

29. The bT scholia at *Il.* 1.366 indicate that Achilles *intended* to attack Chrysē but that he was prevented from doing so by Athena, who revealed that Apollo would not permit him to sack the city.

30. On the philosophical tradition culminating in Schmitt's declaration that "[t]he specific political distinction to which political actions and motives can be reduced is that between friend and enemy" (C. Schmitt 2007: 26), see Derrida 1993 (expanded in Derrida 1997).

31. Taplin 1992: 52.

32. Cf. Nimis 1986: 222: "The *Iliad* articulates a crisis in discourse, which is to say a crisis in the very *form* of social organization . . ."

33. As I noted in chapter 1, *epiakhein* does not belong to the system of response formulas we find in the *Odyssey*. Its presence in the *Iliad* can be understood as another sign of the exceptional circumstances that prevail during the time of the narration. As in the case of *epeuphēmein*, the ambivalence of the term is tied to the fact that it represents an exception to the norm; but it is a less acute case of exception.

34. On *handanein*, see my comments in chapter 1.

35. See Bynum 1987.

36. See Agamben 2005: 57 for the "zone of absolute indeterminacy."

37. In dealing with a term that has a single, unique referent—in essence a kind of proper name—we confront the breakdown of the dialectic between *langue* and *parole* on which linguistic signification is based. The structural relations of *langue* both determine and are determined by the specific applications of *parole*. A truly singular expression, however, exists outside of this dialectic. For the analogy between the political state of exception and the relation between *langue* and *parole*, see Agamben 2005: 36–37, 39–40; Agamben 1998: 20.

38. *IG* XII 3.326, 27–28 (Thera, AD 149). The simplex *euphēmein* can denote acclamation more generally: see Roueché 1984: 181, 193.

39. φέρτε δὲ χερσὶν ὕδωρ, εὐφημῆσαί τε κέλεσθε, / ὄφρα Διὶ Κρονίδῃ ἀρησόμεθ᾽, αἴ κ᾽ ἐλεήσῃ ("Bring water for our hands and bid [all] to be silent, / that we may pray to Zeus son of Kronos for pity," *Il.* 9.171–72). Here, however, the word could also mean "to utter what is ritually correct."

40. On the "ambivalence" of the term *euphēmia*, see Montiglio 2000: 16.

41. The alternative to killing Agamemnon—"putting an end to *kholos* and restraining his *thumos*"—would not just be a decision not to exercise homicidal violence; it would be a decision not to quarrel any further and thus to accept Agamemnon's supremacy. In the event, the (verbal) continuation of the quarrel is marked by the narrator's words, "[Achilles] did not yet cease from *kholos*" (*Il.* 1.224).

42. See Scully 1984: 18 and Wilson 2002: 60.

43. Athena had proposed that Achilles resort to words to express his discontent (*Il.* 1.211). The subsequent narrative emphasizes that the quarrel is a matter of words: cf. 1.223 and 304.

44. Wilson 2002: 64 notes that Achilles appropriates Chryses as a model in his dispute with Agamemnon. His contradictory position of being separate but still belonging can be compared with the "topological structure" of the state of exception defined for Agamben 2005: 35 by the term "ecstasy-belonging."

45. Friedrich and Redfield 1978: 278.

46. The situation becomes considerably more complex in the *Odyssey*, which is intensely interested in the act of narration. Odysseus can narrate events that have already been narrated by another speaker (*Od.* 7.249 ff. ~ 5.131 ff.), and he can quote the preceding diegesis (*Od.* 7.268 = 5.279). (Note that in many cases of near quotation, the fact that Odysseus narrates in the first person requires minor changes.) But the pattern can also be reversed, so that the diegesis can actually paraphrase events whose primary narration has already been given by Odysseus (*Od.* 23.310 ff.). Other human narrators (but only after death) also have the power to retell events that have been narrated by Odysseus (*Od.* 11.63–65 ~ 10.558–60) or by the diegesis (*Od.* 24.125 ff.).

47. Martin 1989: 223; at 170 Martin notes Achilles' tendency to use "expressions elsewhere used exclusively by gods in speeches, or by the narrator in diegesis." Cf. Redfield 1994: 221; Mackie 1996: 139, 155; Scodel 2002: 104.

48. Cf. Hes. *Th.* 27–28.

49. The seashore is "antisocial" because it stands outside the Greek camp, at the farthest possible extreme from the *agorē*, the central space that defines the Achaean community. (Cf. *Il.* 11.5–6 and 806–8: the Achaean *agorē* is next to Odysseus' ship, which is located in the exact center of the camp. For the importance of the center to the spatial definition of the community, see Detienne 1965.) The text emphasizes Achilles' isolation from human company (*Il.* 1.349).

50. At *Il.* 1.474, the phrase *phrena terpesthai* is used of the pleasure Apollo takes in *hearing* a performance; likewise at Hes. *Th.* 37 and 51, the Muses, as performers of a song, please (*terpein*) the mind of their audience (Zeus).

51. The symposion, which could also provide a context for the performance of Homeric poetry, might have been less public than, for instance, a religious festival, but it was still social in a way that cannot be attributed to either of Achilles' performances.

52. Wilson 2002: 85.

53. See Scodel 1989, who sees the omission as deriving from Odysseus' political sensibility. Her argument leads her to a similar conclusion regarding the linguistic nature of the conflicts driving the *Iliad*'s plot: "The silence of Odysseus . . . leads to a profound misunderstanding between Achilles and the other Achaeans. . . . the calamitous outcome is the result of a social failure, of misunderstood statements and distorted communications" (99).

54. Ajax begins and ends his appeal with invocations of *philotēs* (*Il.* 9.630, 642); Achilles acknowledges that his remarks are in harmony with his own sentiments (πάντά τί μοι κατὰ θυμὸν ἐείσαο μυθήσασθαι ["all you have said is in accordance with my heart"], *Il.* 9.645). Here more than anywhere else we see the truth of Sinos' (1980) understanding of Achilles as the embodiment of *philotēs*.

55. Whitman 1958: 192.

56. δμηθήτω· Ἀΐδης τοι ἀμείλιχος ἠδ' ἀδάμαστος, / τοὔνεκα καί τε βροτοῖσι θεῶν ἔχθιστος ἁπάντων ("Let him be subdued: Hades, to be sure, is relentless and unsubduable, / and for that reason most hateful to mortals of all the gods," *Il.* 9.158–59): cf. Taplin 1992: 70, Wilson 2002: 85–86. Achilles speaks as though he had heard the words of Agamemnon.

57. A. Parry 1956.

58. Against Parry, see Reeve 1973, Claus 1975. For specific features of Achilles' speech, see Hogan 1976, Friedrich and Redfield 1978, Scully 1984; also Nimis 1986 and esp. Martin 1989: 146–205.

59. Nimis 1986: 220–21.

60. O. Cramer 1976: 302 notes several passages that reveal the importance to Achilles of "not concealing" and the connection of this motif to the full disclosure of thought in speech. The injunction to ἐξαύδα, μὴ κεῦθε νόῳ, ἵνα εἴδομεν ἄμφω ("speak out, do not conceal [it] in your mind, that we may both know," Il. 1.363, 16.19; cf. 18.74) occurs in several key exchanges between Achilles and Thetis, and Achilles and Patroklos. The opposition transparency/concealment thus serves to contrast Achilles' relationships to Thetis and Patroklos—relationships that are marked by Achilles' poetic performances as alternatives to properly social interactions—with his relationship to the Achaean community as represented by the embassy. Achilles can achieve the transparency he desires only in these eremitic contexts.

61. A. Parry 1956: 6.

62. Scodel 1989: 97.

63. Ibid., 98–99.

64. I revisit here certain points made at the end of chapter 1.

65. See chapter 2. That the etymological meaning persists in Homeric usage can be perceived from the fact that, on the synchronic level of Homeric diction, the adjective occupies the same contexts as and functions as a rough equivalent for anainesthai, the negative form of *ainesthai, "make an ainos."

66. Cf. Muellner 1996: 117: "This time Achilles is swearing that Agamemnon is acting antisocially . . ."

67. For the semantic restriction of the term and its link to the mēnis theme, see Muellner 1996: 117n48 and Nagy 1999: 73–76.

68. Cf. Il. 18.450 (ἔνθ' αὐτὸς μὲν ἔπειτ' ἠναίνετο λοιγὸν ἀμῦναι ["then he was refusing to ward off devastation himself"]), spoken by Thetis: note that the charge of denying ainos is laid against Achilles by the two people with whom he shares a special bond, Patroklos and Thetis.

69. Nagy 1999: 73 (§8n2).

70. Rabel 1988, Wilson 2002: 69 (Wilson's book explores the reasons why Achilles cannot accept Agamemnon's offer).

71. Achilles' relation to the "para-narrative" (I take the term from Alden 2000) of Chryses is analogous to his relation to the Meleager story as told by Phoenix (Il. 9.529–99). As has often been noted, Achilles takes as a positive example a figure who was offered as a negative one.

72. Wilson 2002: 31; cf. Redfield 1994: 167–68.

73. Wilson 2002: 78.

74. The hesitation among the ambassadors as to whether to use the term apoina or poinē reflects the ambivalence of Achilles' position, which in turn recalls the ambivalence of Chryses' position as I described it earlier in the chapter: is Achilles friend (in which case poinē is the appropriate mechanism of conciliation) or foe (in which case the

offering of *apoina* is appropriate)? Here again we observe the basic political indeterminacy that is produced by the state of exception.

75. Cf. Wilson 2002: 10: "the compensation theme is developed in the poem to present Agamemnon's refusal of Chryses' *apoina* as epitomizing a social dysfunction and as initiating a sequence of rejections of *apoina* . . ."

CHAPTER 4: SOCIAL ORDER AND POETIC ORDER

1. Russo 1978, esp. pp. 47–49 (quoted in chapter 3).

2. Ibid., 48.

3. The traditional plot of the *Iliad* is characterized within the poem as "destiny": cf. Redfield 1994: 133, Finkelberg 1998: 136, Scodel 2002: 68. I return to this point below.

4. For the Homeric distinction between the *agorē* and the *boulē*, and its possible connection to the historical practice (as at Athens) of *probouleusis*, see Sealey 1969: 260 and Jeanmaire 1939: 16.

5. Kullmann 1955.

6. Ibid., 260, 272; see also Nagy 1990b: 72–73 and the definitive study of Burgess 2001. Following Burgess, I assume that, regardless of the dates at which the poems of the Cycle were fixed in writing, the underlying traditions developed alongside those represented by the *Iliad* and *Odyssey*. The *Iliad* can therefore evoke an episode that was recounted in, e.g., the *Cypria*, even if the *Cypria* was textualized at a later point than the *Iliad*. In referring to attested poems of the Epic Cycle, I am treating them as representative of the underlying traditions.

7. *Cypria* arg. 61 ed. Bernabé.

8. *Cypria* fr. 29 ed. Bernabé; for a reconstruction of the story and argumentation regarding its relevance to the *Iliad*, see Kullmann 1955, esp. pp. 260–62.

9. Knox and Russo 1989 argue that Agamemnon refers to a custom that may have Near Eastern roots. Barker (2009: 62–63), however, points out that appeals to *themis* often serve as cover for a speaker's assertion of what ought to be permitted, rather than as descriptions of what is, in fact, established custom.

10. Other Homeric passages attest to the fact that the "testing" signified by *peirâsthai* results in "knowing" (*gignōskein*): cf. *Il.* 22.381–82, *Od.* 16.304–7.

11. Cf. Kullmann 1955: 254.

12. Eustathius, however, approved of Agamemnon's subterfuge: "the plan is a good one, shrewd in a way typical of Homer, and truly appropriate to a general" (1.266.23–24 ed. van der Valk).

13. Cf. the activity of the heralds in the trial scene on Achilles' shield. They likewise "restrain the *laos*" (*Il.* 18.503), presumably so that the speakers can be heard.

14. Cf. *Il.* 3.395–420 (Helen follows Aphrodite to Paris' bedchamber), 4.208–9 (Makhaon answers Agamemnon's summons to tend Menelaus' wound), etc. The individualizing force of the phrase *thumon orinein* is evident also in descriptions of reactions to battlefield boasts, as for instance at *Il.* 14.458–59 (ὣς ἔφατ', Ἀργείοισι δ' ἄχος γένετ' εὐξαμένοιο / Αἴαντι δὲ μάλιστα δαΐφρονι θυμὸν ὄρινε ["thus he spoke, and his boast brought grief to the Argives, / but he especially stirred the *thumos* of fierce-minded

Ajax"]; cf. *Il.* 13.417–18, 14.486–87), where Ajax's personal reaction is contrasted with the general reaction of the group.

15. *Il.* 2.155–56. Reference to poetic tradition is implicit not only in the adverb *hupermora*, "contrary to destiny," but also in the term *nostos*, which can mean not only "return" but also "song of return." Thus the poem preceding the *Odyssey* in the Epic Cycle, which told of the homecomings of other Achaean heroes, was titled *Nostoi*, "The Returns."

16. Lang 1989: 7 and Morrison 1992: 69 note the functional equivalence of Achilles' deliberation in Book 1 to the counterfactual "reversal passage" in Book 2 (for bibliography on such passages, see Morrison 1997: 285nn25, 26). *Od.* 9.299–305 combines these two methods for introducing possible alternatives to the story by including both deliberation (with an echo of Achilles' dilemma) and a counterfactual "reversal" statement.

17. See chapters 6 and 7.

18. In doing so, Odysseus reminds the *basilēes* of Agamemnon's instructions in the *boulē* (reading *Il.* 2.194 as a question rather than a statement: cf. Kirk 1985 ad loc.), pointing to the fact that *they* should be the ones doing the restraining according to Agamemnon's original plan.

19. For *muthos* as command, see Martin 1989, who glosses the term on p. 66 as "important speech of social control."

20. Cf. Lincoln 1994: 16–21.

21. Marks 2005, who contends that Thersites is a *basileus*, provides a recent overview of the problem, with useful bibliographical references to works supporting both sides of the issue.

22. Cf. Thalmann 1988, Detienne 1996: 103, Lincoln 1994: 21, 33, and Stuurman 2004.

23. Cf. Kirk 1985: 138–39 and Marks 2005, who develops a wide-ranging argument in favor of a noble Thersites. Notoriously, the *Iliad* does not identify Thersites' father or fatherland, a circumstance that has often been taken as an indication of low status; cf. Higbie 1995: 11.

24. Apollod. 1.8.2, 4–5; Pherecyd. *FGrH* 3 F 123.

25. Cf. Lincoln 1994: 33–34. An ancient commentator saw the violence inflicted by Odysseus as a definite indication of Thersites' low social status (bT scholia at *Il.* 2.212).

26. The name of Thersites' father, Agrios (meaning roughly "Wild Man"), expresses the disruptive force represented by Thersites himself.

27. Cf. S. Edmunds 1990: 38. Diomedes bestowed the rule on Oineus' son-in-law Andraimōn; he himself was evidently ineligible for the kingship, either as a citizen of Argos, or because his father Tydeus was in fact an illegitimate son of Oineus (Apollod. 1.8.5–6). In the Catalogue of Ships, the Calydonian contingent is led by Thoas, son of Andraimōn, "for the sons of great-hearted Oineus were no more" (*Il.* 2.641).

28. Apollod. 1.71–73 gives two versions for the sequel to the hunt, in both of which the sons of Agrios cause the quarrel. According to Pherecydes, as cited by the bT scholia at *Il.* 2.212, Meleager cast Thersites off a precipice for fleeing from the confrontation with the boar. This too is an indication of the threat Thersites poses to the integrity of the group: like a hoplite battle, a boar hunt depends for its success on the coordination and solidarity of the warriors forming the cordon.

29. *Aithiopis* arg. 6–8 ed. Bernabé.

30. See Vian 1959: 21–22. This quarrel represents another instance of the theme of Achilles' involvement in disturbances that threaten the integrity of the community, a theme that begins in the *Cypria* with Achilles' quelling of the mutiny and continues with his Iliadic quarrel with Agamemnon. Diomedes, as we shall see in chapter 5, is also connected to the theme of *epainos*, which lends added significance to his quarrel with Achilles in the *Aithiopis*.

31. Nagy 1999: 253–64.

32. Ibid., 263.

33. See chapter 2. For *kosmos* as applied to Thersites' speech, see Ford 1992: 123, Mackie 1996: 18.

34. Ruzé 1997: 52–55 approximates this point of view. She suggests that Thersites speaks out in a context that does not license debate (52) but also that he belongs to a class that is not ordinarily permitted to speak in the assembly (54–55).

35. Achilles accommodates Antilokhos by awarding a special prize to Eumēlos; similarly, the dispute among the gods at the beginning of Book 4 is resolved by balancing the destruction of Troy against the destruction of one of Hera's cherished cities.

36. Lincoln 1994: 9.

37. Cf. *Il.* 2.95–100, 18.503.

38. Whitman 1958: 161 refers to the "scepter of kingly violence." Kings are *skēptoukhoi* "scepter-bearing" in the *Iliad* (1.279, 2.86), but note that the elders sitting in judgment on Achilles' shield hold "the scepters of the loud-voiced heralds" (18.505; cf. 7.277 and 23.568, where scepters are wielded by heralds).

39. On the *Iliad*'s construction of a space for dissent, see Barker 2009: 31–88.

40. Hector uses the same formula, κλέος οὔ ποτ᾽ ὀλεῖται ("fame will never perish"), to refer to the epic fame he envisions for himself (*Il.* 7.91), but the most explicit indication of the connection between this formula and poetic tradition comes from the *Odyssey*, with reference precisely to the tradition represented by that poem. In the underworld, after hearing the suitor Amphimedon relate his experience of the events of the poem, Agamemnon praises Penelope: ὡς ἀγαθαὶ φρένες ἦσαν ἀμύμονι Πηνελοπείῃ, / κούρῃ Ἰκαρίου, ὡς εὖ μέμνητ᾽ Ὀδυσῆος, / ἀνδρὸς κουριδίου. τῷ οἱ κλέος οὔ ποτ᾽ ὀλεῖται / ἧς ἀρετῆς, τεύξουσι δ᾽ ἐπιχθονίοισιν ἀοιδὴν / ἀθάνατοι χαρίεσσαν ἐχέφρονι Πηνελοπείῃ ("How noble in intention was blameless Penelope, / daughter of Ikarios, that she remained always mindful of Odysseus, / her wedded husband; as a result her fame will never perish, / [the fame] of her virtue, and the gods will craft among men a pleasing song / in honor of loyal Penelope," *Od.* 24.194–98).

41. The single instance of Trojan *epainos* presents a similar instance of ratification of more than just an immediate course of action: see chapter 7.

42. When Athena searches out Odysseus, she finds him standing still: "he, at least, did not take hold of his black, well-benched ship, since grief came over him in his heart and *thumos*" (*Il.* 2.170–71). See Haft 1990: 41–42 for the "poignant irony" of these lines.

43. Book 10, the most "Odyssean" section of the *Iliad*, has often been characterized as an interpolation, but I take it to be an authentic component of Iliadic tradition. In support of this view, see Petegorsky 1982: 175–254 and especially Dué and Ebbott 2010.

44. For the epithet and the unusual use of the article, see Haft 1990: 45–50.

45. For Barker 2009: 59, "it is as if Odysseus threatens to hijack this, his rival's, narrative."

46. Note that, in the *Cypria*, Odysseus was presented as so reluctant to fight at Troy that he feigned madness (*Cypria* arg. 30–33 ed. Bernabé).

47. See, e.g., Feldman 1947, Whitman 1958: 161, Patzek 1992: 132, Schadewaldt 1987: 152, Lowenstam 1993: 78, Barker 2009: 60. Thersites closes his speech with a line used also by Achilles (*Il.* 2.242 = 1.232).

48. The irony would be even greater if, as Ebert 1969: 170–73 hypothesized, Thersites appeared as Achilles' opponent in the mutiny scene of the *Cypria*.

49. His commands can be put into effect even without the fully efficient response because they are implicit in the proposal Odysseus made and the audience approved. One wonders if the tone of Agamemnon's speech is not connected to its failure to receive *epainos*. Odysseus' speech seems more like an exhortation than a command. Agamemnon issues commands in a series of impersonal-sounding third-person imperatives and concludes with a threat to kill anyone he finds willingly keeping back from battle. Ruzé 1997: 58 notes that Agamemnon never formulates the decisive proposal in deliberation.

50. Benardete 1963: 7–8; cf. Fränkel 1977: 19–20. Note, too, the simile at *Il.* 2.209–10, which marks an intermediate stage in the return to order. The waves are no longer on the open sea but not yet as organized as they are in the third and final simile. For the whole series of similes, see Moulton 1977: 38–42.

51. Even if the singular verb and participle suggest that the simile refers to a southeast wind (cf. Fränkel 1977: 20n1), in Homeric cosmography such a wind is a product of the interaction of two distinct winds.

52. On the cohesive group identity implied by such "*tis*-speeches," see Elmer 2012, with further references.

53. See Nimis 1987: 33–42 for the communal meal in Homer as "an expression of social harmony, the physical and spiritual continuity of a group which is dedicated to some concerted action" (33).

54. Note the adverb κλαγγηδόν in the bird simile (*Il.* 2.463): as we saw above, κλαγγή typifies the group as it gathers for the assembly but before it is brought to order.

55. For the significance of *dia*, see Chantraine 1963: 95. The idea of distribution or completeness is secondary. At *Il.* 2.126, *diakosmeîn* likewise means "organize in distinct groups."

56. *Kosmeîn: Il.* 2.704, 3.1, 12.87, 14.379, etc. *Diakosmeîn* is used of marshaling troops only here in Homer, doubtless because here alone is the organization of troops a matter of dividing up a larger group.

57. For "the Catalogue's combined evocation of the sailing and the muster," see Heiden 2008 (quotation from p. 146).

58. On the sequence of thought in the invocation, see Ford 1992: 73.

59. Agamemnon and Menelaus: *Il.* 1.16, 375; Homer: *Certamen* 338 (ed. Allen). Cf. Ford 1992: 86, and 122–23 on the many kinds of order encompassed by the term *kosmos;* Mackie 1996: 19–20, who recognizes the Catalogue as both "an icon of the mustering" and "a poetic *kosmos*"; and Elmer 2010: 290–95, esp. p. 294.

60. Cf. Gaertner 2001: 302.

CHAPTER 5: IN SEARCH OF *EPAINOS*

1. On the Trojan *klangē*, see Mackie 1996: 15–16.

2. The convergence of Achaeans and Trojans around a common set of interests represents in fact the establishment of a transitory Greco-Trojan "supercommunity," expressed here and elsewhere in the collective responses attributed to Achaeans and Trojans alike: see Elmer 2012.

3. Cf. Reinhardt 1961: 107, Morrison 1992: 69.

4. Paris acknowledges defeat privately to Helen (*Il.* 3.439), but his disappearance from the battlefield results in a lack of visible evidence for Menelaus' victory, apart from the helmet he seizes. Agamemnon's *phainetai* rings unmistakably hollow.

5. Essential on this point is Bergold 1977: 98–99.

6. See chapter 1.

7. Cf. *Il.* 9.17–28 and 14.75–79, where Agamemnon proposes abandoning the war, as in Book 2.

8. An example of "Jørgensen's Law," which stipulates that human actors (as opposed to divine actors or the narrator) use the terms *daimōn, theos,* or "Zeus" as generic designations for the divine cause of an event.

9. Cf. *Il.* 7.419 (Ἀργεῖοι). The specification of a *kritos laos* at 7.434 is curious, but it does not seem to alter the picture of concerted action on the part of the Achaeans as a whole (cf. Kirk 1990 ad loc.).

10. ἀλλ᾽ οὐκ Ἀτρεΐδῃ Ἀγαμέμνονι <u>ἥνδανε</u> θυμῷ ("but this did not <u>please</u> the heart of Agamemnon, son of Atreus"), *Il.* 1.24. The echo is amplified by the overall similarity of the two scenes: in each case, a non-Greek figure enters the Achaean camp, seeks a conciliatory exchange, and is rejected.

11. The loose cohesion signaled by the prefixed form *epihandanein* is evident also at *Il.* 7.45, where the verb refers to a temporary agreement between Athena and Apollo, whose interests nevertheless remain opposed—thus, the coordination of divergent points of view, rather than the establishment of a collective purpose.

12. For a more detailed reading of the wall, see chapter 9. *Il.* 2.768–69 speaks in very similar terms about the wrath (*mēnis*) of Achilles as the poem's defining parameter.

13. Cf. Ford 1992: 151–52.

14. For the complementary relationship between the wall as *mētis* and the *biē* of Achilles, see Nagy 1999: 48; Nagy's book presents a detailed exposition of the thematics of *biē* and *mētis* in Homeric epic. The Iliadic representation of the wall should be understood in the context of a more general pattern of thought, convincingly demonstrated by Ellinger 1993: 208–11, that opposes the technical contrivance of a defensive wall to the ideal self-sufficiency of a company of warriors. For a reading of the Achaean wall partly in terms of this opposition, see Elmer 2008.

15. As in Book 2, the simile correlates the confusion created by the interaction of multiple winds with the disintegration of the social body (see my comments in chapter 4). The expression ἐδαΐζετο θυμός ("[their] *thumos* was divided / torn apart") is parallel both semantically and functionally to τοῖσι δὲ θυμὸν . . . ὄρινε ("he stirred their *thumos*") at *Il.* 2.142, a phrase whose "atomizing" force I discussed in chapter 4. Fränkel 1977: 20n1 believes "Boreas and

Zephyros" to be a hendiadys for a northwest wind, noting that they are both said to blow from Thrace. Homeric similes, however, are extraordinarily sensitive to distinctions of number (see Muellner 1990: 71 and Elmer 2008: 420–21). The specification of multiple winds expresses the divisions created by conflicting impulses among the Achaeans.

16. In the preceding chapter, I argued that Odysseus' function as the one who prevents a premature *nostos* in Book 2 has the effect of emphasizing the absence of Achilles, who occupies that role in the *Cypria*. Diomedes' appearance in Book 9 serves the same purpose. Christensen 2009 discusses Diomedes' behavior as speaker in Book 9 in connection with his function as a "replacement Achilles," noting that "there is a gap throughout most of the epic . . . that *should* have Achilles developing and completing *muthoi*" (152). When Achilles' death makes his absence permanent, Nestor fills his shoes: in Agamemnon's narration of the funeral of Achilles, in the so-called Second *Nekuia* of the *Odyssey*, Nestor is the one who prevents a premature embarkation (*Od.* 24.50–53). I note that Nestor, Odysseus, and Diomedes are the only Achaeans to achieve *epainos* in the *Iliad*. (Achilles and Agamemnon manage only the "imperfect" form.)

17. For a detailed investigation of the nuances and layers of meaning implied by the phrase *telos muthōn*, see Christensen 2009, many of whose points I summarize and build on here. On the *telos muthōn* in the broader context of the relationship between Nestor and Diomedes in both the *Iliad* and the *Odyssey*, see Frame 2009: 195.

18. Contrast the subjunctives that conclude Agamemnon's speech at *Il.* 9.26–7 (= 2.139–40) or the second-person plural imperative at the end of Odysseus' climactic speech in Book 2 (*Il.* 2.331). These constructions are the norm for deliberative speeches.

19. Christensen 2009: 149–50. Diomedes' speech includes both lexical (words such as *analkis* and *daimonios*) and syntactic (a rhetorical question and imperative addressed to Agamemnon) markers of invective. For *oneidos* ("reproach"), a noun cognate with the verb *oneidizein*, as the term for a distinct speech genre, see Martin 1989: 17–18.

20. The sentiment bears an unmistakable resemblance to Achilles' wish that he and Patroklos might alone survive to take Troy (*Il.* 16.99–100). The correspondence is part of the strategy, noted above, of highlighting the absence of Achilles by the presence of his stand-in, Diomedes.

21. Wilson 2002: 75–83 elucidates the various problems with Agamemnon's offer, which is decidedly short on "soothing words," including as it does the demand that Achilles "yield to me, inasmuch as I am more kingly" (*Il.* 9.160). Even the gifts seem designed to establish a position of superiority for Agamemnon. The designation of the episode as a *mētis* may signal the disingenuous, manipulative character of Agamemnon's offer, or it may point to the way the ambassadors to Achilles, and principally the "trickster" Odysseus, are implicitly charged with disguising its true significance (Wilson 2002: 81–82).

22. On the notion of sequence as captured by the metaphorical language of weaving, see Nagy 2002: 70–74.

23. Cf. Nagy 1999: 48. Previously in his speech, Achilles did single out the wall for special criticism (*Il.* 9.346–52); note especially the verb *phrazesthai* (9.347), which, as Nagy (ibid.) indicates, is "a verb of *mētis*."

24. Phoenix thus taps into one of the poem's central themes, the father-son relationship, a point developed at length by Wilson 2002.

25. Note that Agamemnon has just addressed Odysseus as *poluainos* ("man of many *ainoi*," *Il.* 9.673), as though in hopeful expectation of a positive result.

26. On the incremental changes in Achilles' position, see Eustathius 2.821.6–13 van der Valk; Muellner 1996: 150–55. In response to Ajax, the last ambassador to speak, Achilles backs away from any mention of an imminent departure and claims that he will reenter the fighting when Hector threatens his own ships (*Il.* 9.650–55). This reply is not reported to the Achaeans, however.

27. This is, of course, a startling reversal of the paradigm established by the *Cypria*. The reversal affects Odysseus as well: in reporting Achilles' words, he becomes himself a kind of advocate for retreat, even though elsewhere he works actively to hold the army together.

28. This is not the place to undertake a thorough review of the notorious problem of the dual forms in the Embassy scene (*Il.* 9.192, etc.). I note, however, that the duals might be understood, synchronically at least, as an anticipation of the ultimate failure of the embassy (by anticipating the loss of Phoenix). For a diachronic explanation, see Nagy 1999: 49–55.

29. For this structural principle, see chapter 1.

30. That is, the political life proper: the funeral games of Book 23 furnish an important window on Achaean social relations, and an important instance of *epainos*, but in a context that might be termed "parapolitical."

31. The significance of the assembly is also marked by the phraseology describing Achilles' summons: ὦρσεν δ' ἥρωας Ἀχαιούς ("he stirred the Achaean heroes," *Il.* 19.41). In the *Iliad*, *ōrse* (aorist of *ornunai*) almost always takes a god as subject (thirty out of thirty-two occurrences recorded in Prendergast 1875). Moreover, as Mühlestein (1987: 24) has shown, the Homeric phrase ὄρνυθι λαούς ("stir up the fighting men"), addressed by Agamemnon to Achilles at *Il.* 19.139, represents a syntagm of considerable antiquity, crystallized in the Mycenaean personal name *e-ti-ra-wo* = *Erti-lawos* and its Homeric equivalent *Laertēs* (see also von Kamptz 1982: 77). In the *Odyssey*, Laertes plays a similar role to Achilles as the embodiment of sociality (paradoxically represented as living in isolation) whose reintegration into the social structure (expressed in terms of inclusion in a troop of fighting men) marks the restoration of a normative community.

32. Here I follow Clay 1995: 72–73, although I disagree with the characterization that it is Agamemnon who intends "to privatize the quarrel with Achilles": Achilles has already spoken as though the quarrel were simply a private matter. For the *meson* as the locus of public speech, see Detienne 1965 and 1996: 90–102. The position from which Agamemnon speaks has been much discussed; for an overview of possible interpretations, see Edwards 1991: 243–44. An attractive possibility not considered by Edwards is put forward by Lateiner (1995: 97; cf. Clay 1995): remaining seated is a way of asserting dominance or saving face. My reading, which places more emphasis on the failure to appear "in the middle," is compatible with this view. Porphyry, in his explanation of the passage, also relies on the notion that Agamemnon's speech to Achilles bears primarily on a private matter (*Homeric Questions ad* 19.79ff.).

33. Edwards 1991: 245 infers from Agamemnon's preamble that the Achaeans have applauded Achilles' speech, but Agamemnon's words are open to any number of other interpretations. In any case, the *khairein* formula is distinct from the system of deliberative responses, in that the latter describe an observable response (or unresponsiveness),

while *khairein* designates only an affective state. Collective decision making, it should be noted, requires some way of observing the preferences of decision makers.

34. For an examination of these oath-sacrifices, with particular attention to the relationship between ritual practice and epic narrative, see Kitts 2005: 115–56.

35. Cf. Wilson 2002: 78: "offers of *apoina* conventionally presuppose a situation of hostility. . . . By offering *apoina* to Achilleus, Agamemnon casts him in the thematic role of the enemy." At 192n100, however, Wilson speculates that "in the real world . . . *apoina* may have been exchanged among insiders, such as in cases of debt bondage." For a critique of Wilson, see Cairns 2011.

36. For the ritual and social significance of meals in the Homeric poems, see Seaford 1994: 42–53, esp. p. 44 on the function of sacrificial eating as "agent and sign of the identity and cohesion of a group." Note that an elaborately described *deipnon* follows the scene in Book 2 in which Odysseus restores order and achieves *epainos:* this meal provides a final sign of revived solidarity. Odysseus may be trying to repeat that success here. Moreover, in urging Achilles to address the assembly, Odysseus may be attempting to reconfigure the private dialogue between Achilles and Agamemnon as public deliberation, scripting Achilles as the one who produces *epainos*. In the event, Achilles does as Odysseus suggests but without any socially significant effect.

37. Both *brōtus* and *brōsis* are *hapax legomena* in the *Iliad. Il.* 19.210 presents a variant of an Odyssean formula (βρῶσίν τε πόσιν τε ["food and drink"], also attested in the nominative) whose usage provides ample evidence that *brōsis* designates "food" precisely in contexts evacuated of social meaning. It is food consumed by sailors on shipboard (*Od.* 10.176, 12.320, 13.72), or individuals in other similarly liminal, extramural situations: cf. *Od.* 1.191 (Laertes in the countryside); 6.209, 246, 248 (Odysseus on the seashore).

38. Cf. Redfield 1994: 218, Alvis 1995: 44, Wilson 2002: 116.

39. Muellner 1976: 106. This use of *anainesthai* should be connected with the occurrences of this verb in the Embassy. For a more detailed reading of the shield scene, see chapter 8.

40. On the persistence of Achilles' alienation, see also Scully 1990: 126–27, who offers a slightly different perspective on the relation between Achilles' shield and his problematic relation to the community.

41. Redfield 1994. On Achilles' isolation as an expression of cultural contradiction, see pp. 99–109, esp. p. 104: "In the story of Achilles the poet dramatizes a fundamental contradiction: communities, in the interest of their own needs, produce figures who are unassimilable, men they cannot live with and who cannot live with them." On the relation between ceremony and art, as cultural expressions of different orders, see pp. 160–67. On the purely formal nature of the poem's resolution, see pp. 218–23, esp. p. 219.

CHAPTER 6: A CONSENSUS OF FOOLS

1. On the relationship between Pouludamas and Hector and the sequence of scenes leading up to this one, see Schofield 1999: 17–21 and Clark 2007.

2. The *epainos* that begins the first day of battle (*Il.* 2.335) occurs in a morning assembly. Nevertheless, when we understand that assembly as a narrative unit (the perspective

taken in chapter 4), it becomes clear that here as elsewhere consensus functions as a *closural* element that brings to an end one narrative movement while simultaneously looking ahead to the next. I return to this point in chapter 9.

3. On *kosmos* as poetic order, see chapter 4.

4. Mackie 1996 offers an "ethnography of speaking" (5) that establishes the differences between the Greek and Trojan communities, especially with regard to their political conduct. For the contrasting arrangement of assembly and council scenes, see pp. 21–26.

5. Mackie's table (1996: 22–23), which omits the *boulē* and considers only the full Greek assembly that happens later in the book, obscures the force of the contrast.

6. For *akritos* in the sense of "lacking a *krisis*" or decisive outcome, cf. *Il.* 14.205 and Hes. [*Sc.*] 311. As Doug Frame points out to me, it seems significant that our first view of the Trojans' political life should be focalized by Iris in the guise of Politēs, the "man of the *polis*"; cf. Seaford 1994: 111–12.

7. Contrast the ultimately successful struggle of the Achaeans to reach the "*telos* of *muthoi*"—a phrase that signals, among other things, an executable proposal—described in chapter 5.

8. Cf. Mackie 1996: 16 and 21, Ross 2005.

9. Cf. Mackie 1996: 23: "the formulas generally used to construct Homeric assembly scenes are strangely lacking from the *Iliad*'s accounts of Trojan assemblies. . . . [Trojan assemblies] are, moreover, governed by practices that seem abnormal, unorthodox, or possibly just less political in nature than those endorsed by the Achaeans."

10. On the meaning of *pepnumenos*, see Dale 1982: 208–9; cf. Heath 2001: 133–34. Antēnōr receives the epithet *pepnumenos* at *Il.* 3.203 as well.

11. *Il.* 7.350–51: δεῦτ᾽ ἄγετ᾽ Ἀργείην Ἑλένην καὶ κτήμαθ᾽ ἅμ᾽ αὐτῇ / δώομεν Ἀτρεΐδησιν ἄγειν ("come, let us give back Argive Helen and the valuables with her, for the Atreids to take"). Note that Antēnōr appeals to the oaths sworn in Book 3.

12. Note that when Idaios delivers his message before the Achaeans, he highlights the discrepancy between Paris' offer and the collective will of the Trojans (*Il.* 7.392–93).

13. On Hector's authoritarianism, see Mackie 1996: 26.

14. The distinctly Trojan quality of the response is noted by the AbT scholia at *Il.* 8.542; cf. my comments in chapter 1.

15. Griffin 1980: 13.

16. Quotation from the b scholia at *Il.* 8.523.

17. The ability to look both "before and behind" may indicate an ability to contextualize events in terms of a temporal continuum extending from past to likely future events. Such an ability, as noted in the introduction, is fundamental to the operation of consensus.

18. Echoes of earlier scenes: *Il.* 18.284 = 12.230; 18.285 ~ 7.357. Hector refers with bitter irony to Pouludamas' own words at 18.303 (cf. 18.277) and 18.306 (cf. 18.278): see Edwards 1991: 181.

19. The bT scholia at *Il.* 18.296 characterize Hector's threat as a manifestation of the same tyrannical impulse they detected in Book 8: "In a tyrannical fashion [τυραννικῶς], he has not left the decision to the multitude, but has diverted it to his own authority."

20. S. Edmunds 1990, esp. pp. 60–88.

21. See Mackie 1996: 24 for this "irregularity."

22. The final, climactic expression of Trojan solidarity on the occasion of Hector's funeral (see chapter 8) produces a similar effect: *après moi, le déluge*.

23. The major exception is the Achaean *epainos* for Agamemnon's proposed settlement in Book 3, discussed in the previous chapter.

24. For Athena's part in Book 2, see chapter 4. On her similar role elsewhere in the poem, see chapter 7.

25. This is an ironic reversal of the rhetoric employed by both Paris and Hector, who claim that "the gods themselves have taken away the *phrenes*" of Antēnōr and Pouludamas, respectively (*Il.* 7.360, 12.234).

26. Quotation from the bT scholia at *Il.* 18.312–13.

27. See Erbse 1978: 24 and 34, and, for complete argumentation, Nagy 1999: 145–47. Nagy points out that the association of the Trojans with defensive rather than offensive action is encoded also in their prayer to Athena *erusiptolis* ("protector of the city," *Il.* 6.305) in Book 6.

28. This pattern, of course, must be inferred, since the *Iliad*'s telescoped narrative centers precisely on the irregular period of Trojan aggression. Hector refers to the Trojans' normal defensive posture with the weariness of long habituation at *Il.* 18.287.

29. Both cases are discussed in chapter 5. In the chariot race of Book 23, Achilles is the higher power who overrules *epainos* for his own proposal, after Antilokhos' objection: more on this scene in chapter 8.

CHAPTER 7: THE VIEW FROM OLYMPUS

1. On the general resemblance between divine and human political communities, see Vlachos 1974: 46, 124–25.

2. Only Hera among the gods expresses direct opposition to Zeus' plan to honor Thetis' request, but Zeus makes clear that he has arrived at his decision without consideration of *any* of the other gods (*Il.* 1.549).

3. Compare *Il.* 1.566 with 1.28, and 1.568 with 1.33.

4. For detailed consideration of the articulation of this scene and its implications for the dynamics of *epainos*, see Elmer 2012.

5. The connection between Zeus' "attempt" (ἐπειρᾶτο, *Il.* 4.5) to nettle Hera and the *diapeira* of Agamemnon in Book 2 (cf. πειρήσομαι, *Il.* 2.73) was noted by Wilamowitz (Wilamowitz-Moellendorff 1920: 298). See also Marks 2001: 55–56.

6. Taplin 1992: 132.

7. Cf. Morrison 1997: 288: "The consequences [of Zeus' acting against the group will]? Not that Zeus would violate the dictates of destiny, not that the vault of heaven would come crashing down, but that none of the gods would approve." In a footnote, Morrison speculates that Zeus fears a challenge to his sovereignty by the other gods, "who in an extreme case might physically fetter him" (n. 31). Even Martin (1989), who elsewhere recognizes the essential role of *epainos* in decision making (cf. 55–56), characterizes Hera's warning as simply "the threat of public blame" (178).

8. For Marks 2001: 53–56, even this claim is part of Zeus' deceptive ploy to gain concessions from Hera at no cost to himself. Without discounting the rhetorical effect of Zeus' remark, I prefer to see it as a sign of a genuine ambivalence, for reasons made clear below.

9. Flaig 1994; see my comments on Flaig's article in the introduction. At pp. 25–26, Flaig emphasizes that, although this scene articulates the principle of consensus, it does not portray complete consensus: a certain "affective dissonance" remains.

10. By means of what Morrison calls "reversal passages" (Morrison 1992). Cf. Redfield 1994: 221: "The distant inclusive perspective of the Olympian gods . . . becomes an Archimedean point where the poet, his audience, and even his hero can stand aside from the human world and judge it."

11. Cf. Redfield 1994: 133, Finkelberg 1998: 136, Scodel 2002: 68. Marks 2001 distinguishes between "fate" as an index of the general outline of Trojan War tradition as a whole (including the specific traditions underlying the Cyclic epics) and the "plan of Zeus" as an index of the plot of the *Iliad*. I speak here of "Iliadic performance" rather than "performance of the *Iliad*" in order to distinguish our text of the *Iliad* from the tradition that produced it.

12. The debates over Troy, Sarpedon, and Hector occur on the first, third, and fourth days of fighting, respectively. The second day begins with Zeus commanding all the gods to "approve" (αἰνεῖτ', *Il.* 8.9) his plan. I discuss this attempt to impose *epainos* later in this chapter. On the tripartite segmentation of the narrative and the possible compositional significance of the distribution of *epainos* scenes, see chapter 9.

13. Flaig 1994: 25–26.

14. At least, he does not overtly question it, although his characterization of the destruction of Troy as the preference of "you goddesses" (*Il.* 7.32, presumably with reference to Hera and Athena) might suggest that this outcome is not sanctioned by the community as a whole. Zenodotus' reading (ἀθανατοῖσι, as reported in the A scholia) mitigates the subversive undertones of the remark.

15. Cf. Murnaghan 1997, Nagy 1999: 82 (§25n2), and the concise statement of Marks 2001: 7: "the supreme god's perspective is more or less coextensive to that of the singer of the epic." References to Zeus' *noos* ("mind") can serve the same function: at the end of the Hesiodic *Theogony*, for instance, the phrase μεγάλου δὲ Διὸς νόος ἐξετελεῖτο ("and the mind of great Zeus was accomplished," 1002) is used with reference to the story of Jason and Medea in a way that matches precisely line 5 of the *Iliad*'s proem (Διὸς δ' ἐτελείετο βουλή ["and the will of Zeus was accomplished"]). This reference to an *Argonautica* tradition is embedded in the catalogue of heroes with which the *Theogony* proper concludes. It appears to inaugurate a brief survey of heroic sagas represented metonymically by their principal heroes, Jason, Phōkos (*Phōkais?*), Achilles (*Iliad*), Aeneas (on a possible *Aeneis* tradition see Nagy 1999: 265–75), Odysseus (*Odyssey*), and Odysseus' children (cf. the *Telegony*). At *Works and Days* 661–62, the narrator constructs a comparable equivalence between the *noos* of Zeus and the substance of song (in this case, the *Works and Days* itself).

16. At *Il.* 8.204, Hera refers to Poseidon's past or potential support for the Achaeans with the phrase σὺ δέ σφισι βούλεο νίκην ("you were plotting victory for them" or "plot

victory for them"; the verb may be either imperfect or imperative). Poseidon is thus cast as a potential counterpart to Apollo as an exponent of Achaean interests. Other gods can play a role in dispensing victory (see the examples involving Athena listed by Nagy 2009b: 497–98), but the collocation *boulesthai nikēn*, "plot victory," is distinctive.

17. Cf. *Il.* 11.79, 12.174, 16.121, and especially 15.596, where the narrator gives a particularly expansive account of the plot ordained by Zeus. At *Il.* 23.682 the βούλετο νίκην formula is used of Diomedes' hope for a particular outcome in the boxing match.

18. On the significance of Apollo's prominence in this alternative proem, see Marks 2002: 17n40: "the causal chain begins with the transfer of Apollo's μῆνις to Achilleus, thus making the anger of Apollo at the beginning of the *Iliad* independent of the plan of Zeus." See also Marks 2001: 46, and especially Muellner 1996: 96–102, who places Aristoxenos' proem in the context of a broader "interpenetration of Zeus and Apollo" in Iliadic tradition. For an illuminating discussion of the alternative proem in connection with the scope of the will of Zeus, see Nagy 2010b: 103–27, esp. pp. 109–19.

19. Van der Valk 1964: 365–66 recognizes the pro-Trojan perspective implied by Aristoxenos' text. He also believes the alternative proem is a "falsification." From my perspective, it is a variant that can be considered authentic to the extent that it is generated by genuinely Iliadic thematics. Cf. Muellner 1996: 97, Nagy 2010b: 109–19.

20. The fragment of the *Cypria* referred to here most likely belongs to the proem of that work, although scholars have expressed differing views on this point: see Marks 2002: 6–7.

21. See the A and D scholia at *Il.* 1.5–6. The polemical remark in the A scholia about *hoi neōteroi* must refer to poems (above all the *Cypria*), whose "fictions" Aristarchus firmly rejected, rather than "newer critics" (*pace* Clay 1999: 40; cf. Severyns 1928: 66–68, Nagy 2009b: 281–82). The intervention of Aristophanes and Aristarchus implies that other scholars (perhaps including their predecessor Zenodotus) were inclined to connect the Iliadic *Dios boulē* with the *Cypria*.

22. See the D scholia at *Il.* 1.5, lines 13–29 (ed. Heyne). Cf. Eustathius 1.33.15–24 ed. van der Valk and J. Cramer 1837: 405.6–406.7 (a commentary on *Il.* 1 in the Bodleian Library's MS. Barocci 162). The most compelling modern proponent of this view is Kullmann 1955.

23. Exhibit A is Zeus' statement of his intentions at *Il.* 15.59–71, which concludes with the sack of Troy. The many suggestions that the destruction of Troy will be consequent on Hector's death also support this understanding of the *Dios boulē*, as well as the prophecy of Troy's destruction reported at *Il.* 2.324–29; cf. Redfield 1979: 107–8. Clay 1999 sketches the arguments in favor of all three of the views outlined above (as well as a fourth, that the "will of Zeus" means simply "fate," which she rejects). See also Alvis 1995: 11–12.

24. Marks 2002: 13–16. The most important of the ambiguities identified by Marks is the correlative for the relative temporal expression ἐξ οὗ ("from the time when," *Il.* 1.6). If this expression is taken to refer to the statement that "the will of Zeus was being accomplished," then the *Dios boulē* is clearly subordinate to Achilles' wrath: "And the will of Zeus was being accomplished / from the time when the two first quarreled . . ." If, on the other hand, the phrase refers back to the imperative in 1.1, then it merely identifies

the prescribed starting point for the Muse's narrative, and no temporal limitation is put on the *Dios boulē* (but cf. Redfield 1979: 96).

25. Clay 1999 asserts that the *Iliad* sustains all three of these visions simultaneously; Marks 2002 argues that the proem's initial open-endedness eventually gives way to a more precise vision of the *Dios boulē,* which corresponds, in the terms I have used, either to the medium- or the long-term perspective.

26. Cf. Clay 1999: 43–44.

27. To the extent that *epainos* is, formally, *ainos* in response to (*epi-*) a primary speech act, the response Zeus calls for would amount to this most decisive form of approval. Why then does Zeus use the simplex *aineîn* rather than the compound form *epaineîn?* He appears to be acknowledging the existence of unbridgeable differences among the gods that make impossible the establishment of a true consensus. Unlike the compound form, which is always used of a group (with one significant exception at *Il.* 21.290, discussed below), and therefore always implies collective sentiment, the simplex verb can be predicated of individuals (cf. *Il.* 24.30). Here, therefore, it suggests the temporary coordination of divergent interests rather than a proper consensus.

28. The coincidence is not complete, however: Zeus stresses that once the Achaeans are again hemmed in at the ships "I myself will devise word and deed / so that the Achaeans may again have respite from toil" (*Il.* 15.234–35).

29. On the meaning of *ēpios,* which I here translate as "in accord," see S. Edmunds 1990 (esp. p. 24): cognate with Latin *apiscor, aptus,* etc., the word means, etymologically, something approximating "connecting." The addition of a negative prefix gives *nēpios,* on which see my remarks in chapter 6.

30. Aristarchus' editorial judgment is confirmed by the *obeloi* at lines 8.28–40 in the Venetus A manuscript of the *Iliad* and the scholion at *Il.* 8.28 in the same manuscript; cf. the T scholia at *Il.* 8.37. The A scholia indicate at *Il.* 8.40 that Zeus is simply "speaking ironically." See also Synodinou 1986: 159.

31. According to the grammar of reception outlined in chapter 1.

32. Cf. Synodinou 1986: 157n1.

33. These are the only two instances of the word *hupermoros* in the poem. In *Il.* 20.30, some editors prefer to write ὑπὲρ μόρον, which also has manuscript support.

34. Murnaghan 1995. On p. 77, Murnaghan outlines an instructive contrast between the complementarity of Athena and Zeus in the *Odyssey* and the more tense relationship between Thetis and Zeus in the *Iliad.*

35. Cf. esp. *Od.* 24.473–81: Athena asks how Zeus intends to resolve the situation on Ithaca; Zeus, pointing out that that situation is the result of Athena's own *noos,* invites her to proceed as she sees fit—but he goes on to dictate the ending he deems most "fitting." This scene, which emphasizes the complementarity of Athena and Zeus, particularly in bringing about a resolution of the plot's action, has much in common with the exchange in *Iliad* 22.

36. Note that the shift from events narrated within the poem to events lying outside its ambit is marked by a shift from the future indicative (*Il.* 15.64, 65, 68) to the optative (15.70).

37. For Aeneas as the hero of his own localized epic tradition, see Nagy 1999: 265–75 and, with reference specifically to the traditions of Lesbos, Aloni 1986: 69–107.

38. See Nagy 1999: 274.

39. The technique is the same as the one at work in the Trojan assembly of Book 7, in which the lack of response formulas speaks to the Trojans' inability to conduct their business in terms of collective will: see chapter 6. Davies 1981: 59 comments on the fact that there is no positive sign of agreement or reconciliation among the gods.

40. So, too, is the twelve-day period that elapses between the initial onset of the dispute and the subsequent debate. This interval recalls the twelve days in Book 1 that separate Achilles' complaint to Thetis from her appearance before Zeus on Olympus. The parallel underscores the fact that Zeus' decision to compel the ransoming of Hector's corpse finally puts an end to the chain of events initiated by his promise to Thetis. For a discussion of this kind of "ring-composition" in the *Iliad*, see Whitman 1958: 249–84, esp. p. 257; Haubold 2000: 95, with references.

CHAPTER 8: THE RETURN TO NORMALCY AND
THE *ILIAD*'S "BOUNDLESS PEOPLE"

1. Cf. Murnaghan 1997: 38–39.

2. Wilson 2002: 132.

3. See Podlecki 1971: 82 and, for the term "reverse simile," H. Foley 1978.

4. Achilles had ransomed Andromache's mother after the sack of Thēbē (*Il.* 6.425–27); compare the words he addresses at *Il.* 21.99–105 to Lykaōn, whom he had previously captured and released (though not for *apoina*—he had sold Lykaōn into slavery at Lemnos). See also Wilson 2002: 31.

5. There is no meal associated with the animals killed at Patroklos' funeral (*Il.* 23.166–74). The meal served by Achilles to the embassy in Book 9 significantly omits the moment of greatest ritual significance—the sacrificial slaughter of the animals (Achilles prepares the meat of animals that have already been killed)—although it does include the burning of *thuēlai*, "sacrificial offerings."

6. *Il.* 24.623–24 = 7.317–18. Note that the restoration of social norms coincides with the reassertion of formulaic conventions.

7. See chapter 5.

8. There are additional signs of a return to normal social life for Achilles. When he retires, Briseis sleeps beside him (*Il.* 24.676). Moreover, Achilles refers to the possibility that he will be visited in the night by "councilors" of the Achaeans, although it is difficult to assess the force of these words, embedded as they are in a speech that he delivers ἐπικερτομέων, "teasingly" (*Il.* 24.649).

9. Note that the Achaean *boulē* concludes with the *epainos* of the *basilēes* (*Il.* 7.344). Typically for the Trojans, their assembly scene includes no corresponding expression of collective sentiment, only the statement that they "heard Priam and obeyed" (7.379).

10. See the discussion of this scene in chapter 5.

11. So Agamemnon's insistence that corpses ought to be committed to the pyre as soon as possible (*Il.* 7.409–10) deepens the pathos of the denial of these rites to Hector, much like Hector's own plea that his body be returned for burial (*Il.* 22.338–43).

12. Another divergence concerns the overt display of emotion in Book 24: in Book 7, Priam instructs the Trojans to bury their dead in silence, without any expression of grief (*Il.* 7.427–28).

13. See Muellner 1976: 105–6 and Andersen 1976: 11–16: both relate the shield scene to Achilles' quarrel with Agamemnon and place it in the context of other references to *poinē* and *apoina* in the *Iliad*. Nagy 1997 argues for the multivalence of the shield's image with respect to Achilles, who can be imagined as occupying the position of either the "defendant," the "plaintiff," or the victim. Haubold 2000: 81 notes the contrast between the public setting of the scene on the shield and the privacy of the ransom scene in Book 24.

14. For overviews of the critical discussion, see Hommel 1969 and Edwards 1991: 213–18.

15. See the bT scholia at *Il.* 18.499–500, an interpretation followed by, e.g., Bonner and Smith 1930: 32–35, Wolff 1946: 37, and Cantarella 2001. See also the authorities cited by Muellner 1976: 102n8.

16. See, e.g., Benveniste 1969: 2.240–42, Andersen 1976: 11–15, Hammond 1985: 80–81, Westbrook 1992: 53–54.

17. A point made convincingly by Dareste 1902: 5–6. Cantarella 2001: 478 attempts to reconcile this publicity with an understanding of the dispute as a question of fact: "given the fact that the delivery of the compensation is a solemn, public ceremony, the dispute can hardly concern *whether* it was paid; it rather concerns whether *all* of it was paid." But here she is contradicted by her own rendering of *Il.* 18.500, "the other claimed that he had received *nothing*" (476, emphasis added). The Greek simply doesn't permit the kind of nuance pleaded by Cantarella. On this point, see Andersen 1976, who offers as well other objections to the question-of-fact hypothesis.

18. Muellner 1976: 105–6; cf. Edwards 1991: 215–16, Nagy 1990b: 252–54.

19. Cf. Nagy 1997 on the interrelationship between the Iliadic plot and the shield scene, which he characterizes in terms of the mutual influence of "tenor" and "vehicle" (see esp. p. 203, with reference to the work of Muellner 1976).

20. See chapter 5. For the semantics of the root and the morphology of its derivatives, see chapter 2.

21. Full discussion in chapter 5.

22. For possible distinctions between these two terms, see Lejeune 1965, Westbrook 1992: 74. The evidence of Linear B suggests that *dēmos* at *Il.* 18.500 can be taken not simply as a general reference to the community at large but specifically as a designation for the community as a legal entity capable of action in a juridical procedure: see Lejeune 1965: 12 (Mycenaean *dāmos* designates "une entité administrative dourée, notamment, de la personalité juridique"), Muellner 1976: 104, Westbrook 1992: 74–75.

23. Edwards 1991: 218. Although this is the natural interpretation of the pronouns in *Il.* 18.508, and the one most often put forward by commentators, some prefer nevertheless to see the gold as a prize for the disputant whose claim prevails (e.g., Dareste 1902: 8, Cantarella 2001: 478).

24. It has been suggested: that the *histōr* mentioned in *Il.* 18.501 is the one who determines the best judgment (Andersen 1976: 11); that the best judgment will be determined

by mutual consent of the parties to the dispute (Pflüger 1942: 148; Hommel 1969: 30); that the elders themselves will decide (Hirzel 1907: 69–70); and, finally, that the best judgment will be the one that wins the approval of the assembled community (Wolff 1946: 40–43, with Germanic parallels; Edwards 1991: 218; Ruzé 1997: 92; Allan 2006: 11). I support this last view.

25. It is possible to reconcile this view, as held by Edwards and others (see previous note), with the view of Andersen that the *histōr* decides which of the *gerontes* has given the best judgment. By analogy with the awarding of prizes in the chariot race of Book 23 (to be discussed shortly), we can suppose that the *histōr* first makes a proposal concerning the awarding of the gold as prize for the best judgment and that the *dēmos* responds with *epainos*. The decision would ultimately rest with the community. A medieval Irish juridical procedure for responding to royal petitions provides a striking parallel for this interpretation: after a suit has been presented, one of the druids pronounces a judgment (the druids are multiple, like the *gerontes*); the king affirms this judgment (like the *histōr*); and the people in attendance then affirm the king's decision (Ó Cathasaigh 2005; I am grateful to Joseph Nagy for this reference). Alternatively, the *histōr* may be the elder whose judgment prevails and who thus provides the "limit" (*peirar*) to the quarrel sought by the disputants (*Il.* 18.501). The difference between these possibilities is minimal: according to the latter, the *histōr* himself formulates the "straightest judgment"; according to the former, he identifies it.

26. Muellner 1976: 106 (emphasis original).

27. Following immediately on Priam's entreaty that he accept *apoina* (*Il.* 24.555–56), Achilles' assertion that "I am myself minded to release Hector" sounds very much like an attempt to claim that his release of the corpse is independent of any compensation: in this way, like the figure on the shield, Achilles can persist in refusing to accept anything that could be equated with the loss of Patroklos. In a subsequent address to Patroklos, however, Achilles does acknowledge the acceptance of *apoina* (*Il.* 24.592–95).

28. Westbrook 1992; Edwards 1991: 216.

29. See Nagy 1997, and cf. Andersen 1976: "*There must be an end to revenge*, whether one thinks of continuous blood feud, as it is still an issue on the Shield, or one considers Achilles maiming the dead Hector" (16; emphasis original).

30. See, e.g., Dareste 1902: 9–11, Gernet 1948: 182, Vélissaropoulos-Karakostas 2003: 16–17.

31. Dareste 1902: 8–9. Most scholars understand the fact that the shield depicts *two* "talents," or measures of gold, as an indication that they have been supplied by the two parties to the dispute. Some (including Dareste) have used the analogy with the wager of Idomeneus and Ajax to argue that the gold is intended not as a prize for the "straightest" judgment but instead as a kind of juridical wager, analogous to the Roman *sacramentum*, to be awarded to the litigant who pleads his case "most straightly." This view runs counter to the interpretation I have proposed here, according to which the two measures of gold should be compared instead with the prizes that await the contestants in the race. It would be a mistake, however, to insist too much on the force of analogy in either case.

32. It is tempting to make some inferences about the function of the *histōr* on the shield on the basis of Agamemnon's role in the chariot race. If Agamemnon is being

called upon to authenticate the result of the race—to pronounce formally the winner—this might suggest that the *histōr* on the shield is supposed likewise to pronounce a formal verdict as to which of the elders has given the "straightest" judgment. But again, this would doubtless press the analogy too far. We cannot and need not correlate every aspect of these two scenes. For a thorough consideration of the significance of the *histōr* figure on the shield, in terms both of the *Iliad*'s thematics and the broader semantics of *histōr* and related words in Greek, see Nagy 1990b: 250–73.

33. Wilson 2002: 124–25 and passim.

34. Eumēlos' right to the title of "best of the Achaeans" in the context of chariot racing is established at the conclusion of the Catalogue of Ships, when the narrator specifies that his horses were in fact the "best" (ἄρισται), after those of Achilles (*Il.* 2.763–70; the Catalogue, however, does not take account of Diomedes' Trojan horses, captured from Aeneas in Book 5). The qualification about Achilles' preeminence is seconded at the start of the race by Achilles himself, who declares that, if he were competing, he would certainly win, insofar as his horses excel all others in *aretē* (*Il.* 23.274–78).

35. In a strict application of Wilson's scheme of "fixed" versus "fluid" ranking systems (cf. Wilson 2002: 37), we would have to say that Achilles is searching for a way to reconcile the two: thus Diomedes is to receive the first prize on the basis of demonstrated achievement (the "fluid" system), while Eumēlos is to be recognized for his "fixed" position in the hierarchy. Wilson herself characterizes the funeral games as an ideal image of the "fluid" system (142–43), although her comments on the spear-throwing contest (*Il.* 23.884–97), in which Agamemnon is awarded a prize without having actually to compete, leave some room for the "fixed" system (125).

36. One of the later contests similarly engages with the economics of Book 1. In setting the prizes for the duel in arms, Achilles stipulates that, while the sword of Asteropaios is to be awarded to the one who first draws blood, the arms of Sarpedon are to be held "in common" (τεύχεα δ᾽ ἀμφότεροι ξυνήϊα ταῦτα φερέσθων ["let both take these arms as a prize held in common"], *Il.* 23.809). This, the only other instance of the adjective *xunēios* in the poem, clearly looks back to the ξυνήϊα κείμενα that were lacking in Book 1 (*Il.* 1.124). When the duel threatens to turn deadly, the availability of this "common" prize serves to resolve the tension (see 23.822–23).

37. Kurke 1991: 108–16. On the relation between Pindaric and Homeric poetics in general terms, see Nagy 1990b.

38. On Pindar's use, here and elsewhere, of the accusative ἄποινα in a quasi-prepositional sense, see Kurke 1991: 110n8, who states, "we should not suppose that the fixity of the phrase reflects a blunting of the metaphorical force of the term." On *ainos/epainos* and *aineîn/epaineîn* as designations for epinician poetry, see Nagy 1999: 222–23.

39. See chapter 2 for the inclusion of epinician poetry in a larger system of exchange.

40. Kurke 1991. For a succinct statement of this thesis, cf. pp. 6–7: "Everything in epinikion aimed at the defusion and resolution of these same tensions [between *oikos* and *polis*], for its goal was the successful integration of the athlete into a harmonious community." See also Kurke 1998: 141 and Crotty 1982: 121 for the epinician ode as an "act of inclusion."

41. Kurke 1991: 110.

42. Frame 2009: 131–72 connects Nestor's *ainos* to the larger context of the chariot race by interpreting it as a coded message referring to Nestor's own youthful race against the twin sons of Aktōr (see esp. 158n52). The importance of *ainos* to the thematics of the episode as a whole can be seen also in the prominence of the adjective *apēnēs*, which is used first by Idomeneus with reference to Ajax's quarrelsomeness during their dispute (*Il.* 23.484) and subsequently by Menelaus in denial of his own quarrelsomeness (23.611).

43. The flaw is indicated already by the imperfect tense of the verb at *Il.* 23.539 (I discuss the difference between aorist and imperfect tenses of the verb in chapter 1).

44. The issue is similar to the one surrounding Eumēlos: Menelaus claims that he *ought* to have finished second, since Antilokhos' horses are "worse" (*Il.* 23.572, 577). Antilokhos responds to Menelaus' demand for an oath by acknowledging the latter's superiority (23.588) and offering to give him the prize (which he nevertheless claims to have won, 23.592). This strategy of appeasement, by which Antilokhos is eventually able to retain the prize, achieves a kind of reconciliation of the "fixed" and "fluid" points of view: Antilokhos is recognized for his actual achievement, while Menelaus is able to assert his absolute position in the hierarchy.

45. Haubold argues of the Homeric *laoi* that "the *Iliad* sees their situation as deeply problematic and fundamentally beyond reform" (2000: 143). Nevertheless, he finds that the epic offers "glimpses of a more permanent solution" (100). In both poems, "aetiological progress is in the air" but "this progress is never narrated" (144). Although I would distance myself from Haubold's pessimistic view of an epic world "fundamentally beyond reform" (the state of exception implies that successful mechanisms have operated in the past and will again in the future), I am fully in agreement that the teleology of the poems is fulfilled not within the narrative but only in the real-world context in which the poems are performed.

46. Ibid., 119 (emphasis original). Clines 1997 offers a remarkably similar reading of the Pentateuch. For Clines, the sacred book of the Jewish people articulates a teleology that remains unfulfilled within the text precisely because it awaits fulfillment in the readers' here and now.

47. Nagy 1997: 207.

48. The text stresses that Achilles himself takes part in the preparation of the body (*Il.* 24.589; cf. Richardson 1993: 337–38), which is indeed remarkable. On the continuity of the mourning rituals for Patroklos with those for Hector, see also Beck 2005: 246.

49. Although the narrator uses the verb *phasthai*, "speak," to designate the utterances of the mourners (see the discussion of the response formulas below), the overall context is one of song rather than speech: the performances are initiated by the song of the *aoidoi*, "singers," who lead the *thrēnos* (*Il.* 24.720–24). In describing the mourners' words as song rather than speech, I follow Alexiou 1974: 11–13, who characterizes the *thrēnos* in this passage as the formal song of professional mourners, as opposed to the *goos* (a less formal but still sung lament) of Hector's relatives, each of whom is said to "lead the *goos*" (*Il.* 24.723, 747, 761); see also Nagy 2010a: 30. Richardson 1993: 350 speaks of "individual spoken laments." Tsagalis 2004: 5 distinguishes *thrēnoi* from *gooi* in terms of song versus speech.

50. Cf. Beck 2005: 245. See Alexiou 1974: 12–13 and 131–35 for contextualization of the antiphonal element in the *Iliad*'s laments. Alexiou suggests (13, 132) that the Homeric representation of solo song followed by refrains that are only signaled (not quoted) may obscure the more developed antiphony of ritual practice and that this Homeric image may be motivated by tendencies or preoccupations peculiar to epic. If this suggestion is correct, we might speculate that the representation of lament has been shaped in part by the isomorphism with deliberative responses.

51. Other important scenes of mourning are Thetis' lament for Achilles at *Il.* 18.51–64, Hecabe's lament for Hector at *Il.* 22.431–36, and the expressions of grief that are formally connected to Patroklos' funeral in the first part of Book 23. Here, however, I focus specifically on those instances that highlight the relation between individual performance and group response. From this point of view, Thetis' lament in 18, Hecabe's in 22, and Achilles' lament at *Il.* 23.19–23 are of only incidental significance, since in each case the lament concludes without any specification of a group response.

52. I noted above that the first ritual acts of Hector's funeral rites are performed by Achilles and his servants when he ransoms the corpse. The funeral itself thus begins in Achilles' tent and ends in the full view of the Trojan people. The public dimension of Hector's funeral at Troy sets off by contrast the strictly private nature of the ransom scene.

53. The gender-based coordination of performer and audience applies also in the case of the lament by Hecabe that intervenes between those of Priam and Andromache (*Il.* 22.431–36). Although the lament concludes without any indication of a group response, the narrator does indicate that Hecabe "led the clamorous lamentation among the Trojan women" (22.430). In a forthcoming paper comparing ritual lament in the *Iliad* and the *Mahābhārata*, Nikolay Grintser draws attention to the avoidance of the expected group-response formula in this passage. I note that the violation of formulaic expectations in Book 22 seems to prefigure the similar avoidance of the expected group-response formula after Hecabe's lament in Book 24, which I discuss below. (My thanks to Nikolay Grintser for providing me with a copy of his manuscript.)

54. Even the public demonstrations of grief for Patroklos are generally restricted to the Myrmidons, to the exclusion of the other Achaeans (see, e.g., *Il.* 23.1–23). It must be admitted, however, that Patroklos is not so central a figure among the Achaeans as a whole as Hector is among the Trojans.

55. On the social and political aspects of lament, see Alexiou 1974: passim and Versnel 1980. For the socially integrative function of lament within the *Iliad*, see Seaford 1994: 159–80. On the transformation of personal into collective experience as "a fundamental feature of lament," see Dué 2002: 81.

56. Note, for instance, the frequent use of this term to indicate simply the confused mass of soldiers (both Achaeans and Trojans) on the battlefield, as at *Il.* 11.469, 13.338, 20.47, etc.

57. See chapter 4 on the response to Agamemnon's speech in the assembly of Book 2.

58. For a detailed application of Durkheim's principle of *anomie* to the funeral of Germanicus, see Versnel 1980.

59. The bounded nature of the shield's images is signaled in the text by the double references to the *antux*, "border," which begin and end the description (*Il.* 18.479, 608).

60. For similar arguments, see Pantelia 2002, Dué 2006: 44. On Helen's self-awareness as a subject of epic song and her affinity with epic composition, see Clader 1976: 6–9, Jenkins 1999, Elmer 2005.

61. Haubold 2000. Cf. esp. p. 144: "Outside Homer, the *laoi* leave behind their suffering to become what we might call the 'founding people' of successful institutional structures."

62. Nagy 2010b: 266–72 points to another component of this strategy: the *peplos* offered by the Trojan women to Athena in *Iliad* 6 evokes the Panathenaic *peplos*, the garment presented to Athena at the festival of the Great Panathenaia, the premier occasion for the performance of the *Iliad* in the classical period. In Nagy's words, "the ad hoc presentation of the peplos to Athena in Troy is a ritual failure; in terms of the festival of the Panathenaia, on the other hand, the seasonally recurring presentation of the peplos to Athena in Athens is notionally always a ritual success. In other words, the *text* is imperfect, but the *subtext* is notionally perfect" (272; italics original).

63. It is highly significant in this regard that Bacchylides (9.30) describes the Panhellenic audience in attendance at the Nemean games as "the boundless [*apeirōn*] circle of the Hellenes."

CHAPTER 9: THE POLITICS OF RECEPTION

1. Nagy 2009a: 283. See also my comments in the introduction.

2. Nagy 1999, which explores the tension between the Panhellenizing tendencies of Homeric epic and the local orientation of hero cult, is the most influential formulation of this perspective on the Homeric poems. See also Nagy 1990b: 52–81; Scodel 2002: 45–46, 49–51. "Panhellenism" in this sense refers to the broad pattern of increasing interconnectedness among the Greek *poleis*, first attested archeologically in the eighth century BCE and manifested, e.g., by the Olympic games and the Delphic oracle.

3. See, e.g., Beecroft 2006.

4. Nagy 2009a: 275.

5. For a discussion of the contrast between the *Iliad* and the *Aithiopis* in terms of the more Panhellenic outlook of the former and the more local orientation of the latter, see Nagy 2005: 80–81.

6. Brillante 2010 is a fascinating discussion of the interplay between Panhellenic and epichoric perspectives in the development of the Homeric tradition. On the similar tension in Greek religion, see Schachter 2000. Nagy 1999: 7, following Rohde, cites the Homeric portrayal of the Olympian gods as an exemplary expression of the poems' Panhellenic orientation; see also Clay 2006: 9–11 (and passim), who traces the Panhellenic orientation of the Olympian pantheon in the politics of the Homeric Hymns. Sienkewicz 1991 identifies a comparable tension between local and supralocal perspectives in the tradition of the West African *Sunjata* epic, which he offers as a parallel for the situation of early Greek epic traditions.

7. By "Homeric verses" (Ὁμηρείων ἐπέων), Herodotus may have meant to refer primarily to the poems of the Theban cycle (the *Thebais* or *Epigonoi*), in which Argos played a major role—see, e.g., Cingano 1985, Brillante 2010: 62. Nevertheless, the phrase seems

deliberately chosen to be as inclusive as possible. Given the frequency with which the Homeric poems make reference to the "Argives," it is not difficult to imagine that Kleisthenes' measure covered the rhapsodic repertoire as a whole, including the *Iliad* and the *Odyssey* (cf. Dion 1977: 155–59; Jensen 2011: 237). In any case, the anecdote clearly reflects a tension between epichoric and Panhellenic perspectives, since the Theban cycle was not inherently anti-Sikyonian.

8. Hesychius, s.v. Βραυρωνίοις, attests to the rhapsodic performance of the *Iliad* at the Brauronia. For the *Homēridai*, see Nagy 1990b: 22–23. Amateur rhapsodic contests took place, e.g., at the Athenian Apatouria (Plato, *Timaeus* 21b).

9. Von Sydow 1948: 12–15 (originally published in Swedish in 1932). As a folklorist, von Sydow was particularly interested in the kinds of testimony passive tradition bearers could provide to the collector. Von Sydow's work is notable for its consistent conceptualization of oral tradition in biological and ecological terms, a vivid example of which is his notion of the "oicotype," which is of major importance in modern folkloristics.

10. Ibid., 14.

11. Ibid., 14–15.

12. Cf. ibid., 14 on the importance of the "good-will and sympathy" of passive tradition bearers, who provide the "resonance" necessary for the survival of the tradition.

13. Jakobson and Bogatyrev 1980: 5.

14. For the various kinds of "infelicity," see J. L. Austin 1975: 12–24.

15. Vansina 1965: 28. I quote these formulas as reported in the notes (207, n. 4): "'We have indicated to those whose work it is to take up the words of the king. And/you/notables/ if you have anything to say, then say it,' says the king. At the end he asks: 'My mother's clan, is it not thus?' 'The mountains are thus, are thus,' is shouted in reply. The king continues: 'And you, come along. Confirm what I have said.' The dignitaries *mbeem* and *mbyeeng* rise and declare that he has spoken the truth."

16. In the tradition of "gathering-house chanting" among the Kuna Indians of Panama, performances consist of a dialogue between a principal chanter and a "responder," who intones the word *teki*, "indeed," after each verse (Sherzer 1987: 106). In the Candaini tradition of Chhattisgarh (a region of central India), a respondent "joined in the last words of every line" sung by the principal performer (Flueckiger 1999: 138).

17. Grimble 1957: 204–5 (cf. Finnegan 1977: 82–83) offers a remarkable description of poetic composition among the Gilbert Islanders: after pondering his poem overnight, the poet performs a "rough draft" for a group of friends, who "interrupt, criticize, interject suggestions, applaud, or howl down, according to their taste."

18. Marks 2010: 300–305. Marks' exploration of the way the Iliadic text accommodates an awareness of local traditions on the part of the audience nicely brings to the fore questions of framing and reception. See esp. p. 301, on the way "audiences would at times be required to set aside other accounts," and p. 319, on the "responsiveness" of the poem to its audiences. For the epichoric framing of Panhellenic tradition at Argos, see Brillante 2010: 56–59. Bakker 2001 discusses the constraint of an emerging Panhellenic narrative in terms of the creation of an author-figure (Homer), who embodies that constraint.

19. In principle, one could argue that locally oriented performances would be similarly liable to be perceived as autonomous and innovative with respect to Panhellenic

tradition. Two considerations, however, point up the limited saliency of this kind of autonomy by comparison with that of Panhellenic tradition. For the local audience, epichoric tradition would be guaranteed by the facts of local cult and ritual. Meanwhile, an epichoric tradition could only appear as "innovative" to an audience unfamiliar with it—i.e., an audience grounded in a *different* set of epichoric standards, more familiar with the Panhellenic "synthetic" narrative than the tradition in question. Philostratus' *Hērōikos* suggests that, as late as the end of the second century CE, the autonomy of local traditions vis-à-vis the Homeric account could be seen as a matter of adherence to a more authentic tradition rooted in local cult. Jenkins 1999: 216–17 points out, however, that local variants could come to seem innovative to "later readers" (who lack a grounding in local cult).

20. Janko 1994: 108; cf. Kullmann 1960: 70–71, who also stresses the antiquity of these traditions, and especially Marks 2010: 315–17.

21. An epigram from the *Peplos* attributed to Aristotle, no. 19 in Rose's edition (Rose 1886: 400), suggests the existence of a cult site in Boeotia. Nestor's advice that the bones of fallen warriors should be brought back to their respective homes (*Il.* 7.334–35) may be thought of as an attempt to take account of these local cult sites.

22. On the "truths" of local tradition as contrasted with the potential "lies" of Panhellenic epic, see Beecroft 2006: 55–66.

23. For the difficulty of associating the *Iliad*'s vision of consensus-based politics directly with archaic political and social formations, see Flaig 1994: 30–31 and my comments in the introduction.

24. See the discussion in chapter 5.

25. On Nestor's plan as a *mētis* or stratagem designed to meet the emergency occasioned by Achilles' withdrawal, see Nagy 1999: 48. If the wall is "built against the will of the immortal gods" (*Il.* 12.8–9), it is in a sense not foreseen by the will of Zeus and so marked as a departure from the plot as conceived by the supreme god.

26. An identical compositional pattern links this passage with the conclusion of Book 3. In both cases, the narration of an innovative proposal leads to a shift to Olympus, where the gods consider what the consequences of the innovation might be and whether or not they should nullify them.

27. On *kleos* as "'glory' *as conferred by poetry*" (emphasis original), see Nagy 1999: 16–17 (esp. §2n3; quotation from p. xii, §16n1).

28. For the Achaean camp as a "temporary *polis*," see Raaflaub 1993: 47–48 and 1998: 101.

29. Schmid 1947 offers an overview of attested *ktisis* traditions. Dougherty 1993, a study of narrative traditions relating to city foundations, claims that "foundation poetry did not exist as an autonomous genre in the archaic period" (15), on the grounds that "genre in the archaic period was determined by occasion . . . and there was no specific occasion for performing foundation poetry" (27n1). Bowie 1986: 27–34, however, makes a convincing case for the existence of the "*ktisis* genre" (32) and the performance of poems belonging to that genre at public festivals.

30. Nagy 1999: 140 (§28n3).

31. While the notion of an epichoric *ktisis* tradition about the city of Troy may be simply a construct of the *Iliad*, Poseidon's association with this hypothetical tradition has a

basis in attested traditional narratives: the god plays a prominent role in the local tradi-tions of a variety of cities as a contestant for the divine patronage of the city's primordial territory (Cook 1995: 129–30). Poseidon's concern that the Achaeans' evident failure to consult the gods will lead mortals in general not to "communicate their mind and de-signs to the immortals" (*Il.* 7.447) may be connected to a prominent motif in *ktisis* tradi-tions, namely, the consultation of an oracle (see Schmid 1947: 148–53).

32. For "the functional identity of the Achaean Wall with the plot of the *Iliad*"—a point of view to which I return below—see J. Porter 2011, which also provides an excel-lent overview of the controversies surrounding the wall in ancient and modern criticism. Ford 1992: 147–57 likewise equates the wall with the poem (which he conceives as a writ-ten text). On the way in which the destruction of the wall marks a rupture between the heroic age and the world of the poem's audiences, see Scodel 1982.

33. Nagy 1990a: 52. According to Proclus, as paraphrased in the scholia on Hesiod's *Works and Days* (text in Gaisford 1823: 361.21–25; cf. Aristotle fr. 565 ed. Rose), the de-struction of Askra was discussed by Aristotle in the *Constitution of the Orkhomenians* and by Plutarch. Buck 1979: 98–99 places the destruction of Askra "probably between 700 and 650." The intervention of the Thespians may have involved mainly the displace-ment of the local population: archeological surveys have produced evidence of more or less continuous use of the site from the Early Iron Age into the Hellenistic period (Bintliff and Snodgrass 1988: 60–61). The salient point for my purposes is that the tra-dition preserved by Proclus attests to the destruction of the community of Askra in precisely that period in which the poetry of Hesiod is beginning to acquire Panhellenic significance.

34. At the same time, according to the logic of the passage, the destruction of the wall will also be the foundation of *Poseidon's* Panhellenic fame. This I take to be the im-plication of the sequence of remarks Zeus makes by way of reassurance. I am indebted to J. Porter 2011 for much of my thinking on the Achaean wall; see pp. 12–23 for a different understanding of the wall's metapoetic reference (Porter thinks not of *ktisis* poetry but of the poems of the Epic Cycle). For different reasons, Porter arrives at a conclusion similar to my own: the wall "is endowed with an indelible *kleos*, a lasting fame that lives on, not even if the wall vanishes, but precisely *because* the wall vanishes" (33).

35. The collaboration of the two gods (as well as Zeus) in the destruction of the Achaean wall is described at greater length at the beginning of Book 12 (17–35), making it clear that the demolition represents the reinstitution of a unified divine will. Poseidon refers again to his past collaboration with Apollo at *Il.* 21.441–57 but appears there to take sole credit for the walls of Troy.

36. On the question of the book-divisions, see Jensen 1999 (with the subsequent contributions of her discussants); for larger-scale divisions, see Taplin 1992: 11–31 (with useful introductory comments on 11–14), Richardson 1993: 1–4, and Heiden 1996: 5–8.

37. Heiden 1996 has a useful discussion of the discrepancies between the various three-movement schemes. Frame 2009: 561–75 has recently made a strong case for a division into six units of four books each (at 575–76, he discusses the possibility of recon-ciling these six units with a three-day performance scheme). West 2011: 75–76 prefers to think in terms of four units of six books each (for West, however, these units are purely

a matter of rhapsodic convenience in the context of serial performance at the Panathe-naia and are not an organic part of the compositional structure).

38. Cf. Nagy 1996a: 87–88, 2002: 62–64.

39. Again, Heiden 1996 provides the most convenient survey of proposed schemes. Heiden himself opts for boundaries at Books 8/9 and 15/16 (extended argumentation in Heiden 2008).

40. Such speculation might also help to explain why the collective decisions that determine the forward development of the plot appear more as closural devices than as preludes to the action they determine. In Book 2, *epainos* leads directly to the execution of the decision, but elsewhere the decisions that shape the plot happen at night, as the concluding event of the day's action, and their consequences take effect only on the following day. Such an arrangement would make sense, however, if these decision-making scenes coincided with the conclusion of performative segments: the *epainos* of the embedded audience for the proposed course of action would then dovetail with the (presumed) approval of the external audience for the preceding performance.

41. On the question of the historicity of the rhapsode Ion, see Rijksbaron 2007: 99.

42. Nagy 2002: 25 (with a discussion of ten examples of rhapsodic language on pp. 25–31).

43. Cf. *Ion* 536d6, and the similar usage of the noun *epainetēs* at 536d3 and 542b4. Nagy 2002: 27 glosses this usage as "to 'quote' Homer *in medias res*, in a specific context and for a specific purpose." Rijksbaron (2007: 188, *ad* 536c7–d3), with no mention of LSJ or Nagy, understands *epainein/epainetēs* simply as "eulogize/eulogist." Plato's phrasing does not rule out such an interpretation. I note, however, that the activity denoted by *epainein/epainetēs* is regarded as part of Ion's professional competence as a rhapsode (this is implicit in the nature of the debate over whether Ion is a "formidable *epainetēs*" by *tekhnē* or by divine inspiration). It is therefore not equivalent to the simple "praise" of Homer but is something that can only be done in virtue of a rhapsode's knowledge of the Homeric tradition. Independent confirmation of this typically rhapsodic expression comes from Lycurgus, *Against Leocrites* 102: βούλομαι δ' ὑμῖν καὶ τὸν Ὅμηρον παρασχέσθαι ἐπαινῶν ("I wish also to put Homer in evidence, quoting [*epainein*] him"; this is the reading of the manuscripts, which some editors emend, although the expression is perfectly intelligible). As Lycurgus proceeds with the prefatory remarks to his quotation of Homer, he speaks specifically of rhapsodic performance at the Panathenaia. For commentary on this passage, see Nagy 2010b: 23–26.

44. Nagy 1990b: 217n18 identifies precisely the same understanding of the significance of performance in the Ionic usage of the noun *apodexis*, as observed in Herodotus: the noun reflects "a conflation of *apo-deik-numai* 'present publicly, make public' and *apo-dek-omai* 'accept or approve a tradition.' . . . the implication is not only that whatever is accepted is made public but also that whatever is made public is accepted. *Such acceptance is the presupposition of a living tradition*" (italics added).

45. Socrates' previous formulations of critical approval/disapproval have favored impersonal verbal adjectives (cf. ἀποκριτέον, 377c2; παραδεκτέον, 378d5; ἀποδεκτέον, 379c9), so that this expression stands out even more against its context.

46. I should stress that I am not attributing to Plato a commitment to consensus as the determinant of collective values. Plato clearly has a top-down conception of how the norms that govern the community are to be constituted. What is essential is that Plato subordinates the Iliadic tradition to the values that govern the community (even if those values themselves are not determined collectively), that he views reception as a process that shapes tradition, and that he exploits the metapoetic value of the *Iliad*'s own terminology to make these points.

47. The title *Homeri et Hesiodi Certamen* ('Ομήρου καὶ Ἡσιόδου ἀγών) is Stephanus'; the sole medieval manuscript (Laur. 56.1) bears the title περὶ Ὁμήρου καὶ Ἡσιόδου καὶ τοῦ γένους καὶ ἀγῶνος αὐτῶν, that is, "On Homer, Hesiod, their Birth, and their Contest" (West 1967: 433n1).

48. Nietzsche 1870: 536–40. West 1967: 433n2 notes that the wording of the reference to Hadrian at line 33 (ed. Allen) implies that "Hadrian is dead but of fresh memory."

49. P. Petrie 1.25 (= P. Lit. Lond. 191), dated to the third century BCE, gives a version of lines 68–101 and thus provides a *terminus ante quem* for the contest narrative. P. Mich. inv. 2754 (published in Winter 1925), dated to the second or early third century CE, has the end of our *Certamen* (with some differences in phrasing), followed by some opaque concluding remarks and the subscription [Ἀλκι]δάμαντος περὶ Ὁμήρου. A new papyrus (P. Ath. Soc. Pap. inv. M2), first published in Mandilaras 1990 and dated no later than 100 BCE, contains the account of Hesiod's death (lines 227–35, with minor differences) but contributes nothing new to the discussion of dating or authorship.

50. Concise accounts of the arguments and evidence for Alcidamas' role and his possible relationship to earlier traditions may be found in West 1967, Richardson 1981, O'Sullivan 1992: 63–64, and Graziosi 2001: 58–60; for a review of earlier scholarship, see Avezzù 1982: 84–87. Graziosi 2002: 176–200 situates the core of the *Contest* narrative in democratic (fifth- and fourth-century) Athens. Debiasi 2001 maintains that Alcidamas likely drew on an earlier version of the story by Theagenes of Rhegium (sixth century BCE), a version that was itself rooted in Euboean traditions arising from the Lelantine War.

51. Potentially significant for my argument are the claims of Heldmann 1982. While acknowledging that the contest narrative is at least as early as Aristophanes' *Frogs* (he denies that our text can be traced to Alcidamas), Heldmann maintains that the judgment of Panēdēs has been introduced by the second-century compiler. (See below for the importance of this episode and the spelling of the name.) Richardson 1984, rightly stressing the evidence of the Flinders Petrie papyrus, outlines the weaknesses of this case.

52. Graziosi 2002: 5; for the *Certamen* in particular, see pp. 168–80.

53. Nagy 1990b: 76; as evidence for the difference in status between Homer and Hesiod, Nagy notes the fact that "we hear only of Homeric poetry, not of Hesiodic, in connection with reports about recitations that are privileged by law at the Panathenaia." See also Nagy 2010b: 50.

54. Cf. Debiasi 2001: 25.

55. J. Porter 2010: 349.

56. Vogt 1959: 199; cf. 201. For the proverbial "judgment of Panēdēs," see West 1967: 439n5, who quotes Apostolius Paroem. 14.11: Πανίδου ψῆφος· ἐπὶ τῶν ἀμαθῶς ψηφιζομένων ("'the judgment of Panidēs': [said] of those who pass judgment ignorantly"). Nietzsche also detected injustice in Panēdēs' verdict (1870: 539); similarly O'Sullivan 1992: 96, who follows Nietzsche in seeing Homer as a representative of Alcidamas' improvisation-oriented pedagogy.

57. West 1967: 443, Graziosi 2001: 71, Ford 2002: 276–77.

58. As Kirchhoff (1892: 887) saw, the form Πανήδης, which is adopted by Rzach in his edition of Hesiod and by Allen in the OCT edition of Homer, is guaranteed by the Petrie papyrus (lines 3–4). The manuscript has Πανοίδης, while Philostratus (*Hērōikos* 43.9), Tzetzes (following Proclus: cf. Gaisford 1823: 7.13, 17.5–6), and Apostolius Paroem. 14.11 attest the form Πανίδης. Some scholars (e.g., Ford 2002: 276) adopt Hermann's emendation Πανείδης, "All-Knowing," which lacks manuscript support. Noting that the name Πανήδης is nowhere else attested, Kirchhoff 1892: 887 describes it as a significant invention that designates one "for whom 'anything goes [*Alles recht ist*],'" who enjoys everything—even the poor and inferior—and thus that characterizes the incapacity to judge of a man who could choose Hesiod over a Homer."

59. See, e.g., Graziosi 2002: 175–76.

60. J. Porter 2011: 21; slightly later, Porter remarks, "the poetic life of the Achaean Wall is (roughly) coextensive with the life of the *Iliad*." See also Ford 1992: 151–52.

61. The monumental scale of the *Iliad* (and the *Odyssey*) is a central concern of Kirk 1962 and is frequently pointed to by other writers. On the ways in which the Homeric poems can be contrasted with the remains of the Epic Cycle, see Griffin 1977.

62. The number of studies addressing the relation between "tradition" and "innovation" in the Homeric poems, with "innovation" necessarily understood in terms of deviation from a traditional background, is immense. Purely for the sake of example, one may cite Russo 1968, Fenik 1978 (a collection of essays by five scholars), Berg and Haug 2000. Combellack 1976 reviews (skeptically) a number of attempts to discern innovations in the poems.

63. Scodel 2002 (esp. pp. 1–41) is perhaps the most sustained interrogation of the analytical usefulness of the rubrics "traditional" and "innovative." Particularly helpful is her warning about the danger of confusing the "invented" with the "contextually bound" (29). See also the remarks of Combellack 1976.

64. Noting that Eustathius speaks not of the "Achaean" but of the "Homeric" wall, J. Porter (2011: 20) wonders, "Might this suggest that the Homeric version of the *Iliad*—our version—distinguished itself from all prior narrations of the war precisely by omitting the story of the sack of Troy and by substituting in its place its prefiguration in the form of a central *teichomachia* around the (possibly never before witnessed) Achaean Wall? . . . Poseidon's expression of fear in book 7 should be taken . . . as a kind of meta-poetical highlighting on the part of a poet eager . . . to draw attention to one of the major criterial differences between his own poem and the traditional (cyclic or other) versions of the epic material."

65. Cf. the remarks of Russo 1978, quoted in chapters 3 and 4.

66. Haubold 2000 argues, from a slightly different perspective, for a similar relationship between the Achaeans as a political community and the *polis*-communities that were their notional descendants: see chapter 8.

67. Scodel 2002.

AFTERWORD: *EPAINOS AND THE ODYSSEY*

1. Bolling 1946: 343; cf. Martin 1989: 14.

2. I restate here several observations made in chapter 1.

3. Wonder at Telemachus' public speaking is expressed by the formula ὣς ἔφαθ', οἱ δ' ἄρα πάντες ὀδὰξ ἐν χείλεσι φύντες / Τηλέμαχον θαύμαζον ("thus he spoke, and they all, biting their lips, / wondered at Telemachus," *Od.* 1.381–82, 18.410–11, 20.268–69); the tension between Odysseus and his companions by ὣς ἐφάμην, τοῖσιν δὲ κατεκλάσθη φίλον ἦτορ ("thus I spoke, and their dear hearts broke," *Od.* 10.198, 10.566, 12.277). It is not always clear whether the context for these responses is properly deliberative, but I am taking a broad view of the dynamics of response.

4. Cf. *Od.* 13.16, 16.406, 18.290, 20.247, 21.143, 21.269; also 18.422. The only instance in which the formula refers to a group other than the Suitors is 13.16, where it describes the response to a speech made by Alkinoos, king of the Phaeacians. The application to this idealized community of a formula otherwise associated with the Suitors' dysfunctional political culture seems at first glance problematic, but plausible explanations can be found. The avoidance of the definitively efficacious *epainein* formula may be intended to sustain the suspense surrounding Odysseus' return (Alkinoos begins his speech by predicting a successful homecoming for Odysseus); or *epihandanein* may have been selected in order to emphasize that Alkinoos' proposal is a matter of coordinated but *individualized* action (cf. ἀνδρακάς "man by man," 13.14). In any case, the frequency with which the formula is applied to the Suitors seems clearly intended to cast an uncomplimentary light on their deliberations.

5. For the semantics of *handanein*, see chapter 1.

6. Telemachus' command recalls that of Zeus at the beginning of *Iliad* Book 8 (discussed in chapter 7). The *Odyssey* does not observe the distinction, described in chapter 1, between the aorist and imperfect tenses of *epainein*.

7. As in the *Iliad*, it is Athena who intervenes: through a dream vision, she reassures Penelope that she will prevent the Suitors from executing their plan (*Od.* 4.824–29), and she similarly reassures Telemachus (*Od.* 15.27–35). Although Zeus refers to Athena's direct involvement in the frustration of the Suitors' designs (*Od.* 5.25–27), the poem never actually narrates the means by which she intervenes. The cultivation of suspense continues with Telemachus' foreboding thoughts as he sails for Ithaca (*Od.* 15.300). On the similarly suspenseful effect of the *epainos* that concludes *Iliad* 3, see my comments in chapter 5.

8. According to Ruzé 1997: 20, only about one-ninth of the *Odyssey* is devoted to deliberative scenes (broadly defined), as opposed to about one quarter of the *Iliad*.

9. See chapter 1.

10. It is worth noting that there is a comparable moment in the *Iliad*, when the "silence" formula may be taken to signal the conclusion of a unique and unrepeatable poetic

performance. When Achilles concludes his great *rhēsis* in Book 9—the defiant speech in which he rejects Agamemnon's offer of reconciliation, which is the longest speech in the poem—his audience responds with silence (*Il.* 9.430). As Martin 1989 has shown, in this speech above all Achilles demonstrates a mastery of poetic language that is on a par with that of the Iliadic narrator. And in fact his addressees have real difficulty in transmitting his words back to Agamemnon: Scodel 1989 points out that the failure of the ambassadors to transmit his position in full is in a certain way responsible for Patroklos' death.

11. On the way the epithet reinforces the meaning of the name, see Scully 1981: 74. Cf. the comment recorded in the Q scholia at *Od.* 8.44 (ed. Dindorf): οἰκεῖον τὸ ὄνομα διὰ τὴν παρὰ τῷ δήμῳ ὑποδοχήν ("the name is appropriate on account of his acceptance among the people").

12. For *muthos* as the designation for a "performative," see chapter 1, with reference to Martin 1989.

13. Cf. the *dokimos humnos*, "acceptable hymn," of Pind. *Nem.* 3.11, which Pindar promises to "share" or "make common" (κοινάσομαι, line 12): the "acceptability" of the song is the measure of its ability to circulate in human communities. Suggestive also in this connection is the participial form of *dekhesthai* at *Il.* 9.191, in reference to Patroklos as he is "waiting for Achilles to finish singing" (δέγμενος Αἰακίδην ὁπότε λήξειεν ἀείδων). On the potentially rhapsodic overtones of this usage, see Nagy 1996b: 72 and 2002: 60.

14. It should be noted, however, first, that Telemachus does attribute some agency to Phēmios in choosing his songs (cf. ὅππῃ οἱ νόος ὄρνυται ["as his mind inclines"], *Od.* 1.347), and, second, that Penelope seems to have heard the song before (cf. αἰεί ["always"], *Od.* 1.341). Bakker 2002: 142 notes a possible suggestion that the song departs from "established poetic tradition." Cf. Ford 1992: 109 on the "palpable irony" of Telemachus' remark. For a different perspective on Telemachus' use of the term *neos*, "new," see Nagy 1990b: 69.

15. See, e.g., Pucci 1987: 230–31, Bakker 1997: 137–38, Finkelberg 1998: 54–57, Assaël 2001.

16. It might seem that there is a slight contradiction between Phēmios' claim here and Telemachus' argument in Book 1 that Phēmios ought not to be faulted, since he sings only to please his audience. The contradiction is resolved when viewed from a different angle, however: in both cases the point is that Phēmios must be evaluated independently from the Suitors and their predilections. Moreover, as I noted above, the notion that the song that pleases the Suitors is "new" works to detach it from the traditions embodied in the singer.

17. On the singer as upholder of social order, see Scully 1981.

18. *Od.* 1.356–59 = 21.350–53, with the substitution of τόξον, "bow," in the latter passage for μῦθος, "speech," in the former. On the connection between these scenes, expressive of a strategy whereby a normative vision of gender relations (and the violence they entail) is asserted, see Nagler 1993: 250–52.

19. With *Od.* 21.430 compare *Od.* 1.152, the only other occurrence of the expression τὰ γάρ τ' ἀναθήματα δαιτός ("for these are the adornments of a feast").

20. Cf. Haubold 2000: 100–44. Nagler 1990 and 1993 describes a somewhat darker vision of the destructive violence visited on Odysseus' associates—darker because the violence is more deliberate. I suggest that the violence Odysseus deliberately inflicts on the Suitors is part of a broader symptomology of social dysfunction, which is also expressed in the performer-group relations examined here. Pazdernik 1995 explores the way in which Odysseus' own framing, as a performer, of violence resonates with the fates of the Companions and the Suitors; Pazdernik notes that Odysseus employs a "profoundly different poetic strategy" than other speakers or the narrator himself (360).

21. *Od.* 10.34–46 and 12.339–52. In the former case, the leaderless quality of the deliberation is expressed by the casting of the proposal in the form of an anonymous "*tis*-speech," a device unparalleled by any other decision-making scene in the Homeric corpus. On the way in which such "*tis*-speeches" encapsulate collective sentiments, see Elmer 2012.

22. *Il.* 23.539–42, discussed in chapter 1.

23. Odysseus' subjection to *biē* in a sense reverses his own use of force in silencing Thersites, the sole obstacle to the establishment of *epainos* in *Iliad* 2: see chapter 4.

24. Among intimates, of course—including Telemachus, Eumaios, and ultimately Penelope—Odysseus is a remarkably good communicator, but this only underscores my point, since poetic performance is precisely a matter of embodying the traditions of the community. (I am grateful to Doug Frame for reminding me of this important point.)

25. So in the case of Aiolos' sack of winds (leading directly to one of the Companions' bad decisions), and again in the case of Skylla (*Od.* 12.223–25).

26. Haubold 2000: 133–34 comments insightfully on the reciprocal relationship between Odysseus' *kleos* and the fate of the Companions; see also Pazdernik 1995.

Bibliography

Adkins, A. W. H. 1960. *Merit and Responsibility: A Study in Greek Values.* Oxford: Clarendon.

Agamben, Giorgio. 1998. *Homo Sacer: Sovereign Power and Bare Life.* Translated by Daniel Heller-Roazen. Stanford, CA: Stanford UP.

———. 2005. *State of Exception.* Translated by Kevin Attell. Chicago: U of Chicago P.

Alden, Maureen Joan. 2000. *Homer Beside Himself: Para-Narratives in the "Iliad."* Oxford: Oxford UP.

Alexiou, Margaret. 2002. *The Ritual Lament in Greek Tradition.* 2nd ed. Lanham, MD: Rowman and Littlefield.

Allan, William. 2006. Divine Justice and Cosmic Order in Early Greek Epic. *Journal of Hellenic Studies* 126: 1–35.

Allan, William, and Douglas Cairns. 2011. Conflict and Community in the *Iliad.* In *Competition in the Ancient World.* Edited by N. Fisher and H. van Wees. Swansea: Classical Press of Wales.

Allen, T. W., ed. 1931. *Homeri Ilias.* 3 vols. Oxford: Clarendon.

Aloni, Antonio. 1986. *Tradizioni arcaiche della Troade e composizione dell'Iliade.* Milano: Edizioni UNICOPLI.

Alvis, John. 1995. *Divine Purpose and Heroic Response in Homer and Virgil: The Political Plan of Zeus.* Lanham, MD: Rowman and Littlefield.

Andersen, Øivind. 1976. Some Thoughts on the Shield of Achilles. *Symbolae Osloenses* 51: 5–18.

Assaël, Jacqueline. 2001. Phémios autodidaktos. *Revue de philologie, de littérature et d'histoire anciennes* 75 (1): 7–21.

Austin, J. L. 1975. *How to Do Things with Words.* 2nd ed. Cambridge, MA: Harvard UP.

Austin, N. 1975. *Archery at the Dark of the Moon: Poetic Problems in Homer's "Odyssey."* Berkeley: U of California P.

Avezzù, Guido. 1982. *Alcidamante: orazioni e frammenti.* Bolletino dell'Istituto de filologia greca, Supplemento 6. Rome: "L'Erma" di Brentschneider.

Bader, Françoise. 1978. De 'protéger' a 'razzier' au néolithique indo-européen: phraséologie, etymologies, civilization. *Bulletin de la Société de linguistique de Paris* 33: 103–219.

———. 1980. Rhapsodies homériques et irlandaises. In *Recherches sur les religions de l'antiquité classique.* Edited by Raymond Bloch. Geneva: Droz.

———. 1989. *La langue des dieux, ou, l'hermétisme des poètes indo-européens.* Testi linguistici 14. Pisa: Giardini.

Bailey, F. G. 1965. Decisions by Consensus in Councils and Committees: With Special Reference to Village and Local Government in India. In *Political Systems and the Distribution of Power*. Edited by Michael Banton. London: Tavistock.

Bakker, Egbert J. 1997. *Poetry in Speech: Orality and Homeric Discourse*. Ithaca: Cornell UP.

———. 2001. Homer, Hypertext, and the Web of Myth. In *Varieties and Consequences of Literacy and Orality: Franz H. Bäuml zum 75. Geburtstag*. Edited by U. Schaefer and E. Spielmann. Tübingen: Narr.

———. 2002. Polyphemos. *Colby Quarterly* 38 (2): 135–50.

Barker, Elton. 2004. Achilles' Last Stand: Institutionalising Dissent in Homer's *Iliad*. *Proceedings of the Cambridge Philological Society* 50: 92–120.

———. 2009. *Entering the Agon: Dissent and Authority in Homer, Historiography and Tragedy*. Oxford: Oxford UP.

Beck, Deborah. 1999. Speech Introductions and the Character Development of Telemachus. *Classical Journal* 94 (2): 121–41.

———. 2005. *Homeric Conversation*. Washington, DC: Center for Hellenic Studies.

Beecroft, Alexander J. 2006. 'This Is Not a True Story': Stesichorus' *Palinode* and the Revenge of the Epichoric. *Transactions of the American Philological Association* 136 (1): 47–69.

Benardete, Seth. 1963. Achilles and the *Iliad*. *Hermes* 91 (1): 1–16.

Benveniste, Émile. 1966. Don et échange dans le vocabulaire indo-européen. In *Problèmes de linguistique générale*, vol. 1. Paris: Gallimard.

———. 1969. *Le vocabulaire des institutions indo-européens*. 2 vols. Paris: Éditions de Minuit.

Berg, Nils, and Dag Haug. 2000. Innovation vs. Tradition in Homer—An Overlooked Piece of Evidence. *Symbolae Osloenses* 75: 5–23.

Bergold, Wolfgang. 1977. *Der Zweikampf des Paris und Menelaos: Zu Ilias Γ 1 - Δ 222*. Habelts Dissertationsdrucke, Reihe Klassische Philologie 28. Bonn: Habelt.

Bernabé, Albertus. 1996. *Poetarum epicorum Graecorum testimonia et fragmenta*, pars I. Corrected ed. Stuttgart: Teubner.

Bintliff, John, and Anthony Snodgrass. 1988. Mediterranean Survey and the City. *Antiquity* 62 (234): 57–71.

Blanc, Alain. 1985. Étymologie de ἀπηνής et προσηνής. *Revue de philologie, de littérature et d'histoire anciennes* 59: 255–63.

———. 1995. Formes de la racine *h₂en-* 'consentir': une concordance gréco-germanique. *Bulletin de la Société de linguistique de Paris* 90: 179–229.

Bloomfield, Maurice. 1897. *Hymns of the Atharva-Veda: Together with Extracts from the Ritual Books and the Commentaries*. Sacred Books of the East 42. Oxford: Clarendon.

Boehm, Christopher. 1996. Emergency Decisions, Cultural-Selection Mechanics, and Group Selection. *Current Anthropology* 37 (5): 763–93.

Bolling, George Melville. 1946. The Personal Pronouns of the *Iliad*. *Language* 22 (4): 341–43.

Bonazzi, Mauro. 2006. La concordia di Antifonte: cura di sé e degli altri fra democrazia e oligarchia. In *Amicizia e concordia: etica, fisica, politica in età preplatonica*. Edited by Emidio Spinelli. Rome: Euroma.

Bonner, Robert J., and Gertrude Smith. 1930. *The Administration of Justice from Homer to Aristotle*, vol. 1. Chicago: U of Chicago P.

Bowie, E. L. 1986. Early Greek Elegy, Symposium and Public Festival. *Journal of Hellenic Studies* 106: 13–35.

Brenkman, John. 2007. *The Cultural Contradictions of Democracy: Political Thought since September 11*. Princeton, NJ: Princeton UP.

Brillante, Carlo. 2010. Diomede, la poesia epica e le tradizioni argive. In *Tra panellenismo e tradizioni locali: generi poetici e storiografia*. Edited by Ettore Cingano. Alessandria: Edizioni dell'Orso.

Buck, Robert J. 1979. *A History of Boeotia*. Edmonton, Alberta: U of Alberta P.

Burgess, Jonathan S. 2001. *The Tradition of the Trojan War in Homer and the Epic Cycle*. Baltimore: Johns Hopkins UP.

Burkert, Walter. 1976. Das hunderttorige Theben und die Datierung der Ilias. *Wiener Studien* 89: 5–21.

Bynum, David E. 1987. Of Sticks and Stones and Hapax Legomena Rhemata. In *Comparative Research on Oral Traditions: A Memorial for Milman Parry*. Edited by John Miles Foley. Columbus, OH: Slavica.

Cairns, Douglas. 2011. Ransom and Revenge in the *Iliad*. In *Sociable Man: Essays on Ancient Greek Social Behaviour in Honour of N. R. E. Fisher*. Edited by S. D. Lambert. Swansea: Classical Press of Wales.

Calder, William M., III. 1984. Gold for Bronze: *Iliad* 6.232–36. In *Studies Presented to Sterling Dow on His Eightieth Birthday*. Edited by Kent J. Rigsby. Durham: Duke University.

Cantarella, Eva. 1979. *Norma e sanzione in Omero: contributo alla protostoria del diritto greco*. Milan: A. Giuffrè.

———. 2001. Private Revenge and Public Justice. *Punishment & Society* 3 (4): 473–83.

Carlier, Pierre. 1984. *La royauté en Grèce avant Alexandre*. Strasbourg: AECR.

———. 1999. *Homère*. Paris: Fayard.

———. 2006. Ἄναξ and Βασιλεύς in the Homeric Poems. In *Ancient Greece: From the Mycenaean Palaces to the Age of Homer*. Edited by Sigrid Deger-Jalkotzy and I. S. Lemos. Edinburgh: Edinburgh UP.

Cartledge, Paul. 1996. La nascita degli opliti e l'organizzazione militare. In *I Greci: storia, cultura, arte, società*. Turin: Giulio Einaudi.

———. 2009. *Ancient Greek Political Thought in Practice*. Key Themes in Ancient History. Cambridge: Cambridge UP.

Cassio, Albio Cesare. 2009. Early Editions of the Greek Epics and Homeric Textual Criticism in the Sixth and Fifth Centuries BC. In *Omero tremila anni dopo: personaggi e strutture narrative*. 2nd ed. Edited by Franco Montanari. Rome: Edizioni di storia e letteratura.

Catanzaro, Andrea. 2008. *Paradigmi politici nell'epica omerica*. Politeia 34. Florence: Centro editoriale toscano.

Caton, Steven C. 1990. *"Peaks of Yemen I Summon": Poetry as Cultural Practice in a North Yemeni Tribe*. Berkeley: U of California P.

Chantraine, Pierre. 1963. *Grammaire homérique, tome II: syntaxe*. Paris: Klincksieck.

———. 2009. *Dictionnaire étymologique de la langue grecque: histoire des mots*. New ed. Paris: Klincksieck.

Christensen, Joel. 2009. The End of Speeches and a Speech's End: Nestor, Diomedes, and the *Telos Muthōn*. In *Reading Homer: Film and Text*. Edited by Kostas Myrsiades. Madison, NJ: Fairleigh Dickinson UP.

Cingano, Ettore. 1985. Clistene di Sicione, Erodoto e i poemi del Ciclo tebano. *Quaderni urbinati di cultura classica* ns 20 (2): 31–40.

Clader, Linda Lee. 1976. *Helen: The Evolution from Divine to Heroic in Greek Epic Tradition*. Mnemosyne Supplementum 42. Leiden: Brill.

Clark, Matthew. 2007. Poulydamas and Hektor. *College Literature* 34 (2): 85–106.

Claus, David B. 1975. Aidōs in the Language of Achilles. *Transactions of the American Philological Association* 105: 13–28.

Clay, Jenny Strauss. 1995. Agamemnon's Stance (*Iliad* 19.51–77). *Philologus* 139 (1): 72–75.

———. 1999. The Whip and Will of Zeus. *Literary Imagination* 1 (1): 40–60.

———. 2006. *The Politics of Olympus: Form and Meaning in the Major Homeric Hymns*. 2nd ed. London: Bristol Classical Press.

Clines, David J. A. 1997. *The Theme of the Pentateuch*. 2nd ed. Sheffield: Sheffield Academic Press.

Combellack, Frederick M. 1976. Homer the Innovator. *Classical Philology* 71 (1): 44–55.

Cook, Erwin F. 1995. *The Odyssey in Athens: Myths of Cultural Origins*. Ithaca: Cornell UP.

———. 2004. Near Eastern Sources for the Palace of Alkinoos. *American Journal of Archaeology* 108 (1): 43–77.

Cramer, J. A. 1837. *Anecdota Graeca e codd. manuscriptis Bibliothecarum Oxoniensium*, vol. 4. Oxford.

Cramer, Owen C. 1976. Speech and Silence in the *Iliad*. *Classical Journal* 71 (4): 300–304.

Crotty, Kevin. 1982. *Song and Action: The Victory Odes of Pindar*. Baltimore: Johns Hopkins UP.

Cunliffe, Richard John. 1924. *A Lexicon of the Homeric Dialect*. London: Blackie and Son.

Čolaković, Zlatan. 2004. Ćor Huso ili Avdo, rapsod ili aed? *Almanah* 27: 47–68.

———. 2007. The Singer Above Tales. In *Epika Avda Međedovića: kritičko izdanje / The Epics of Avdo Međedović: A Critical Edition*. Edited by Zlatan Čolaković. Podgorica: Almanah.

Dale, Annette Teffeteller. 1982. Homeric Ἐπητής/Ἐπητύς: Meaning and Etymology. *Glotta* 60 (3/4): 205–14.

Danek, Georg. 2010. Sänger, Dichter, Schreiber: Die Homerische Frage. In *Musiker und Tradierung: Studien zur Rolle von Musikern bei der Verschriftlichung und Tradierung von literarischen Werken*. Edited by Regine Pruzsinszky and Dahlia Shehata. Wiener Offene Orientalistik 8. Vienna: Lit.

Dareste, Rodolphe. 1902. *Nouvelles études d'histoire du droit*. Paris: L. Larose.

Davies, Malcolm. 1981. The Judgement of Paris and *Iliad* Book XXIV. *Journal of Hellenic Studies* 101: 56–62.

Davreux, Juliette. 1942. *La légende de la prophétesse Cassandre d'après les textes et les monuments*. Liège: Faculté de philolosophie et lettres.

Debiasi, Andrea. 2001. Variazioni sul nome di Omero. *Hesperia* 14: 9–35.

Derrida, Jacques. 1993. Politics of Friendship. *American Imago* 50 (3): 353–91.

———. 1997. *Politics of Friendship*. London: Verso.

Detienne, Marcel. 1965. En Grèce archaïque: géométrie, politique et société. *Annales: économies, sociétés, civilisations* 20 (3): 425–41.

———. 1996. *The Masters of Truth in Archaic Greece*. Translated by Janet Lloyd. New York: Zone.

Dion, Roger. 1977. *Aspects politiques de la géographie antique*. Paris: Les Belles Lettres.

Doniger O'Flaherty, Wendy. 1976. *The Origins of Evil in Hindu Mythology*. Berkeley: U of California P.

Donlan, Walter. 1989. The Unequal Exchange between Glaucus and Diomedes in Light of the Homeric Gift-Economy. *Phoenix* 43 (1): 1–15.

———. 1997. The Homeric Economy. In *A New Companion to Homer*. Edited by Ian Morris and Barry Powell. Leiden: Brill.

Dougherty, Carol. 1993. *The Poetics of Colonization: From City to Text in Archaic Greece*. New York: Oxford UP.

Dué, Casey. 2002. *Homeric Variations on a Lament by Briseis*. Lanham, MD: Rowman and Littlefield.

———. 2006. *The Captive Woman's Lament in Greek Tragedy*. Austin: U of Texas P.

Dué, Casey, and Mary Ebbott. 2010. *"Iliad" 10 and the Poetics of Ambush: A Multitext Edition with Essays and Commentary*. Washington, DC: Center for Hellenic Studies.

Dumézil, Georges. 1943. *Servius et la fortune: essai sur la fonction sociale de louange et de blâme et sur les éléments indo-européens du cens romain*. Paris: Gallimard.

———. 1969. *Idées romaines*. Paris: Gallimard.

Ebeling, H., ed. 1885. *Lexicon Homericum*. Leipzig: B. G. Teubner.

Ebert, Joachim. 1969. Die Gestalt des Thersites in der Ilias. *Philologus* 113 (3/4): 159–75.

Edmunds, Lowell. 1985. The genre of Theognidean Poetry. In *Theognis of Megara: Poetry and the Polis*. Edited by Thomas J. Figueira and Gregory Nagy. Baltimore: Johns Hopkins UP.

Edmunds, Susan. 1990. *Homeric Nēpios*. Harvard Dissertations in Classics. New York: Garland.

Edwards, Mark W. 1969. On Some "Answering" Expressions in Homer. *Classical Philology* 64 (2): 81–87.

———. 1991. *The "Iliad": A Commentary*, vol. 5. Cambridge: Cambridge UP.

Ellinger, Pierre. 1993. *La légende nationale phocidienne: Artémis, les situations extrêmes et les récits de guerre d'anéantissement*. Bulletin de Correspondance hellénique, Supplément 27. Athens: École française d'Athènes.

Elmer, David F. 2005. Helen *Epigrammatopoios*. *Classical Antiquity* 24 (1): 1–39.

———. 2008. *Epikoinos*: The Ball Game *Episkuros* and *Iliad* 12.421–23. *Classical Philology* 103 (4): 414–23.

———. 2010. *Kita* and *Kosmos*: The Poetics of Ornamentation in Bosniac and Homeric Epic. *Journal of American Folklore* 123 (489): 276–303.

———. 2012. Building Community across the Battle-Lines: The Truce in *Iliad* 3 and 4. In *Maintaining Peace in Archaic and Classical Greece*. Edited by Julia Wilker. Mainz: Verlag Antike.

Erbse, Hartmut. 1978. Ettore nell'Iliade. *Studi classici e orientali* 28: 13–34.

Farenga, Vincent. 2006. *Citizen and Self in Ancient Greece: Individuals Performing Justice and the Law.* Cambridge: Cambridge UP.

Feldman, Abraham. 1947. The Apotheosis of Thersites. *Classical Journal* 42 (4): 219–21.

Fenik, Bernard C. 1978. *Homer: Tradition and Invention.* Leiden: Brill.

Fick, August. 1877. Zum s-Suffix im Griechischen. *Beiträge zur Kunde der indogermanischen Sprachen* 1: 231–48.

Finkelberg, Margalit. 1998. *The Birth of Literary Fiction in Ancient Greece.* Oxford: Clarendon.

Finley, Moses I. 1977. *The World of Odysseus.* 2nd ed. London: Chatto and Windus.

Finnegan, Ruth H. 1977. *Oral Poetry: Its Nature, Significance and Social Context.* Cambridge: Cambridge UP.

Fish, Stanley. 1980. *Is There a Text in This Class?: The Authority of Interpretive Communities.* Cambridge, MA: Harvard UP.

Flaig, Egon. 1993. Die spartanische Abstimmung nach der Lautstärke: Überlegungen zu Thukydides 1, 87. *Historia* 42 (2): 139–60.

———. 1994. Das Konsensprinzip im homerischen Olymp: Überlegungen zum göttlichen Entscheidungsprozess Ilias 4.1–72. *Hermes* 122 (1): 13–31.

———. 1995. Entscheidung und Konsens: zu den Feldern der politischen Kommunikation zwischen Aristokratie und Plebs. In *Demokratie in Rom?: die Rolle des Volkes in der Politik der römischen Republik.* Edited by Martin Jehne. Historia Eizelschriften 96. Stuttgart: F. Steiner.

Flueckiger, Joyce Burkhalter. 1999. Appropriating the Epic: Gender, Caste, and Regional Identity in Middle India. In *Epic Traditions in the Contemporary World: The Poetics of Community.* Edited by Margaret Beissinger, Jane Tylus, and Susanne Wofford. Berkeley: U of California P.

Foley, Helene P. 1978. "Reverse Similes" and Sex Roles in the *Odyssey. Arethusa* 11 (1/2): 7–26.

Foley, John Miles. 1990. *Traditional Oral Epic: The Odyssey, Beowulf, and the Serbo-Croatian Return Song.* Berkeley: U of California P.

———. 1995. Sixteen Moments of Silence in Homer. *Quaderni urbinati di cultura classica* 50 (2): 7–26.

Ford, Andrew. 1992. *Homer: The Poetry of the Past.* Ithaca: Cornell UP.

———. 2002. *The Origins of Criticism: Literary Culture and Poetic Theory in Classical Greece.* Princeton: Princeton UP.

Frame, Douglas. 2009. *Hippota Nestor.* Washington, DC: Center for Hellenic Studies.

Fränkel, Hermann. 1977. *Die homerischen Gleichnisse.* Göttingen: Vandenhoeck and Ruprecht.

Friedrich, Paul, and James Redfield. 1978. Speech as a Personality Symbol: The Case of Achilles. *Language* 54 (2): 263–88.

Friedrich, Rainer. 2007. *Formular Economy in Homer: The Poetics of the Breaches.* Hermes Einzelschriften 100. Stuttgart: F. Steiner.

Froehde, F. 1877. Etymologien. *Zeitschrift für vergleichende Sprachforschung auf dem Gebiete der indogermanischen Sprachen* 23 (3): 310–12.

Gaertner, Jan Felix. 2001. The Homeric Catalogues and Their Function in Epic Narrative. *Hermes* 129 (3): 298–305.

Gaisford, Thomas. 1823. *Poetae Minores Graeci*, vol. 2. Leipzig: Kuehn.

Gallavotti, C. 1977. Scritture della Sicilia ed altre epigrafi arcaiche. *Helikon* 17: 97–136.

García-Ramón, J. L. 1992a. Homérico κόσμος, κεδνός y las pretendidas raíces IE *ḱes- 'anordnen' y *ḱed- 'id.' In *Homerica: Estudios lingüísticos*. Edited by E. Crespo, J. L. García-Ramón, H. Maquieira, and J. de la Villa. Madrid: Universidad Autónoma de Madrid.

———. 1992b. Mycénien *ke-sa-do-ro* /Kessandros/, *ke-ti-ro* /Kestilos/, *ke-to* /Kestōr/: grec alphabétique Αἰνησιμβρότα, Αἰνησίλαος, Αἰνήτωρ et le nom de Cassandre. In *Mykenaïka: Actes du IXe Colloque international sur les textes mycéniens et égéens organisé par le Centre de l'antiquité grecque et romaine de la Fondation hellénique des recherches scientifiques et l'École française d'Athénes*. Edited by Jean-Pierre Olivier. Paris: École francaise d'Athénes.

———. 1993. Lat. *cēnsēre*, got. *hazjan* und das idg. Präsens *ḱéns-e-ti (und *ḱn̥s-éi̯e-ti?) 'verkündigt, schätzt,' Stativ *ḱn̥s-eh₁- 'verkündigt, geschätzt sein / werden.' In *Indogermanica et Italica: Festschrift für Helmut Rix zum 65. Geburtstag*. Edited by G. Meiser. Innsbruck: Institut für Sprachwissenschaft der Universität Innsbruck.

Geddes, A. G. 1984. Who's Who in "Homeric" Society? *Classical Quarterly* 34 (1): 17–36.

Gernet, Louis. 1948. Jeux et droit (remarques sur le XXIIIe chant de l'Iliade). *Revue historique de droit français et étranger* 26 (3/4): 177–88.

———. 1955. *Droit et société dans la Grèce ancienne*. Publications de l'Institut de droit romain de l'Université de Paris 13. Paris: Recueil Sirey.

González, José M. 2013. *The Epic Rhapsode and His Craft: Homeric Performance in a Diachronic Perspective*. Hellenic Studies 47. Washington, DC: Center for Hellenic Studies.

Graziosi, Barbara. 2001. Competition in Wisdom. In *Homer, Tragedy and Beyond: Essays in Honour of P. E. Easterling*. Edited by F. Budelmann and P. Michelakis. London: Society for the Promotion of Hellenic Studies.

———. 2002. *Inventing Homer: The Early Reception of Epic*. Cambridge: Cambridge UP.

Green, Jeffrey E. 2010. *The Eyes of the People: Democracy in an Age of Spectatorship*. Oxford: Oxford UP.

Griffin, Jasper. 1977. The Epic Cycle and the Uniqueness of Homer. *Journal of Hellenic Studies* 97: 39–53.

———. 1980. *Homer on Life and Death*. Oxford: Clarendon.

Griffith, Mark. 1990. Contest and Contradiction in Early Greek Poetry. In *Cabinet of the Muses: Essays on Classical and Comparative Literature in Honor of Thomas G. Rosenmeyer*. Edited by Mark Griffith and Donald J. Mastronarde. Atlanta, GA: Scholars Press.

Grimble, Arthur. 1957. *Return to the Islands*. London: John Murray.

Grote, George. 1869. *A History of Greece; From the Earliest Period to the Close of the Generation Contemporary with Alexander the Great*, vol. 2. A new ed. London: J. Murray.

Haebler, Claus. 1967. Kosmos: eine etymologisch-wortgeschichtliche Untersuchung. *Archiv für Begriffsgeschichte* 11 (2): 101–18.

Haft, Adele J. 1990. "The City-Sacker Odysseus" in *Iliad* 2 and 10. *Transactions of the American Philological Association* 120: 37–56.

Hammer, Dean. 2002. The "Iliad" as Politics: The Performance of Political Thought. Norman: U of Oklahoma P.

Hammond, N. G. L. 1985. The Scene in Iliad 18.497–508 and the Albanian Blood-Feud. Bulletin of the American Society of Papyrologists 22 (1–4): 79–86.

Haubold, Johannes. 2000. Homer's People: Epic Poetry and Social Formation. Cambridge: Cambridge UP.

Havelock, Eric A. 1963. Preface to Plato. Cambridge, MA: Harvard UP.

Heath, John. 2001. Telemachus ΠΕΠΝΥΜΕΝΟΣ: Growing into an Epithet. Mnemosyne 54 (2): 129–57.

Heiden, Bruce. 1991. Shifting Contexts in the Iliad. Eranos 89: 1–12.

———. 1996. The Three Movements of the Iliad. Greek, Roman and Byzantine Studies 37 (1): 5–22.

———. 2008. Homer's Cosmic Fabrication: Choice and Design in the "Iliad." Oxford: Oxford UP.

Heldmann, Konrad. 1982. Die Niederlage Homers im Dichterwettstreit mit Hesiod. Hypomnemata 75. Göttingen: Vandenhoeck and Ruprecht.

Higbie, Carolyn. 1995. Heroes' Names, Homeric Identities. Albert Bates Lord Studies in Oral Tradition 10. New York: Garland.

Hirzel, Rudolf. 1907. Themis, Dike und Verwandtes: Ein Beitrag zur Geschichte der Rechtsidee bei den Griechen. Leipzig: S. Hirzel.

Hogan, James C. 1976. Double πρίν and the Language of Achilles. Classical Journal 71 (4): 305–10.

Hölkeskamp, Karl-Joachim. 2000. Zwischen Agon und Argumentation: Rede und Redner in der archaischen Polis. In Rede und Redner: Bewertung und Darstellung in den antiken Kulturen. Edited by Christoff Neumeister and Wulf Raeck. Möhnesee: Bibliopolis.

———. 2009. 'Ptolis' and 'Agore': Homer and the Archaeology of the City-State. In Omero tremila anni dopo: personaggi e strutture narrative. 2nd ed. Edited by Franco Montanari. Rome: Edizioni di storia e letteratura.

Hommel, H. 1969. Die Gerichtsszene auf dem Schild des Achilleus: Zur Pflege des Rechts in homerischer Zeit. In Politeia und Res publica: Beiträge zum Verständnis von Politik, Recht, und Staat in der Antike, dem Andenken Rudolf Starks gewidmet. Edited by P. Steinmetz. Palingenesia 4. Wiesbaden: F. Steiner.

Huffer, Elise, and Asofou So'o. 2003. Consensus versus Dissent: Democracy, Pluralism and Governance in Sāmoa. Asia Pacific Viewpoint 44 (3): 281–304.

Jacoby, Felix. 1931. Theognis. Sitzungsberichte der preussischen Akademie der Wissenschaften, philosophisch-historische Klasse 10: 90–180.

Jaeger, Werner. 1945. Paideia: The Ideals of Greek Culture, vol. 1. 2nd ed. Translated by Gilbert Highet. New York: Oxford UP.

Jakobson, Roman, and Petr Bogatyrev. 1980. Folklore as a Special Form of Creation. Translated by John M. O'Hara. Folklore Forum 13 (1): 1–21.

Janko, Richard. 1994. The "Iliad": A Commentary, vol. 4. Cambridge: Cambridge UP.

Jeanmaire, H. 1939. Couroi et Courètes: essai sur l'éducation spartiate et sur les rites d'adolescence dans l'antiquité hellénique. Lille: Bibliothèque universitaire.

Jenkins, Thomas E. 1999. *Homēros ekainopoiēse:* Theseus, Aithra, and Variation in Homeric Myth-Making. In *Nine Essays on Homer.* Edited by Miriam Carlisle and Olga Levaniouk. Lanham, MD: Rowman and Littlefield.

Jensen, Minna Skafte. 1980. *The Homeric Question and the Oral-Formulaic Theory.* Copenhagen: Museum Tusculanum.

———. 1999. Dividing Homer: When and How Were the *Iliad* and the *Odyssey* Divided into Songs? *Symbolae Osloenses* 74: 5–91.

———. 2011. *Writing Homer: A Study Based on Results of Modern Fieldwork.* Copenhagen: Det Kongelige Danske Videnskabernes Selskab.

Johnson, Barbara. 1980. *The Critical Difference: Essays in the Contemporary Rhetoric of Reading.* Baltimore: Johns Hopkins UP.

Kelly, Adrian. 2007. *A Referential Commentary and Lexicon to "Iliad" VIII.* Oxford: Oxford UP.

King, Preston. 1987. Sovereignty. In *The Blackwell Encyclopaedia of Political Thought.* Edited by David Miller. Oxford: Basil Blackwell.

Kirchhoff, A. 1892. Der Roman eines Sophisten. *Sitzungsberichte der preussischen Akademie der Wissenschaften* Jahrg. 1892 (2): 865–91.

Kirk, G. S. 1962. *The Songs of Homer.* Cambridge: Cambridge UP.

———. 1985. *The "Iliad": A Commentary,* vol. 1. Cambridge: Cambridge UP.

———. 1990. *The "Iliad": A Commentary,* vol. 2. Cambridge: Cambridge UP.

Kitts, Margo. 2005. *Sanctified Violence in Homeric Society: Oath-Making Rituals and Narratives in the Iliad.* Cambridge: Cambridge UP.

Knox, Ronald, and Joseph Russo. 1989. Agamemnon's Test: *Iliad* 2.73–75. *Classical Antiquity* 8: 351–58.

Kouklanakis, Andrea. 1999. Thersites, Odysseus, and the Social Order. In *Nine Essays on Homer.* Edited by Miriam Carlisle and Olga Levaniouk. Lanham, MD: Rowman and Littlefield.

Kullmann, Wolfgang. 1955. Die Probe des Achaierheeres in der Ilias. *Museum Helveticum* 12 (4): 253–73.

———. 1960. *Die Quellen der Ilias.* Wiesbaden: F. Steiner.

Kurke, Leslie. 1991. *The Traffic in Praise: Pindar and the Poetics of Social Economy.* Ithaca: Cornell UP.

———. 1998. The Economy of *Kudos.* In *Cultural Poetics in Archaic Greece: Cult, Performance, Politics.* Edited by Carol Daugherty and Leslie Kurke. New York: Oxford UP.

Lang, Mabel. 1989. Unreal Conditions in Homeric Narrative. *Greek, Roman and Byzantine Studies* 30 (1): 5–26.

Lateiner, Donald. 1995. *Sardonic Smile: Nonverbal Behavior in Homeric Epic.* Ann Arbor: U of Michigan P.

Lejeune, Michel. 1965. Le ΔΑΜΟΣ dans le société mycénienne. *Revue des études grecques* 78 (1): 1–22.

Lesky, Albin. 1961. *Göttliche und menschliche Motivation im homerischen Epos.* Sitzungsberichte der Heidelberger Akademie der Wissenschaften, philosophisch-historische Klasse, Jahrg. 1961, Bericht 4. Heidelberg: C. Winter.

Lévêque, Pierre, and Pierre Vidal-Naquet. 1996. *Cleisthenes the Athenian: An Essay on the Representation of Space and Time in Greek Political Thought from the End of the Sixth Century to the Death of Plato.* Translated by David Ames Curtis. Atlantic Highlands, NJ: Humanities Press.

Lincoln, Bruce. 1994. *Authority: Construction and Corrosion.* Chicago: U of Chicago P.

Loraux, Nicole. 1990. La majorité, le tout et la moitié: sur l'arithmétique athénienne du vote. *Le Genre humain* 22: 89–110.

———. 2002. *The Divided City: On Memory and Forgetting in Ancient Athens.* Translated by Corinne Pache with Jeff Fort. New York: Zone.

Lord, Albert B. 2000. *The Singer of Tales.* 2nd ed. Edited by Steven Mitchell and Gregory Nagy. Cambridge, MA: Harvard UP.

Lowenstam, Steven. 1981. *The Death of Patroklos: A Study in Typology.* Königstein: Hain.

———. 1993. *The Scepter and the Spear: Studies on Forms of Repetition in the Homeric Poems.* Lanham, MD: Rowman and Littlefield.

Machacek, G. 1994. The Occasional Contextual Appropriateness of Formulaic Diction in the Homeric Poems. *American Journal of Philology* 115 (3): 321–35.

Mackie, Hilary. 1996. *Talking Trojan: Speech and Community in the "Iliad."* Lanham, MD: Rowman and Littlefield.

Mandilaras, Basil G. 1990. A New Papyrus Fragment of the *Certamen Homeri et Hesiodi.* *Platon* 42 (83/84): 45–51.

Marks, James Richard. 2001. Divine Plan and Narrative Plan in Archaic Greek Epic. Ph.D. thesis, University of Texas, Austin.

———. 2002. The Junction between the *Kypria* and the *Iliad. Phoenix* 56 (1/2): 1–24.

———. 2005. The Ongoing *Neikos:* Thersites, Odysseus, and Achilleus. *American Journal of Philology* 126 (1): 1–31.

———. 2010. Context as Hypertext: Divine Rescue Scenes in the *Iliad. Trends in Classics* 2 (2): 300–322.

Martin, Richard P. 1989. *The Language of Heroes: Speech and Performance in the "Iliad."* Ithaca: Cornell UP.

———. 1993. The Seven Sages as Performers of Wisdom. In *Cultural Poetics in Archaic Greece.* Edited by Carol Dougherty and Leslie Kurke. Cambridge: Cambridge UP.

Mauss, Marcel. 1921. Une forme ancienne de contrat chez les Thraces. *Revue des études grecques* 34 (159): 388–97.

———. 1990. *The Gift: The Form and Reason for Exchange in Archaic Societies.* Translated by W. D. Halls. New York: Norton.

Meillet, Antoine. 1967. *The Comparative Method in Historical Linguistics.* Translated by Gordon B. Ford, Jr. Paris: Librairie Honoré Champion.

Montiglio, Silvia. 2000. *Silence in the Land of Logos.* Princeton: Princeton UP.

Morris, Ian. 1986. The Use and Abuse of Homer. *Classical Antiquity* 5 (1): 81–138.

Morrison, James V. 1992. Alternatives to the Epic Tradition: Homer's Challenges in the *Iliad. Transactions and Proceedings of the American Philological Association* 122: 61–71.

———. 1997. *Kerostasia,* the Dictates of Fate, and the Will of Zeus in the *Iliad. Arethusa* 30 (2): 273–96.

Moulton, Carroll. 1977. *Similes in the Homeric Poems*. Göttingen: Vandenhoeck and Ruprecht.

Muellner, Leonard. 1976. *The Meaning of Homeric EUXOMAI through Its Formulas*. Innsbrucker Beiträge zur Sprachwissenschaft 13. Innsbruck: Institut für Sprachwissenschaft der Universität Innsbruck.

———. 1990. The Simile of the Cranes and Pygmies: A Study of Homeric Metaphor. *Harvard Studies in Classical Philology* 93: 59–101.

———. 1996. *The Anger of Achilles: Mēnis in Greek Epic*. Ithaca: Cornell UP.

Mühlestein, Hugo. 1987. *Homerische Namenstudien*. Frankfurt am Main: Athenäum.

Murnaghan, Sheila. 1995. The Plan of Athena. In *The Distaff Side: Representing the Female in Homer's "Odyssey."* Edited by Beth Cohen. New York: Oxford UP.

———. 1997. Equal Honor and Future Glory: The Plan of Zeus in the *Iliad*. In *Classical Closure: Reading the End in Greek and Latin Literature*. Edited by Deborah H. Roberts, Francis M. Dunn, and Don Fowler. Princeton: Princeton UP.

Murphy, William P. 1990. Creating the Appearance of Consensus in Mende Political Discourse. *American Anthropologist* 92 (1): 24–41.

Murray, Oswyn. 1965. Philodemus on the Good King According to Homer. *Journal of Roman Studies* 55 (1/2): 161–82.

Nagler, Michael N. 1990. Odysseus: The Proem and the Problem. *Classical Antiquity* 9 (2): 335–56.

———. 1993. Penelope's Male Hand: Gender and Violence in the *Odyssey*. *Colby Quarterly* 29 (3): 241–57.

Nagy, Gregory. 1974. *Comparative Studies in Greek and Indic Meter*. Harvard Studies in Comparative Literature 33. Cambridge, MA: Harvard UP.

———. 1976a. Formula and Meter. *Oral Literature and the Formula*. Edited by B. A. Stolz and R. S. Shannon III. Ann Arbor: Center for the Coordination of Ancient and Modern Studies.

———. 1976b. Iambos: Typologies of Invective and Praise. *Arethusa* 9 (2): 191–205.

———. 1981. An Evolutionary Model for the Text Fixation of Homeric Epos. In *Oral Traditional Literature: A Festschrift for Albert Bates Lord*. Columbus, OH: Slavica.

———. 1985. Theognis and Megara: A Poet's Vision of His City. In *Theognis of Megara: Poetry and the Polis*. Edited by Thomas J. Figueira and Gregory Nagy. Baltimore: Johns Hopkins UP.

———. 1988. Review of *Naming Achilles*, by David M. Shive. *Phoenix* 42 (4): 364–66.

———. 1990a. *Greek Mythology and Poetics*. Ithaca: Cornell UP.

———. 1990b. *Pindar's Homer: The Lyric Possession of an Epic Past*. Baltimore: Johns Hopkins UP.

———. 1996a. *Homeric Questions*. Austin: U of Texas P.

———. 1996b. *Poetry as Performance: Homer and Beyond*. Cambridge: Cambridge UP.

———. 1997. The Shield of Achilles: Ends of the *Iliad* and Beginnings of the *Polis*. In *New Light on a Dark Age: Exploring the Culture of Geometric Greece*. Edited by Susan Langdon. Columbia: U of Missouri P.

———. 1999. *The Best of the Achaeans: Concepts of the Hero in Archaic Greek Poetry*. Rev. ed. Baltimore: Johns Hopkins UP.

————. 2002. *Plato's Rhapsody and Homer's Music: The Poetics of the Panathenaic Festival in Classical Athens.* Washington, DC: Center for Hellenic Studies.

————. 2005. The Epic Hero. In *A Companion to Ancient Epic.* Edited by John Miles Foley. Malden, MA: Blackwell.

————. 2009a. Hesiod and the Ancient Biographical Traditions. In *Brill's Companion to Hesiod.* Edited by F. Montanari, A. Rengakos, and C. Tsagalis. Leiden: Brill.

————. 2009b. *Homer the Classic.* Hellenic Studies 36. Washington, DC: Center for Hellenic Studies.

————. 2010a. Ancient Greek Elegy. In *The Oxford Handbook of the Elegy.* Edited by Karen Weisman. Oxford: Oxford UP.

————. 2010b. *Homer the Preclassic.* Sather Classical Lectures 67. Berkeley: U of California P.

————. 2012. Signs of Hero Cult in Homeric Poetry. In *Homeric Contexts: Neoanalysis and the Interpretation of Oral Poetry.* Trends in Classics Supplement 12. Edited by F. Montanari, A. Rengakos, and C. Tsagalis. Berlin: de Gruyter.

Nicolai, Walter. 1983. Rezeptionssteuerung in der Ilias. *Philologus* 127 (1): 1–12.

Nietzsche, F. 1870. Der florentinische Tractat über Homer und Hesiod, ihr Geschlecht und ihren Wettkampf. *Rheinisches Museum für Philologie* 25 (4): 528–40.

Nimis, Stephen. 1986. The Language of Achilles: Construction vs. Representation. *Classical World* 79 (4): 217–25.

————. 1987. *Narrative Semiotics in the Epic Tradition: The Simile.* Bloomington: Indiana UP.

Ó Cathasaigh, Tómas. 2005. *Sírrabad Súaltaim* and the Order of Speaking among the Ulaid. In *A Companion in Linguistics: A Festschrift for Anders Ahlqvist on the Occasion of His Sixtieth Birthday.* Edited by Bernadette Smelik. Nijmegen: Stichting Uitgeverij de Keltische Draak.

Ohmann, Richard. 1972. Instrumental Style: Notes on the Theory of Speech as Action. In *Current Trends in Stylistics.* Edited by Braj B. Kachru and Herbert F. W. Stahlke. Edmonton, Alberta: Linguistic Research.

Olson, S. Douglas. 1995. *Blood and Iron: Story and Storytelling in Homer's "Odyssey."* Leiden: Brill.

Opland, J. 1980. Southeastern Bantu Eulogy and Early Indo-European Poetry. *Research in African Literatures* 11 (3): 295–307.

Osborne, Robin. 2004. Homer's Society. In *The Cambridge Companion to Homer.* Edited by Robert Fowler. Cambridge: Cambridge UP.

O'Sullivan, Neil. 1992. *Alcidamas, Aristophanes and the Beginnings of Greek Stylistic Theory.* Hermes Einzelschriften 60. Stuttgart: F. Steiner.

Palmer, L. R. 1979. A Mycenaean "Akhilleid"? In *Serta philologica Aenipontana III.* Edited by Robert Muth and Gerhard Pfohl. Innsbrucker Beiträge zur Kulturwissenschaft 20. Innsbruck: Institut für Sprachwissenschaft der Universität Innsbruck.

Pantelia, Maria C. 2002. Helen and the Last Song for Hector. *Transactions of the American Philological Association* 132 (1/2): 21–27.

Parry, Adam. 1956. The Language of Achilles. *Transactions and Proceedings of the American Philological Association* 87: 1–7.

Parry, Milman. 1971. *The Making of Homeric Verse: The Collected Papers of Milman Parry.* Edited by Adam Parry. Oxford: Clarendon.

Partridge, P. H. 1971. *Consent and Consensus.* London: Pall Mall.

Patzek, Barbara. 1992. *Homer und Mykene: Mündliche Dichtung und Geschichtsschreibung.* Munich: R. Oldenbourg.

Pazdernik, Charles F. 1995. Odysseus and His Audience: *Odyssey* 9.39–40 and Its Formulaic Resonances. *American Journal of Philology* 116 (3): 347–69.

Person, R. J. 1995. The "Became Silent to Silence" Formula in Homer. *Greek, Roman and Byzantine Studies* 36 (4): 327–39.

Petegorsky, Dan. 1982. Context and Evocation: Studies in Early Greek and Sanskrit Poetry. Ph.D. thesis, U of California, Berkeley.

Pflüger, H. H. 1942. Die Gerichtsszene auf dem Schilde des Achilleus. *Hermes* 77 (2): 140–48.

Podlecki, Anthony J. 1971. Some Odyssean Similes. *Greece and Rome* 18 (1): 81–90.

Porter, Andrew E. 2011. "Stricken to Silence": Authoritative Response, Homeric Irony, and the Peril of a Missed Language Cue. *Oral Tradition* 26 (2): 493–520.

Porter, James I. 2010. *The Origins of Aesthetic Thought in Ancient Greece: Matter, Sensation, and Experience.* Cambridge: Cambridge UP.

———. 2011. Making and Unmaking: The Achaean Wall and the Limits of Fictionality in Homeric Criticism. *Transactions of the American Philological Association* 141 (1): 1–36.

Powell, Barry B. 1991. *Homer and the Origin of the Greek Alphabet.* Cambridge: Cambridge UP.

Prendergast, Guy Lushington. 1875. *A Complete Concordance to the "Iliad" of Homer.* London: Longmans, Green, and Co.

Pucci, Pietro. 1987. *Odysseus Polutropos: Intertextual Readings in the "Odyssey" and the "Iliad."* Ithaca: Cornell UP.

Raaflaub, Kurt A. 1993. Homer to Solon: The Rise of the *Polis;* The Written Sources. In *The Ancient Greek City-State: Symposium on the Occasion of the 250th Anniversary of the Royal Danish Academy of Sciences and Letters, July 1–4, 1992.* Edited by M. H. Hansen. Copenhagen: Munksgaard.

———. 1997. Homeric Society. In *A New Companion to Homer.* Edited by Ian Morris and Barry Powell. Leiden: Brill.

———. 1998. A Historian's Headache: How to Read "Homeric Society"? In *Archaic Greece: New Approaches and New Evidence.* Edited by N. Fisher and H. van Wees. London: Duckworth.

Raaflaub, Kurt A., and Robert W. Wallace. 2007. "People's Power" and Egalitarian Trends in Archaic Greece. In *Origins of Democracy in Ancient Greece.* Edited by Kurt A. Raaflaub, Josiah Ober, and Robert W. Wallace. Berkeley: U of California P.

Rabel, Robert J. 1988. Chryses and the Opening of the *Iliad. American Journal of Philology* 109 (4): 473–81.

Redfield, James. 1979. The Proem of the *Iliad:* Homer's Art. *Classical Philology* 74 (2): 95–110.

———. 1994. *Nature and Culture in the "Iliad": The Tragedy of Hector.* Expanded ed. Durham: Duke UP.

Reeve, M. D. 1973. The Language of Achilles. *Classical Quarterly* 23 (2): 193–95.

Reinhardt, Karl. 1961. *Die Ilias und ihr Dichter*. Göttingen: Vandenhoeck and Ruprecht.

Richardson, N. J. 1981. The Contest of Homer and Hesiod and Alcidamas' *Mouseion*. *Classical Quarterly* 31 (1): 1–10.

———. 1984. Review of *Die Niederlage Homers im Dichterwettstreit mit Hesiod*, by Konrad Heldmann. *Classical Review* 34 (2): 308–9.

———. 1993. *The "Iliad": A Commentary*, vol. 6. Cambridge: Cambridge UP.

Riggsby, Andrew M. 1992. Homeric Speech Introductions and the Theory of Homeric Composition. *Transactions of the American Philological Association* 122: 99–114.

Rijksbaron, Albert. 2007. *Plato, "Ion, or, On the 'Iliad.'"* Amsterdam Studies in Classical Philology 14. Leiden: Brill.

Rose, Valentinus. 1886. *Aristotelis qui ferebantur librorum fragmenta*. Leipzig: Teubner.

Ross, Shawn A. 2005. Barbarophonos: Language and Panhellenism in the *Iliad*. *Classical Philology* 100 (4): 299–316.

Rouché, Charlotte. 1984. Acclamations in the Later Roman Empire: New Evidence from Aphrodisias. *Journal of Roman Studies* 74: 181–99.

Rousseau, Philippe. 2001. L'intrigue de Zeus. *Europe: revue littéraire mensuelle* 79 (865): 120–58.

Russo, Joseph A. 1968. Homer against His Tradition. *Arion* 7 (2): 275–95.

———. 1978. How, and What, Does Homer Communicate?: The Medium and Message of Homeric Verse. In *Communication Arts in the Ancient World*. Edited by Eric A. Havelock and Jackson P. Hershbell. New York: Hastings House.

Rüter, Klaus. 1969. *Odysseeinterpretationen: Untersuchungen zum 1. Buch und zur Phaiakis*. Hypomnemata 19. Göttingen: Vandenhoeck and Ruprecht.

Ruzé, Françoise. 1984. *Plethos*, aux origines de la majorité politique. In *Aux origines de l'hellénisme: la Crète et la Grèce. Hommage à Henri van Effenterre*. Paris: Centre G. Glotz.

———. 1997. *Délibération et pouvoir dans la cité grecque: de Nestor à Socrate*. Histoire ancienne et médiévale 43. Paris: Publications de la Sorbonne.

Sacks, R. 1987. *The Traditional Phrase in Homer: Two Studies in Form, Meaning and Interpretation*. Columbia Studies in the Classical Tradition 14. Leiden: Brill.

Said, Edward W. 1975. *Beginnings: Intention and Method*. New York: Basic Books.

Sartori, Giovanni. 1975. Will Democracy Kill Democracy? Decision-Making by Majorities and by Committees. *Government and Opposition* 10 (2): 131–58.

Schachter, Albert. 2000. Greek Deities: Local and Panhellenic Identities. In *Further Studies in the Ancient Greek Polis*. Edited by Pernille Flensted-Jensen. Stuttgart: F. Steiner.

Schadewaldt, Wolfgang. 1987. *Iliasstudien*. Darmstadt: Wissenschaftliche Buchgesellschaft.

Schmid, Benno. 1947. *Studien zu griechischen Ktisissagen*. Fribourg: Paulusdruckerei.

Schmitt, Carl. 2005. *Political Theology: Four Chapters on the Concept of Sovereignty*. Translated by George Schwab. Chicago: U of Chicago P.

———. 2007. *The Concept of the Political*. Expanded ed. Translated by George Schwab. Chicago: U of Chicago P.

Schmitt, Rüdiger. 1967. *Dichtung und Dichtersprache in indogermanischer Zeit.* Wiesbaden: O. Harrassowitz.

Schofield, Malcolm. 1999. *Saving the City: Philosopher-Kings and Other Classical Paradigms.* London: Routledge.

Schwartz, Martin. 2003. Encryptions in the Gathas: Zarathustra's Variations on the Theme of Bliss. In *Religious Themes and Texts of Pre-Islamic Iran and Central Asia: Studies in Honour of Professor Gherardo Gnoli on the Occasion of His 65th Birthday on 6th December 2002.* Edited by C. Cereti, M. Maggi, and E. Provasi. Wiesbaden: Reichert.

Scodel, Ruth. 1982. The Achaean Wall and the Myth of Destruction. *Harvard Studies in Classical Philology* 86: 33–50.

———. 1989. The Word of Achilles. *Classical Philology* 84 (2): 91–99.

———. 2002. *Listening to Homer: Tradition, Narrative, and Audience.* Ann Arbor: U of Michigan P.

———. 2008. *Epic Facework: Self-Presentation and Social Interaction in Homer.* Swansea: Classical Press of Wales.

Scully, Stephen. 1981. The Bard as the Custodian of Homeric Society: *Odyssey* 3,263–272. *Quaderni urbinati di cultura classica* 8: 67–83.

———. 1984. The Language of Achilles: The ΟΧΘΗΣΑΣ Formulas. *Transactions of the American Philological Association* 114: 11–27.

———. 1990. *Homer and the Sacred City.* Ithaca: Cornell UP.

Seaford, Richard. 1994. *Reciprocity and Ritual: Homer and Tragedy in the Developing City-State.* Oxford: Clarendon.

Sealey, Raphael. 1957. From Phemius to Ion. *Revue des études grecques* 70: 312–55.

———. 1969. Probouleusis and the Sovereign Assembly. *California Studies in Classical Antiquity* 2: 247–69.

Segal, Charles. 1994. *Singers, Heroes, and Gods in the "Odyssey."* Ithaca: Cornell UP.

Severyns, Albert. 1928. *Le cycle épique dans l'école d'Aristarque.* Liège: É. Champion.

Sherzer, Joel. 1987. Poetic Structuring of Kuna Discourse: The Line. In *Native American Discourse: Poetics and Rhetoric.* Edited by Joel Sherzer and Anthony C. Woodbury. Cambridge: Cambridge UP.

Shive, David. 1987. *Naming Achilles.* New York: Oxford UP.

Sienkewicz, Thomas J. 1991. The Greeks Are Indeed Like the Others: Myth and Society in the West African *Sunjata.* In *Myth and the Polis.* Edited by D. C. Pozzi and J. M. Wickersham. Ithaca: Cornell UP.

Sinos, Dale S. 1980. *Achilles, Patroklos and the Meaning of* Philos. Innsbrucker Beiträge zur Sprachwissenschaft 29. Innsbruck: Institut für Sprachwissenschaft der Universität Innsbruck.

Snell, Bruno. 1953. *The Discovery of the Mind: The Greek Origins of European Thought.* Translated by T. G. Rosenmeyer. Cambridge, MA: Harvard UP.

Snodgrass, Anthony M. 1974. An Historical Homeric Society? *Journal of Hellenic Studies* 94: 114–25.

———. 2006. *Archaeology and the Emergence of Greece.* Ithaca: Cornell UP.

Stuurman, Siep. 2004. The Voice of Thersites: Reflections on the Origins of the Idea of Equality. *Journal of the History of Ideas* 65 (2): 171–89.

Synodinou, Katerina. 1986. The Relationship between Zeus and Athena in the *Iliad*. *Dodone* 15: 155–64.

Taplin, Oliver. 1992. *Homeric Soundings: The Shaping of the "Iliad."* Oxford: Clarendon.

Thalmann, William G. 1988. Thersites: Comedy, Scapegoats, and Heroic Ideology in the *Iliad*. *Transactions of the American Philological Association* 118: 1–28.

———. 1998. *The Swineherd and the Bow: Representations of Class in the "Odyssey."* Ithaca: Cornell UP.

Tideman, Nicolaus. 2006. *Collective Decisions and Voting: The Potential for Public Choice*. Aldershot: Ashgate.

Tsagalis, Christos. 2004. *Epic Grief: Personal Laments in Homer's Iliad*. Untersuchungen zur antiken Literatur und Geschichte 70. Berlin: de Gruyter.

Ulf, Christoph. 2002. Herkunft und Charakter der grundlegenden Prämissen für die Debatte über die historische Auswertung der homerischen Epen. *Klio* 84 (2): 319–54.

———. 2011. Die Diskussion über Ilias und Homer: alte Thesen—neue Zugänge. In *Lag Troia in Kilikien? Der actuelle Streit um Homers Ilias*. Edited by Christoph Ulf and Robert Rollinger. Darmstadt: WBG.

van der Valk, Marchinus. 1964. *Researches on the Text and Scholia of the "Iliad,"* vol. 2. Leiden: Brill.

Vansina, Jan. 1965. *Oral Tradition: A Study in Historical Methodology*. Chicago: Aldine.

van Wees, Hans. 1992. *Status Warriors: War, Violence and Society in Homer and History*. Dutch Monographs on Ancient History and Archaeology 9. Amsterdam: J. C. Gieben.

———. 2002. Homer and Early Greece. *Colby Quarterly* 38 (1): 94–117.

Vélissaropoulos-Karakostas, Julie. 2003. Homère et Anaximandre de Milet: Aux origines de la justice grecque. In *Symposion 1999: Vorträge zur griechischen und hellenistischen Rechtsgeschichte (Pazo de Mariñán, La Coruña, 6.-9. September 1999)*. Edited by Gerhard Thür and Francisco Javier Fernández Nieto. Cologne: Böhlau.

Verdenius, W. J. 1962. ΑΙΝΟΣ. *Mnemosyne* 15 (4): 389.

Versnel, H. S. 1980. Destruction, *Devotio* and Despair in a Situation of Anomy: The Mourning for Germanicus in Triple Perspective. In *Perennitas: studi in onore di Angelo Brelich*. Rome: Edizioni dell'Ateneo.

Vian, Francis. 1959. *Recherches sur les Posthomerica de Quintus de Smyrne*. Études et commentaries 30. Paris: Klincksieck.

Vlachos, Georges C. 1974. *Les sociétés politiques homériques*. Paris: Presses universitaires de France.

Vogt, Ernst. 1959. Die Schrift von Wettkampf Homers und Hesiods. *Rheinisches Museum für Philologie* 102: 193–221.

von der Mühll, P., ed. 1962. *Homeri Odyssea*. Basel: Helbing and Lichtenhahn.

von Kamptz, Hans. 1982. *Homerische Personennamen: Sprachwissenschaftliche und historische Klassifikation*. Göttingen: Vandenhoeck and Ruprecht.

von Sydow, Carl Wilhelm. 1948. On the Spread of Tradition. In *Selected Papers on Folklore Published on the Occasion of His 70th Birthday*. Edited by Laurits Bødker. Copenhagen: Rosenkilde and Bagger.

Walsh, Thomas R. 2005. *Fighting Words and Feuding Words: Anger and the Homeric Poems*. Lanham, MD: Lexington.

Watkins, Calvert. 1976. The Etymology of Irish *Dúan*. *Celtica* 11: 270–77.

———. 1995. *How to Kill a Dragon: Aspects of Indo-European Poetics*. New York: Oxford UP.

———, ed. 2000. *The American Heritage Dictionary of Indo-European Roots*. Boston: Houghton Mifflin.

Weber, Max. 1978. *Economy and Society: An Outline of Interpretative Sociology*, vol. 1. Edited by Guenther Roth and Claus Wittich. Berkeley: U of California P.

Węcowski, Marek. 2011. On the Historicity of the "Homeric World": Some Methodological Considerations. In *The "Dark Ages" Revisited: Acts of an International Symposium in Memory of William D. E. Coulson, University of Thessaly, Volos, 14–17 June 2007*. Edited by Alexander Mazarakis Ainian. Volos: U of Thessaly P.

West, M. L. 1967. The Contest of Homer and Hesiod. *Classical Quarterly* 17 (2): 433–50.

———. 1978. *Hesiod: Works and Days*. Oxford: Clarendon.

———. 1990. Archaische Heldendichtung: Singen und Schreiben. In *Der Übergang von der Mündlichkeit zur Literatur bei den Griechen*. Edited by Wolfgang Kullmann and Michael Reichel. Tübingen: G. Narr.

———. 1995. The Date of the *Iliad*. *Museum Helveticum* 52 (4): 203–19.

———. 2011. *The Making of the "Iliad": Disquisition and Analytical Commentary*. Oxford: Oxford UP.

Westbrook, Raymond. 1992. The Trial Scene in the *Iliad*. *Harvard Studies in Classical Philology* 94: 53–76.

White, James Boyd. 1984. *When Words Lose Their Meaning: Constitutions and Reconstitutions of Language, Character, and Community*. Chicago: U of Chicago P.

Whitman, Cedric H. 1958. *Homer and the Heroic Tradition*. Cambridge, MA: Harvard UP.

Whitmarsh, Tim. 2004. *Ancient Greek Literature*. Cambridge: Polity.

Wickersham, John M., and Dora C. Pozzi. 1991. Introduction. In *Myth and the Polis*. Edited by Dora C. Pozzi and John M. Wickersham. Ithaca: Cornell UP.

Wilamowitz-Moellendorff, Ulrich von. 1920. *Die Ilias und Homer*. Berlin: Weidmann.

Wilson, Donna. 2002. *Ransom, Revenge, and Heroic Identity in the "Iliad."* Cambridge: Cambridge UP.

Winter, J. G. 1925. A New Fragment on the Life of Homer. *Transactions and Proceedings of the American Philological Association* 56: 120–29.

Wolff, H. J. 1946. The Origin of Judicial Litigation among the Greeks. *Traditio* 4: 31–87.

Index

Achaeans: decisions among, de iure/de facto distinction, 4, 65; distinguished from Trojans, 33–34, 38, 133, 135, 144, 243n37, 263nn4, 9; point to external audience, 130, 204

Achaean society: Achilles' isolation from, 75–78, 85, 99–100, 115, 128–30, 253n49; hierarchy in, 93; norms of, 84–85, 194; not historical, 12. *See also* "Homeric society"

Achilles: committed to transparency, 79–80, 254n60; death of, *epainos* of Trojans and, 142–43; as embodiment of *philotēs*, 70, 77–78, 85, 115, 177, 194, 251n24, 253n54; isolation of, 75–78, 85, 99–100, 115, 253n49; and language, 76–81, 253nn47, 53, 254nn58, 60; as narrator, 76–77; not reintegrated into Achaean society, 128–30; "two–fold dooms" of, 142–43. *See also* shield of Achilles

Aeneas: confrontation with Achilles, 167–69, 171; as hero of independent tradition, 167, 265n15, 267n37

Agamben, Giorgio, 68–69, 250n14, 251nn17–18, 252nn36–37, 44

Agamemnon: achieves provisional *epainos*, 109–13; autocratic and counterconsensual disposition of, 69–70, 90–92, 100, 220, 237n50, 251n22, 258n49; as dysfunctional leader, 33, 42–43, 111–13, 243n35

agorē ("assembly"): vs. *boulē*, 113–14, 116, 124–25, 255n4, 263nn4–5; as marker of deliberative context, 24

aineîn/ainos, 22; and *apoina/poinē*, 184, 190–92; as "praise," 48–49, 53–56, 60–62, 190–92, 245nn2–3, 247n30, 248n37; semantic range of, 57, 59–62; as socially constructive speech, 44, 47, 82–83, 122;

Zeus' appeal to, 159–60, 267n27. *See also anainesthai; apēnēs*

ainesthai ("make an *ainos*"), 57–58, 62, 184, 254n65

Aithiopis, 94, 205, 257nn29–30, 274n5. *See also* Epic Cycle

akritos ("lacking a *krisis*"), 134, 263n6

Alcaeus, 8; *fr. 348*, 237n50

Alcidamas, 219, 279nn49–51, 280n56

an-, root, 44, 57–58, 184

anainesthai ("deny, refuse"), 44–47, 57–58, 122, 129–30, 183–84, 192, 244–45n46, 254nn65, 68, 262n39. See also *apēnēs*

anomie, 69, 251n19, 273n58

apeirōn ("without limit, boundless"), points to present of performance, 17, 202–3, 274n63. See also *dēmos apeirōn*

apēnēs ("unyielding"), 44–47, 82–84, 193, 244–45n46, 248n51, 249n52, 272n42; cognate with *ainos*, 82; cognate with *anainesthai*, 44, 57–58. See also *anainesthai*

apoina ("compensation, ransom"), 70, 83–85, 128, 177–79, 181–83, 190–92, 251n25, 254–55n74 , 255n75, 262n35, 268n4, 269n13, 270n27; in Pindar, 190–91, 271n38. See also *poinē*

Apollo: in alternative *Iliad* proem, 155–56, 266n18; substitutes for Zeus as architect of plot, 155, 167

Apollodorus, 94, 256nn24, 27–28

Apologoi, 226–28

Apostolius Paroemiographus, 280nn56, 58

Archilochus: *174.1*, 249n59; *185.1*, 249n59

Aristarchus, 157, 162, 266n21, 267n30

Aristophanes, *Frogs*, 279n51